Airline
Recognition Guide

Jane's Recognition Guides

Aircraft
Guns
Special Forces
Tank
Train
Vintage Aircraft
Warship

Airline
Recognition Guide

Günter Endres and
Graham Edwards

Collins

An Imprint of HarperCollinsPublishers

www.collins.co.uk

ISBN-10: 0-00-720442-6
ISBN-13: 978-0-00-720442-7

www.harpercollins.com

ISBN-10: 0-06-113729-4 (in the United States)
ISBN-13: 978-0-06-113729-7

FIRST U.S. EDITION: HarperCollins books may be purchased
for educational, business, or sales promotional use. For
information in the United States, please write to:
Special Markets Department, HarperCollins Publishers,
10 East 53rd Street, New York, NY 10022.

The name of the "Smithsonian," "Smithsonian
Institution," and the sunburst logo are registered
trademarks of the Smithsonian Institution.

Text © HarperCollins Publishers, 2006

www.janes.com

Design: Graham Edwards, Susie Bell
Proofreading: Jodi Simpson
Editorial: Louise Stanley

Printed and bound by Printing Express, Hong Kong

10 09 08 07 06
8 7 6 5 4 3 2 1

Contents

A-Z of Airlines

ABX Air (Airborne Express) United States
Adamair Indonesia
Adria Airways Slovenia
Aegean Airlines Greece
Aer Arann Ireland
Aer Lingus Ireland
Aero Airlines Estonia
Aero Asia International Pakistan
Aero California Mexico
Aerocaribbean Cuba
Aeroflot Russian Airlines Russian Federation
Aeroflot-Don Russian Federation
Aeroflot-Nord Russian Federation
Aerolineas Argentinas Argentina
Aeromar Mexico
Aeromexico Mexico
Aeropelican Australia
Aeropostal-Alas de Venezuela Venezuela
AeroRepública Colombia
Aerosucre Colombia
Aerosur Bolivia
Aerosvit Airlines Ukraine
African International Airways Swaziland
African Safari Airways Kenya
Afriqiyah Airways Libya
Aigle Azur France
Air Adriatic Croatia
Air Algérie Algeria
Air Alps Aviation Austria
Air Arabia United Arab Emirates
Air Astana Kazakhstan
Air Atlanta Icelandic Iceland
Air Austral Réunion
Air Bagan Myanmar
AirBaltic Latvia
Air Berlin Germany
Air Botswana Botswana

Air Burkina Burkina Faso
Air Cairo Egypt
Air Calédonie New Caledonia
Air Calédonie International (Aircalin) New Caledonia
Air Canada Canada
Air Canada Jazz Canada
Air Caraïbes French West Indies
Air Central (ANA Connection) Japan
Air China China
Air Creebec Canada
Air Deccan India
Air Do (Hokkaido International Airlines) Japan
Air Dolomiti Italy
Air Europa Spain
Air Europe Italy
Air Fiji Fiji
Air Finland Finland
Air France France
Air Gabon Gabon
Air Greenland Greenland
Air Guinée Express Guinea
Air Guyane Express/Air Antilles Express French Guiana/French West Indies
Air Hongkong Hong Kong
Air Iceland (Flugfélag Islands) Iceland
Air-India India
Air-India Express India
Air Inuit Canada
Air Italy Italy
Air Ivoire (Nouvelle Air Ivoire) Côte d'Ivoire
Air Jamaica Jamaica
Air Japan Japan
Air Kiribati Kiribati
Air Koryo North Korea
Air Labrador Canada
Air Lithuania Lithuania
Air Macau Macau

Air Madagascar Malagasy Republic
Air Madrid Spain
Air Malawi Malawi
Air Malta Malta
Air Mandalay Myanmar
Air Marshall Islands Marshall Islands
Air Mauritanie Mauritania
Air Mauritius Mauritius
Air Méditerranée France
Air Memphis Egypt
Air Moldova Moldova
Air Moorea French Polynesia
Air Namibia Namibia
Air Nauru Nauru
Air New Zealand New Zealand
Air New Zealand Link New Zealand
Air Nippon Japan
Air Niugini Papua New Guinea
Air North Canada
Air One Italy
Air Pacific Fiji
Air Paradise International Indonesia
Air Philippines Philippines
Air Plus Comet Spain
Air Pullmantur Spain
Air Rarotonga Cook Islands
Air Sahara India
Air Scotland United Kingdom
Air Sénégal International Senegal
Air Seychelles Seychelles
Air Slovakia Slovak Republic
Air Sofia Bulgaria
Air Southwest United Kingdom
Air Tahiti French Polynesia
Air Tahiti Nui French Polynesia
Air Tanzania Tanzania
Air Transat Canada
Air Transport International (ATI)
  United States
Air Vallee Italy
Air Vanuatu Vanuatu

Air VIA Bulgaria
Air Wales United Kingdom
Air Zimbabwe Zimbabwe
AirAsia Malaysia
AirBridgeCargo Russian Federation
AIRES Colombia Colombia
Airkenya Aviation Kenya
Airlinair France
Airlines of PNG Papua New Guinea
AirTran Airways United States
Alaska Airlines United States
Albanian Airlines Albania
Alitalia Italy
Alitalia Express Italy
All Nippon Airways Japan
Allegiant Air United States
Alliance Air India
Alliance Airlines Australia
Aloha Airlines United States
AlpiEagles Italy
Amakusa Airlines Japan
AMC Airlines Egypt
Amerer Air Austria
American Airlines United States
American Connection United States
American Eagle Airlines United States
AmeriJet International United States
Antonov Airlines Ukraine
Ariana Afghan Airlines Afghanistan
ArkeFly (TUI Airlines Netherlands)
  Netherlands
Arkia Israeli Airlines Israel
Armavia Armenia
Arrow Cargo (Arrow Air) United States
Aserca Airlines Venezuela
Asiana Airlines South Korea
Asian Spirit Philippines
Astar Air Cargo United States
Astraeus United Kingdom
ATA Airlines United States
Atlantic Airlines United Kingdom

Atlantic Airlines Nicaragua/Honduras

Atlantic Air Transport (Air Atlantique)
 United Kingdom

Atlantic Airways Faroe Islands

Atlant-Soyuz Airlines Russian
 Federation

Atlas Air United States

Atlas Blue Morocco

Atlasjet International Airways Turkey

Aurigny Air Services Channel Islands

Austral Lineas Aéreas Argentina

Australian Airlines Australia

Austrian Airlines Austria

Austrian arrows Austria

Aviacsa Mexico

Avianca Colombia

Aviogenex Serbia and Montenegro

Avior Airlines (Aviones de Oriente)
 Venezuela

Axis Airways France

Azerbaijan Airlines Azerbaijan

Azteca Airlines (Lineas Aéreas Azteca)
 Mexico

Bahamasair Bahamas

BAL Bashkirian Airlines Russian
 Federation

Bangkok Airways Thailand

Batavia Air Indonesia

Bearskin Airlines Canada

Belair Airlines Switzerland

Belavia Belarusian Airlines Belarus

Bellview Airlines Nigeria

Big Sky Airlines United States

Biman Bangladesh Airlines
 Bangladesh

Binter Canarias Spain

Blue Dart Aviation India

Blue Line France

Blue Panorama Airlines Italy

Blue Wings Germany

Blue1 Finland

Bluebird Cargo Iceland

BMED (British Mediterranean
 Airways) United Kingdom

bmibaby United Kingdom

bmi british midland United Kingdom

bmi regional United Kingdom

Bouraq Indonesia Airlines Indonesia

BRA Transportes Aéreos Brazil

Brit Air France

Britannia Airways Sweden

British Airways United Kingdom

British Airways CitiExpress United
 Kingdom

BritishJet.com Malta

Buddha Air Nepal

Buffalo Airways Canada

Bulgaria Air Bulgaria

Bulgarian Air Charter Bulgaria

BWIA West Indies Airways Trinidad
 and Tobago

CAL Cargo Air Lines Israel

Calm Air Canada

Cameroon Airlines Cameroon

Canadian North Canada

CanJet Airlines Canada

Cape Air United States

Cargojet Airways Canada

Cargolux Airlines International
 Luxembourg

Caribbean Star Airlines Antigua

Caribbean Sun Airlines United States

Carpatair Romania

Caspian Airlines Iran

Cathay Pacific Airways Hong Kong

Cayman Airways Cayman Islands

CCM Airlines France

Cebu Pacific Air Philippines

Centralwings Poland

Centurion Air Cargo United States

Chalk's Ocean Airways United States
Chanchangi Airlines Nigeria
Channel Express United Kingdom
China Airlines Taiwan
China Cargo Airlines China
China Eastern Airlines China
China Postal Airlines China
China Southern Airlines China
China Xinhua Airlines China
China Yunnan Airlines China
Cielos Airlines (Cielos del Peru) Peru
Cimber Air Denmark
Cirrus Airlines Germany
City Airline Sweden
CityJet Ireland
Click Mexicana Mexico
Coast Air Norway
Comair South Africa
Condor Flugdienst Germany
Continental Airlines United States
Continental Connection United States
Continental Express United States
Continental Micronesia Micronesia
Conviasa Venezuela
Copa Airlines Panama
Corsair France
Cosmic Air Nepal
CR Airways Hong Kong
Croatia Airlines Croatia
CSA Czech Airlines Czech Republic
Cubana de Aviación Cuba
Cygnus Air Spain
Cyprus Airways Cyprus

Daallo Airlines Djibouti
Dalavia Far East Airways Russian
  Federation
Danish Air Transport (DAT) Denmark
Darwin Airline Switzerland
DAS Air Cargo Uganda
Dauair Germany

dba (Deutsche BA) Germany
Delta Air Lines United States
Delta Connection United States
Denim Airways Netherlands
DHL Air United Kingdom
Domodedovo Airlines Russian
  Federation
Donbassaero Ukraine
Dragonair (Hong Kong Dragon
  Airlines) Hong Kong
Druk Air (Royal Bhutan Airlines)
  Bhutan

Eastern Airways United Kingdom
easyJet United Kingdom
EAT–European Air Transport Belgium
Edelweiss Air Switzerland
EgyptAir Egypt
EirJet Ireland
EL AL Israel Airlines Israel
Emerald Airways United Kingdom
Emirates Airline United Arab Emirates
Era Aviation United States
Eritrean Airlines Eritrea
Estafeta Carga Aérea Mexico
Estonian Air Estonia
Ethiopian Airlines Ethiopia
Etihad Airways United Arab Emirates
Eurocypria Airlines Cyprus
Eurofly Italy
euroLOT Poland
EuroManx Isle of Man
Europe Airpost France
European Air Express (EAE) Germany
Eurowings Germany
EVA Air Taiwan
Evergreen International Airlines
  United States
Excel Airways United Kingdom
Express.Net Airlines United States
Falcon Air Sweden

Falcon Air Express United States
Far Eastern Air Transport (FAT) Taiwan
Farnair Europe Hungary/Switzerland
FedEx (Federal Express) United States
Finnair Finland
Finncomm Airlines Finland
First Air Canada
First Choice Airways United Kingdom
Fischer Air Polska Poland
Flightline United Kingdom
Florida West International Airways
   United States
Fly Air (Fly Airlines) Turkey
FlyGlobespan United Kingdom
FlyBaboo Switzerland
FlyBE (British European) United
   Kingdom
FlyJet United Kingdom
FlyLAL (Lithuanian Airlines) Lithuania
FlyMe Sweden
FlyNordic Sweden
Focus Air United States
Four Star Air Cargo U.S. Virgin Islands
Free Bird Airlines Turkey
Freedom Air New Zealand
Frontier Airlines United States
Frontier Flying Service United States
Futura International Airways Spain

Garuda Indonesia Indonesia
GB Airways Gibraltar
Gemini Air Cargo United States
Georgian Airlines Georgia
Germanwings Germany
Global Supply Systems United
   Kingdom
GOL Linhas Aéreas Inteligentes Brazil
Golden Air Sweden
Great Lakes Airlines United States
Gulf Air Bahrain/Oman
Gulf Traveller Bahrain/Oman

Hainan Airlines China
Hamburg International Germany
Hapag-Lloyd Express Germany
Hapagfly (Hapag-Lloyd Flug)
   Germany
Harbour Air Seaplanes Canada
Harmony Airways Canada
Hawaiian Airlines United States
HeavyLift Cargo Airlines Australia
Helios Airways Cyprus
Hello Switzerland
Helvetic Airways Switzerland
Hemus Air Bulgaria
Hewa Bora Airways Democratic
   Republic of Congo
Hifly Portugal
Hola Airlines Spain
Hongkong Express Hong Kong
Hooters Air United States
Horizon Air United States

Iberia Spain
Iberia Regional (Air Nostrum) Spain
Iberworld Airlines Spain
Ibex Airlines Japan
Icelandair Iceland
Iceland Express Iceland
Independence Air United States
Indian Airlines India
Inter Airlines Turkey
InterSky Austria
IranAir Iran
Iran Air Tour Iran
Iran Aseman Airlines Iran
Iraqi Airways Iraq
Ishtar Airlines Iraq
Island Air United States
Island Aviation Services Maldives
Isles of Scilly Skybus United Kingdom
Israir Airlines Israel
Jagson Airlines India

J-Air Japan
JAL Express Japan
JALways Japan
Japan Air Commuter Japan
Japan Airlines Domestic Japan
Japan Airlines International Japan
Japan Asia Airways Japan
Japan TransOcean Air Japan
Jat Airways Serbia and Montenegro
Jatayu Airlines Indonesia
Jazeera Airways Kuwait
Jet Airways India
Jetair (TUI Airlines Belgium) Belgium
JetBlue Airways United States
Jetstar Australia
Jetx Iceland
Jet2 United Kingdom
Jordan Aviation Jordan

Kabo Air Nigeria
Kalitta Air United States
Karat Air Russian Federation
Karthago Airlines Tunisia
KD-Avia (Kaliningradavia) Russian
  Federation
Kenn Borek Air Canada
Kenya Airways Kenya
Kibris Türk Hava Yollari (Cyprus
  Turkish Airlines) Northen Cyprus
Kingfisher Airlines India
Kinshasa Airways Democratic
  Republic of Congo
Kish Air Iran
Kitty Hawk Aircargo United States
KLM Royal Dutch Airlines Netherlands
KLM cityhopper Netherlands
KMV (Kavminvodyavia) Russian
  Federation
Kolavia (Kogalymavia) Russian
  Federation
Korean Air South Korea

KrasAir (Krasnoyarsk Airlines) Russian
  Federation
Kuban Airlines Russian Federation
Kulula.com South Africa
Kuwait Airways Kuwait
Kuzu Airlines Cargo Turkey
Kyrghyzstan Airlines Kyrghyzstan

LAB–Lloyd Aéreo Boliviano Bolivia
LADE–Lineas Aéreas del Estado
  Argentina
LAI–Linea Aérea IAACA Venezuela
LAM–Linhas Aéreas de Moçambique
  Mozambique
LAN Airlines Chile
LAN express Chile
LAO Airlines Laos
LASER–Linea Aérea de Servicio
  Ejecutivo Regional Venezuela
LatCharter Airlines Latvia
Lauda Air Austria
Lauda Air Italia Italy
LIAT Antigua
Libyan Arab Airlines Libya
Lineas Aéreas Suramericanas
  Colombia
Lion Air (PT Lion Mentari Airlines)
  Indonesia
Livingston Italy
Loganair United Kingdom
LOT Polish Airlines Poland
Lotus Air Egypt
LTA–Línea Turística Aerotuy Venezuela
LTU International Airways Germany
Lufthansa Germany
Lufthansa Cargo Germany
Lufthansa Regional Germany/Italy
Luxair Luxembourg

Macair Airlines Australia
Mahan Air Iran

Malaysia Airlines Malaysia
Maldivian Air Taxi Maldives
Malév Hungarian Airlines Hungary
Malmö Aviation Sweden
Mandala Airlines Indonesia
Mandarin Airlines Taiwan
Martinair Netherlands
Mas Air Mexico
MAT-Macedonian Airlines Macedonia
MaxJet United States
Maya Island Air Belize
MenaJet United Arab Emirates
Meridiana Italy
Merpati Indonesia
Mexicana (Cia Mexicana de Aviación)
  Mexico
MIAT Mongolian Airlines (MEA)
  Mongolia
Middle East Airlines Lebanon
Midwest Airlines United States
Midwest Connect United States
MK Airlines Ghana
MNG Airlines/MNG Cargo Turkey
Moldavian Airlines Moldova
Monarch Airlines United Kingdom
Montenegro Airlines Serbia and
  Montenegro
Myair (My Way Airlines) Italy
Myanma Airways Myanmar
Myanmar Airways International
  Myanmar
MyTravel Airways Denmark
MyTravel Airways United Kingdom
MyTravelLite United Kingdom

National Jet Systems Australia
Nationwide Airlines South Africa
NatureAir Costa Rica
Neos Italy
Nightexpress Germany
Niki Austria

Nippon Cargo Airlines Japan
Nok Air Thailand
Nordeste Linhas Aéreas Regionais
  Brazil
Nordic Leisure/Nordic Regional
  Sweden
North American Airlines United States
North Cariboo Air Canada
Northern Air Cargo United States
Northwest Airlines United States
Northwest Airlink United States
Norwegian Norway
Nouvelair Tunisia
Novair (Nova Airlines) Sweden

Ocean Airlines Italy
OceanAir Brazil
O'Connor Airlines Australia
Odessa Airlines Ukraine
OLT Ostfriesische Lufttransport
  Germany
Olympic Airlines Greece
Oman Air Oman
Omni Air International United States
Omskavia Russian Federation
One-Two-Go Thailand
Onur Air Turkey
Orient Thai Airlines Thailand
Origin Pacific Airways New Zealand

Pacific Airlines Vietnam
Pacific Blue Airlines New Zealand
Pacific Coastal Airlines Canada
Pakistan International Airlines
  Pakistan
Palestinian Airlines Palestinian
  Authority
Pantanal Linhas Aéreas Brazil
PBair Thailand
Pegasus Airlines Turkey

PenAir (Peninsula Airways) United States
Perimeter Airlines Canada
Perm Airlines Russian Federation
PGA–Portugália Airlines Portugal
Philippine Airlines Philippines
Phuket Air Thailand
PLUNA Líneas Uruguayas de Navegación Aérea Uruguay
Polar Air Cargo United States
Polet Airlines Russian Federation
Polynesian Airlines Western Samoa
Precision Air Services Tanzania
Provincial Airlines Canada
Pulkovo Aviation Enterprise Russian Federation

Qantas Airways Australia
QantasLink Australia
Qatar Airways Qatar

Regional Air Lines Morocco
Regional Air Services Tanzania
Régional Compagnie Aérienne Européenne France
Regional Express Australia
RegionalLink Australia
Rico Linhas Aéreas Brazil
Rio-Sul Serviços Aéreos Regionais Brazil
Rockhopper Channel Islands
Romavia Romania
Royal Air Maroc Morocco
Royal Brunei Airlines Brunei Darussalam
Royal Jordanian Airlines Jordan
Royal Nepal Airlines Nepal
Royal Wings Airlines Jordan
Russian Sky Airlines Russian Federation

Rutaca Airlines (Rutas Aéreas CA) Venezuela
Rwandair Express Rwanda
Ryanair Ireland
Ryan International Airlines United States

Safair South Africa
Samara Airlines Russian Federation
Santa Barbara Airlines Venezuela
Saravia (Saratov Airlines) Russian Federation
SAS Braathens Norway
SAS Scandinavian Airlines Norway/ Denmark/Sweden
SATA Air Açores Azores
SATA International Azores
Satena Colombia
Saudi Arabian Airlines Saudi Arabia
Scenic Airlines United States
Scot Airways United Kingdom
Shaheen Air International Pakistan
Shandong Airlines China
Shanghai Airlines China
Shenzhen Airlines China
Siberia Airlines Russian Federation
Sichuan Airlines China
Siem Reap Airways International Cambodia
SilkAir Singapore
Singapore Airlines Singapore
Skippers Aviation Australia
Sky Airlines Turkey
SkyEurope Airlines Slovak Republic
SkyKing Airlines Turks and Caicos Islands
Skymark Airlines Japan
Skyservice Airlines Canada
Skyways Express Sweden
Skywest Airlines Australia
Slok Air International The Gambia

Slovak Airlines Slovak Republic
Smart Wings Czech Republic
SN Brussels Airlines Belgium
Snowflake Denmark/Norway/Sweden
Solomon Airlines Solomon Islands
Sonair Angola
Song United States
Sosoliso Airlines Nigeria
South African Airlink South Africa
South African Airways South Africa
South African Express Airways
  South Africa
Southwest Airlines United States
Spanair Spain
SpiceJet India
Spirit Airlines United States
Spring Airlines China
SriLankan Airlines Sri Lanka
Star Airlines France
Sterling Denmark
Styrian Spirit Austria
Sudan Airways Sudan
Sun Air Fiji
Sun Country Airlines United States
Sun D'Or International Airlines Israel
SunExpress Turkey
Sun-Air of Scandinavia Denmark
Surinam Airways Suriname
Swedline Express Sweden
Swiss International Air Lines
  Switzerland
Syrianair (Syrian Arab Airlines) Syria

TAAG Linhas Aéreas de Angola Angola
TACA International Airlines El Salvador
TACA Regional Airlines Costa Rica/
  Guatemala/Honduras/Nicaragua/
  Panama
TACV Cabo Verde Airlines Cape Verde
  Republic
TAF Linhas Aéreas Brazil

Tajikistan Airlines Tajikistan
TAM Linhas Aéreas Brazil
TAM Mercosur Paraguay
TAME Linea Aérea del Ecuador
  Ecuador
TAMPA Cargo Colombia
TANS Perú Peru
TAP Portugal Portugal
TAROM Romanian Air Transport
  Romania
Ted United States
Thai Airways International Thailand
Thomas Cook Airlines Belgium
Thomas Cook Airlines United
  Kingdom
Thomsonfly United Kingdom
Tiger Airways Singapore
Tikal Jets Airlines Guatemala
Titan Airways United Kingdom
TNT Airways Belgium/Spain
Tobago Express Trinidad and Tobago
Total Linhas Aéreas Brazil
Tradewinds Airlines United States
Trans Maldivian Airways Maldives
Transaero Airlines Russian Federation
Transafrik International São Tomé e
  Principe
TransAsia Airways Taiwan
Transavia Airlines Netherlands
Transmile Air Services Malaysia
Travel Service Airlines Czech Republic
TRIP Linhas Aéreas Brazil
Tropic Air Belize
Tuninter Tunisia
Tunisair Tunisia
Tunisavia Tunisia
Turkish Airlines Turkey
Turkmenistan Airlines Turkmenistan

Ukraine International Airlines Ukraine
UM Air Ukraine

UNI Airways Taiwan
United Airlines United States
United Express United States
Universal Airlines Guyana
UPS Airlines (United Parcel Service) United States
Ural Airlines Russian Federation
US Airways United States
US Airways Express United States
US Airways Shuttle United States
USA 3000 Airlines United States
USA Jet Airlines United States
uTair Aviation Russian Federation
Uzbekistan Airways Uzbekistan

Valuair Singapore
Vanair Vanuatu
VARIG (Viação Aérea Rio-Grandense) Brazil
VARIG Log Brazil
Viaggio Air Bulgaria
Vietnam Airlines Vietnam
Viking Airlines Sweden
VIM Airlines Russian Federation
Virgin Atlantic Airways United Kingdom
Virgin Blue Airlines Australia
Virgin Express Belgium
Virgin Nigeria Nigeria
Vladivostok Air Russian Federation
VLM Airlines Belgium
Volar Airlines Spain
Volareweb.com (Volare Airlines) Italy
Volga-Dnepr Airlines Russian Federation
Vueling Airlines Spain

WDL Aviation Germany
Welcome Air Austria
West Air Sweden Sweden
West Coast Air Canada

WestJet Airlines Canada
White Portugal
White Eagle Aviation Poland
Widerøe's Flyveselskap Norway
Winair Netherlands Antilles
Wind Jet Italy
Wizz Air Hungary
World Airways United States

Xiamen Airlines China

Yakutia Airlines Russian Federation
Yamal Airlines Russian Federation
Yangon Airways Myanmar
Yemenia (Yemen Airways) Yemen
Yeti Airlines Nepal

Zambian Airways Zambia
Zoom Airlines Canada

1time Airline South Africa

Foreword

Over nearly 100 years, aircraft markings adopted by both large and small airlines have evolved to form a rich and diverse palette that is continuously being extended. These range from highly imaginative, expansive, and colorful designs to more simplistic and modest arrangements, with every variation in between. All have one thing in common. They are an outward expression of the virtues the airline wants to project to its passengers and the world at large, be that a desire to convey safety and reliability, comfort, strong service culture, and/or a wish to project an image that identifies it with its country of origin.

As keen observers of airlines, readers will be aware that the industry is dynamic and fast changing, with new carriers being formed almost on a weekly basis, with some disappearing just as frequently. Airline markings are also being changed on a regular basis to follow the latest trends, or to reflect a change of ownership. We would ask the reader, therefore, to accept those color schemes in the book that may be outdated, or those of airlines no longer operating at the time of publication, as a useful historic record, rather than an error on our part. The changes that will have taken place during the production process will be accounted for in the next edition. Airline fleets are also a movable feast and will possibly have changed, in some cases, by the time the book is published.

The book covers only the standard markings of each airline. The minor variations on a theme, special commemorative aircraft, hybrid schemes usually on leased aircraft, and those serving as giant flying advertisements would fill a separate volume. To avoid too many repetitions of liveries, those regional airlines operating on behalf of majors are not listed separately, but have been included under the operating name: for example, Delta Connection, United Express, US Airways Express, and others.

Keeping track of some 700-plus airlines has been a mammoth task, but we believe that the coverage is as accurate as we could make it. A book of this magnitude, however, has never before been attempted and any comments/additions on the operations and history of the airlines included, and on the color schemes, their rationale, and the significance of airline symbols, which we may in some instances have interpreted differently, would be welcome.

Günter Endres MRAeS and Graham Edwards
January 2006

From Dull to Dazzling

There have always been functional elements to the painting of aircraft, although these are perhaps of lesser importance today than previously when a coat of paint on wood and fabric-covered aircraft provided a modicum of protection from inclement weather. Heat generation rather than weather on modern high-speed and high-flying aircraft are a problem minimized by light-colored or white upper fuselages, which reflect the rays of the sun, while aircraft bellies, prone to be splattered by dirt from runways and taxiways, are usually gray or darker shades. There are, of course, always exceptions to the rule, with a few designers having created imaginative, if less practical, schemes. Some airlines have experimented with using a bare-metal finish to save weight and, therefore, fuel burn, which with today's high fuel prices has taken on even greater importance than previously.

The application of a company symbol was a very early development, even if aircraft remained otherwise unadorned. A number of these still form the key element of modern designs, the Lufthansa crane and the KLM Royal Dutch Airlines crown being notable examples. Throughout the history of aviation, winged creatures, whether real or mythical, have featured on the tailfin of aircraft. Graceful seabirds, birds of prey, and even the less aerodynamic puffin adorn aircraft even today. Famous among the legendary animals is Qantas Airways' flying kangaroo, South Africa Airways' winged springbok, and the garuda of Thailand and Indonesia, a bird with a human face said to be the reincarnation of the Hindu god Vishnu. Pegasus, the winged horse of Greek mythology, is yet another example of these immortal breeds. Incongruous though it may seem, even the earthbound elephant has featured on aircraft.

Airlines gradually adopted house colors, which, in the case of government-owned national airlines and many others, often were those of the national flag, either faithfully reproduced or in an adaptive representation. The flag has always been central to representing the home country and is still applied in a smaller rendition by almost all airlines at various locations on the aircraft. The Swiss took the patriotic fervor a little too far, insisting that all airlines had to cover the tailfin

BOAC VC10

with the flag, an edict that was removed only fairly recently. Specialist operators, including those involved in polar and mountain flying, preferred strong and highly visible colors, such as orange and red, for enhanced recognition, a concept that has been adapted by many airlines to ensure that their brand stands out from others at the airport.

Another aspect of corporate identity was soon taken on board and is now accepted throughout the industry. This is the "total concept," whereby instant recognition of all facets of an airline's operation is the name of the game, and involves a consistent presentation of aircraft, signage, ground vehicles, stationery and sales offices; in short, every item visible or handled by staff and public.

For the first 50 years, color schemes remained fairly conventional, with the name of the airline emblazoned, usually on the cabin roof, sometimes above colored cheatlines that ran along the lower fuselage, and the airline symbol displayed on the tailfin or alongside the title. Of note in the 1960s was the sober, businesslike BOAC scheme in dark blue and gold (illustrated on previous page), with the "Speedbird" prominent on the fin. But along came Braniff International of the United States (below) and Luton, UK–based Court Line (bottom), which,

Braniff Boeing 747

although both eventually consigned to history, nevertheless left a lasting legacy. Braniff's management believed that bright and interesting color schemes enhanced passenger appeal and proceeded to paint its aircraft in seven different pastel shades. On the other side of the Atlantic, Court Line decided to completely

Court Line BAC 1–11

Mohawk/Gas Light DC3

Overseas National Airways DC8 in bicentennial markings

change its image to reflect its position as a holiday charter airline and, although this was perhaps taken to the extreme, its overall turquoise, pink, orange, and lilac aircraft, like those of Braniff, were recognized everywhere they landed.

Themed designs also made their appearance, with Mohawk Airlines probably being the first, introducing a rather imaginative service and livery on its Douglas DC-3s (illustrated above) to combat increased competition on its routes from jet aircraft. The "Gas Light Service" introduced Victoriana décor and hostesses dressed in period costumes, while the matching exterior featured a gas lamp on the tailfin and a floral design on the aircraft and engines. In 1976, Overseas National Airways painted two Douglas DC-8s (illustrated above) in a strikingly patriotic livery to celebrate the bicentennial of the United States of America. Braniff also took note of the anniversary by having celebrated U.S. artist Alexander Calder cover the aircraft with an abstract painting using the red, white, and blue of the Stars and Stripes. This was known as the "The Flying Colors of the United States," but other original works of art by Calder on aircraft followed ("The Flying Colors of South America" is illustrated overleaf). However, this trend was not taken up again until much later.

The clean and sleek shapes of modern jet aircraft soon inspired a phalanx of corporate image consultants, which found increasing employment by airlines wishing to project a modern image that reflected their origin and service culture, while also being memorable and instantly recognizable. They were also trying to

Braniff DC8 "The Flying Colours of South America"

appear more innovative, progressive, and dynamic than their competitors. Perhaps the best known among the brand and creative design consultants is California-based Landor, which has been responsible for some of the more outstanding liveries, such as those for Cathay Pacific, Gulf Air, Garuda Indonesia, Thai International, Japan Airlines, and VARIG. Many smaller design consultancies have also contributed to today's rich canvas of airline liveries.

But airlines wanted to set themselves apart from each other, and more color appeared in the sky. A large proportion of major and minor airlines now have at least one aircraft in their fleet in a special color scheme, commemorating a special event, an anniversary, a new destination, membership of an alliance, television characters, and much more. The reasons for a distinctive paint scheme are endless and these special liveries would justify a book on their own. Art was again introduced many years later, by both established artists and children, but British Airways made a massive, if ultimately unsuccessful, leap by introducing its "World of Colours" identity, commissioning artists across the world to decorate the tailfin of their aircraft in distinctive designs, representing the cultures, trad-itions, and customs of the nations served by the airline (below). However, the variety of schemes diluted BA's identity, and the disapproval of a former British prime minister compelled the airline to abandon these colorful designs for a patriotic representation of the Union Jack. Other trailblazers included All Nippon Airways with the "Marine Whale" design created by 12-year-old Yukie Ogaki, Qantas with the "Wunala Dreaming" aircraft, and South African Airways' Boeing 747-300 "Ndizani," specially painted for the 1996 Olympic Games in Atlanta.

British Airways Boeing 747 in "Ndebele" design

The advent of low-fare airlines added further interest and variations. A most noticeable departure for some was in the names given to airlines. Short, trendy, catchy, and easily remembered was the mantra for designers, who came up with names such as Hello, Song, Snowflake, and Ted. Low-fare airlines, now often referred to as low-cost carriers (LCCS), also needed to supplement revenues and

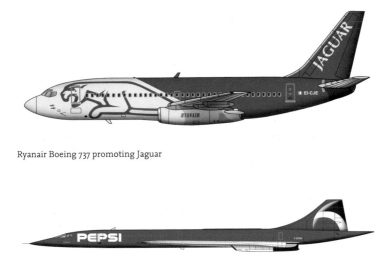

Ryanair Boeing 737 promoting Jaguar

Air France Concorde in special Pepsi promotional colors

hit on the idea to use some of their aircraft as giant advertising hoardings, alongside their standard image. There was nothing new in this, as advertising by aircraft goes back to the very beginning of aviation, but today's airlines have elevated this concept to a new level, as in Ryanair's Jaguar (top) and Air France's Concorde promotions (above).

The genie is now out of the bottle, and we can expect the skies to become yet more varied and colorful in the future.

International Civil Aircraft Markings

An organized, systematic approach to the registration of civil aircraft was first proposed as early as 1912 but, due to the intervention of the First World War, it was not instituted until the Paris Air Convention in 1919. It was then recommended that all aircraft should have five letters with the first denoting the nationality. Letters after the nationality mark were usually an alphabetical sequence starting with AAAA, AAAB, and so on. All letters were to be painted in black on white as large as possible on both sides of the fuselage, as well as on the top surface and underside of the wings. In addition, the nationality letter was to be painted on each side of the tailfin. Privately owned aircraft had to have the last four letters underlined.

As a result of the rapid development of civil aviation, almost all countries owned aircraft by 1929 and the regulations were revised accordingly. Two-letter nationality codes had to be introduced. Gradually, however, many of the rules were forgotten, with registrations becoming smaller and the nationality letter on the tail disappearing altogether. The present standards, adopted by the International Civil Aviation Organization (ICAO) on 8 February 1949, call for the registration to be applied on the lower surface only of wings, on either side of the fuselage between wings and tail surface, or on the upper half of the vertical tail surface. They should also be clean, clearly visible, and identifiable, although no minimum size has been mandated. On rear-engined aircraft, the registration is sometimes painted on the engine itself.

With the exception of the national prefix, which is adhered to by all the member nations, the individual aircraft registration is issued subject to countries' own internal regulations for civil aircraft. These are usually in the form of three or four letters or numbers, depending on whether a one- or two-digit national prefix is allocated, either in alphabetical or numerical sequence. Some nations have their own subdivisions, which serve to group individual aircraft types and thus assist in recognition (i.e. SE-H.. for helicopters). In many countries, major airlines are given a special sequence that makes them instantly recognizable, such an example being ZS-SA for South African Airways.

AP	Pakistan	B	China–Taiwan
A2	Botswana	B-H	Hong Kong
A3	Tonga Friendly Islands	B-M	Macau/Macao
A4O	Oman	C	Canada
A5	Bhutan	CC	Chile
A6	United Arab Emirates	CN	Morocco
A7	Qatar	CP	Bolivia
A8	Liberia	CS	Portugal
A9C	Bahrain	CU	Cuba
B	China	CX	Uruguay

C2	Nauru	J8	St. Vincent and
C3	Andorra		Grenadines
C5	Gambia	LN	Norway
C6	Bahamas	LV	Argentina
C9	Mozambique	LX	Luxembourg
D	Germany	LY	Lithuania
DQ	Fiji	LZ	Bulgaria
D2	Angola	N	United States
D4	Cape Verde Islands	OB	Peru
D6	Comoros	OD	Lebanon
EC	Spain	OE	Austria
EI	Eire	OH	Finland
EK	Armenia	OK	Czech Republic
EP	Iran	OM	Slovakia
ER	Moldova	OO	Belgium
ES	Estonia	OY	Denmark, including
ET	Ethiopia		Greenland and
EW	Belarus		Faroe Islands
EX	Kyrgyzstan	P	Korea (North)
EY	Tajikistan	PH	Netherlands
EZ	Turkmenistan	PJ	Netherlands Antilles
E3	Eritrea	PK	Indonesia
F	France and Overseas	PP/PR/PT	Brazil
	Territories	PZ	Suriname
G	Great Britain	P2	Papua New Guinea
HA	Hungary	P4	Aruba
HB	Switzerland and	RA	Russian Federation
	Liechtenstein	RDPL	Laos
HC	Ecuador	RP	Philippines
HH	Haiti	SE	Sweden
HI	Dominican Republic	SP	Poland
HK	Colombia	ST	Sudan
HL	Korea (South)	SU	Egypt
HP	Panama	SU-Y	Palestine
HR	Honduras	SX	Greece
HS	Thailand	S2	Bangladesh
HV	Vatican	S5	Slovenia
HZ	Saudi Arabia	S7	Seychelles
H4	Solomon Islands	S9	São Tomé e Principe
I	Italy	TC	Turkey
JA	Japan	TF	Iceland
JU	Mongolia	TG	Guatemala
JY	Jordan	TI	Costa Rica
J2	Djibouti	TJ	Cameroon
J3	Grenada	TL	Central African Republic
J5	Guinea Bissau	TN	Congo Brazzaville
J6	St. Lucia	TR	Gabon
J7	Dominica	TS	Tunisia

TT	Chad	ZP	Paraguay
TU	Ivory Coast	ZS/ZU	South Africa
TY	Benin	Z3	Macedonia
TZ	Mali	3A	Monaco
T2	Tuvalu	3B	Mauritius
T3	Kiribati	3C	Equatorial Guinea
T7	San Marino	3D	Swaziland
T8A	Palau	3X	Guinea
T9	Bosnia and Herzegovina	4K	Azerbaijan
UK	Uzbekistan	4L	Georgia
UN	Kazakhstan	4R	Sri Lanka
UR	Ukraine	4X	Israel
VH	Australia	5A	Libya
VN	Vietnam	5B	Cyprus
VP-A	Anguilla	5H	Tanzania
VP-B	Bermuda	5N	Nigeria
VP-C	Cayman Islands	5R	Madagascar
VP-F	Falkland Islands	5T	Mauritania
VP-G	Gibraltar	5U	Niger
VP-L	British Virgin Islands	5V	Togo
VP-M	Montserrat	5W	Western Samoa
VQ-T	Turks and Caicos Islands	5X	Uganda
VT	India	5Y	Kenya
V2	Antigua and Barbuda	6O	Somalia
V3	Belize	6V	Senegal
V4	St. Kitts and Nevis	6Y	Jamaica
V5	Namibia	7O	Yemen
V6	Micronesia	7P	Lesotho
V7	Marshall Islands	7Q	Malawi
V8	Brunei	7T	Algeria
XA/XB/XC	Mexico	8P	Barbados
XT	Burkina Faso	8Q	Maldives
XU	Cambodia	8R	Guyana
XY	Myanmar	9A	Croatia
TA	Afghanistan	9G	Ghana
YI	Iraq	9G	Malta
YJ	Vanuatu	9J	Zambia
YK	Syria	9K	Kuwait
YL	Latvia	9L	Sierra Leone
YN	Nicaragua	9M	Malaysia
YR	Romania	9N	Nepal
YS	El Salvador	9Q/9T	Democratic Republic of Congo
YU	Serbia and Montenegro		
YV	Venezuela	9U	Burundi
Z	Zimbabwe	9V	Singapore
ZA	Albania	9XR	Rwanda
ZK	New Zealand and Cook Islands	9Y	Trinidad and Tobago

Explanation of Airline Presentations

Two-letter code
The two-letter code after the airline name is that allocated by the International Air Transport Association (IATA), generally serving as the flight-number prefix for scheduled services.

Three-letter code
The three-letter code after the airline name is that allocated by the International Civil Aviation Organization (ICAO). It also serves as a flight-number prefix.

Nationality prefix
The letter(s), or combination of letters and numbers, is the unique nationality prefix assigned by the ICAO. It is applied to each aircraft registered in that country.

Aircraft designations
Space limitations have necessitated the use of abbreviations for aircraft manufacturers in the fleet section. These are as follows:

A = Airbus
AN = Antonov
B = Boeing
BAC = British Aircraft Corporation
BAE = British Aerospace
CRJ = Bombardier (Canadair)
Dash/DHC = Bombardier (de Havilland Canada)
DC = Douglas (McDonnell Douglas)
EMB/ERJ = Embraer
F = Fokker/Fairchild
FD = Fairchild Dornier
IL = Ilyushin
KA = Kamov
L = Lockheed
MD = McDonnell Douglas
Mi = Mil
SA = Swearingen Aircraft (later Fairchild)
TU = Tupolev
Yak = Yakovlev

Fleet numbers
Numbers in parentheses are aircraft on firm order at 1 January 2006.

Airlines

Eos Airlines (EO/XXU)

U.S. carrier offering a luxurious transatlantic service between
New York JFK and London Stansted airports with three Boeing
757-200s. Eos Airlines operated its first flight on 18 October 2005.

Ghana International Airlines (GO/GHB)

Ghanaian flag-carrier that began operations on 29 October 2005
with a daily service from Accra to London Gatwick, using a
single Boeing 757 on lease from Ryan International Airlines.

GoAir (G8)

Indian low-fare airline that began operations on 4 November
2005 from Mumbai to Ahmedabad. Other early destinations
included Coimbatore and Goa, all flown with an Airbus A320.

Interjet

Mexican low-fare airline linking Cancun, Guadalajara, Monterrey,
and Toluca with leased Airbus A320s. Ten new A320s have been
ordered. The first service was flown in December 2005.

ABX Air (Airborne Express) (GB/ABX)

UNITED STATES (N)

Major u.s. cargo carrier, operating overnight express parcel services and cargo charters from its main base at the privately owned Airborne Air Park in Wilmington, Ohio, and 11 other hubs in the United States. Services cover more than 130 destinations in the u.s., Canada, Puerto Rico, and the u.s. Virgin Islands. Connections to international destinations are available on other carriers at the main gateway airports. The airline was established as Airborne Express on 17 April 1980 when the Airborne Freight Corporation acquired Midwest Air Charter. The present operating name was adopted in 2003.

FLEET:

21 X B767-200, 5 X B767-200ER, 4 X B767-200SF, 12 X DC-8-63CF, 2 X DC-9-10, 43 X DC-9-30, 29 X DC-9-40

FEATURES:

ABX Air uses the company colors of red and black in a simple, yet striking arrangement, with the first letter A in a flowing hand-drawn style covering the red tailfin in white with a black shadow. A straight cheatline culminates forward in the company title, with the large A drawn in red, and the rest in contrasting black against the white aircraft. The design was created by the airline's employees.

Adamair (KI/DHI)

INDONESIA (PK)

Privately owned Indonesian domestic carrier providing low-fare services from Jakarta to more than 10 other major cities, among them Denpasar, Medan, Pontianak, Surabaya, and others spread across the main Indonesian islands. Adamair is the operating name of Adam Sky Connection Airlines, which was established on 21 November 2002 by Agung Laksono and Sandra Ang. Operations started on 19 December that same year, with two Boeing 737s leased from GE Capital Aviation Services, from Jakarta to Medan, and the main tourist destinations of Denpasar and Yogyakarta.

FLEET:
6 X B737-200A, 2 X B737-300, 5 X B737-400, 1 X B737-500

FEATURES:
The orange-red cabin roof, separated from the lower white fuselage, carries white and lime green *Adamair* titles, before changing to golden yellow at the rear, the transition between the two colors being effected with red bands set into the gold. The airline's notable emblem is a large white winged human figure poised to take off from the orange-red tailfin. The orange-red engines are used to create a vertical balance in the design.

Adria Airways (7L/AZX)

SLOVENIA (S5)

National airline of Slovenia established in 1961 in what was then the Yugoslav Federation, initially under the local title of Adria Aviopromet. Between 1968 and 1986, when associated with the trading group Interexport, the airline operated under the title of Inex-Adria Airways. Based at Brnik Airport in the capital city of Ljubljana, Adria Airways operates scheduled services to more than 20 destinations in 17 European countries. Charter flights extend to resorts in the Mediterranean basin, especially to Greece and Turkey, but also reach as far away as the Canary Islands. Regional member of the global Star Alliance.

FLEET:
3 X A320-200, 1 X CRJ100LR, 6 X CRJ200LR

FEATURES:
The large and bold *Adria* titles in blue on the clean, all-white fuselage provide high visibility from a distance, while the name of the country at the rear leaves no one in doubt as to the origin of the airline. The flowing symbol on the tailfin depicts the first letter in the airline's name in blue, reflected in the turquoise waters of the Adriatic Sea, which touches the country on its south-western tip through the Gulf of Venice. The symbol is repeated on the engine cowlings.

Aegean Airlines (A3/AEE)

GREECE (SX)

Major Greek airline, operating scheduled services from Athens and Thessaloniki to the principal mainland and island destinations within Greece, and to cities in Germany and Italy. Founded in 1977 as a business/VIP operator under the name of Aegean Aviation, the present title was adopted in March 1999 for the start of scheduled services with Avro RJ100s the following May. In December 1999, Air Greece was merged into Aegean Airlines, and an agreement was reached in April 2001 to join with Cronus Airlines (founded in 1995). Operations continued for a time as Aegean Cronus Airlines.

FLEET:
(8) X A320-200, 5 X B737-300, 7 X B737-400, 6 X RJ100

FEATURES:
This smart livery uses Mediterranean blue to good effect on the largely snow-white fuselage. Two seagulls are depicted in graceful flight against the outline background of the sun, which rises on the tailfin. This logo is repeated on the engine cowlings and on the forward fuselage below the cockpit. The airline's name, of course, comes from the Aegean Sea, a stretch of water in the eastern Mediterranean between mainland Greece and Turkey.

Aer Arann (RE/REA)

IRELAND (EI)

Irish regional airline operating a network of scheduled services from Cork and Dublin to several cities within the Irish Republic, and to major UK destinations. A number of UK points are also served from smaller Irish provincial cities. Aer Arann was originally founded in 1970 to operate exclusively to the Aran Islands off the west coast of Ireland, which is being continued by Aer Arann Islands, but a regional base at Dublin was added on 2 March 1998, initially operating wet-lease flights for Manx Airlines, before being chosen by the Department of Public Enterprise to operate a service between Dublin and Donegal.

FLEET:
5 X ATR 42-300, 6 X ATR 72-200, 2 X BN-2A Islander, 1 X BN-2B Islander, 2 X F50

FEATURES:
The elegant sweep of two-tone blue representing sky and sea is intended to convey a business-like approach in its service to passengers. The engines are painted in the darker blue, providing a balanced contrast to the white fuselage. Aer Arann Islands uses the same two-tone blue colors, but differentiates itself with two interlinked circles with arrow heads pointing the way to the islands.

Aer Lingus (EI/EIN)

IRELAND (EI)

Irish flag-carrier operating a comprehensive European scheduled passenger and cargo network and a number of long-haul flights across the North Atlantic. The airline offers low fares to more than 20 destinations in mainland Europe and on frequent connections between the Irish Republic and the United Kingdom. A domestic route system is also operated. Aer Lingus was founded on 22 May 1936 and began operations across the Irish Sea with a de Havilland Dragon five days later. The name is an anglicization of the Gaelic *Aer Loingeas*, meaning "air fleet." Member of the global oneworld alliance.

FLEET:
21 X A320-200, 6 X A321-200, 3 X A330-200, 4 X A330-300, 3 X B737-500

FEATURES:
Developed by Luxon Carra, the livery captures the essence of the airline: Irish, vibrant, dynamic, responsive, natural, and "green." It features the inevitable shamrock with fluid and natural lines on the tailfin and soft colors of three shades of green, petrol blue, and gray. This is said to evoke a lush and verdant landscape, interspersed with clean lakes and rivers and overcast with mist-laden skies.

Aero Airlines (EE/EAY)

ESTONIA (ES)

Finnair-backed airline operating turboprop flights across the Gulf of Finland serving the Finnish capital Helsinki and Tallinn in Estonia. Aero has also taken over some services within Finland, which are being operated on behalf of Finnair, and there are plans to extend its network to other points in Scandinavia and mainland Europe. Aero Airlines was established on 21 December 2000 to serve the Baltic area, reviving the well-known name of the Finnish flag-carrier used until 1953. Operations began with two ATR 72-200 turboprop aircraft on 31 March 2002 with a flight from Helsinki to Tallinn.

FLEET:
9 X ATR 72-200

FEATURES:
The Aero livery uses the same colors as Finnair, with the blue on the tailfin and engines suggesting the cloudless sky over the snowy landscape (represented by the arctic white aircraft fuselage). A freely drawn white lowercase *a*, denoting the first letter in the name, raises the visual impact of the blue tail. By contrast, the full name on the forward upper fuselage, which revives the old title of Finnair, is rather understated. The blue engine cowlings provide a balanced contrast to the scheme.

Aero Asia International (E4/RSO)

PAKISTAN (AP)

Pakistani carrier operating a small network of scheduled passenger and cargo services from Karachi's Jinnah International Airport to Pakistan's main cities, and to destinations in the neighboring Persian Gulf States of Qatar, Oman, and the United Arab Emirates. A second base is maintained at Dubai International Airport. The airline also promotes tourism between Pakistan and India. Aero Asia was founded by the Tabani Group during 1993 and began operations on 6 May that year with two Romanian-built 1-11s. It was the first low-fare airline to be established in Pakistan.

FLEET:
3 X B737-200A, 3 X DC-9-50, 1 X MD-81, 2 X MD-82, 1 X Yak-42

FEATURES:
An attractive fan-shaped design in blue, yellow, and red on the tailfin, and between large red *Aero Asia* titles across the forward fuselage, is the airline signature, intended to emphasize its motto of "friendly people, friendly service."

Aero California (JR/SER)

MEXICO (XA)

Mexico's third-largest airline, operating a comprehensive domestic network centered on Mexico City, Guadalajara, and on Tijuana in the Baja California peninsula, where routes radiate out to more than 30 towns and cities across the country. Two cross-border routes to the United States are also operated. Non-flying activities include maintenance and overhaul of aircraft, engines, and components. Aero California was established in 1960 as a charter and air-taxi company and launched domestic schedules in June 1982, before adding flights across the border to the United States in 1989.

FLEET:
10 x DC-9-10, 11 x DC-9-30

FEATURES:
A stylish livery of bright sunshine colors makes the Aero California aircraft stand out wherever they land. Narrow cheatlines of four colors graduating from deep red via orange to yellow extend along the fuselage and sweep up over the cabin roof. A similar arrangement is repeated on the engine cowlings and, in a straighter rendition, on the tailfin. Simple *Aero California* titling in dark red appears on the forward fuselage alongside its stylized bird motif.

Aerocaribbean (7L/CRN)

CUBA (CU)

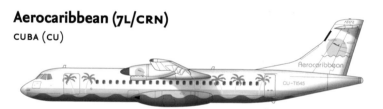

State-owned Cuban regional airline, which operates scheduled domestic passenger services and international flights from Havana's José Marti International Airport to Grand Cayman, Haiti, Nicaragua, and the Dominican Republic. Charters for passengers and cargo are operated to anywhere in the Caribbean and Central America. Aerocaribbean was set up by the Cuban government in 1982 to supplement the services of national carrier Cubana, and to assist in the development of tourism. Operations started with Soviet aircraft on 2 December that same year.

FLEET:
1 x AN-24RV, 2 x AN-26,
2 x ATR 42-300, 2 x ATR 72-210,
2 x IL-18D, 1 x IL-18E, 6 x Yak-40

FEATURES :
The Aerocaribbean aircraft serve as a canvas for a typical scene in the Caribbean islands, with the gentle waves of blue seas washing up onto sandy beaches scattered with green palm trees. On the tailfin, an aircraft takes off against the sun rising from the sea. Blue *Aerocaribbean* titles appear only on the base of the tailfin so as not to detract from the beach painting along the white fuselage.

Aeroflot Russian Airlines (SU/AFL)

RUSSIAN FEDERATION (RA)

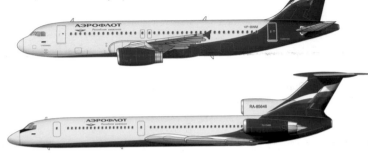

Russia's principal international airline, flying to some 140 destinations in 75 countries and providing 60% of all international passenger routes served by the country's airlines. Air bridges connect Moscow with around 40 cities in Russia and the CIS. Aeroflot-Don and Aeroflot-Nord are regional subsidiaries. Aeroflot's history goes back to 14 March 1923 and the founding of Dobrolet, which began operations between Moscow and Nishnij Novgorod. On 29 October 1930, Dobrolet became Grazdansii Vozdusnyj Flot, absorbing the Ukrainian airline Ukvozduchput, which had begun flying on 15 April 1925. Aeroflot, as it became known on 26 March 1932, grew to become the largest aviation enterprise by far, at its peak operating some 3,500 aircraft throughout the vast territory of the Soviet Union and to all corners of the globe, and another 5,000 light aircraft and helicopters on all types of aerial work. Aeroflot was also responsible for some 120 "national economy" tasks, and ran all airfields, maintenance, and training. The vast Aeroflot empire broke up with the collapse of Communism, and a much reduced Aeroflot was restyled in July 1992 as Aeroflot Russian International Airlines, with the International dropped from the title in 2000. All non-flying activities were delegated to independent companies, especially airport operators.

FLEET:
8 x A319-100, 7 x A320-200, 3 x B737-400, 9 x B767-300ER, 1 x B777-200ER, 2 x IL-86, 10 x IL-96-300, 4 x DC-10-30CF, (30) x RRJ 95, 13 x TU-134A, 1 x TU-134B-3, 26 x TU-154M

FEATURES:
The livery, by London agency Identica, has been designed to reposition the airline as a quality carrier that has shrugged off its Soviet past, although the winged hammer-and-sickle motif has been retained. A stylized flag, on which a more friendly orange has replaced the red, flutters on the dark blue fin.

Aeroflot-Don (D9/DNV)

RUSSIAN FEDERATION (RA)

Rostov-on-Don-based southern subsidiary of Aeroflot Russian Airlines operating scheduled and charter passenger and cargo services to some of Russia's main cities and abroad to the Caucasian republics, Ukraine, Germany, Israel, the Persian Gulf, and Africa. Aeroflot-Don was formed as a joint-stock company in May 1993 as the successor to the North Caucasian Civil Aviation Directorate/Rostov-on-Don United Air Detachment under the name of Donavia. Aeroflot acquired a controlling 51% stake in the ailing carrier in early 2000 and the airline started operations under its new name and ownership on 13 April that year.

FLEET:
1 X AN-12BP, 5 X TU-134A-3, 8 X TU-154B-2, 4 X TU-154M, 1 x Yak-40

FEATURES:
Two stylized delta-winged aircraft in dark and light blue, streaking past the sun as illustrated on the tailfin, is the most notable design on the white aircraft. Cheatlines in the Russian red and blue colors start under the cockpit windows and run through to the rear, and are repeated around the front of the engines. *Aeroflot-Don* titles in blue are carried in Cyrillic lettering on the port side and in English on the starboard.

Aeroflot-Nord (5N/AUL)

RUSSIAN FEDERATION (RA)

Arkhangelsk-based northern subsidiary of Aeroflot Russian Airlines operating scheduled and charter passenger, cargo, and mail flights to Moscow and other main cities in Russia, with international connections to the neighboring Scandinavian countries, and to the Black Sea resort of Simferopol. The airline was founded in May 1991 as Arkhangelsk Airlines, when the airline operations were separated from the Arkhangelsk First United Airguard. The new name was adopted in April 2004, when Aeroflot acquired a controlling 51% interest, with the remaining stake being held by Aviainvest.

FLEET:
4 X AN-24RV, 2 X AN-26B, (3) X IL-114, 7 X TU-134A-3, 5 X TU-154B-2, 1 x Yak-40

FEATURES:
The white aircraft has been given a blue paint scheme edged in orange that starts on the underside at the front and gradually flares out to encompass the rear engines and part of the tailfin, leaving space for the charming white and ice blue snowflake design. *Aeroflot-Nord* titling is applied in orange and blue in English on the starboard and Cyrillic on the port side.

Aerolineas Argentinas (AR/ARG)
ARGENTINA (LV)

National airline operating scheduled passenger and cargo services throughout the Americas. Routes are also flown across the Atlantic to several European capital cities, and across the Pacific to Australia and New Zealand. Main domestic routes are those between the capital Buenos Aires and major provincial cities, backed up by further extensive services to over 30 towns and cities through an alliance with Austral. The airline was established in May 1949 from the unifications of ZONDA, Aeroposta, ALFA, and FAMA, and began operations with an inherited fleet of 70 motley aircraft on 7 December 1950.

FLEET:
2 X A310-300, (6) X A340-600, 4 X A340-200, 19 X B737-200A, 2 X B747-200B, 3 X B747-400, 4 X MD-88

FEATURES:
The only splash of color on the white aircraft is the light blue on the tailfin and engines, and in the *Aerolineas Argentinas* titles. The traditional condor insignia is set into the blue tail. The white and blue recall the national flag, which is painted under the cockpit. It incorporates the "Sun of May," which symbolizes the start of the country's struggle for independence.

Aeromar (VW/TAO)
MEXICO (XA)

Mexico's largest commuter airline, linking the capital Mexico City to more than 20 towns and cities with scheduled passenger and cargo services, catering mainly for business travelers. A single cross-border extension is also operated to Texas in the U.S., with other connections available through code-share agreements. Aeromar was established on 29 January 1987 and began flying on 5 November that year with an ATR 42 between Toluca and Acapulco. Following domestic deregulation, Aeromar restructured its route system into a hub-and-spoke operation from Mexico City in April 1991.

FLEET:
5 X ATR 42-300, 10 X ATR 42-500

FEATURES:
The simple business-like color scheme features the airline's AM initials in sky blue with a black shadow written in calligraphic form alongside the fuselage and ending in a long flourish, with black *Aeromar* titling to the rear of the white aircraft. The AM is repeated in a curtailed form on the tailfin.

Aeromexico (AM/AMX)

MEXICO (XA/XB)

Mexico's major airline, serving a vast domestic network of 40 towns and cities, together with scheduled cross-border services to the United States, to points in South America and across the Atlantic to Madrid and Paris in Europe. The domestic network is supported with feeder services by subsidiary Aeroliteral. Based at Benito Juarez International Airport, Mexico City, Aeromexico was founded on 15 September 1934 as Aeronaves de Mexico SA. Pan Am acquired a major stake on 12 September 1940, but this passed to the Mexican government upon nationalization in 1959. The present name was adopted on 28 January 1972.

FLEET:
19 (10) X B737-700,
(4) X B737-800, 5 X B757-200,
5 X B767-200ER, 1 X B767-300ER,
5 X MD-82, 8 X MD-83,
16 X MD-87, 10 X MD-88,
8 X DC-9-32

FEATURES:
The central feature is the famous Mexican birdman motif on a mid-blue tailfin, with the airline name at the base, given an emphasis of speed through a blue-and-white graduation of the word *Aero*. The colors reflect the national flag, where the "three guarantees" stand for religion, independence, and unity.

Aeropelican (OT/PEL)

AUSTRALIA (VH)

Australian commuter airline providing a high-frequency service in New South Wales between Sydney and Newcastle, giving access to some of Australia's most magnificent coastal areas, Lake Macquarie, and the Hunter Valley. The airline, based at Aeropelican Airfield near Pelican Point on the shoreline of Lake Macquarie, was established 23 October 1968 by Keith Hilder, who had operated a flying school and air charters since 25 July 1962. Aeropelican operated its first scheduled flight on 1 June 1971 with an eight-passenger Cessna 402.

FLEET:
1 X DHC-6-300 Twin Otter,
1 X EMB-110P1 Bandeirante,
1 X SA227DC Metro 23

FEATURES:
The airline's white and blue livery depicts the Southern Hemisphere's Southern Cross constellation on the blue tailfin and Aeropelican's web address on the lower fuselage, with *Aeropelican* enlarged to aid recognition. The engines are also painted in blue.

Aeropostal-Alas de Venezuela (VH/LAV)

VENEZUELA (YV)

Leading Venezuelan airline operating scheduled passenger and cargo services linking the capital Caracas with all major points in the country, as well as with Miami in Florida, and destinations in Central and South America. The airline's long history dates back to 1933 and the establishment of Linea Aeropostal Venezolana as a branch of the Ministry of Labour and Communications to take over the routes of French company Cie Générale Aéropostale, which had been operating in Venezuela since 1930. Operations ceased in August 1994, but the airline was reactivated in January 1997.

FLEET:
3 X B727-200A, 3 X DC-9-20, 6 X DC-9-30, 1 X DC-9-34F, 12 X DC-9-50, 4 X MD-82, 1 X MD-83

FEATURES:
The livery of blue, mustard yellow, and red draws its inspiration from the national flag. A red pencil line separates the gray underside of the aircraft from the white upper fuselage, but the dominant feature is the dark blue tailfin, which incorporates the airline's yellow bird symbol. Bold, matching blue *Aeropostal* titles on the cabin roof are sandwiched between the bird symbol and the national flag.

AeroRepública (P5/RPB)

COLOMBIA (HK)

Colombia's third-largest domestic airline, operating a network of passenger and cargo services from the capital Bogotá to 10 major destinations, and on the coffee axis with an operation from Pereira. The airline also serves other Latin American countries on a charter basis and offers tourist packages to well-known beaches and historic sights. AeroRepública was established on 23 November 1992 and became the first new airline in Colombia for 25 years when it started operations on 19 June 1993, flying from Bogota to San Andrés, Santa Marta, and Cartagena with three Boeing 727-100s.

FLEET:
2 X DC-9-30, 5 X MD-81, 2 X MD-83

FEATURES:
The orange aft fuselage and rear engines are hemmed in broad blue, providing a pleasing color combination that is maintained on the orange tailfin, with interlinked AR initials set into a blue disc. *Aero República Colombia* titles in orange and blue take up the forward fuselage. The colorful yellow, blue, and red Colombian flag with the unusual red ring surrounding the state arms appears under the cockpit.

Aerosucre (6N/KRE)

COLOMBIA (HK)

Colombian all-cargo airline operating scheduled services from Bogotá to other points within the country and to neighboring areas in Central America and the Caribbean. The airline also operates extensively within Latin America and to the United States on a charter basis, carrying livestock, automotive parts, and general cargo. Aerosucre was formed in 1970 as a third-level operator in Sincelejo, northern Colombia, with a Piper Cherokee, and later restructured to become a cargo operator.

FLEET:
2 X B727-100F, 1 X B727-200F, 3 X B737-200QC

FEATURES:
A triple cheatline of purple, red, and orange runs along the aircraft fuselage before fanning out to fill the entire tailfin. Large *Aerosucre* titles appear on the cabin roof, preceded by the word *Colombia* to indicate the airline's South American origin.

Aerosur (5L/RSU)

BOLIVIA (CP)

Private Bolivian airline linking its home city of Santa Cruz de la Sierra with 10 other major destinations within the country, with international extensions scheduled to Argentina, Brazil, and Peru, where flight connections are available to North America and across the South Atlantic to Europe. A tourist route, flown with a Douglas DC-3, serves Rurrenabaque, El Salar de Uyuni, Sucre, and the Imperial city of Potosi. Aerosur was established in April 1992 to take advantage of the deregulation of Bolivia's air transport, and started flying on 24 August that year between Santa Cruz and Potosi.

FLEET:
1 X B727-100, 5 X B727-200A, 1 X B737-200A, 1 X DC-3, 3 X LET L-410 UVP-E, 1 X SA227DC Metro 23

FEATURES:
The dark cyan tailfin and white fuselage convey a fresh, clean image. Set into a white disc on the tailfin is an A in which the first upward stroke has been fashioned into a dark cyan condor. Blue-green *Aerosur* titles are applied under the forward cabin windows.

Aerosvit Airlines (vv/aew)
UKRAINE (UR)

Majority Ukrainian-owned airline providing a growing network of passenger and cargo services from Kiev Borispol to more than 20 destinations in Europe, the Commonwealth of Independent States, and North Africa. International charters are flown and the airline also maintains a domestic network linking all major towns in the Ukraine. Some domestic routes are flown in code-share arrangements with other local airlines. Aerosvit was established on 25 March 1994 and started operations in April initially in cooperation with the now defunct Air Ukraine. It acquired its own fleet in October that same year.

FLEET:
(5) X AN-140, 1 X B737-200A, 1 X B737-300, 5 X B737-400, 2 X B737-500, 2 X B767-300ER

FEATURES:
An azure winged arrow rises in front of a golden yellow sun on the tailfin of the largely white aircraft, taking its colors from the Ukrainian flag, which leads the blue *Aerosvit* titling on the forward fuselage. The colors represent the country's golden yellow cornfields under a blue sky. The airline name is applied in the Ukrainian language on the port side and in English on the starboard side.

African International Airways (AIN)
SWAZILAND (3D)

All-cargo airline operating ad hoc and contract charter flights on a worldwide basis but with a strong emphasis on the African continent, carrying a wide variety of freight from animals (for which the airline is specially equipped) to dry cargo including fresh produce, car parts, and humanitarian relief supplies. The airline is licensed for cargo operations between Africa and the United States. African International was established in Swaziland in 1985 and subsequently licensed by South Africa. Until 1996 it operated as a contract carrier providing supplementary capacity for scheduled airlines.

FLEET:
2 X DC-8F-54, 3 X DC-8-62F

FEATURES:
A simple sky blue cheatline, interrupted forward by the airline's web address, extends along the full length of the fuselage before sweeping up the tailfin to a stylized red globe alluding to its worldwide operations. *African International* titles appear in red on the mid-fuselage.

African Safari Airways (ASA/QSC)
KENYA (5Y)

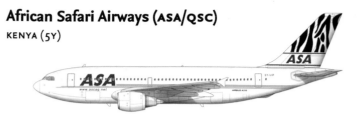

Holiday airline providing up-market charter and inclusive-tour services between Europe and Kenya, serving the East African game parks, beach resorts, and other attractions on behalf of its owner, the Swiss African Safari Club. Flights operate every weekend between London Gatwick and Mombasa, and from other European gateways including Vienna, Basel, Frankfurt, and Milan several times a week. ASA was founded on 1 August 1967 as an associate of the African Tourist Development Co. and African Safari Lodges, and began operations on 31 December 1967 with a McDonnell Douglas DC-10-30 flight from Zurich to Mombasa.

FLEET:
1 x A310-300

FEATURES:
There is no mistaking the *raison d'être* of the airline with the distinctive zebra stripes on the tailfin heralding its services to the game parks of East Africa. Bold blue italicized *Asa* titles are painted near the front of the aircraft, underlined by red and blue pencil lines. *Asa* initials between pencil lines also decorate the base of the fin.

Afriqiyah Airways (8U/AAW)
LIBYA (5A)

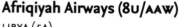

Libya's second airline formed to provide regional and long-haul links from the capital Tripoli to points in Africa, Europe, the Middle East, and Asia. Scheduled services are presently operated to West, Central, and East Africa, and to France, Belgium, Switzerland, and the UK. Some flights originate in Benghazi. Long-haul flights are under consideration. Afriqiyah Airways was formed by the Libyan government in April 2001 and began scheduled passenger services on 1 December that same year.

FLEET:
2 x A320-200

FEATURES:
Afriqiyah is the Arabic for "African," denoting the airline's aim of providing a service for the continent. The striking colors of its aircraft are appropriately those of Africa, with the red symbolizing the struggles of its forefathers, green its agriculture, yellow its natural resources, and black its freedom. The repeated numeral 9s and full stops applied to the tailfin and engines refer to the Declaration of United African States made at Sirte in Libya on 9 September 1999 – that is, 9.9.99.

Aigle Azur (ZI/AAF)

FRANCE (F)

French scheduled and charter airline operating domestic services from Paris, together with scheduled flights to and within Algeria. Wet-lease and cargo services are also provided. The airline's history goes back to 1969 and the formation of Lucas Air Transport, which provided air-taxi flights, charters, and flight training, until it added a seasonal scheduled service between Deauville and London Gatwick in 1975. It then used the name of Lucas Aigle Azur, before being renamed again.

FLEET:
1 X A320-200, 3 X A321-200, 1 X B737-300QC, 1 X B737-400

FEATURES:
An azure and deep blue representation of an eagle hovers above the azure sky of the lower part of the tailfin, framed in deep blue at the top and below. The same symbol is repeated on the blue engines, while the aircraft winglets are also painted blue. The conversion of the horizontal stroke in the letter a into the shape of an aircraft has added interest to the *Aigle Azur* titles on the forward fuselage.

Air Adriatic (AHR)

CROATIA (9A)

Croatian charter airline serving the tourist industry with flights to Dubrovnik, Rijeka, and Pula, all gateways to the Croatian coastal resorts along the Adriatic. The airline has contracts with some 15 tour operators providing regular flights from more than 20 points in Germany, Ireland, Sweden, Norway, and the United Kingdom. Charter flights are also undertaken to Russia and North Africa, and Air Adriatic provides an additional air-taxi service with small Piper aircraft. Air Adriatic was the first private airline in Croatia when it was established in March 2002. Operations began the following month.

FLEET:
4 X MD-82, 2 X MD-83

FEATURES:
The airline uses the mid-red, blue, and white of the national flag, with bold *Air Adriatic* titles taking up the front half of the white aircraft. The only other ornamentation is the application on the tailfin of the initials AA, again in red and blue, surrounded by two dynamic swirls in the same colors.

Air Algérie (AH/DAH)

ALGERIA (7T)

National flag-carrier operating scheduled passenger and cargo services to destinations in North and West Africa, Europe, and the Middle East. An extensive domestic network is also operated, together with air-taxi and agricultural flying. Air Algérie was established in 1946 as Compagnie Générale de Transports Aériens and changed to the present name in April 1953 after a merger with Compagnie Air Transport. CAT had been founded after the war by Air France and CGT, the French Steamship Line, and operated a similar network. Air Algérie is based at Houari Boumedienne Airport in the capital Algiers.

FLEET:
1 x A310-200, 1 x A310-300,
1 x A320-200, 5 x A330-200,
6 x ATR 72-500, 5 x 727-200A,
7 x 737-200A, 1 x 737-200C,
5 x B737-600, 11 x B737-800,
1 x B747-200B, 3 x 767-300,
7 x Fokker F27-400M,
2 x L100-30 Hercules

FEATURES:
The paint scheme uses the national colors of red, green, and white, with two thin red stripes separated by a green band. The upper red cheatline sweeps up and over the rear fuselage into a wide sash. The tail displays the company's insignia, said to represent its code AH in a bird shape.

Air Alps Aviation (A6/LPV)

AUSTRIA (OE)

Independent Austrian regional airline based at Innsbruck in the Tirol linking its home base and the cities of Linz and Salzburg with destinations in neighboring Italy, Germany, and Switzerland. The airline also operates hubs at Amsterdam and Rome, from which services radiate in association with KLM and Alitalia respectively. Air Alps Aviation was founded in 1998 with a commercial cooperation with KLM and began operations as KLM Alps on 28 March 1999 . Following a new agreement with KLM in 2001, the KLM Alps brand was dropped in favor of the present title.

FLEET:
7 x FD 328-110

FEATURES:
The simple color scheme is notable for the bold *Air Alps* titles in a business-like silver gray and blue, where the letter *I* has been replaced by an attention-drawing exclamation mark. The titles are unusually applied towards the rear. The only other marks on the alpine white aircraft are the large blue exclamation mark on the tailfin and the words *discover the sky* under the forward windows.

Air Arabia (G9/ABY)

UNITED ARAB EMIRATES (A6)

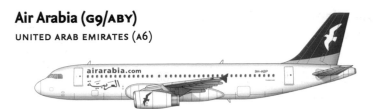

Sharjah, United Arab Emirates-based low-fare airline providing scheduled passenger services to points in the Middle East, North Africa, and the Indian subcontinent. Countries served are Bahrain, Egypt, Kuwait, Lebanon, Oman, Qatar, Saudi Arabia, Sri Lanka, Sudan, and Syria. Bus services are available from the emirates of Dubai, Abu Dhabi, and Al Ain to ferry passengers to Air Arabia's flights out of Sharjah. The airline was established on 3 February 2003 by the Sharjah Civil Aviation Department and the Sharjah Airport Authority and began flight operations on 28 October that year.

FLEET:
5 X A320-200

FEATURES:
The inspiration for the name comes from an underlying vision of creating an airline that bridges the gap between the people of the region, replacing nationalistic ideals with a more all-embracing attitude. The red and white colors are those of Sharjah International Airport, which is its base of operations, with a white seagull highlighted on the red tailfin of the aircraft.

Air Astana (4L/KZR)

KAZAKHSTAN (UN)

Major Kazakhstan airline serving a domestic network and international flights from the main city of Almaty to destinations in Western Europe, the Middle East, the Indian subcontinent, and the Far East. Some schedules to Western Europe are also operated from the capital Astana and the towns of Atyrau, Karaganda, Kostanay, and Oral. Seasonal summer services are flown to the European points, while a winter service operates to Thailand. Air Astana was set up on 11 September 1991 as a joint venture between the Kazakhstan Government and the UK's BAE Systems.

FLEET:
2 X B737-700, 1 X B737-800, 4 X B757-200, 5 X F50

FEATURES:
The livery makes use of the national colors of blue and gold, representing the endless sky over the country's steppes. The airline's initials, drawn in gold and white in the form of a traditional national ornamentation and turned to represent arrows moving forward, decorate the blue tailfin of the aircraft. The symbol is repeated in front of the web address on the forward fuselage.

Air Atlanta Icelandic (cc/abd)

ICELAND (TF)

International wet-lease specialist providing passenger and cargo capacity to airlines and tour operators on an aircraft, crew, maintenance, and insurance basis. Although most flying is done in the markings of customer airlines, Air Atlanta also offers charters from Kevlavik in its own colors for Icelandic tour operators. Air Atlanta Icelandic was founded by Captain Arngrim Johansson and Thora Gudmundsdottir on 10 February 1986. Islandsflug, founded in 1991 through the amalgamation of Eagle Air Domestic and Flugtak, was merged into Air Atlanta on 1 January 2005.

FLEET:
1 X A310-300, 1 X B737-300QC, 1 X B737-400, 2 X B747-200B, 2 X B747-200F, 2 X B747-300, (4) X B777-200LRF

FEATURES:
The airline symbol on the blue tailfin is a globe in which the curve and momentum of the a, the initial letter in the name, refer to speed and flexibility, while the line through it forms a trip around the world in a reference to its worldwide operations. Blue is the color of sky and sea, while the golden color conveys a feeling of stability and trust and may also be seen as the landmass of the the earth.

Air Austral (uu/reu)

RÉUNION (F-O)

Regional airline based on the island of Réunion in the Indian Ocean off the southern African coast providing scheduled passenger and cargo services from St. Denis de la Réunion to Mayotte, Mauritius, Madagascar, Comores, Seychelles, and South Africa. A long-haul service also links Réunion with Paris. Air Austral was established as Réunion Air Service in October 1974 and operated as Air Réunion from March 1987 until 1990 when the present title was adopted. It was certified in March 1975 for air-taxi and air-ambulance flights and began scheduled passenger services on 8 August 1977.

FLEET:
1 X ATR 72-500, 1 X B737-300, 1 X B737-500, 3 X B777-200ER

FEATURES:
The mid-blue tailfin incorporates the airline's mirrored AA logo in a light blue and white, which is repeated on the similarly colored aircraft engines. A light blue cheatline rides above the darker underside, with the French and European Union flags at the rear. The word austral means "coming from the south."

Air Bagan (W9)

MYANMAR (XY)

Prominent domestic airline operating a comprehensive network linking the capital Yangon to 12 cities along the length and breath of Myanmar. The airline's name derives from the ancient city of Bagan, whose hundreds of temples rival those of Angkor Wat in Cambodia. Air Bagan was established in June 2004 as a joint venture between the Ministry of Transport and Htoo Trading, primarily to develop the country's tourist industry. The first commercial flights were undertaken from Yangon on 15 November that same year.

FLEET:
2 X ATR 42-320, 1 X ATR 72-200, 2 X F100

FEATURES:
The turquoise tailfin on the mostly white aircraft is distinguished by an artistic representation of the lotus flower, which in Myanmar culture symbolizes purity and the promise of man to strive for the highest achievements. It communicates a synthesis of bold, modern entrepreneurial principles and a desire to be the best. Strong turquoise *Air Bagan* lettering across the white fuselage is notable for the freehand script.

AirBaltic (BT/BTI)

LATVIA (YL)

Latvian flag-carrier providing international scheduled passenger and cargo services from the capital Riga and neighboring Vilnius in Lithuania, to cities in northern Europe. Services are operated in a strategic partnership with Scandinavian Airlines (SAS), which holds a major financial stake, under the "Well connected with SAS" banner. AirBaltic was established on 28 August 1995 as a joint venture between the Latvian government and SAS, taking over from Baltic International Airlines and government-owned Latavio. The first service was flown on 1 October that same year.

FLEET:
7 X B737-500, 7 X F50

FEATURES:
The present identity, developed by Stockholm Design Lab and inspired by the Baltic Sea, features a simple lime green tailfin with white *Baltic* titles, to provide a vivid, contemporary, eye-catching image that illustrates the airline's confidence and accentuates its regional status. Deep blue and gray *airBaltic.com* titles, an arrow symbol signifying a forward-looking attitude, and silver engine cowlings are the only other adornments on the white aircraft.

Air Berlin (AB/BER)

GERMANY (D)

Fast-growing German low-fare airline, serving all the major leisure destinations in the Mediterranean basin, as well as the Canary Islands, Madeira, and Portugal. The Majorca Shuttle operates daily flights from 12 German airports, while the City Shuttle connects nine German airports with major European cities. Air Berlin was founded on 11 July 1978 in the U.S. because after WWII only aircraft from the Allied powers were allowed to land in Berlin. Operations were started on 28 April 1979 with a Boeing 707 flight to Palma de Mallorca. The airline was incorporated in Germany on 16 April 1991.

FLEET:
5 (55) x A320-200, 5 x B737-400, 3 x B737-700, 38 x B737-800

FEATURES:
The Air Berlin livery has not changed markedly since its foundation and features a burgundy underbelly and pencil line above that sweep up the rear of the tailfin. Similarly colored *Air Berlin* titles with a dash in between take up most of the fin and are repeated above the forward cabin windows. The web address underneath is a concession to the Internet age.

Air Botswana (BP/BOT)

BOTSWANA (A2)

National airline operating scheduled domestic services from the capital Gaborone, together with regional flights to Zimbabwe and South Africa to assist in the economic development of the country and promote tourism. Of particular importance is the route from Johannesburg to Maun, which serves the magnificent wetland wilderness of the Okavango Delta. Air Botswana was set up in August 1972 following the reorganization of Botswana Airways, established in 1969 to succeed Botswana National Airways. It was taken over by the government in April 1988 and has since been partially privatized.

FLEET:
3 x ATR 42-500, 1 x BAE 146-100, 1 x Beech 1900D, 1 x F28-4000

FEATURES:
The livery has been inspired by the blue, black, and white of the national flag, which symbolizes the equality and unity of the black and white populations under the country's blue sky. The zebra stripes in blue and black on the white tailfin refer to Botswana's richness in animals roaming free in the wild. *Air Botswana* titles in black break the blue and black cheatlines running the length of the fuselage.

Air Burkina (2J/VBW)

BURKINA FASO (XT)

National airline of the West African state of Burkina Faso providing a small regional network from the capital Ouagadougou to other West African countries, together with a long-haul flight to Paris. A domestic shuttle links Ouagadougou with the country's second city of Bobo-Dioulasso. The airline was formed as Air Volta on 17 March 1967, when Burkina Faso was still called Upper Volta, with the assistance of Air Afrique and the independent French airline UTA. Operations began with local routes around Ouagadougou. The present name was adopted following the country's change of name in 1984.

FLEET:
1 x A319-100, 1 x F28-4000

FEATURES:
Red, green, and yellow are the national pan-African colors, signifying the break with the colonial past and unity with other African former colonies. The red stands for the revolution, green, for the abundance of natural riches, and yellow (from the star in the flag) as a guiding light. The symbol on the tailfin represents a local tribal mask.

Air Cairo (MSC)

EGYPT (SU)

Subsidiary of national airline EgyptAir providing low-cost charter flights to the Egyptian holiday resorts and ancient cities, such as Sharm el Sheikh, Hurgada, Luxor, and Aswan, from Europe, Africa, and Asia. Flights are also undertaken within Egypt. Air Cairo was initially established in 1997 by a group of local travel agents and began operations with Tupolev TU-204-120s leased from Sirocco Aviation. Majority control was acquired by EgyptAir in 2003.

FLEET:
2 x A321-200

FEATURES:
The bright blue tail, engines, and winglets, together with blue and red *Air Cairo* titles in English and Arabic on the forward fuselage, give the aircraft a smart and balanced look. However, the *Cairo* logo, comprising a red C enclosing the remaining golden letters, applied on the tailfin and engine cowlings, has not been drawn very artistically and detracts somewhat from the otherwise pleasing appearance. The red, white, and black Egyptian flag has been painted at the rear.

Air Calédonie International (Aircalin) (sb/aci)

NEW CALEDONIA (f-o)

International carrier of the French Overseas Territory of New Caledonia in the southwest Pacific Ocean providing scheduled services from the capital Noumea to other Pacific islands including Fiji, Wallis and Futuna, Vanuatu, and Tahiti, together with longer flights to Japan, Australia, and New Zealand. The airline was established in September 1983 and inaugurated its first flight on 2 December that year with a service to Melbourne in partnership with Qantas using a Boeing 747. Its first owned aircraft, a Caravelle 10B, arrived in October 1984.

FLEET:
1 X A320-200, 2 X A330-200, 1 X DHC-6 Twin Otter 300

FEATURES:
A beautiful red hibiscus decorates the tailfin and engines of the aircraft, symbolizing a young, dynamic company at home in Oceania. Blue *Aircalin* titles are applied on the forward upper fuselage with the airline's full title in gray below the cabin windows.

Air Calédonie (ty/tpc)

NEW CALEDONIA (f-o)

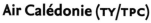

Regional airline of the French Overseas Territory of New Caledonia in the southwest Pacific Ocean operating scheduled services to more than 10 destinations from Magenta Airport in the capital Noumea on the main island to the Loyalty Islands, Isles de Pins, North Province, and Tontouta. Air Calédonie was founded in October 1954 as Société Caledonienne de Transports Aériens (Transpac) and began operations on 25 September 1955 between Noumea, Mare, and Lifou with a de Havilland DH.89A Dragon Rapide. The name was changed to the present title on 30 October 1967.

FLEET:
3 X ATR 42-300, (1) X ATR 42-500, (2) X ATR 72-500, 1 x Dornier 228-200

FEATURES:
The intriguing symbol on the tailfin is dominated by a yellow and orange sun that is setting behind a native carving similar to those decorating the top of the huts of the great chiefs. It signifies that the airline is devoted entirely to the inhabitants of these paradise islands. The only other splash of color on the white aircraft is a Pacific blue cheatline with inset *Air Calédonie* titles, also in blue.

Air Canada (AC/ACA)

CANADA (C)

Canada's largest airline providing passenger and cargo flights to the u.s. and the Caribbean, together with trans-Pacific routes to the Far East, and services across the North Atlantic to Europe. All major domestic points are scheduled, with feeder services provided by Air Canada Jazz. Air Canada Jetz is the premium business brand, serving corporate clients, and special-interest groups with specially configured aircraft and high-quality service. Air Canada was formed on 10 April 1937 as Trans-Canada Airlines and began operations on 7 July that year with survey flights. Scheduled passenger services between Montreal and Vancouver were inaugurated on 1 April 1939. The present title was adopted on 1 January 1965 to reflect its status as the national airline. It was privatized in July 1989 and acquired Canadian Airlines in January 2000. Canadian Airlines was formed as Canadian Pacific Air Lines on 31 January 1942 by the Canadian Pacific Railway to take over and unify a group of 10 small operators. The 10 were Arrow Airways, Canadian Airways, Dominion Skyways, Ginger Coote Airways, Mackenzie Air Services, Prairie Airways, Quebec Airways, Starratt Airways, Wings, and Yukon Southern Air Transport. The name was changed to cp Air in 1968 and the airline grew substantially in 1987, when it adopted the Canadian Airlines name.

FLEET:
48 X A319-100, 52 X A320-200, 10 X A321-200, 8 X A330-300, 10 X A340-300, 2 X A340-500, (3) X A340-600, 3 X B747-400M, 6 X B767-200, 7 X B767-200ER, 32 X B767-300ER, (18) X B777, (14) X B787, 22 X CRJ100ER, 9 (6) X EMB 175LR, (45) X EMB 175LR

FEATURES:
Air Canada's livery, designed by FutureBrand Worldwide, features fresh clean lines and lighter colors, reflecting a new modernity and added energy. It symbolizes Air Canada's approach to streamlining customer service and developing innovative products through simplification. The distinctive red maple leaf on the tailfin is complemented by a graphic dot patterned representation called the "frosted leaf," symbolizing Canada, its people, and its strength. The Air Canada Jetz aircraft have blue *Jetz* titles under the Air Canada logo.

Air Canada Jazz (QK/ARN)
CANADA (C)

One of the world's largest regional airlines serving some 70 destinations in Canada and the United States from operational bases across Canada at Vancouver, Calgary, Toronto, London, Montreal, and Quebec City. The network provides seamless connections with the worldwide network of its parent company and other Star Alliance members. The airline was formed on 1 January 2001 from the merger of four regional airline brands – AirBC, Air Nova, Air Ontario, and Canadian Regional Airlines – all operating under the Air Canada Connector brand. It was initially known as Air Canada Regional.

FLEET:
10 X BAE 146-200, 3 X CRJ100ER, 10 X CRJ200ER, 15 X CRJ200LR, 10 (5) X CRJ705LR, 42 X Dash 8 100, 25 X Dash 8 300

FEATURES:
An attractive scheme that features a large maple leaf on the white tailfin and the word Jazz painted freely across the rear fuselage under the Air Canada logo. The web address is carried above the forward cabin windows. The fleet is painted in four colors – red, orange, yellow, and green – in reference to its four ancestor airlines.

Air Caraïbes (TX/FWI)
FRENCH WEST INDIES (F-O)

Principal airline in the French West Indies offering scheduled and charter flights within the Caribbean and Central America, together with a long-haul connection to Paris. Air Caraïbes was founded in 1970 as Air Guadeloupe but adopted the present name in July 2000 after merging with Air Martinique and Air St. Barthelemy. Air Martinique was established in 1974 as Compagnie Antillaise d'Afretements Aériens and changed its name on 20 October 1993, while Air St. Barthelemy started operations on 1 october 1981. Air Caraïbes started flying across the Atlantic in December 2003.

FLEET:
2 X A330-200, (1) X A330-300, 1 X ATR 42-500, 3 X ATR 72-500, 6 X Dornier 228-200, 2 X ERJ 145MP

FEATURES:
The mid-blue underside of the aircraft graduates to sky blue as it sweeps up the tailfin, whose lower half is covered in the airline's symbol of palm fronds over stylized blue and yellow wings. This design is repeated over forward Air Caraïbes titles, which graduate from darker blue at the top to sky blue. The aircraft engines are painted in mid-blue.

Air Central (ANA Connection) (NV)

JAPAN (JA)

Regional airline providing scheduled passenger and cargo services from Nagoya on the main Japanese island of Honshu to some 10 other cities across Japan. All services are operated on behalf of All Nippon Airways under the ANA Connection banner. The airline was initially founded by the Nagoya Railroad Company and ANA on 12 May 1988 as Nakanihon Airlines and began commuter services on 23 April 1991. In November 2004, ANA acquired a controlling stake. The carrier was renamed along with the opening of the new Chubu Centrair International Airport serving Nagoya on 17 February 2005.

FLEET:
4 x Fokker 50

FEATURES:
Air Central aircraft are painted in the basic ANA scheme, comprising an angular cheatline in two shades of blue that runs up the white upper fuselage until it takes over the whole of the tail, incorporating the ANA logo in white. The logo also appears on both sides of the front fuselage.

Air China (CA/CCA)

CHINA (B)

China's flag-carrier serving mostly regional and intercontinental passenger and cargo services from Beijing's Capital Airport to more than 30 cities in Asia, Australia, Europe, Canada, and the United States. Other Chinese cities linked into the international network are Dalian, Guangzhou, Kunming, Shanghai, and Xiamen. An extensive domestic trunk network is also operated. The airline was founded on 2 November 1949 as part of the Civil Aviation Administration of China and adopted its present title on 1 July 1988. It is the major carrier within China National Aviation Holding.

FLEET:
1 (5) x A319-100, (20) x A330-200, 1 x A330-300, 3 x A340-300, 5 x B737-300, (9) x B737-700, 11 (7) x B737-800, 4 x B747-400, 8 x B747-400M, 5 x B767-200ER, 4 x B767-300, 5 x B767-300ER, 10 x 777-200, (15) x B787-8

FEATURES:
The white tailfin is dominated by the sacred phoenix of Chinese legend, which flies over towering Kunlun Mountain and crosses the vast expanses of the China Sea, alluded to by the blue cheatlines below. The phoenix is said to bring good fortune, joy, and peace.

Air Creebec (YN/CRQ)

CANADA (C)

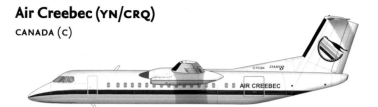

Quebec-based airline providing vital air links to some 17 destinations in northern Ontario and Quebec, contributing to the social and economic development of the Cree nation. Also operates VIP and speciality charters and cargo flights. Air Creebec was established in 1979 by the Cree Regional Authority and Austin Airways, following the James Bay and Northern Quebec Agreement, Canada's first modern aboriginal land-claim settlement approved by the Cree and Inuit. Operations began on 5 July 1982. The airline became wholly Cree owned in 1988.

FLEET:
1 X BAE 748-2A, 4 x Dash 8 100, 1 x Dash 8 Q300, 3 x EMB 110P1 Bandeirante, 1 x Beech 1900D

FEATURES:
The interesting symbol on the white tailfin depicts the outline of a Cree drum and a Canada goose flying above a triple line of red, orange, and yellow, repeated in the form of a cheatline along the lower part of the aircraft and engines. Black *Air Creebec* titles are applied at the rear.

Air Deccan (DN/DKN)

INDIA (VT)

Indian low-fare airline operating a growing network of services from Bangalore to more than 30 points in southern India, with other services extending to Delhi and places further north, as well as parts of eastern India. Major destinations include Delhi, Mumbai, Kolkata, Hyderabad, Chennai, Cochin, Srinagar, and others. Air Deccan, a unit of Deccan Aviation, India's largest private helicopter-charter company, was established in 2003 and began flying on 27 August that year. The parent company uses helicopters for charters, tourist flights, emergency medical, and offshore services.

FLEET:
5 X ATR 42-300, 7 X ATR 42-500, (30) X ATR 72-500, 5 (35) X A320-200

FEATURES:
The airline symbol in blue and yellow on the white tailfin comprises two open hands in a blue disc spread wide in a welcoming gesture, emphasizing its wish to provide a friendly service. A sky blue windowline graduates towards the white of the main body of the aircraft, with blue *Air Deccan* titles applied above the forward cabin.

Air Do (Hokkaido International Airlines) (HD/ADO)

JAPAN (JA)

Independent domestic airline established on 14 November 1996 to take advantage of the impending deregulation of the Japanese domestic market. The airline operates several daily services on the high-density trunk route between Tokyo Haneda and Sapporo. Other points served from Tokyo are Asahikawa and Hakodate, like the capital Sapporo also on the northernmost island of Hokkaido. The brainchild of a successful poultry farmer on Hokkaido, Air Do began flying with a single Boeing 767-200 on 20 December 1998.

FLEET:
1 x B737-400, 1 x B767-300, 2 x B767-300ER

FEATURES:
The bright livery is highlighted by a straight double cheatline of blue and yellow and a tailfin where the two colors are divided diagonally with the yellow predominant. Black *Air Do* titles straddle the tail colors, while the airline's official title *Hokkaido International Airlines*, sits above the forward cabin windows.

Air Dolomiti (EN/DLA)

ITALY (I)

Largest regional airline in Italy, providing domestic services in northern and central Italy from its base at Verona. It also flies across the Alps to points in Europe, particularly in Germany. The airline is a wholly owned subsidiary of Germany's flag-carrier Lufthansa and operates extensive feeder flights to its parent company's hubs at Frankfurt, Munich, and Vienna. It operates as part of the Lufthansa Regional strategic grouping, although it has been allowed to retain its own strong brand. Air Dolomiti was founded by the Leali steel group in January 1989 and began scheduled operations two years later.

FLEET:
8 x ATR 42-500, 8 x ATR 72-500, 3 x BAE 146-300

FEATURES:
The light blue and white colors reflect the cloudless sky over the snow-covered mountains of the Dolomites, after which the airline has been named. The blue ribbons draped around the aircraft fuselage lead to the similarly colored tailfin, which incorporates the company symbol of three diamonds forming an arrow in flight and *Air Dolomiti* titles below, repeated under the windows.

Air Europa (UX/AEA)

SPAIN (EC)

Palma de Mallorca based independent airline specializing in inclusive-tour services between northern Europe and the Balearic and Canary islands. Scheduled services also serve all major domestic towns and cities, and there are long-haul flights to North America and the Caribbean. Air Europa was founded on 17 February 1984 as Air España and began flying in November 1986. Originally part of the Airlines of Europe Group, it was acquired by Spanish investors in 1991. Scheduled passenger services were added on 1 November 1993 following liberalization of the domestic market.

FLEET:
(2) x A330-200, 1 x A340-200, 2 x B737-400, 28 (22) x B737-800, 5 x 767-300ER

FEATURES:
With the emphasis moving away from inclusive-tour flights, the previous sunshine colors have been replaced by a smarter and simpler scheme to convey the airline's progress into the scheduled-services market. Handwritten and entwined *ae* initials in sky blue are followed by bold *Air Europa* titles in red, both on the forward fuselage and covering the majority of the white tailfin of the aircraft.

Air Europe (PE/AEL)

ITALY (I)

Italian leisure airline operating scheduled and charter passenger services for major tour operators out of Milan Malpensa and Rome Fiumicino airports. Scheduled services link both cities with Mauritius, while Milan has a direct service to Cuba. Charter flights operate to Egypt and Zanzibar. Air Europe, now a member of the Volare Group, was founded in 1988 and began operations on 19 December 1989 as part of the UK-based Airlines of Europe Group, but became Italian owned in March 1991. Operations ceased in November 2004 but were restarted on a smaller scale on 27 December.

FLEET:
1 x B767-300ER

FEATURES:
The airline's interesting logo featuring a series of orange swirls takes pride of place on the white tailfin but is also applied on the blue engine cowlings and ahead of the blue and orange *Air Europe* titles on the forward cabin roof. The main body of the aircraft is painted white, with the underside in dark blue.

Air Fiji (PC/FAJ)
FIJI (DQ)

Largest and longest-serving domestic airline operating an interisland network, with 65 daily flights radiating from Nadi and Nausori on the largest island of Viti Levu to some 15 other exotic islands. A regional route is operated to Tuvalu. Charter flights within the Fiji Islands and to other parts of the South Pacific are also offered. The airline was founded on 10 July 1967 and was known as Air Pacific until 29 March 1971, when it adopted the Fiji Air name. The two words were transposed in February 1995, concurrent with a major expansion.

FLEET:
2 X BN-2A Islander,
4 X EMB 110P1 Bandeirante,
3 X EMB 110P2 Bandeirante,
1 X EMB 120ER Brasilia,
2 x Hamc Y-12 II

FEATURES:
The airline's beautifully drawn tropical symbol, displayed on the tailfin, shows a green seabird in sunshine flying above the green of the islands. Flashes in the same three colors continue the design through to the rear of the fuselage. Some aircraft carry *Pacific Link* titles and other slogans, but there are also several special schemes within the fleet.

Air Finland (OF/FIF)
FINLAND (OH)

Finnish airline specializing in leisure flights to southern destinations in the Mediterranean, the Canary Islands, and the European resorts most popular with Finnish travelers. The airline also flies holiday packages for many of the country's major tour operators. Air Finland was founded on 13 June 2002 and started flying with a single Boeing 757 on 30 March 2003.

FLEET:
2 X B757-200

FEATURES:
The simple but effective color scheme features an orange sun on a Mediterranean blue tailfin, alluding to the airline's leisure-based activities. The Mediterranean blue is reiterated on the engine cowlings, as well as in the airline titles on the upper forward fuselage. *Air Finland* titles are also set in part into the sun and in part into the blue fin.

Air France (AF/AFR)

FRANCE (F)

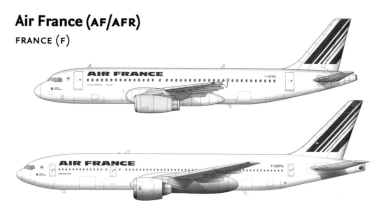

National carrier operating services to some 200 destinations in more than 80 countries from main hubs at Paris Charles de Gaulle and Orly airports, with a particularly strong presence in Europe, Africa, and the French Overseas Departments in the Caribbean, Indian, and Pacific oceans. An extensive domestic network is supplemented by several regional franchises. Air France was founded on 30 August 1933 when Société Centrale pour l'Exploitation de Lignes Aériennes, itself formed on 17 May 1933 by an amalgamation of Air Orient, Air Union, CIDNA, and SGTA, purchased the assets of Compagnie Génerale Aéropostale, a South Atlantic pioneer, which had been founded in 1927. The oldest predecessor was CFRNA, which was founded on 23 April 1920 and became CIDNA on 25 January 1925. Domestic carrier Air Inter, which had started flying on 17 March 1958; Air Charter, set up as a subsidiary on 7 February 1966; and long-haul airline UTA (Union de Transports Aériens), formed on 1 October 1963 through the merger of Union Aéromaritime de Transports and Compagnie de Transports Aériens Intercontinentaux; merged into the Air France Group on 12 January 1990. In May 2004, Air France and Dutch airline KLM completed a merger, becoming the Air France-KLM Group, although each retains its individual brand.

FLEET:
15 (3) X A318-100, 45 X A319-100, 13 X A320-100, 54 X A320-200, 5 X A321-100, 8 X A321-200, 14 X A330-200, 2 X A330-300, 20 X A340-300, (10) X A380-800, 13 X B737-500, 3 X B747-200C, 8 X B747-200F, 2 X B747-300M, 10 X B747-400, 5 X B747-400ERF, 6 X B747-400M, 25 X 777-200ER, (5) X B777-200LRF, 10 (10) X B777-300ER

FEATURES:
Based on the French tricolor, the pure white overall fuselage finish is highlighted by bold blue *Air France* titles in uppercase lettering, led by its long-established winged sea horse symbol in blue. The aircraft's major design element is a splash of color in the form of blue and red stripes in varying widths sweeping up the tailfin. Freighter aircraft carry additional *Cargo* titles after the name, rendered in a striped font to suggest speed. The Air France aircraft now also carry the SkyTeam Alliance logo behind the cockpit windows.

Air Gabon (GN/AGN)

GABON (TR)

Flag-carrier of Gabon operating international services from Libreville to regional points throughout West Africa and further afield to South Africa and Europe. A small domestic network links the major towns. Its history goes back to 1951 and the foundation of Compagnie Aérienne Gabonaise, later becoming known as Société Nationale Transgabon, before adopting the present title on 1 June 1977 following Gabon's withdrawal from the Air Afrique consortium. Operations under the new name began on 2 June and the airline was designated Gabon's international carrier on 23 December that year.

FLEET:
1 X AN-12B, 1 X B737-200C,
1 X B737-400, 1 X B767-200ER

FEATURES:
The pure white finish of the aircraft fuselage is further freshened by the airline's stylized green parrot symbol on the tailfin, and *Air Gabon* titles in blue. A patriotic tricolor cheatline in the green, yellow and red colors of the national flag runs below the windows and extends the length of the fuselage. The color green stands for the Gabonese forests, yellow for the warm sun, and blue for the abundant sea.

Air Greenland (GL/GRL)

GREENLAND (OY)

Greenland-based air carrier providing concessional air services to all local communities and the only link between this huge Arctic island and the Kingdom of Denmark of which it forms a part (although enjoying relative independence). Air Greenland also performs charter, air-taxi, air-ambulance, search-and-rescue, and other flights with fixed-wing aircraft and helicopters, as well as contract operations for the u.s. Air Force to the Thule Airbase. It was established as Greenlandair (Grønlandsfly) on 7 November 1960 and began flying on 1 May 1962. The present name was adopted in 2002.

FLEET:
1 X A330-200, 1 X B757-200,
2 X DHC-6 Twin Otter 300,
6 X DHC-7-100

FEATURES:
The airline's striking red overall aircraft livery is contrasted with a pattern of white dots of different sizes on the tailfin, making the connection with the icy landscape bathed in the midnight sun. Red and white are also the colors of the national flag. Lowercase *Air Greenland* titles are highlighted in white on the forward fuselage below the windowline.

Air Guinée Express (J9/GIB)

GUINEA (3X)

Flag-carrier of the West African state of Guinea, connecting the capital Conakry with other capital cities in West Africa. A comprehensive domestic route system also radiates from Conakry to all parts of the country. Air Guinée was established by government decree on 31 December 1960 following an agreement reached the previous March with the Soviet Union for the supply of aircraft and technical assistance. Operations started with two Ilyushin IL-14s over two domestic routes linking Conakry with Boake and Kankan.

FLEET:
1 X AN-24V, 1 X B737-200A,
1 x Dash 7-110, 1 X XAC Y-7-100

FEATURES:
As befits a national airline, Air Guinée uses the green, yellow, and red colors of the flag to good effect. The cheatline along the side of the fuselage uses all three colors, but the dominant feature is the tailfin, which displays an outline of Africa in yellow on green, with the country's location within the continent marked in red. The yellow stripes represent speed and dynamism. *Air Guinée Express* titles are applied in red.

Air Guyane Express/Air Antilles Express (3S/GUY)

FRENCH GUIANA/FRENCH WEST INDIES (F-O)

Regional airline operating scheduled services in French Guiana, linking the capital Cayenne with three other major towns in the country, as well as providing charter flights within South America and the southern Caribbean. Subsidiary Air Antilles Express provides a similar service connecting the islands of the French West Indies in the Caribbean with each other and linking them to Santo Domingo in the Dominican Republic. Both operations were established by Christian Marchand, owner of Guyane Aero Invest and Antilles Aero Invest, in co-operation with local tourist and trade organizations.

FLEET:
1 X ATR 42-300, 1 X ATR 42-500,
1 X BN-2A Islander,
3 X DHC-6 Twin Otter 300,
1 x Reims F406 Caravan II

FEATURES:
The aircraft of both airlines are instantly recognizable by the colorful floral design scattered across the tailfin and lower rear fuselage. More sober *Air Guyane* or *Air Antilles* titles in blue capital letters are preceded by a red bird in flight against a blue circle, the latter symbol also being repeated on the engine cowling.

Air Hongkong (LD/AHK)

HONG KONG (B-H)

Hong Kong's only dedicated all-cargo airline operating a network of scheduled cargo services in Asia and serving destinations in Thailand, Malaysia, Singapore, Taiwan, Japan, and South Korea. The airline carries mostly express packages in a business partnership with DHL Express Worldwide, forged in October 2002. General cargo is also carried and some charter flights are undertaken. Air Hongkong was established in 1986 to provide cargo charter flights between Asia and Europe and began operations on 4 February 1988. Scheduled services were added on 18 October 1989. The airline is now a subsidiary of Cathay Pacific Airways.

FLEET:
7 (2) X A300-600GF

FEATURES:
The livery represents a smart interpretation of the paint scheme of DHL, using the yellow and red DHL house colors, while maintaining the Air Hongkong identity through strong red titles on the forward white fuselage. The yellow of the tailfin wraps around the rear fuselage and incorporates the DHL marque. The yellow engines complement the overall effect.

Air Iceland (Flugfélag Islands) (NY/FXI)

ICELAND (TF)

Regional airline providing a domestic service to nine destinations, with links to Greenland and the Faroe Islands. It also offers a wide variety of Getaway packages and day tours to all parts of Iceland. Air Iceland was established in 1997 through the merger of Icelandair's domestic operations and Flugfélag Nordurlands. The latter had been founded by Tryggi Helgason on 1 November 1959 as Nordur-flug, which initially provided air-taxi and ambulance flights with a single Piper Apache, before quickly moving into scheduled operations. It adopted the Flugfélag Nordurlands title on 1 May 1975.

FLEET:
2 x DHC-6 Twin Otter 300,
1 x Metro III, 6 x F50

FEATURES:
The central motif of the airline is a flying horse with a yellow ocher outline, which emerges from the blue half of the tailfin. The blue, underscored by an ocher band, sweeps down and along the fuselage, ending in a razor point about halfway along. Blue *Flugfélag Islands* titles, the Icelandic equivalent of the anglicized name, appear on both sides of the fuselage.

Air-India (AI/AIC)

INDIA (VT)

India's international flag-carrier providing extensive passenger and cargo services from Ahmedabad, Bangalore, Kolkata (Calcutta), Chennai (Madras), Delhi, Goa, Hyderabad, Mumbai (Bombay), and Thiruvananthapuram to destinations in the Asia Pacific region, the Middle East and Persian Gulf, Africa, Europe, and North America. Established on 15 October 1932 as Tata Airlines, it became Air-India on 29 July 1946 and Air-India International on 8 March 1948, after which it started international flights to London Heathrow on 8 June that year. It was nationalized on 1 August 1953. International was dropped from the name in 1962.

FLEET:
20 X A310-300, (4) X B737-800, 2 X B747-200B, 2 X B747-300M, 11 X B747-400, 1 X B747-400M, 3 X B777-200ER

FEATURES:
The windows are fashioned into graceful Rajasthani-style arches that produce the effect of a row of Jharoka-type balconies, recalling the Hawa Mahal balconies of Jaipur. The whole design is framed in red. The name is painted in Hindi along the fuselage and in English atop a red fin flash. The centaur, a stylized version of Sagittarius, the archer, symbolizes movement and speed.

Air-India Express (IX/AXB)

INDIA (VT)

Subsidiary of Air-India operating low-fare services between major Indian cities and the Persian Gulf and southeast Asia. An increasing number of destinations are served from five Indian cities, Calicut, Kochi, Thiruvananthapuram, Mumbai, and Delhi, primarily serving the non-resident Indian market within four hours' flying time. The low-cost arm of the national flag-carrier was established at the end of 2004 under the operating authority of Air-India Charters and began flying on 29 April 2005 with an inaugural flight between Thiruvananthapuram and Abu Dhabi in the UAE.

FLEET:
3 X B737-800

FEATURES:
The orange and yellow tailfins stand out because of the variety of designs adopted, each side painted differently, with designs including a sitar, flying kites in rainbow colors, a pair of drums, an elephant head and trunk decorated for a festive occasion, the head of a camel dressed in traditional colors, and more as new aircraft are delivered. Common to all aircraft are the red folds of "fabric" draped around the rear fuselage, and red *Air-India Express* titling.

Air Inuit (3H/AIE)

CANADA (C)

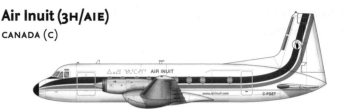

Inuit-owned airline providing essential passenger, charter, cargo, and emergency transportation in the Nunavik area in northern Quebec, which takes up almost 40% of territorial Quebec. Nearly 20 communities are served along the eastern Hudson Bay coast, southern shore of Hudson Strait, and the Ungava coasts. Air Inuit, owned collectively by the Inuit through the Makivik Corporation, was founded in 1978 with a single de Havilland Beaver floatplane, following the James Bay and Northern Quebec Agreement, Canada's first modern land-claim settlement conferring territorial rights on the Inuit. It was reorganized in 1985.

FLEET:
4 X BAE 748-2A, 7 x Dash 8 100, 2 x DHC-2 Beaver, 2 x DHC-3 Otter, 7 x DHC-6 Twin Otter 300

FEATURES:
From a point at the nose, the broad red windowline and narrower terracotta band speed along the fuselage and sweep up the center of the tailfin. The gold pencil line runs straight through, adding a streamlining effect. In the center of the fin is the symbol of the Makivik Corporation, showing an Inuit figure fronting the outline of the Nunavik area. The attractive local script precedes English *Air Inuit* titles.

Air Italy (AEY)

ITALY (I)

One of Italy's newest private airlines operating leisure flights for leading tour operators and other charter airlines out of Turin, as well as out of Milan Malpensa, where the airline maintains a technical base. The first service was flown on 29 May 2005 on behalf of leading Italian tour operator Francorosso, linking Turin Caselle with Budapest, the capital of Hungary.

FLEET:
2 X B757-200

FEATURES:
The patriotic palette of the Italian tricolor is used to good effect, with three green bands of varying widths and a single red band covering most of the tailfin, angled in line with the leading edge. Black *Air Italy* titles are riding above the green. The only other design on the white fuselage and engines is black *Air Italy* lettering over a segment of the tailfin coloring and the slogan "It's nice to fly with friends again!" at the rear cabin roof.

Air Ivoire (Nouvelle Air Ivoire) (VU/VUN)

CÔTE D'IVOIRE (TU)

National airline operating a small network of scheduled passenger and cargo services from Abidjan, the main commercial center, to other West African cities, with an extension to France. Air Ivoire was set up on 14 December 1960 to take over local services from French airline Transports Aeriens Intercontinentaux and began operations in August 1964 with de Havilland DH.89A Rapides over three domestic routes. It came into government ownership in January 1976. The airline suspended operations in September 1999 but was later reformed as Nouvelle Air Ivoire, trading under its original name.

FLEET:
3 × F28 MK4000

FEATURES:
The most notable feature on the airline's aircraft is the "speedbird" design, which has changed little in its history other than being drawn in a more modern form. The colors used are those of the national flag, which was adopted just prior to the country's independence from France on 7 August 1960. The orange stands for progress and the northern part of this West African country, while the green signifies hope and the forests of the south. White stands for unity.

Air Jamaica (JM/AJM)

JAMAICA (6Y)

National airline providing regional services from Kingston and Montego Bay to points in the Caribbean, Central America, and the U.S., as well as across the Atlantic to London. Interisland services were operated by subsidiary Air Jamaica Express. Air Jamaica was born in 1968 to succeed a company of the same name that had been established with the help of BOAC and BWIA in 1962. Operations began on 1 April 1969. It was partially privatized in November 1994. Air Jamaica Express, founded as Jamaica airtaxi and later known as Trans-Jamaican Airlines, was closed on 14 October 2005.

FLEET:
8 × A320-200, 6 × A321-200, 2 × A340-300

FEATURES:
The "Jamaican Flair" colors were introduced following privatization to convey facing the future with confidence. The splash of bright Caribbean colors graduate, in bands of varying size, from golden yellow to orange, magenta, and royal blue, ending in a sweep at the rear. The royal blue covers the tailfin and is interspersed with magenta and lighter blue stripes. On the tail is Air Jamaica's symbol, the doctor bird, a native of Jamaica.

Air Japan (NQ/AJX)

JAPAN (JA)

Member of the All Nippon Airways Group providing low-fare scheduled and seasonal charter services from Tokyo-Narita and Osaka-Kansai to the Hawaiian Islands, Guam, Hong Kong, and South Korea. Various destinations in China are also served. Air Japan is the reincarnation of charter subsidiary World Air Network, which was established on 29 June 1990 and operated its inaugural flight on 1 March 1991 between Oita on Kyushu, the southernmost of Japan's four main islands, and Singapore. Services under the Air Japan title were begun on 1 January 2001 between Osaka-Kansai and Seoul.

FLEET:
B767-300ER leased from All Nippon Airways as required

FEATURES:
As Air Japan uses aircraft from the parent company, it does not have its own identity, although aircraft sometimes carry additional *Air Japan* titles. The angular cheatline in two shades of blue broadens along the white upper fuselage until it takes over the whole of the tail, incorporating the ANA logo in white. The logo, alongside two-tone blue lines, also appears on both sides of the front fuselage.

Air Kiribati (4A)

KIRIBATI (T3)

National airline of the Republic of Kiribati, formerly known as the Gilbert Islands, a group of 33 coral atolls spread over a vast area of the Pacific Ocean, straddling the Equator. Scheduled services are flown from the capital Tarawa to all the Kiribati islands except to the Line and Phoenix islands. Air Kiribati also undertakes charters, medical evacuation, and search-and-rescue flights providing a vital service to these isolated communities. The airline was established by the government on 1 April 1995 to take over from the national carrier Air Tungaru, which had been founded on 31 October 1977.

FLEET:
1 X ATR 72-200, 2 X C-212-200 Aviocar, 1 x Harbin Y-12-II

FEATURES:
The livery is memorable for the striking representation of the national flag on the tailfin of its aircraft. A yellow sun rises above the white breakers of the blue Pacific Ocean, with a frigate bird flying overhead. Large blue *Air Kiribati* titles are set into the white fuselage at the front. Kiribati is the local pronunciation of the word "Gilbert."

Air Koryo (JS/KOR)

NORTH KOREA (P)

National airline of the Democratic People's Republic of Korea (North Korea), providing a small international network of scheduled passenger and cargo services from the capital Pyongyang to points in China, Thailand, and Russia's far east, together with charter flights, both commercial and for the government, to Asian, African, and some European countries. A small domestic route system is also maintained. The airline was organized in 1950 initially as a joint Soviet/Korean undertaking under the title of SOKAO but was renamed Chosonminhang in 1954. The present name was taken in 1993.

FLEET:
5 X AN-24RV, 2 X AN-24V, 1 X IL-18D, 1 X IL-18V, 4 X IL-62M, 3 X IL-76MD, 2 X TU-134B-3, 3 X TU-154B, 1 X TU-154B2

FEATURES:
Air Koryo is one of only a few airlines that have retained the drab and traditional Communist-era livery, although it has dabbled with applying a blue flying crane symbol on the tail. The only adornment on its aircraft is the national flag on the tailfin and a red cheatline trimmed with blue. The red band and star in the flag stand for Communism, while white suggests purity and blue represents hope of peace.

Air Labrador (WJ/LAL)

CANADA (C)

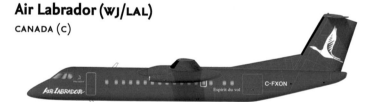

Labrador-based airline operating scheduled passenger and cargo services to some 30 communities in Newfoundland and Labrador, more than any other carrier. It also has an extensive charter business offering flights to remote and off-strip locations with ski-, wheel-, and float-equipped aircraft. Air Labrador was founded in 1948 as Newfoundland Airways and began with mail and cargo flights from its base at Gander using float-equipped aircraft. Scheduled services soon followed. Following a change of ownership in 1983, the airline moved its operation to Goose Bay.

FLEET:
3 x Dash 8 100, 1 x DHC-6 Twin Otter 100, 3 x DHC-6 Twin Otter 300, 1 x Beech 1900C-1, 1 x Beech 1900D

FEATURES:
It is rare to see an aircraft painted a single color, but the overall metallic blue Air Labrador craft stand out from the rest. A small number of white elements feature a representation on the tailfin of the Canada goose, which is prevalent in southern Canada; the airline title under the cockpit; and the "Esprit du vol" (Spirit of flight) slogan and the aircraft registration at the rear.

Air Lithuania (TT/KLA)

LITHUANIA (LY)

Regional airline operating scheduled passenger and cargo services from Kaunas and Palanga in western Lithuania to destinations in Scandinavia and Germany. Charter flights and aircraft leasing is also part of its flying business. Air Lithuania was founded as a state-owned company from the reorganization of the former subdivision of Aeroflot's Kaunas Joint Air Detachment. Charter flights were inaugurated on 15 February 1992, followed by the first scheduled service from Kaunas to Budapest in February 1993. On 17 July 1995 the airline was transformed into a joint-stock company but was privatized in May 2004.

FLEET:
2 X ATR 42-300

FEATURES:
A broad red band and thinner line start at the rear top of the tailfin and flow down and along the lower fuselage before ending at the nose of the aircraft. The bird symbol, outlined against a red sun, flies on the tail. Red *Air Lithuania* titles are applied on the forward cabin roof, preceded by the Lithuanian flag, in which yellow stands for the country's wheat fields, green for the forests, and red for patriotism. Collectively, the colors represent hope for the future, freedom from oppression, and courage.

Air Macau (NX/AMU)

MACAU (B-M)

Sole carrier of Macau, a Special Administrative Region of the People's Republic of China at the mouth of the Pearl River, operating scheduled passenger and cargo services to China, the Philippines, and points in Southeast Asia. It also provides a one-stop link between Taiwan and mainland China. Following the building of new casinos, and the inclusion of Macau in the list of the World Cultural Heritage sites, the airline also promotes this former Portuguese colony as a trade and tourist destination. Air Macau was founded on 13 September 1994 and began operations on 9 November 1995.

FLEET:
3 X A300B4-200F, 4 X A319-100,
1 X A320-200, 4 X A321-100,
3 X A321-200, 1 X B727-200F

FEATURES:
Air Macau's logo in red, white, and blue, which takes up the whole of the tailfin of the otherwise pristine white aircraft, is a fusion of a lotus flower (the symbol of Macau) and a white dove, alluding to international peace. The high-flying dove represents the airline's vision of the highest standards of safety, reliability, and quality of service to the passenger, and its ambition to become a preferred airline.

Air Madagascar (MD/MDG)

MALAGASY REPUBLIC (5R)

National carrier of the Malagasy Republic connecting the island of Madagascar with points in Europe, neighboring southern Africa, and other Indian Ocean states. An extensive domestic network serves more than 40 destinations, criss-crossing the island from the capital Antananarivo. The airline was formed as Madair in 1961 by the Malagasy government, Air France, and a predecessor company of the same name dating from 1947. The first service was inaugurated on 20 October 1961 to Paris, initially by the French carrier TAI with a Douglas DC-7C. The present name was adopted on 1 January 1962.

FLEET:
3 X ATR 42-300, (1) X ATR 42-500, (2) X ATR 72-500, 2 X B737-300, 2 X B767-300ER, 4 X DHC-6 Twin Otter 300

FEATURES:
The attractive image developed by Lufthansa Consulting combines elements from the airline's history and the qualities needed to access the global market. Its lively central symbol is the Ravenala tree, also known as the traveler's tree, which is unique to this island, and is prominently displayed in green on the tailfin. The green and red color mix has been supplemented with silver, signifying modernity.

Air Madrid (NM/DRI)

SPAIN (EC)

Spanish low-fare airline connecting the capital Madrid with a number of destinations in Central and South America, serving, among others, points in Costa Rica, the Dominican Republic, Panama, Colombia, Ecuador, Peru, and Brazil. Air Madrid was established in 2003 by Herminio Gil with the support of retail groups and several hotels. Operations began on 31 May 2004 with a flight to White End in the Dominican Republic using an Airbus A330.

FLEET:
1 X A310-300, 2 X A330-200, 1 X A340-300

FEATURES:
The simple livery comprises a bright red ribbon on the tailfin, engines, and winglets, and large blue Air Madrid titles on the forward fuselage. The airline's web address is painted on the lower rear fuselage. The aircraft is otherwise painted all in white.

Air Malawi (QM/AML)

MALAWI (7Q)

National airline operating a small domestic network and regional flights from Blantyre and Lilongwe to destinations in Kenya, Tanzania, Mozambique, Zambia, Zimbabwe, South Africa, and the Democratic Republic of the Congo. Holiday packages are also available for the East African markets. Air Malawi was formed on 1 September 1967 following the dissolution of the Central African Airways Corporation to succeed another airline with the same name, which had been established in March 1964 to take over local services in the newly independent state of Malawi, formerly Nyasaland.

FLEET:
1 X ATR 42-300, 1 X B737-200A, 1 X B737-300, 1 X LET L-410UVP-E

FEATURES:
The tailfin of the aircraft is decorated with the airline symbol of the M for *Malawi* riding a stylized bird flying across a red sun. The gradually widening cheatline uses the black, red, and green colors of the national flag, while understated *Air Malawi* titles in red are applied to the forward roof.

Air Malta (KM/AMC)

MALTA (9H)

National carrier with a network of scheduled and charter passenger and cargo flights within Europe, and extending to North Africa and the Middle East, with a strong emphasis on tourist traffic to the Maltese islands. Air Malta was established on 30 March 1973 and started flights with chartered British Airways Tridents. Independent operations followed on 1 April 1974 using wet-leased Boeing 720Bs. An interisland helicopter service, flown by Malta Air Charter (Gozo Wings), provided frequent daily links between Malta and the neighboring island of Gozo from July 1990 until 31 October 2004.

FLEET:
7 X A319-100, 5 X A320-200, 5 X 737-300

FEATURES:
The Air Malta corporate symbol is the eight-pointed, four-armed Maltese Cross, representing the four Christian values of prudence, justice, fortitude, and temperance. It is displayed in white on a red field, covering the upper two thirds of the tailfin and underscored by three solid blue stripes, alluding to the three islands of Malta, Gozo, and Comino. The corporate identity was introduced in 1989.

Air Mandalay (6T/MGL)

MYANMAR (XY)

Regional airline linking all major tourist centers in Myanmar and providing a cross-border connection between Yangon and Chiang Mai in northern Thailand. Charter flights to nearby countries are also undertaken. Air Mandalay was established on 6 October 1994 and began operations on the popular tourist round-trip between Yangon, Bagan, and Mandalay 12 days later.

FLEET:
1 X ATR 42-300, 2 X ATR 72-210

FEATURES:
The maroon and yellow color scheme of the aircraft is highlighted by the representation on the tailfin of the hintha, the mythological wild goose of Burma. According to legend, hintha was ridden by the Hindu god Brahma and was also the emblem of the Mons kings of Bago, a one-time capital of the country. The name of the airline is derived from the town but was also inspired in part by the famous poem by Rudyard Kipling, who wrote: "On the road to Mandalay, where the flying-fishes play."

Air Marshall Islands (CW/MRS)

MARSHALL ISLANDS (V7)

National airline of the Marshall Islands, a scattered group of 900 atolls, islands, and coral reefs in the mid-Pacific Ocean, and designated flag-carrier of the Government of Tuvalu. Services link the capital Majuro to more than 30 atolls and islands in the Ratak, or "sunshine chain" to the east and the Ralik, or "sunset chain" to the west. An extension is also scheduled to Tarawa in the Kiribati Islands. The airline was formed in 1980 as Airline of the Marshall Islands and started operations with small Australian-built GAF Nomad aircraft. The new name was adopted in 1989.

FLEET:
1 x Dash 8 100,
2 x Dornier 228-200

FEATURES:
The tail markings are representative of the national flag adopted on independence in 1979. The orange and white stripes are symbolic of the two side-by-side island chains, the Ratak and Ralik, with the blue field standing for the surrounding Pacific Ocean. The white star has a point for each of the 24 districts that make up the Marshall Islands.

Air Mauritanie (MR/MRT)

MAURITANIA (5T)

National airline of the Islamic Republic of
Mauritania in northwest Africa, operating a small
regional network to the capital cities of Senegal,
Benin, Mali, Côte d'Ivoire, and Congo, with
extentions to the Canary Islands, Casablanca in
Morocco, and Paris, France. All major domestic
towns are also linked with the capital Nouakchott.
Air Mauritanie was established in September 1962
to take over and expand a small internal network
previously operated by Air France and Union
Aeromaritime de Transport. Operations started in
October 1963.

FLEET:
2 X B737-700, 1 X F28-4000,
1 X F28-6000

FEATURES:
Three shades of green, the
Muslim color of hope and well-
being, sweep up from the
underside of the otherwise
brilliant white aircraft and
continue in narrower form before
broadening again and wrapping
themselves around the rear roof.
The airline logo, comprising the
traditional Muslim crescent and
five-pointed star, both in green,
and incorporating a yellow-
golden "dart" streaming upwards,
provides a neat contrast to the
white tail.

Air Mauritius (MK/MAU)

MAURITIUS (3B)

National airline providing international and
regional flights from Sir Seewoosagur Ramgoolam
Airport to points within the Indian Ocean area,
southern and East Africa, Europe, the Middle East,
the Indian subcontinent, the Far East, and Australia.
Flights within the island of Mauritius, mainly in
support of tourism, are operated with helicopters.
Air Mauritius was set up on 14 June 1967, but its
activities were initially limited to handling aircraft
operating into the island. Local airline operations
were inaugurated in August 1972, with international
flights added the following year.

FLEET:
2 X A319-100, 5 (3) X A340-300,
2 X ATR 42-500, 1 X ATR 72-500,
2 X B767-200ER

FEATURES:
Air Mauritius titles are promoted
alongside the national flag on the
forward fuselage above a bright
red windowline and pinstripe.
The flag, adopted on independence in 1968, features four
colors: red for the martyrs of
independence, blue for the sea,
yellow for freedom, and green for
the fertile soil. The airline's Paille
en Queu tropical bird symbol
flies across a white band on a
quartered, red tail.

Air Méditerranée (BIE)

FRANCE (F)

French non-scheduled airline based at Lourdes-Tarbes International, specializing in passenger charter flights to destinations around the Mediterranean and Africa. Flights are undertaken for FRAM and other major tour operators from Paris, Lourdes, Lyon, Marseille, and Nantes. The airline also provides passenger subcharters for other airlines, together with some cargo and mail flights. Another important business sector is the transportation of pilgrims to the Catholic shrine at Lourdes. Air Méditerranée was established in 1997.

FLEET:
1 X A320-200, 3 X A321-100, 2 (1) X A321-200, 2 X B737-200, 1 X B737-200C

FEATURES:
A very simple livery applied to an all-white aircraft, comprising the stylized letters A and M in turquoise and dark blue on the tailfin, and *Air Méditerranée* titles with a trailing line in dark blue on the forward fuselage. The colors suggest the azure skies and blue waters of the Mediterranean.

Air Memphis (MHS)

EGYPT (SU)

Egyptian charter airline bringing tourists from Europe and Africa to the famous resorts of Sharm el Sheikh and Hurghada on the Red Sea and the ancient cities along the Nile, including Luxor, Abu Simbel, and Aswan. Air Memphis was founded by private interests in August 1995 and began operations in March 1996.

FLEET:
2 X A320-200, 1 X B707-320C, 1 X DC-9-30

FEATURES:
The capital A, the first letter in the name, lends itself ideally to the shape of the tailfin. It is rendered in a rich blue and red, highlighted by a white star at the top. *Air Memphis* titles are applied on the cabin roof. The airline takes its name from the ancient capital of the Old Kingdom of Egypt, which is believed to have been the largest city in the world from its foundation in 3100 BC until 2250 BC. The ruined city lies 12 miles southwest of Cairo.

Air Moldova (9U/MLD)
MOLDOVA (ER)

Flag-carrier of the Republic of Moldova operating scheduled passenger services from Chisinau International Airport to destinations in Western Europe and the Middle East. Charter flights for passengers and cargo are also undertaken, and the airline is active in the package-holiday market with flights to the Black Sea resorts during the summer season. Air Moldova was established soon after the country won its independence from the Soviet Union on 27 August 1991. The first services were flown in May 1992 from Chisinau to Frankfurt with Tupolev twin-engined TU-134AS and TU-154 trijets.

FLEET:
2 X A320-200, 1 X AN-26B,
1 X EMB 120ER Brasilia,
1 X EMB 120RT Brasilia,
8 X TU-134A-3

FEATURES:
The stylish livery divides the aircraft diagonally into two halves of blue and white, with *Air Moldova* titles set in white into the upper blue fuselage. The airline's motif on the tailfin comprises the national colors of blue, yellow, and red, which have been formed into a flying wing.

Air Moorea (VT/TAH)
FRENCH POLYNESIA (F-O)

Local airline in French Polynesia operating a frequent air shuttle between Tahiti and the neighboring island of Moorea, just 11 miles and seven minutes' flying time away. The airline operates up to 40 daily flights for people commuting between the islands and to serve the tourist industry on Moorea, one of the most beautiful of the Polynesian islands. Flights also serve the island of Tetiaroa. Night flights are operated to connect with long-haul flights arriving at Papeete. Air Moorea, a subsidiary of Air Tahiti, was formed in 1968 by local businessmen. It was first known as Air Tahiti.

FLEET:
2 x Dornier 228-200,
4 x DHC-6 Twin Otter 300

FEATURES:
This striking color scheme features a tropical island scene with blue sky and sea on the tailfin and rear of the aircraft, fading into white. Several orange hibiscus flowers, the "Queen of the Tropics," are drifting across the forward fuselage, with a white hibiscus on the fin.

Air Namibia (sw/nmb)

NAMIBIA (V5)

National airline maintaining a small regional network of scheduled passenger and cargo services in southern Africa, together with long-haul flights from the capital Windhoek to Europe. An extensive domestic network links all major points from Windhoek International and Eros airports. Air Namibia was established in 1946 as South West Air Transport, later Southwest Airways, and began scheduled services two years later. The carrier merged with Namib Air in late 1978 under the latter's name. Following the country's independence from South Africa, the airline adopted its present name in October 1991.

FLEET:
2 X A340-300, 4 X B737-200A, 1 x Beech 1900C, 2 x Beech 1900D, 1 X MD-11

FEATURES:
The tailfin is essentially a representation of the national flag in blue, red, green, and white, with the sun symbol, representing the country's diverse ethnic groups, set into the blue field at the top of the fin. Simple *Air Namibia* titles are displayed in blue on the forward cabin roof, preceded by the airline's logo of a flamingo flying across a sun disc.

Air Nauru (on/ron)

NAURU (C2)

National airline of the island republic of Nauru, the world's smallest independent country, lying in the Melanesian basin of the central Pacific. Main services link Nauru with several destinations in Australia, with other flights scheduled to the Marshall Islands, Fiji, Kiribati, and Norfolk Island. Air Nauru was formed by the government in 1970 and began an experimental service on 14 February with a Dassault Falcon to Brisbane, Australia. This route was upgraded to a scheduled service, before other destinations were added. Aircraft are operated under an Australian air operator's certificate.

FLEET:
1 X B737-400

FEATURES:
The aircraft is draped in the yellow, blue, and white colors of the national flag. The yellow stripe in a blue field on the tailfin is symbolic of the country's geographical position almost on the Equator. The 12 points of the white star stand for the 12 indigenous tribes of the island. The underside of the aircraft is also painted blue with a yellow stripe. Blue *Air Nauru* titles are displayed above the forward cabin windows.

Air New Zealand (NZ/ANZ)

NEW ZEALAND (ZK)

National carrier flying international services from Auckland, Wellington, Christchurch, and Queenstown, mainly to points in Australia and the South Pacific, but extending to North America and Europe. Extensive domestic services are also flown throughout New Zealand's North and South islands. Air NZ was founded in 1939 as Tasman Empire Airways Ltd. and began operations to Australia with flying boats on 30 April 1940. The present name was adopted on 1 April 1965. New Zealand National Airways, founded on 7 December 1945, and Safe Air, founded on 8 November 1950, were absorbed on 1 April 1978.

FLEET:
9 (3) x A320-200, 15 x B737-300, 8 x B747-400, 9 x 767-300ER, (8) x B777-200ER, (2) x B787-8

FEATURES:
A key element in the Air New Zealand livery is the "Pacific wave" in blue and turquoise, running through deep blue titling on a clean white fuselage, symbolizing the meeting of sea and shore around the islands of the Pacific. The deep blue tailfin bears a redesigned koru, the strong, curved spiral that dominated the beautifully etched canoe prows of the Maori and signifies new life and replenishment.

Air New Zealand Link (NZ)

NEW ZEALAND (ZK)

Provincial network of services operated by three regional airlines wholly owned by Air New Zealand. Air Nelson was founded in 1976 and operates throughout North Island from bases at Auckland, Napier-Hastings, Nelson, Tauranga, and Plymouth. Hamilton-based Eagle Airways, established in 1969, covers both islands from hubs at Auckland, Wellington, and Christchurch. Mount Cook Airline is the oldest having been founded as long ago as 1920 under the name of New Zealand Aero Transport. It provides scheduled services throughout the country, but mainly covering the tourist areas on South Island.

FLEET:
11 x ATR 72-500, 16 x Beech 1900D, 1 (16) x Dash 8 Q300, 17 x Saab 340A

FEATURES:
All three subsidiaries have adopted the basic Air New Zealand livery with the "Pacific wave" in blue and turquoise, and the koru of the Maori canoes, but with the individual airline names under the cockpit. The word Link has been added in gray on the rear fuselage.

Air Nippon (EL/ANK)
JAPAN (JA)

Regional subsidiary of All Nippon Airways (ANA) operating a mixture of jets and turboprops to some 45 points on Japan's main islands and smaller islands lying off its shores. Further destinations will be added as ANA rationalizes its main services. Air Nippon, known until spring 1987 as Nihon Kinkyori Airways, was formed on 13 March 1974 by ANA, Japan Airlines, Toa Domestic, and others, initially to provide subsidized feeder services. The operations of subsidiary Air Nippon Network, which started feeder services around Hokkaido Island in July 2002, are being integrated.

FLEET:
3 x A320-200, 23 x B737-500, 1 x B737-400, 2 x DHC-6 Twin Otter 300, 4 x Dash 8 Q300, 3 x YS-11A-200, 3 x YS-11A-500

FEATURES:
All Air Nippon aircraft carry the ANA markings, comprising an angular cheatline in two shades of blue that broadens along the white upper fuselage until it takes over the whole of the tail, incorporating the ANA logo in white. The logo also appears on both sides of the front fuselage. An interesting touch is a cartoon of a dolphin on the engines.

Air Niugini (PX/ANG)
PAPUA NEW GUINEA (P2)

National airline of Papua New Guinea operating a small number of international routes to destinations in Australia, the Solomon Islands, the Philippines, Singapore, and Japan, together with a comprehensive 20-point domestic network from Port Moresby and Lae. Holiday packages are also offered in support of the local tourist industry. Air Niugini was established by the PNG government and Australia's main airlines and started operations on 1 November 1973 when a small Fokker F27 Friendship lifted off from Jackson Airport at Port Moresby on a flight to Lae, Rabaul, and Kieta in the eastern part of the country.

FLEET:
1 x B767-300ER, 4 x Dash 8 200, 5 x F28-4000, 2 x F100

FEATURES:
As the national carrier, the airline's symbol, taken from the country's flag and prominently displayed on the tailfin of its aircraft, is the remarkably beautiful and fiery red Greater Bird of Paradise with its long trailing plumes and colorful collar which inhabits the dark rainforests of Papua New Guinea. With few exceptions, the many species of bird of paradise are found nowhere else in the world. Niugini is the accepted Pidgin English spelling of "New Guinea."

Air North (4N/ANT)

CANADA (C)

Canadian airline operating scheduled passenger and cargo services from its base at Whitehorse to other points in the Yukon Territory, with extensions to Juneau and Fairbanks in neighboring Alaska and to major cities in western Canada, including Calgary, Edmonton, and Vancouver. A thriving charter business is also operated. The airline was founded as Air North Charter and Training in 1977 and started operations that same year. Scheduled services were added on 17 January 1986.

FLEET:
3 x BAE 748-2A, 2 x B737-200A, 1 x Beech 99

FEATURES:
The key element of the aircraft livery is the blue compass pointing north, which is prominently displayed on the tailfin. Blue *Air North* titles are accompanied by the words *Yukon's Airline* in sienna, and the blue web address.

Air One (AP/ADH)

ITALY (I)

Independent airline operating an extensive domestic network along the length and breadth of Italy from its hubs at Milan Linate, Milan Malpensa, and Rome Fiumicino airports. The airline is a Lufthansa partner, with some services connecting with the German carrier's flights at Frankfurt and Munich. Air One's history goes back to 1983 and the formation of Aliadriatica at Pescara, then operating a light-aircraft training school. Scheduled and jet charter services were begun in June 1994, before the present name was adopted on 23 November 1995 with an inaugural service on the Milan–Rome route.

FLEET:
3 x B737-200A, 6 x B737-300, 21 x B737-400

FEATURES:
Midnight blue and golden yellow are the dominant colors of the Air One corporate identity. Large blue elongated *Air One* titles sit atop the windows on a white fuselage extending to below the wings, where the white gives way to gray paint. The letter o in the title incorporates a yellow sun disc. Flying across the all-blue tailfin is the company's yellow flamingo motif.

Air Pacific (FJ/FJI)
FIJI (DQ)

Fiji's national airline connecting Nadi International Airport on the largest island of Viti Levu to the nearby South Pacific island nations of the Solomon Islands, Tonga, Samoa, and Vanuatu, with longer flights serving destinations in Australia, New Zealand, Japan, Hawaii, and the Pacific coasts of Canada and the United States. Air Pacific, known until 31 July 1971 as Fiji Airways, was founded by Australian aviation pioneer Harold Gatty in September 1951. Operations began with de Havilland DH.89A Dragon Rapide biplanes.

FLEET:
1 X B737-700, 2 X B737-800, 2 X B747-400, 1 X B767-300ER

FEATURES:
For an airline whose home is in the exotic islands of the South Pacific, Air Pacific has adopted a rather plain livery, the only acknowledgment of the vibrant colors of the islands are understated bands of yellow, orange, magenta, and ocean blue at the rear of the tailfin, extending down under the otherwise white fuselage. Blue *Fiji* titles are displayed on the fin, while *Air Pacific*, also in blue, is applied above the forward cabin.

Air Paradise International (AD/PRZ)
INDONESIA (PK)

Indonesian carrier established in June 2002 to re-invigorate tourism to the island of Bali, a popular destination for holidaymakers, particularly from Australia. Services are operated to several cities in Australia and to South Korea and Japan, with future plans including services to other Asian destinations, with China top of the list. Charter flights for tour operators are also provided. Air Paradise International was established by Kadek Wiranatha, popularly known as Babak Kadek, in June 2002 and started flying from Denpasar International Airport to Perth and Melbourne on 16 February 2003.

FLEET:
2 X A300-600R, 2 X A310-300

FEATURES:
As the name would suggest, a stylized depiction of the remarkable bird of paradise with its long trailing plumes and beautiful collar adorns the yellow golden tailfin of the airline's aircraft. The gold sweeps down to meet the blue and red straight-through cheatlines, which slope down at the front to follow the aircraft contours, ending in a sharp needle point. The blue and red are repeated in the airline name on the forward cabin roof.

Air Philippines (2P/GAP)

PHILIPPINES (RP)

Privately owned low-fare airline operating a growing domestic network from Manila and Cebu to some 15 destinations throughout the Philippines. The airline is also the designated Philippine carrier to Hong Kong and Thailand, although services have not yet started. Air Philippines was set up on 13 February 1995 to take advantage of deregulation of domestic air transport and began operations on 1 February 1996 with Boeing 737-200 flights to Subic Bay, Iloilo, and Zamboanga under a temporary operator's permit. It was granted a full certificate for the operation of scheduled services on 4 June 1997.

FLEET:
2 X B737-200, 9 X B737-200A, 1 X B737-300

FEATURES:
This attractive scheme makes use of the colors of the national flag, where the blue and red stand for magnanity and courage, white for liberation, the gold stars for the main regions, and the eight rays of the sun for the first provinces to revolt against Spain. A striking representation of an eagle in red flying against the golden sun is the corporate symbol displayed on the mid blue tailfin. The eagle was chosen for its strength, agility, and ability to fly at high altitudes.

Air Plus Comet (A7/MPD)

SPAIN (EC)

Spanish holiday airline operating a mix of scheduled and charter services from Madrid and Palma de Mallorca, principally to destinations in North America, the Caribbean, and Latin America. Scheduled flights also service some major cities in Europe. Air Plus Comet was established in December 1996 by Grupo Marsans, which is active in the tourist industry and also has interests in Argentina. Flights began in March 1997 with two Airbus A310-300s.

FLEET:
3 X A310-300, 2 X B737-300, 4 X B747-200B, 1 X MD-88

FEATURES:
With interests in South America, the airline has chosen the native condor as its central theme, a stylized depiction of which is reversed out in white on the dark blue tailfin. The large airline title on the forward fuselage is painted in three distinct parts, comprising a bold blue *Air*, followed by the red *Plus*, which is drawn in a more florid style, and the rather more understated *Comet* below.

Air Pullmantur (PLM)

SPAIN (EC)

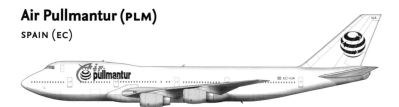

Spanish long-haul scheduled and charter operator serving popular resorts in Cuba, Mexico, and the Dominican Republic. Flights to the Dominican Republic connect with the group's cruise ships for Caribbean cruises taking in Puerto Rico, the U.S. Virgin Islands, Antigua, and islands of the French West Indies. Air Pullmantur was set up in 2003 and started operations in June that year.

FLEET:
2 X B747-200C, 1 X B747-300

FEATURES:
The simple but attractive livery features, on the white tailfin, a large stylized globe in red, which is given a dynamic feel by the arrowed latitudes. The airline's name in blue and red is wrapped around a smaller rendition of the globe. Sky blue engines and underside of the aircraft provide a contrast to the pristine white fuselage.

Air Rarotonga (GZ)

COOK ISLANDS (ZK)

Private airline operating scheduled passenger services in the Cook Islands, a group of 15 widely spread islands and atolls lying in the middle of the South Pacific to the east of Tonga. Flights serve nine islands in the Northern and Southern groups, radiating from Rarotonga and Aitutaki. International connections to Auckland and Los Angeles are available at Rarotonga. Charters are also provided to the neighboring island states of Tahiti, Niue, Tonga, and Samoa, and scenic flights are offered over Rarotonga, together with tours to the outlying islands. Air Rarotonga was founded in February 1978.

FLEET:
2 X EMB 110P1 Bandeirante, 1 X Saab 340A

FEATURES:
Two sweeps of turquoise and blue on the tailfin and an all-white fuselage are intended to bring to mind the white sandy beaches of the islands, the cloudless blue sky, and the turquoise waters of the Pacific Ocean. At the top of the tailfin is the airline's symbol, which is a triple rendition in its natural magenta of a *tipani*, or frangipani, a Pacific flower of exceptional beauty.

Air Sahara (S2/SHD)
INDIA (VT)

Fast-growing private Indian carrier connecting its main metropolitan hubs of Delhi, Mumbai, Hyderabad, Bangalore, and Kolkata to more than 20 destinations spread right across India. A regional service is also operated to neighboring Sri Lanka. Helicopters are available for charter flights and aerial photography. Air Sahara is part of the diversified Sahara India Pariwar conglomerate and was founded on 20 September 1991 as Sahara Airlines. Operations commenced with two Boeing 737-200s on 3 December 1993 following the government's decision to open the skies to the private sector. To be taken over by Jet Airways.

FLEET:
4 X B737-300, 3 X B737-400,
8 X B737-700, 3 (2) X B737-800,
4 X CRJ200ER, 2 X CRJ200LR

FEATURES:
Air Sahara has adopted a patriotic livery, with colors matching those of the Indian flag, which is displayed at the rear of the aircraft. Triple cheatlines of blue, orange, and green, separated by white, flow along the lower fuselage before ultimately angling up and widening to cover the tailfin. Winged *Air Sahara* lettering in blue, accompanied by the angled lines from the tailfin, fills the forward cabin roof.

Air Scotland (HLN)
UNITED KINGDOM (G)

Low-cost Scottish airline promoting inbound travel to Scotland and operating holiday flights from Glasgow and Edinburgh to the Mediterranean resorts and the Canary Islands. A service is also operated between Glasgow and Paris. Services are flown under the licence of Greece Airways. Air Scotland was established in November 2002 and launched services on 29 March 2003 in cooperation with Electra Airlines of Greece and later Air Holland, both of which ceased flying. Air Scotland aims to have its own air operator's certificate and become "totally Scottish."

FLEET:
1 X B757-200

FEATURES:
This patriotic scheme features the Scottish saltire flag, also known as the historic Cross of St. Andrew, first hoisted in 1512. It is set into the blue tail, which is itself highlighted by a luminous center section. The blue of the tailfin meets the white fuselage in an elegant scalloped sweep. Bold blue *Air Scotland* titles take up the front half of the aircraft. The painted engine cowlings add a balancing effect to the overall design.

Air Sénégal International (v7/sng)

SENEGAL (6v)

International carrier of the West African state of Senegal flying scheduled services from the capital Dakar to other West African cities and to the Canary Islands, Morocco, and destinations in France. A small domestic network is also operated, together with charter and air-taxi flights. Air Senegal International was established on 2 November 2000 following the restructuring of regional airline Air Senegal after the acquisition of a majority stake by Royal Air Maroc. Air Sénégal's history went back to November 1962, when it succeeded Ardic Aviation. Flights were inaugurated in November 1963.

FLEET:
1 X B737-500, 3 X B737-700

FEATURES:
This simple but pleasing livery comprises a white upper aircraft that carries fresh green *Air Sénégal International* titles on the cabin roof and a symbol in red and green on the tailfin. This shows two boomerangs arranged to form the shape of a letter S for Senegal. The boomerang displays pure grace and beauty and bird-like flight; once thrown, it returns in circular flight. At the top of the tailfin is the Senegalese flag in the pan-African colors.

Air Seychelles (hm/sey)

SEYCHELLES (s7)

National carrier offering international passenger and cargo services that stretch from the capital Mahé to other islands in the Indian Ocean, and to southern and East Africa, Europe, the Middle East, the Indian subcontinent, and Southeast Asia. The airline also provides domestic flights from Seychelles International Airport to all the main islands on a scheduled and charter basis serving the tourist industry. Helicopters are used for sightseeing flights and aerial photography. Air Seychelles was formed on 15 September 1977 as Seychelles Airlines and adopted the present name in March 1979.

FLEET:
2 X B767-300ER, 3 X DHC-6 Twin Otter 300, 1 x Shorts 360-300

FEATURES:
A pair of pure white fairy terns flying in harmony against the background of the red and green colors of the Seychelles flag is the airline's symbol, applied to the tailfin of its aircraft. Blue *Air Seychelles* titles are displayed on the upper fuselage, together with the national flag, whose broad red band of revolution and progress and lower green alluding to its peoples' reliance on agriculture, enclose a white wavy stripe that symbolizes the resources of the Indian Ocean.

Air Slovakia (GM/SVK)

SLOVAK REPUBLIC (OM)

Main Slovak airline providing scheduled passenger services from M. R. Stefanik Airport in the capital Bratislava to destinations in Cyprus, Israel, Kuwait, Lebanon, India, and the United Kingdom. A domestic service also links the two main cities of Bratislava and Kosice. Holiday charters are flown to the Greek and Spanish resorts, as well as to Bulgarian resorts on the Black Sea. Air Slovakia was formed on 2 June 1993 with Slovak and Czech interests and operated as Air Terrex Slovakia until becoming wholly owned by local investors in 1995. The first service was operated on 1 July 1993.

FLEET:
2 X B757-200

FEATURES:
This elegant livery creates a striking combination of white and two tones of blue. Dark and mid blue flashes are painted diagonally across the side of the largely white aircraft and are complemented by smaller dark blue flashes on each side of a white flash on the mid-blue tailfin.

Air Sofia (CT/SFB)

BULGARIA (LZ)

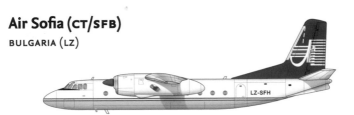

Bulgarian airline operating regular and ad hoc cargo charters to destinations in Europe, Africa, Middle East and Far East, and the Americas, together with some passenger flights. The airline also performs contract work for the United Nations and the Red Cross on humanitarian relief flights, and wet-lease services for other airlines. Another part of its buiness involves tourism, golf, and hotel management. Air Sofia was registered on 11 February 1992 and started cargo flights four days later with AN Antonov AN-12B leased from Russia.

FLEET:
4 X AN-12B

FEATURES:
This latest livery is distinguished by the blue tailfin with an unusual design and the blue tips of the engines and propellers. Twin blue cheatlines separate the lower gray from the upper white fuselage.

Air Southwest (WOW)

UNITED KINGDOM (G)

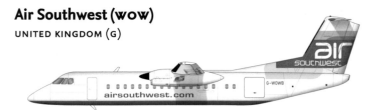

Regional airline based in the West Country, in England's southwest, connecting Plymouth and Newquay to London, northwest England and the Channel Islands. Charter flights and special leisure packages are also offered. Air Southwest was formed in May 2003 to re-establish air links from the West Country after British Airways pulled out and began operations on 26 October that same year with daily flights from Plymouth and Newquay to London Gatwick. The airline is owned by Sutton Harbour Holdings, whose interests span coastal and urban regeneration and regional aviation.

FLEET:
4 x Dash 8 300

FEATURES:
White *Air Southwest* titles, with the emphasis on *Air* are set into a four-layer design across the tailfin and lower rear fuselage, ranging in color from sky blue to a dark mauve. The colors complement the white aircraft, creating a clean and modern look. The airline's website address is added above the mauve aircraft belly.

Air Tahiti (VT/VTA)

FRENCH POLYNESIA (F-O)

Regional airline operating scheduled and charter services to more than 40 islands in the five island groups that comprise French Polynesia. Some of the more remote islands are served by small aircraft via hubs at Hao, Makemo, Rangiroa, and Nuku Hiva. The airline's history goes back to 1953 and the foundation of Reseau Aérien Interinsulaire, when the then colonial government of French Oceania took over the operation of a small private carrier, Air Tahiti, dating from 1950. On 1 January 1970, the name was changed to Air Polynésie, but the name Air Tahiti was revived in January 1987.

FLEET:
4 x ATR 42-500, 6 (3) x ATR 72-500, 2 x Dornier 228-200

FEATURES:
This dramatic and unusual livery displays a "double swirl" design in red below the wings, which tapers to a point at the nose and rear tip of the aircraft. Although not immediately obvious, it represents a mirror image of the letters AP, harking back to the days when the airline was known as Air Polynésie, and is repeated on the tailfin. Small red *Air Tahiti* titles appear on the lower forward fuselage.

Air Tahiti Nui (TN/THT)

FRENCH POLYNESIA (F-O)

Tahiti's only international airline, formed to develop tourism and trade from key world markets to the islands of French Polynesia. Based at Faa'a International Airport in Papeete, Tahiti, the airline connects the South Pacific to destinations on four continents, serving major cities in Japan, Australia, New Zealand, France, and the United States. Majority-owned by the French Polynesian government, Air Tahiti Nui was established on 31 October 1996 and began operations on 20 November 1998 with an inaugural flight to Los Angeles on the u.s. West Coast.

FLEET:
5 X A340-300

FEATURES:
The predominant colors of turquoise and blue suggest the islands' lagoons and surrounding seas, while the curved lines along the fuselage create a feeling of ocean waves. The snowy white tiare, regarded as the queen of flowers and used in leis and floral crowns presented to arriving visitors, is prominently displayed on the tailfin and winglets of the aircraft. The whole adds up to a powerful expression of the Polynesian spirit and pride in the airline shared by all Tahitian people.

Air Tanzania (TC/ATC)

TANZANIA (5H)

Tanzanian flag-carrier operating a small regional network to destinations in Kenya and South Africa, together with domestic flights to all major business and tourist centers in this East African country. The airline was founded by the government on 10 March 1977 to take over services following the collapse of the tri-national East African Airways Corporation as a result of the breakup of the East African Community (EAAC). Commercial operations began on 1 June that same year, initially over a domestic network serving 13 communities, using Fokker F27 Friendships inherited from EAAC.

FLEET:
2 X B737-200A, 1 X B737-200C, 1 X F28-4000

FEATURES:
The smart livery of Air Tanzania is dominated by the colourful tailfin with its arrow symbol, which provides a stark contrast to the clean white of the aircraft fuselage. The colours represent the national flag, where the green and blue represent the fertility of the land and abundance of the sea, with yellow symbolizing the mineral resources and black the largest ethnic group of the country. A small drawing of a giraffe brings to mind the rich wildlife in its national parks.

Air Transat (TS/TSC)

CANADA (C)

Montreal, Canada-based scheduled and charter airline offering flights from Calgary, Edmonton, Halifax, Moncton, Montreal, Quebec City, St. John's, Toronto, and Vancouver, serving some 90 cities in 25 countries. Primary destinations during the summer season are points in Europe and within Canada, while winter flights serve the sunshine destinations in the United States, Caribbean, Mexico, and Central and South America. Air Transat is the designated carrier between Canada and Cuba. The airline was founded in December 1986 and began commercial operations in November 1987 with Lockheed TriStars.

FLEET:
10 X A310-300, 3 X A330-200, 1 X A330-300

FEATURES:
Royal blue and white give the Air Transat aircraft a smart appearance, with the sky blue star, freely drawn in two halves on the royal blue tailfin being the most pleasing visual aspect. The tailfin design is duplicated on the winglets of appropriate aircraft. Bold blue *Air Transat* titles in a classic typeface are highlighted on the white fuselage.

Air Transport International (ATI) (8C/ATN)

UNITED STATES (N)

U.S. non-scheduled airline operating mostly cargo flights and some passenger/cargo combination services worldwide from its main hub of Toledo, Ohio. The airline specializes in ad hoc charters, government and military contracts, long-term contract services to other airlines, logistics organization, and racehorse and other high-value animal transportation. ATI was founded in 1978 as U.S. Airways but changed its name to Interstate Airlines before operations started in 1979. The current name was adopted in 1988, and on 1 October 1994 ATI took over ICX International Cargo Express.

FLEET:
6 X DC-8-63CF, 3 X DC-8-73AF, 4 X DC-8-73CF, 7 X DC-8-73F

FEATURES:
The rather attractive scheme uses midnight blue, sky blue, and turquoise colors which sweep along the lower fuselage and up and over the tailfin. ATI initials are applied forward, with the full title underneath. The letter *a* is given dynamism through graduated stripes in shades of blue and turquoise, while a stylized globe and speed flash form the cross bar of the letter.

Air Vallee (DO/RVL)

ITALY (I)

Regional airline providing scheduled passenger and cargo services from the mountainous Aosta Valley region in northwestern Italy to Turin, Rome, and other Italian cities. A connection is also scheduled to neighboring Austria. Other activities include charter and air-taxi flights, as well as various helicopter services including heli-skiing. Air Vallee was established in June 1987 to promote the commercial development of Aosta's Corrado Gex airport and began operations in June 1988 by opening a link with Rome, using a six-seat Beech c90 King Air.

FLEET:
2 x Fairchild Dornier 328JET

FEATURES:
The key features of the livery are the black and red colors of the flag of the Aosta regional government, here formed into two arrows flying in opposite directions to indicate the round-trip nature of its flights.
Set into the arrow symbol is the lion rampant of the Aosta coat of arms.

Air Vanuatu (NF/AVN)

VANUATU (YJ)

National airline of Vanuatu offering scheduled passenger and cargo services from the capital Port Vila to Australia, New Zealand, and Fiji, plus additional flights to Fiji and New Caledonia in code-share arrangements with Qantas and Aircalin. Air Vanuatu was established in 1980 following the country's independence from the UK and France, with the government initially holding 60% of the shares and Ansett Australia the rest. The former New Hebrides Airways formed the basis of the new airline, which began operations in September 1981 with a flight to Australia.

FLEET:
1 X ATR 42-300, 1 X B737-300

FEATURES:
The airline's origins cannot be mistaken, for the country's name is written large along the height of the tailfin of the white aircraft. Air Vanuatu titles in black are preceded by swirls in the red, black, green, and yellow colors of the national flag formed into the airline's initials. The flag, applied towards the rear, is unusual in that the v shape refers to the shape of the chain of islands making up the republic.

Air VIA (VL/VIM)
BULGARIA (LZ)

Bulgarian holiday airline serving the tourist industry, with flights for tour operators from Germany, Belgium, France, and other European countries to the local resorts, and specifically to Varna and Bourgas on the Black Sea. Flights are also operated to popular destinations in the Mediterranean basin for Bulgarian holidaymakers, and other activities include subcharters for other airlines and leasing services. Air VIA, with its slogan "VIA est vita" (VIA is life), was established on 13 June 1990 as the first private airline in Bulgaria to be licensed for international flights.

FLEET:
5 X TU-154M

FEATURES:
The blackcurrant tailfin with white VIA titles set in is given forward movement by the similarly colored stripes on the center engine of its Tupolev aircraft. The only other color on the predominantly white aircraft is the large VIA in bright green on the forward fuselage.

Air Wales (6G/AWW)
UNITED KINGDOM (G)

Flag-carrier of Wales operating scheduled passenger and cargo services from Cardiff to a growing number of destinations in the UK, Ireland, and France. Important air links are also provided between the West Country and Ireland with flights from Plymouth. Air Wales was founded in 1999 by Swansea property financier Roy Thomas and inaugurated scheduled services in October 2000 between Cardiff Wales Airport and Cork in the Irish Republic, using an Iceland-registered Dornier 228 with seating for 19 passengers. All passenger operations ceased on 23 April 2006.

FLEET:
5 X ATR 42-300

FEATURES:
The highly visible paint scheme is noteworthy for the large rendition on the tailfin of the Welsh dragon in a fiery red, with *Air Wales* titles applied, rather unusually, at the rear of the aircraft, set in white into a wavy red band. The red dragon has a long history and is seen as a symbol of national independence. One of the three standards carried into battle by Henry Tudor, the future King Henry VII of England, featured the red dragon as a tribute to the Welsh people.

Air Zimbabwe (UM/AZW)

ZIMBABWE (Z)

State-owned airline of Zimbabwe providing limited long-haul services from the capital Harare to three points in Europe together with modest regional routes in southern and East Africa. A domestic network incorporates Zimbabwe's main towns and particularly the country's famous tourist resorts. The airline was founded on 1 September 1967 as Air Rhodesia following the dissolution of the multi-national Central African Airways Corporation. It adopted the present name in April 1980 after the country's independence.The first service in the new guise was operated on 2 April to London.

FLEET:
3 X B737-200A, 2 X B767-200ER, 3 X XAC Y-7/M60

FEATURES:
A quadruple cheatline in the national colors of green, yellow, red, and black on a white upper fuselage produces an attractive livery. Commencing at the nose, the stripes step up in broader diagonal bands, ultimately embracing most of the tailfin. Near the top of the tailfin appears the Zimbabwe bird, a soapstone carving of an ancient African culture, fronting the red star of socialism and national aspiration. *Air Zimbabwe* titles are displayed alongside a fluttering portrayal of the national flag.

AirAsia (AK/AXM)

MALAYSIA (9M)

Leading Asian low-fare, no-frills airline and first to introduce ticketless travel in the region. A growing network of services now link the capital Kuala Lumpur and Johor Bahru with destinations in Peninsular Malaysia, Sabah and Sarawak on the island of Borneo, and Singapore, Macau, and Indonesia. A Thailand-based arm, Thai AirAsia, has also been established. AirAsia was founded in 1993 as a national airline to provide regional services and began operations on 18 November 1996. It was transformed into a low-fare carrier following the acquisition by TuneAir on 8 December 2001.

FLEET:
1(59) X A320-200, 21 X B737-300

FEATURES:
The emphasis of this scheme is on the cursive red *AirAsia.com* title splashed across the aircraft fuselage, and the slogan *Now everyone can fly* along the aft cabin roof. The white flourish on the red tailfin is balanced by the red engines, providing a pleasing and recognizable overall design.

AirBridgeCargo (VI/VDA)

RUSSIAN FEDERATION (RA)

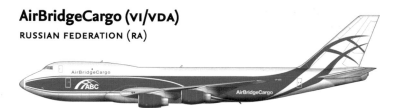

Russia's first scheduled international cargo airline operating a growing network of cargo flights linking Europe with the Far East via Russia, with major hubs established in Luxembourg and Moscow. The airline was established in 2004 as a subsidiary of Volga-Dnepr as part of the group's strategic development plan and to complement its outsize freight business operated by Volga-Dnepr Airlines with Antonov AN-124-100 Ruslan Freighters.

FLEET:
1 X B747-200F, 1 X B747-200SF, (2) X B747-400ERF

FEATURES:
Apart from the roof and most of the tailfin, the aircraft carries a mid-blue paint scheme that runs from the nose of the aircraft towards the rear, where the solid blue splits to create a bridge across the fin. The same stylized bridge design spans the white ABC initials framed in white under the airline's full *AirBridgeCargo* title in blue, which is also repeated low on the aft fuselage, set in white into the blue field.

AIRES Colombia (4C/ARE)

COLOMBIA (HK)

Colombian regional airline, which operates an extensive domestic service covering the entire central, northern, and southwestern part of the country. International services are also operated to the Netherlands Antilles off Colombia's northernmost point, together with holiday packages to the same destinations and to Panama. AIRES (Aerovias de Intergración Regional SA) was established at Ibaque in the Department of Tolima and Huila on 2 October 1980 and began scheduled services on 23 February 1981 between Bogotá and Ibaque with a fleet of two Embraer Bandeirante turboprops.

FLEET:
4 x Dash 8 100, 4 x Dash 8 300, 1 X EMB 110P1 Bandeirante

FEATURES:
The blue and lime-green livery projects the sun as its central theme. Formed ingeniously by the capital letter a from the airline's name, the sun was worshiped by all ancient civilizations in Central and South America. Prominent blue *Aires Colombia* titles on the lower forward fuselage and, without Colombia, at the rear of the white aircraft provide clear visibility from a distance.

Airkenya Aviation (QP)

Privately owned Kenyan airline providing a network of scheduled services throughout Kenya and charter flights within the East African region. Scheduled services from Nairobi cover the main coastal points and the game parks of Amboseli, Nanyuki, Lewa Downs, Meru, Samburu, and the Masai Mara, as well as Kilimanjaro in Tanzania. The airline was formed in 1985 from the merger of Air Kenya, founded in 1966 as Wilkenair, and Sunbird Aviation. Sunbird had come into being in 1979 through the merger of Sunbird Charters and Caspair, one of Kenya's oldest airlines, dating back to 1946.

FLEET:
2 x Dash 7-100, 3 x DHC-6 Twin Otter 300, 1 x Shorts 360-300

FEATURES:
A stylized red and black *colibri* (hummingbird) hovers in the black letter A, which comprises the airline's logo and is applied on the tailfin of the mostly white aircraft. A broad red cheatline edged in black runs the entire length of the aircraft. There are variations between the different types of aircraft operated.

Airlinair (A5/RLA)
FRANCE (F)

Privately owned French regional airline operating a small network of scheduled passenger services out of Paris Orly to six destinations on the French mainland, but the main part of its business is the provision of wet-lease services for both passengers and freight for other companies, including Air France, CCM Airlines, Europe Airpost, Tassili Airlines in Algeria, and many others. Airlinair was established in January 1999 and took to the air in May 1999.

FLEET:
4 X ATR 42-300, 1 X ATR 42-300(F), 9 X ATR 42-500, 1 X ATR 72-200(F)

FEATURES:
A sketchy blue outline of a dove in flight is the central symbol of the airline, featuring on the tailfin of the sparsely decorated white aircraft. At the base of the tailfin is the slogan "Chaque région est capitale," loosely translated as "Every region is capital." Solid blue *Airlinair* titles appear below the cabin windows.

Airlines of PNG (CG/TOK)

PAPUA NEW GUINEA (P2)

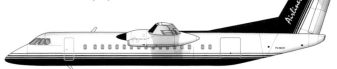

Papua New Guinea's second largest airline serving more than 30 domestic points and an extension to Cairns in Australia on a scheduled basis, and a total of 120 aerodromes on charter flights. The airline operates over 400 scheduled and charter flights per week from its main base of Port Moresby. It was established in 1987 as Milne Bay Air to operate in the resource-development industry and obtained a regular public transport license in September 1992. Following the acquisition of its airline license in March 1997, the name was changed to MBA Airline. Airlines of PNG is wholly owned by its chairman John R. Wild.

FLEET:
1 x Beech King Air 200, 7 x Dash 8 100, 5 x DHC-6 Twin Otter 300

FEATURES:
A not-very-exciting corporate identity, with the aircraft tailfin painted in a dark blue and the airline name reversed out in white along the leading edge. A dark blue base with thin pencil lines are the only other adornments. The color scheme varies between different types of aircraft in the fleet.

AirTran Airways (FL/TRS)

UNITED STATES (N)

Major U.S. low-fare airline operating an extensive network of passenger services to cities throughout the eastern USA and the Midwest from its main base at Orlando International Airport in Florida and a large hub at Hartsfield-Jackson Atlanta International in Georgia. AirTran Airways, as it operates today, was established on 24 September 1997 through a complicated merger of ValuJet and AirTran, the latter's history going back to June 1993 when it was founded as Conquest Sun Airlines, changing to AirTran in August 1994. ValuJet had been founded in 1992 and started operations on 26 October 1993.

FLEET:
83 (4) x B717-200, 15 (42) x B737-700

FEATURES:
The patriotic colors of turquoise, cream, and red have been woven into an attractive design, in which a large, lowercase a on the mid-blue tailfin grabs the attention. Two shades of a different blue with an inset red cheatline contrast with the white upper fuselage, which only presents *AirTran* titles above the forward windows. The web address on the blue engines reinforces the corporate identity. There are minor variations depending on the shape of different aircraft.

Alaska Airlines (AS/ASA)

UNITED STATES (N)

Major u.s. airline operating an extensive network of scheduled passenger and cargo services to nearly 70 destinations in the western u.s., Canada, and Mexico. Passenger charters are flown at night and at weekends. The airline's ancestry dates back to 1930 and the foundation of Star Air Services, which became Star Air Lines in November 1937, having taken over McGhee Airways in 1934. The present name was adopted on 6 June 1944 following the acquisition of three small carriers. In 1968, Cordova Airways and Alaska Coastal Airways were bought, with Jet America taken over on 1 October 1987.

FLEET:
7 x B737-200C, 40 x B737-400, 22 x B737-700, 3 (35) x B737-800, 12 x B737-900, 26 x MD-83

FEATURES:
The face of a friendly Eskimo smiling down from the tailfin evokes the frozen north of the airline's base, which is accentuated by the ice-white aircraft. The name *Alaska* in bold blue italic calligraphic script divides the two-tone straight cheatline on the forward fuselage.

Albanian Airlines (LV/LBC)

ALBANIA (ZA)

Privately owned Albanian airline providing modest international connections between the capital Tirana and destinations in Germany, Italy, Turkey, and Kosovo. Albanian Airlines was established in May 1992 as a joint venture between Albanian state-owned Albtransport and Austrian regional airline Tyrolean Airways but did not inaugurate services until 20 June 1995 with Ilyushin aircraft. It was restructured in 1996 with the Kuwaiti Kharafi Group taking full control. Formerly the national carrier.

FLEET:
1 x BAE 146-100, 1 x BAE 146-200, 1 x BAE 146-300, 1 x Yak-40

FEATURES:
A black cogwheel on the tailfin is a surprising choice for an airline logo, and even the double a set into it in red and gold cannot create an impression of speed. The only concession to flight is the red seagull hovering over the blue airline name. The red Albanian flag behind the front door incorporates a black double-headed eagle and the red star of Communism.

Alitalia (AZ/AZA)

ITALY (I)

National airline providing international passenger and cargo services from hubs at Milan Malpensa and Rome Fiumicino airports to more than 110 cities in 50 countries on all five continents, with a strong emphasis on Europe and the Americas. An extensive domestic network is backed up by regional feeder flights operated by Alitalia Express. Alitalia was established on 16 September 1946 as Aerolinee Italiane Internazionali and started operations on domestic routes on 5 May 1947. On 31 October 1957 it merged with Linee Aeree Italiane (LAI), which had been founded on the same day, but with assistance from TWA. Member of SkyTeam.

FLEET:
12 X A319-100, 11 X A320-200, 23 X A321-100, 1 X B747-200F, 13 X B767-300ER, 10 X B777-200ER, 3 X MD-11C, 2 X MD-11F, 72 X MD-82

FEATURES:
The striking corporate image developed by Landor Associates in the national colors of red, white, and green focuses on a simple, yet bold stylized a in green with a red center, which fills the tailfin as a continuation of a green windowline that fades to a point at the nose. The a is repeated as the first letter in the black *Alitalia* titles on the forward fuselage.

Alitalia Express (XM/SMX)

ITALY (I)

Regional airline subsidiary of Alitalia, operating a mix of domestic and European schedules covering most major and secondary cities in Italy, as well as points in France, Germany, Belgium, Austria, Switzerland, and Spain. Charter flights are also undertaken for the parent company. The airline's history dates back to 1986 and the foundation of Avianova on the island of Sardinia, beginning regional services with three ATR 42s. It came into the ownership of the Alitalia Group in 1993 when purchased by Aero Trasporti Italiani and was reconstituted under the present identity on 1 October 1997.

FLEET:
5 X ATR 42-300, 4 X ATR 72-210, 6 X ATR 72-500, 14 X ERJ 145LR, 6 X EMB 170LR

FEATURES:
The livery is identical to that of the parent company, with the exception of the handwritten form of the word *Express* after *Alitalia* and the positioning of the titling under the windowline.

All Nippon Airways (ANA) (NH/ANH)

JAPAN (JA)

Japan's second largest airline with a comprehensive domestic network linking 35 cities on all Japanese islands with high-frequency services providing some 500 daily flights. Intercontinental and regional routes, introduced in 1986, also link 30 destinations in Asia, Europe, and North America. Services on shorter domestic routes are operated by subsidiary Air Nippon, while low-fare flights are provided by Air Japan out of Osaka. The airline also has arrangements with Air Central and Ibex Airlines, both of which operate feeder services under the ANA Connection banner. ANA was formed on 1 December 1957 through the merger of Japan Helicopter and Aeroplane Transport (JHAT) and Far Eastern Airlines. Both were domestic airlines organized in 1952 after the Japanese Peace Treaty, which permitted the country to re-establish its own commercial air services. Far East Airlines served principally the area south of Osaka, while JHAT linked Osaka and Tokyo with Sapporo. ANA expanded its local network with the acquisition of small carriers Fujita Airlines (founded on 26 April 1952) and Central Japan Airlines in 1963 and 1965 respectively. It also took over the routes of Nagasaki Airways on 1 December 1967. All Nippon Airways is a member of the Star Alliance.

FLEET:

25 X A320-200, 7 X A321-100, 45 B737-700, 1 X B747SR-100B, 2 X B747-200B, 10 X 747-400, 13 X B747-400D, 33 X B767-300, 19 X B767-300ER, 1 (3) X B767-300ERF, 16 (5) X B777-200, 4 X B777-200ER, 7 (2) X 777-300, 2 (8) X B777-300ER, (30) X B787-3, (30) X B787-8

FEATURES:

An angular cheatline in two shades of blue broadens along the white upper fuselage until it takes over the whole of the tail, incorporating the ANA logo in white. The logo also appears on both sides of the front fuselage. Some aircraft carry the full title in English and Japanese, sometimes preceded by the hi-no-maru, or sun disc of the national flag. For more than a thousand years the sun has been a fundamental element. It is the legendary ancestor of the emperor and is the symbol of the "land of the rising sun."

Allegiant Air (G4/AAY)

UNITED STATES (N)

U.S. scheduled air carrier providing affordable non-stop services to Las Vegas from its base at Fresno, California, and from other cities in the United States, together with flights to Orlando, Florida. A large charter program is offered throughout the U.S. and to Canada and Mexico, including contract work for a major gaming company and Apple Vacations. Through its Allegiant Vacations affiliate, the airline also provides complete holiday packages for travel to Las Vegas. Founded in 1997 as WestJet Express, it began operations the following year and adopted the present title during 1999.

FLEET:
2 X MD-82, 10 X MD-83, 2 X MD-87

FEATURES:
An impressive yellow and orange sunburst on the blue tailfin highlights the fact that the airline services the leisure industry. The blue continues the line of the leading edge down and around the rear fuselage, also taking in the rear-mounted engines. A variant of the sunburst forms the *i* in the strong blue *Allegiant* titles low on the forward fuselage, while the smaller web address is applied above the cabin windows. The pleasing effect is one of balance and high visibility.

Alliance Air (CD/LLR)

INDIA (VT)

Low-cost subsidiary of state-owned Indian Airlines providing frequent domestic services to more than 40 destinations centered on the main metropolitan centers of Delhi, Chennai, Kolkata, and Mumbai. Among destinations served are Agra, Ahmedabad, Bangalore, Guwahati, Hyderabad, Jaipur, Jodhpur, Mangalore, Port Blair, Udaipur, and Varanasi. The airline was set up on 1 April 1996 and began operations on 21 June that same year.

FLEET:
4 X ATR 42-300, 10 X B737-200A

FEATURES:
Modern and elegant, the Alliance Air livery features a blue and red tailfin, with the color separation achieved by an attractive scalloped edge, and a broad blue sash edged in red, painted diagonally across the rear fuselage. Blue and red cheatlines at the front are abruptly curtailed upon reaching the cabin door. The orange, white, and green Indian flag on the roof is followed by the airline name in Hindi.

Alliance Airlines (QQ/UTY)

AUSTRALIA (VH)

Australian operator providing a wide range of
aviation services from its Brisbane base including
scheduled passenger services within Queensland,
ad hoc and contract charter flights throughout
Australia and the Pacific, and aircraft maintenance.
Alliance Airlines was established on 25 May 1987 as
Flight West Airlines and started flying on 1 June that
same year with a leased fleet of three Beech Super
King Airs. Flight West Airlines ceased operations on
19 June 2001, but on 5 April 2002 was bought by
Queensland Airline Holdings, which rebranded the
dormant carrier as Alliance Airlines.

FLEET:
4 x Fokker 100

FEATURES:
The golden "flying wing" symbol
set into the blue tailfin,
highlighted by a gold band
following the leading edge down
to wrap around the rear fuselage,
creates an elegant contrast to the
white of the remaining body of
the aircraft. The dot over the *i* in
the blue *Alliance* name has been
replaced by the gold symbol,
further strengthening the
corporate identity.

Aloha Airlines (AQ/AAH)

UNITED STATES (N)

U.S. airline providing a high-frequency all-jet
passenger and cargo service, connecting the five
major airports on the Hawaiian islands of Hawaii,
Oahu, Maui, and Kauai. A transpacific service also
links Honolulu on the island of Oahu to
destinations on the West Coast of the United States
and Canada. The airline was founded on 9 June 1946
under the name of Trans-Pacific Airlines and began
charter operations with Douglas DC-3s on 26 July
that year. Scheduled interisland services were
added on 6 June 1949. The title Aloha Airlines was
officially adopted on 11 February 1959.

FLEET:
10 X B737-200A, 4 X B737-200QC,
10 X B737-700

FEATURES:
The colorful bird-of-paradise
flower in red, blue, green, and
yellow lights up the deep blue
tailfin of the airline's fleet of jet
aircraft. The word *Aloha* drawn
with a flourish across the forward
fuselage in red, means love,
compassion, honesty, and
happiness, but is also a way of life
in the Hawaiian Islands. It is often
dubbed the "spirit of aloha" or the
"way of aloha." The tail design is
reiterated on the winglets where
appropriate, while the engines
are painted only in deep blue.

AlpiEagles (E8/ELG)

ITALY (I)

Privately owned Italian regional carrier operating an all-jet service from its bases at Venice and Verona to other points on the Italian mainland, and to the islands of Sicily and Sardinia. External routes serve mainland Greece, the Greek Islands, and the Mediterranean coasts of France and Spain. AlpiEagles was established in 1979 as an aerobatic team under the name of Pattuglia Aerobatica AlpiEagles but began air-taxi flights in 1987. Scheduled regional services from Venice were introduced in June 1996 following deregulation.

FLEET:
8 x Fokker 100

FEATURES:
As the name would suggest, the eagle forms the key element in the corporate identity, combined with the snow white of the Alps and the blue sky of the domain of this greatest of the birds of prey. The eagle has been expertly transformed into the shape of an aircraft serenely gliding across the blue tailfin, with its gray shadow projected large on the forward fuselage. The *AlpiEagles* titles have been rendered in sky blue and Mediterranean blue, both on the forward cabin roof and on the engine cowlings.

Amakusa Airlines (AMX)

JAPAN (JA)

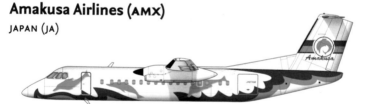

Regional airline linking the breathtaking Amakusa Islands in the Kumamoto prefecture with the main centers on the southernmost main island of Kyushu, including Fukuoka, Kumamoto, and Matsuyama. Amakusa Airlines was established on 9 October 1998 by the municpal government, which has a majority stake, and Japan Airlines, and started operations on 23 March 2000.

FLEET:
1 x Dash 8 100

FEATURES:
This attractive livery is based on the dolphin, acknowledging the fact that around 200 of these friendly and intelligent sea mammals swim off Tsuji Island year-round. Several dolphins frolic above the two-tone blue waves on the lower and rear fuselage, and the dolphin is also depicted as the central symbol inside a blue ring that cuts the two-tone blue band with a red edge on the white tailfin. Red *Amakusa* titles are written underneath.

AMC Airlines (AMV)
EGYPT (SU)

Private charter airline serving the Red Sea holiday resorts of Hurghada and Sharm el Sheikh, and the ancient Egyptian sights of Luxor, Aswan, and others. Flights originate from European countries, particularly from Belgium, France, Germany, and Italy, but also from Africa, the Middle East, and Asia. VIP flights and wet-lease services are also offered. The airline was founded on 11 July 1988 as a maintenance organization under the name of AMC Aviation. Domestic and international passenger flights with a Boeing 737-200 were added in 1992. The present title was adopted on 1 September 1999.

FLEET:
1 X A300B4-200, 1 X A310-300, 1 X B737-200, 2 X MD-83

FEATURES:
A white sunburst splits the red top half of the tailfin from the lower black and incorporates AMC initials, which stand for Aircraft Maintenance Corporation. Black and red cheatlines, which separate the gray belly from the upper white fuselage, run the length of the aircraft before turning down to form a chinstrap at the front. Large joined AMC initials in red break the cheatlines under the forward windows.

Amerer Air (AMK)
AUSTRIA (OE)

Austrian all-cargo airline operating quick-response ad hoc air cargo charter flights, long-term contract charters, and ACMI (aircraft, crew, maintenance, and insurance) wet-lease services throughout Europe and the Mediterranean, and into North Africa and the Middle East. The Linz-based company serves major freight forwarders, express cargo companies, private shippers, integrated parcel carriers, and governments. Road trucking is also undertaken. Amerer Air was founded on 27 February 1995 by Captain Heinz Peter Amerer and began operations with a single Fokker F27 Friendship.

FLEET:
1 X F27-500, 1 X L188A Electra, 1 X L188C Electra

FEATURES:
This economical paint scheme is notable only for the two intertwined letter As in burgundy and gray on the tailfin, derived from the initial letters in the airline name. A version of the symbol follows very small *Amerer Air* titles behind the cockpit.

American Airlines (AA/AAL)

UNITED STATES (N)

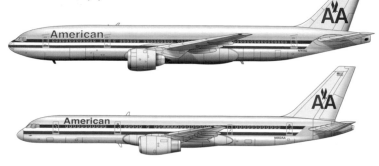

World's second-largest passenger airline with a 160-point international and domestic network operated from hubs at Dallas/Fort Worth, Chicago, Miami, and San Juan, not including feeder services operated by its regional affiliate American Eagle. International schedules are flown to Canada, Mexico, the Caribbean, Central and South America, Europe, Asia, and Australia. American Airlines was organized on 13 May 1934 as a direct successor to American Airways, which had been formed on 25 January 1930 to consolidate the services of numerous companies dating back to the Robertson Aircraft Corporation, which became the first contract mail carrier when it opened a service on 15 April 1926 between Chicago and St. Louis. American Airlines became an influential carrier with a vast network of services throughout the Americas, making contributions to the design of a number of aircraft including several Douglas models. Intercontinental routes were added in May 1982. American Airlines absorbed Trans-Caribbean Airways in 1971 and Reno Air in 1999 before acquiring the assets of another contemporary, Trans World Airlines (TWA), in April 2001. TWA's history went back to 17 April 1926 when the first of its parental foursome, Western Air Express, opened a mail service between Salt Lake City and Los Angeles.

FLEET:

34 x A300-600R, 77 (47) x B737-800, 143 x B757-200, 16 x B767-200ER, 58 x B767-300ER, 54 x B777-200ER, 239 x MD-82, 90 x MD-83, 28 x Fokker 100

FEATURES:

A polished-metal finish provides the backdrop for a straight-through patriotic triple cheatline in red, white, and blue. The long-established blue eagle motif swoops down between the twin peaks of the double red and blue A initials, outlined in white. *American* lettering in red, again with a white outline, is displayed on the cabin roof. The livery dates back to 1969. The American flag is painted at the top of the tailfin.

American Connection (AA)

UNITED STATES (N)

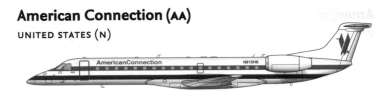

Regional airline network provided by Chautauqua Airlines, RegionsAir, and Trans States Airlines in a cooperative program with American Airlines. All three operate feeder services into American Airlines' St. Louis hub. Chautauqua Airlines was established on 3 May 1973 and began operations on 1 August 1974. RegionsAir was founded in 1996 and began operations in December that year. It was first known as Corporate Express Airlines, and later as Corporate Airlines, before changing to the present name in 2005. Trans States Airlines, initially known as Resort Air, started flying on 11 April 1993.

FLEET:

1 X ATR 42-300, 1 X ATR 72-200, 15 X ERJ 140, 15 X ERJ 145LR, 11 X Jetstream 32, 1 x Jetstream 32EP, 15 x Jetstream 41

FEATURES:

All aircraft operated on American Connection services carry the broad patriotic cheatlines of blue and red, more widely separated on the white fuselage than on American Airlines aircraft. A large rendition of the American Airlines eagle with blue wings adorns the tailfin. *American Connection* titles sit atop the blue windowline.

American Eagle Airlines (MQ/EQF)

UNITED STATES (N)

Affiliate of American Airlines and the world's largest regional airline system serving 135 cities across the United States, Canada, the Bahamas, and Central America, from hubs at Dallas/Fort Worth, Los Angeles, Chicago, Miami, and New York. The airline is the result of the consolidation of Executive Airlines (founded as Executive Air Charter in 1979), Flagship Airlines (founded in 1987 as Nashville Eagle), Simmons Airlines (founded in 1978), and Wings West Airlines (founded in 1975), which had been operating under the American Eagle banner since 1 June 1986.

FLEET:

25 X CRJ700ER, 2 X ERJ 135ER, 37 X ERJ 135LR, 59 X ERJ 140LR, 108 X ERJ 145LR, 33 X Saab 340B

FEATURES:

The American Eagle livery differs from American Airlines in that the patriotic cheatlines of red, white, and blue are relatively broad and more widely separated on the white fuselage. A large rendition of the American Airlines eagle with red and blue wings adorns the tailfin. *American Eagle* titles sit atop the blue windowline.

AmeriJet International (M6/AJT)

UNITED STATES (N)

A leading provider of global cargo transport and logistic services on land, sea, and air. Its scheduled air cargo network out of Miami serves some 45 destinations in the Caribbean and Central and South America, while ad hoc and contract charter flights are operated globally for DHL, Airborne Express, UPS, and other freight companies, as well as for airlines. AmeriJet was founded by David Bassett and a partner in 1974, initially operating air-taxi services for passengers. In 1976, it acquired a single Cessna 401, which flew for Purolator Courier for a number of years before the airline added its own cargo operation in 1982.

FLEET:
7 X B727-200A(F)

FEATURES:
A patriotic scheme emphasizing the red, white, and blue of the American flag, both on the tailfin and the aircraft fuselage. The progress of the triple cheatline is interrupted by large *AmeriJet International* titles in blue and red, where the letter A has been fashioned from the star shape. The cheatlines then continue, gradually flaring out and ending at the base of the bright blue tailfin, which is notable for a repeat of the a-shaped star trailing red, blue, and red bands.

Antonov Airlines (ADB)

UKRAINE (UR)

Commercial airline arm of the O K Antonov Aeronautical, Scientific and Technological Complex, specializing in the carriage of outsize and heavy cargo from its base at Kiev-Gostomel using aircraft from its own production. Humanitarian relief work for the UN and the Red Cross, and flights in support of the Ukrainian government's charity program, are also undertaken. O K Antonov, having produced large freighters, began transporting outsize cargo in the 1960s, but entered the commercial arena in 1993, when it became the second airline in the country to receive its air operators' certificate.

FLEET:
2 X AN-12, 1 X AN-22A, 1 X AN-26, 2 X AN-32P, 1 X AN-74T, 5 X AN-124-100, 1 (1) X AN-225

FEATURES:
The Antonov blue is prevalent on the tailfin of its aircraft, which either have the words *Antonov Design Bureau* reversed out in white (as per illustration), or incorporate the company logo, which comprises the Russian initials superimposed on the globe, with the name in English around the outside. A blue line separates the upper white fuselage from the gray belly.

Ariana Afghan Airlines (FG/AFG)
AFGHANISTAN (YA)

National carrier of Afghanistan, operating a small network of scheduled international services from Kabul to cities in China, Pakistan, India, Iran, Azerbaijan, Turkey, Germany, and Russia. A three-point domestic network is also flown. The airline's history goes back to 27 January 1955 when it was founded by the Afghan government and the Indamer Company of India. Scheduled services were begun in 1956 with three Douglas DC-3s. Its recent history has been marred by conflict with Russia and the U.S.-led war on terror, during which much of its infrastructure and most aircraft were totally destroyed.

FLEET:
3 X A300B4-200, 1 X AN-24RV, 3 X B727-200A, (4) X B737-700, (2) X B757-200

FEATURES:
The simple yet attractive livery features a royal blue paint scheme that broadens from a point on the nose into a sweep of blue that covers a large part of the rear fuselage and tailfin. Set into the tail in white is Ariana's stylized bird motif, which has graced its aircraft since its inception. The name *Ariana* derives from the Aryans, an ancient people who inhabited the lands now taken up by Afghanistan and parts of Tajikistan and Iran.

ArkeFly (TUI Airlines Netherlands) (TFL)
NETHERLANDS (PH)

Dutch charter airline providing seat-only sales and inclusive-tour packages to holiday destinations in the Mediterranean, West Africa, the Caribbean, and Central and South America. Countries regularly served are Greece, Spain, Turkey, Egypt, Gambia, Cuba, Dominican Republic, Jamaica, Mexico, and Brazil. The airline was founded as HollandExel in 2003 and commenced flying in January 2004. Following the demise of the Exel Aviation Group, the airline was acquired by TUI on 14 April 2005 and started operations under the new name with a flight from Amsterdam to Hurghada and Luxor in Egypt.

FLEET:
4 X B767-300ER

FEATURES:
The livery reflects the airline's membership of the World of TUI, with the red smile looking down from the sky blue tailfin. Unlike on other TUI airlines, the fuselage is painted white, rather than blue, and sports large red and blue *Arkefly* titles across the forward part of the aircraft.

Arkia Israeli Airlines (IZ/AIZ)

ISRAEL (4X)

Israel's second-largest airline, operating a small network of passenger and cargo schedules within Israel and to neighboring countries, together with international charter flights, primarily for the tourist industry. Arkia's history goes back to the establishment of the Israeli state and the foundation of Eilata Airlines to link Eilat with the center of the new country. The first service was flown with a Curtiss c-46 on 28 February 1950. Then owned by El Al and the labor federation Histradut, the name was changed to Arkia Airlines in September 1950. Between December 1972 and March 1980 it was known as Kanaf Arkia Airlines.

FLEET:
4 X ATR 72-500, 1 X B757-200, 2 X B757-300, 4 x Dash 7-100

FEATURES:
The company colors have been combined into an attractive scheme, in which the orange speed lines on the blue tailfin and the sketched orange line along the lower fuselage enhance the visual streamlining effect. On the starboard side, the name *Arkia* has been painted across the lower front in English, and in Hebrew at the base of the tailfin, the design being reversed on the port side. The name comes from the Bible and translates as "I will soar (to the canopy of heaven)."

Armavia (U8/RNV)

ARMENIA (EK)

Leading Armenian airline operating international services from Zvartnots Airport, serving the capital Yerevan. Its network incorporates a growing number of destinations in Russia and neighboring former Russian republics and extends to Western Europe and the Near and Middle East. The airline was established in 1996 and began operations in 2001. A major strategic alliance was concluded in October 2002 with Russia's Sibiria Airlines, which acquired a controlling stake. The operations of Armenian International Airways were transferred to Armavia on 1 January 2005.

FLEET:
3 X A320-200

FEATURES:
The "home from home" identity developed by Landor Associates proclaims the airline as the major conduit connecting Armenians with each other and the outside world. The brand is centered on the symbolic significance of Mount Ararat, which is displayed on the tailfin in the orange color of the national flag and is cleverly carried through to the underside of the fuselage. The orange provides warmth and vibrancy. A dynamic representation of the national flag is depicted on the engines.

Arrow Cargo (Arrow Air) (JW/APW)

UNITED STATES (N)

Miami-based all-cargo airline operating scheduled air-cargo services within the United States and to Central and South America and the Caribbean under the trade name of Arrow Cargo. The airline operates to twenty destinations, serving freight forwarders, passenger and cargo airlines, and the U.S. Department of Defense and Postal Service. Arrow Air was founded by George Batchelor in 1947. It suffered several periods of inactivity but in spring 1999 was taken over by Fine Airlines, founded in September 1992. The two entered bankruptcy protection but re-emerged under the Arrow name.

FLEET:
12 X DC-8-63CF, 1 X DC-10-10F, 3 X DC-10-30F

FEATURES:
The airline name ensures that the arrow symbol takes center stage. It is applied in two-tone blue, both on the tailfin and after the *Arrow Cargo* name on the white forward body of the aircraft. The dominant color, however, is a fresh green, which covers the tail and rear fuselage and is attractively edged by a broadening sweep of blue. The engines are also painted in green.

Aserca Airlines (R7/OCA)

VENEZUELA (YV)

Private Venezuelan airline operating from the capital Caracas and its main base of Valencia to all major cities within this South American country, with flights extending into the Caribbean serving Aruba, Curaçao, and the Dominican Republic. Apart from scheduled passenger and cargo services, Aserca also has a charter business. The airline was founded as Aserca-Aeroservicios Carabobo and started flying in 1991 to the holiday island of Margarita off Venezuela's north coast, initially using two Douglas DC-9-30s acquired from U.S. carrier Midway Airlines.

FLEET:
9 X DC-9-30

FEATURES:
This South American airline does a mix-and-match with its three principal corporate colors of red, blue, and gold. Although the stylized blue and gold bird of prey on the tailfin stays constant, the top of the fin, rear tail cone and engines are rendered in red, blue, or gold, with the two bands fronting the rear applied in the other two colors. The airline title is always red and the *Venezuela* beneath always gold.

Asiana Airlines (oz/aar)

SOUTH KOREA (HL)

South Korea's second major airline operating a network of international services now linking the capital Seoul with some 50 destinations in Asia, Australia, Europe, and North America. All major domestic destinations are also served, with the holiday island of Cheju off the southern coast and the principal port of Pusan, also in the south, linked with high-frequency flights. The airline was established as Seoul Air International on 16 February 1988 but renamed on 11 August that year. Operations began, initially on domestic routes, on 23 December.

FLEET:
2 (2) x A320-200, 4 x A321-100,
15 x A321-200, 6 x A330-300,
10 x B737-400, 3 x B737-500,
2 x B747-400, 5 (1) x B747-400F,
6 x B747-400M, 7 x B767-300,
1 x B767-300ER, 1 x B767-300ERF,
6 (4) x B777-200ER

FEATURES:
The "Saektong" multicolored stripes are a traditional motif signifying joy and hospitality. The figure in the emblem, appearing ahead of the airline name, has its white, red, blue, and yellow stripes raised in an open-arm gesture of welcome, displaying the pride Koreans feel in playing host to people from all over the world.

Asian Spirit (6k/rit)

PHILIPPINES (RP)

Philippine domestic airline operating scheduled passenger services from Manila, Clark, and Cebu to more than 20 tourist destinations and secondary and tertiary airports. Further tourist destinations are being added in line with the Department of Tourism's master plan. Asian Spirit was set up in September 1995 as an employee cooperative by 36 Filipino nationals, following deregulation of the local air transport industry. It started operations in April 1996 to Caticlan, providing access to the famous island resort of Boracay.

FLEET:
1 x BAE 146-100, 1 x BAE 146-200,
1 x BAE ATP, 4 x DHC-7-100,
2 x CN-235-200, 1 x L-410 UVP,
2 x L-410 UVP-E, 3 x YS-11A-500

FEATURES:
A colorful tribal mask and headdress dominate the tailfin of the white aircraft. The only other application of color is in the red *Asian Spirit* titles written in cursive lettering across the forward fuselage.

Astar Air Cargo (ER/DHL)

UNITED STATES (N)

Major U.S. cargo carrier providing scheduled flights from its hub at Cincinnati's Northern Kentucky International Airport and gateways at San Francisco, Los Angeles, Miami, and New York, to more than 30 domestic and 20 international destinations. Services are operated for DHL Worldwide Express, the U.S. Postal Service, U.S. Air Force, freight brokers, forwarders, and consolidators. The airline was certificated in 1972 as DHL Airways, initially transporting courier packages between various points in California and Hawaii. The present name was adopted on 14 July 2003 following a management buyout.

FLEET:
6 X A300B4-200F, 25 X B727-200F, 1 X DC-8-73AF, 2 X DC-8-73CF, 6 X DC-8-73F

FEATURES:
The clean design of the markings matches the airline name, with a single five-pointed red star and blue trail on the tailfin the principal highlight on the mostly white aircraft. The star also rises from the *Astar* titles behind the cargo door, partially set into the blue underside.

Astraeus (5W/AEU)

UNITED KINGDOM (G)

Independent UK charter airline serving a wide variety of destinations throughout Europe, Africa, and the Middle East from bases at London Gatwick and Manchester, flying mostly for independent and vertically integrated tour operators. The airline also operates energy-support services to destinations in Kazakhstan, Algeria, and Equatorial Guinea for major oil and gas companies. Scheduled services are flown to Ghana, Liberia, Sierra Leone, and Egypt. Astraeus was established on 17 January 2002 and began operations on 6 April that year.

FLEET:
2 X B737-300, 2 X B737-700, 3 X B757-200

FEATURES:
The most interesting aspect to the livery is the name of the airline, which comes from Greek mythology. Astraeus was the husband of Eos, goddess of dawn and god of the four winds, Boreas, Zephyrus, Eurus, and Notus. The airline, therefore, flies in all four directions, as indicated also by the four-pointed star that forms the *t* in the name and is also applied to the engines. Three golden stars accompany the name and light up the blue sky of the tailfin.

ATA Airlines (TZ/AMT)

UNITED STATES (N)

Tenth-largest u.s. airline providing scheduled and charter services for leisure travelers from Indianapolis International Airport, taking in most major resort cities in the u.s. and Hawaii, as well as well-known destinations in Central America and the Caribbean. Additionally, the airline has a strong charter-only business within the United States, to the Caribbean, and across the Atlantic to Europe. Formed in August 1973 to manage the Ambassadair Travel Club, it received its air carrier certificate in March 1981 and began scheduled flights in 1986. It was known as American Trans Air until 2003.

FLEET:
20 (7) x B737-800, 6 x B757-200, 9 x B757-300, 1 x L1011-100, 4 x L1011-500

FEATURES:
Four gold and orange ribbons flutter on the dark blue tailfin, enclosing ATA initials in the same colors. This striking design is balanced with even larger ATA initials set into the dark blue base and gold and orange cheatline. The same elegant theme is maintained on the engines.

Atlantic Airlines (AAG)

UNITED KINGDOM (G)

British cargo airline offering ad hoc and long-term cargo contracts to customers in the United Kingdom, Europe, and North and South America from its base at Coventry in the West Midlands. The company also specializes in the transport of livestock and other aerial work tasks such as oil-spill response, dispersant spraying, icing trials, remote sensing, economic exclusion zone protection, and airborne control platforms. Atlantic Airlines was established in 1994 as part of the Air Atlantique Group. It was purchased by management in July 2004 and now operates as an independent unit within the group.

FLEET:
1 x AN-72-100D, 2 x L188AF Electra, 3 x L188CF Electra, 2 x L188PF Electra, 1 x TU-204-120S

FEATURES:
Black and green are the two colors applied to good effect on a snow-white fuselage. A fine sketch of an eagle is framed by black and three green pencil lines at the top of the tailfin and wrapped around the fuselage and riding above the black underside of the aircraft. Green *Atlantic Airlines* titling is displayed on the mid-cabin.

Atlantic Airlines (AYN) (ZF/HHA)
NICARAGUA (YN)/HONDURAS (HR)

Regional airline based in Nicaragua, with an affiliate operation in Honduras, operating extensive local flights in Nicaragua, Costa Rica, El Salvador, Honduras, Belize, and Guatemala. Scheduled services radiate out from hubs at San Salvador, San José, Managua, Tegucigalpa, La Ceiba, Guatemala City, and Belize City to reach all major points in these Central American countries. Other activities include passenger and cargo charters, aircraft sales, and maintenance. Atlantic Airlines was established in 1997.

FLEET:
1 X B737-200A, 1 X BAE 748-2B, 2 X F-27F, 1 X F27-500F, 1 X Let L-410 UVP, 13 X Let L-410 UVP-E

FEATURES:
This paint scheme conjures up visions of tropical beaches, with a palm tree swaying gently in the warm breeze against a background of turquoise seas and cloudless blue skies on the tailfin. On the forward fuselage, behind the green and black *Atlantic Airlines* name and a green palm tree, the golden orange sun takes center stage.

Atlantic Air Transport (Air Atlantique) (AAG)
UNITED KINGDOM (G)

Airline operation of Coventry-based Air Atlantique Group providing passenger and cargo charters, supply of aircraft to other scheduled airlines, and oil-industry support in the North Sea. It also operates the Air Atlantique Classic Flight, which owns a number of historic aircraft for display. The company's history goes back to 1969 and the formation of General Aviation Services in Jersey in the Channel Islands. The Air Atlantique name was adopted in June 1977 when it launched into charter work. Trading names within the expanding group were established after a move to mainland Britain.

FLEET:
3 X ATR 42-300, 1 X Convair 440-0, 1 X DC-3C, 1 X DC-6A, 1 X DC-6A/B, 1 X SA227AC Metro III + smaller types

FEATURES:
A sketch drawing of an eagle is framed by a green line at the top of the tailfin and a green cheatline running the length of the aircraft above the black underside. Green *Atlantic* titles are painted at the rear on this aircraft, but generally they are on the cabin roof on other types in the fleet.

Atlantic Airways (RC/FLI)

FAROE ISLANDS (OY)

National airline of the Faroe Islands, an archipelago of 18 islands lying halfway between Iceland and Norway. The airline provides scheduled connections between the capital Vágar and destinations in Denmark, Norway, Iceland, and Scotland, with summer flights also operated to Greenland. A domestic helicopter network provides vital air links between the islands. Atlantic Airways was established in November 1987 and operated its first service on 28 March 1988 to Copenhagen. The government-operated helicopter service, part of Strandfaraskip Landsins, was incorporated into Atlantic in spring 1994.

FLEET:
4 X BAE 146-200A, 1 x Bell 212, 1 x Bell 412EP

FEATURES:
Atlantic Airways uses the colors of the Faroese flag, a "fair red" Scandinavian cross fimbriated dark blue, which can be seen under the forward windows followed by the words *Faroe Islands*. A stylized seabird in blue with suggested red wings flies on the white tail, and again on the engine cowlings. A foreshortened blue underbelly edged in red incorporates the airline's web address. Modest *Atlantic Airways* titles are applied on the forward upper fuselage.

Atlant-Soyuz Airlines (3G/AYZ)

RUSSIAN FEDERATION (RA)

Large Russian airline operating regular and ad hoc passenger and cargo charter flights from Moscow's Sheremetyevo and Domodedovo airports to many countries across the world. Its main cargo markets are China and the United Arab Emirates, but frequent flights are also made to Belgium, Germany, Italy, Spain, Turkey, Egypt, and the United Kingdom. The carriage of cargo accounts for the major part of its business. Atlant-Soyuz Airlines was established on 8 June 1993 and began operations later that same month. It is a joint-stock company in which the Moscow government has a 25% stake.

FLEET:
5 X IL-76M, 10 X IL-76TD, 4 X IL-86, 1 X IL-96-300, (1) X IL-96-400T, 4 X TU-154B-2, (5) X TU-334-100

FEATURES:
The bright blue of the underside of the aircraft extends in a graceful sweep up the tailfin, which also displays a blue-winged a for Atlant. The red cheatline adds distinction to the overall appearance. Of note are the *aviakompaniya pravetel'stva moskvy* subtitle under the airline name and the Moscow city crest on some of its aircraft, referring to its partial ownership by the Moscow government.

Atlas Air (5Y/GTI)

UNITED STATES (N)

Major cargo airline providing scheduled freight flights on contract to other airlines, usually on an ACMI (aircraft, crew, maintenance, and insurance) wet-lease basis, serving more than 100 cities in 46 countries. Charter flights for commercial organizations and the U.S. military are also undertaken. Atlas Air was founded in April 1992 by the late Michael Chowdry to specialize in the long-term outsourcing of its Boeing 747 capacity. Operations started in 1993 with one Boeing 747-200F contracted to China Airlines.

FLEET:
14 X B747-200F, 7 X B747-400F

FEATURES:
As implied by the airline's name, the central feature is a large golden orange depiction of Atlas, a titan from Greek mythology, on the deep blue tailfin. Atlas was compelled to support the sky on his shoulders as punishment for rebelling against Zeus and is used by the airline as a symbol of strength. Bold *Atlas Air* titles in blue and gold take up most of the remaining parts of the white aircraft.

Atlas Blue (8A/BMM)

MOROCCO (CN)

Wholly owned subsidiary of Royal Air Maroc (RAM) operating competitively priced flights from the Moroccan cities of Marrakech and Agadir to a growing number of destinations in the French, Italian, Belgian, Dutch, German, and British markets. The airline plans to add other European countries to its network in the next five years. Atlas Blue was created on 28 May 2004 within the framework of Vision 2010, a national project designed to structure the development of tourism in Morocco. It operated its first flight on 26 July that same year, carrying tourists from Marrakech to Lyon in France.

FLEET:
6 X B737-400

FEATURES:
The bold aircraft livery is notable for a stylized white letter a in a red sun, prominently displayed on the tailfin, and *Atlas-blue.com* titling in blue and red, which covers a large part of the white fuselage. The airline has been named after the country's high but fertile Atlas Mountains.

Atlasjet International Airways (2U/OGE)

TURKEY (TC)

Turkish scheduled and charter air carrier operating year-round services from bases at Antalya and Istanbul mainly to destinations in Germany and other European countries, the Middle East, North Africa, and further afield to Nigeria and the Maldives. A comprehensive domestic network serves all principal Turkish cities. Atlasjet was established by tour operator Öger Holding on 14 March 2001 and started flying on 1 June that year with two Boeing 757-200s.

FLEET:
(2) X A319-100, 2 X A320-200, 2 X B757-200, 3 X B757-200ER

FEATURES:
The dominant color in the airline's paint scheme is a bright red, which fills the tailfin and is used in the large *Atlasjet* titles on the forward fuselage, and in the pinstripe that divides the dark blue underside of the aircraft from the white upper body. *Atlasjet* titles are also applied in white along the leading edge of the fin. The airline's name is derived from the Titan Atlas of Greek mythology, signifying strength and a knowledge of the stars.

Aurigny Air Services (GR/AUR)

CHANNEL ISLANDS (G)

Regional airline operating high-frequency services between the three main islands of Guernsey, Jersey, and Alderney, with connections to the UK mainland and northern France. Contracts are held for mail and newspaper flights, and the airline also operates air-ambulance charters and regular flights to the UK for tour operators. Aurigny Air Services was founded on 1 March 1968 and started commercial operations with nine-seat Britten-Norman Islanders. In July 1971, it became the first operator of the 16-seat Trislander. The airline has been owned by the States of Guernsey since 15 May 2003.

FLEET:
3 X ATR 72-200, 8 X BN-2A MKIII Trislander 2, 1 X Saab 340A

FEATURES:
The small Atlantic puffin, which breeds on the island of Alderney, has been chosen as the airline's symbol. It is depicted in flight on the bright yellow tailfin. The yellow extends to the rear fuselage and rather unusually fades out some way along. The prominent blue and red web address, accompanied by the words *Channel Islands*, takes up virtually the whole length of the aircraft. The name derives from the old French name for Alderney, the airline's home base.

Austral Lineas Aéreas (AU/AUT)
ARGENTINA (LV)

Argentinian domestic and regional airline operating extensive scheduled passenger and cargo services in cooperation with Aerolineas Argentinas out of Buenos Aires Aeroparque Jorge Newbery Airport. Austral was created in June 1971 by the merger of Austral Compania Argentina de Transportes Aéreos and Aerotransportes Litoral Argentina, both of which dated back to 1957. After several recent changes of ownership, the airline is now in the Grupo Air Comet-Marsans stable and is a sister company of Aerolineas Argentinas.

FLEET:
10 X B737-200A, 2 X MD-81, 6 X MD-83

FEATURES:
The only splash of color on the white aircraft is the blue on the tailfin and engines, and in the *Austral* titles on the starboard side of the aircraft, which carry the *Aerolineas Argentinas* name on the port side. The traditional condor insignia is set into the blue tail and engines. The white and blue recall the national flag, which is painted under the cockpit. It incorporates the "Sun of May," which symbolizes the start of the country's struggle for independence.

Australian Airlines (AO/AUZ)
AUSTRALIA (VH)

Cairns, Queensland–based low-cost, full-service, single-class leisure airline providing a growing network of flights from Australia to holiday destinations in Asia. Services link Cairns, the Gold Coast, Sydney, Melbourne, and Perth to points in Indonesia, Singapore, Malaysia, Japan, and Hong Kong. Main tourist destinations include Phuket and Bali. Australian Airlines was established as a wholly owned subsidiary of Qantas Airways in 2001 and began operations on 27 October 2002 with flights from Cairns to Nagoya and Osaka. The Australian Airlines brand was discontinued in July 2006.

FLEET:
5 X B767-300ER

FEATURES:
The kangaroo, the unmistakable icon from down under, is given a sense of dynamism through the addition of multiple dots behind the stylized marsupial outlined against the backdrop of the ocher aircraft. Ocher is recognized as the color of the heart of Australia, conveying a feeling of the Australian outback. The almost handwritten typeface was chosen to emphasize the airline's warm and welcoming style and to capture the relaxed personality for which Australians are famous.

Austrian Airlines (os/aua)

AUSTRIA (OE)

National airline providing scheduled passenger and cargo services from its Vienna hub to close on 70 destinations throughout Europe, and to the Middle and Far East, Africa, and North America. The network is further extended through regional subsidiaries Austrian Arrows and leisure airline Lauda Air. Austrian Airlines was founded on 30 September 1957 when agreement was reached to merge the two projected airline companies, Air Austria and Austrian Airways. Operations began on 31 March between Vienna and London using Vickers Viscount turboprops.

FLEET:
7 X A319-100, 6 X A320-200, 3 X A321-100, 3 X A321-200, 4 X A330-200, 2 X A340-200, 2 X A340-300, (2) X B737-800, 2 X B767-300ER, (1) X B777-200ER, 2 X MD-83, 4 X MD-87, 3 X F70

FEATURES:
The "Spirit of Spring" scheme developed by Landor connects the national colors on the tailfin with the snow-covered mountains, icy glaciers, blue lakes, and abundant rivers of the Austrian landscape. A red chevron, stylizing a plane taking off and reflected in gray below, provides an element of continuity.

Austrian arrows (vo/tyr)

AUSTRIA (OE)

Innsbruck, Tirol-based regional subsidiary of Austrian Airlines, providing a comprehensive domestic network together with services from all major cities in Austria to more than 40 destinations right across Europe. Charter flights are also undertaken. Founded as Aircraft Innsbruck in 1958, the company adopted the Tyrolean Airways name upon the introduction of scheduled services on 1 April 1980. Austrian Airlines acquired full control on 23 March 1999 and later also of Rheintalflug, which was integrated into Tyrolean on 10 January 2002. The rebranding was launched on 16 September 2003.

FLEET:
2 X CRJ100LR, 13 X CRJ200LR, 12 x Dash 8 Q300, 10 x Dash 8 Q400, 6 x F70, 9 x F100

FEATURES:
The aircraft livery is identical to that of the parent company, with the exception of the title, which reads *Austrian arrows* in red. The dynamic arrow and its shadow fly on ahead, while also filling the white center section of the simple red, white, red Austrian flag on the tailfin. The similarity of the scheme aids recognition and harmonizes the brand across the Austrian Airlines Group.

Aviacsa (6A/CHP)

MEXICO (XA/XB)

Major Mexican airline operating a network of services across the length and breadth of the country from hubs at Monterrey, Mexico City, Guadalajara, and León. Services extend from Monterrey and Mexico City across the border to several destinations in the United States. Charter work is also part of the airline's business. Aviacsa was founded on 5 May 1990 and began operations on 20 September that year with a single British Aerospace BAE 146-200. Progress thereafter was swift, leading to a major reorganization in 2000.

FLEET:
5 X B727-200A, 23 X B737-200A

FEATURES :
The key element of the paint scheme is the depiction of an Aztec chief with his splendid headdress of Quetzal feathers emblazoned in blue on the white tailfin. Aviacsa titles forward and a low cheatline, separating the gray belly from the white upper fuselage, are also rendered in the same blue. The Mexican tricolor of green, white, and red, derived from the flag of the "Three Guarantees," flown during the war of independence from Spain, appears mid-fuselage.

Avianca (AV/AVA)

COLOMBIA (HK)

Colombian flag-carrier and one of the world's oldest airlines, operating a domestic network and scheduled flights throughout Latin America, the Caribbean, the U.S., and Europe. The airline's history goes back to the founding on 5 December 1919 by German settlers of Sociedad Colombia-Alemana de Transportes Aereos (SCADTDA), which begun operations with Junkers F 13 float-planes on 12 September 1940. Aerovias Nacionales de Colombia (Avianca) began on 14 June 1940 through the merger of SCADTDA and Servicio Aereo Colombiano, which had operated a small domestic network since 1933.

FLEET:
5 X B757-200, 4 X B767-200ER, 2 X B767-300ER, 13 X MD-83, 6 X F50

FEATURES:
An interesting presentation where the red on the upper part of the forward fuselage gently sweeps up to the roof before reaching the tailfin, leaving the majority of the fuselage in white. Set into the red are white Avianca titles with two waves in red, yellow, and dark blue, the colors of the Colombian flag, which is painted underneath the cockpit. A larger version of the two waves covers part of the red tailfin.

Aviogenex (AGX)

SERBIA AND MONTENEGRO (YU)

Balkan airline providing regular and ad hoc charter flights to and from Belgrade and other cities, mainly for its parent company's travel agency Yugotours. The transport of migrant workers across Europe is also undertaken and a growing part of its business is the wet-leasing of aircraft. Aviogenex was established on 21 May 1968 as the air transport division of Generalexport, an enterprise for trade and tourism, and started flights in April 1969 with two Russian Tupolev TU-134as. UN sanctions and the Kosovo conflict forced a suspension of services for several years, but these were restarted in November 2000.

FLEET:
2 X B727-200A, 1 X B737-200A

FEATURES:
The white aircraft is complemented by the company's terracotta-red color painted on the underside of the fuselage, where it is surmounted by an orange pinstripe, and on the tailfin. The normally red AV motif is promoted on the fin reversed out in white. Black *Aviogenex* titles are applied on the forward cabin roof.

Avior Airlines (Aviones de Oriente) (3B/ROI)

VENEZUELA (YV)

Regional Venezuelan airline operating an extensive domestic network from its base at Barcelona across the whole of the country, and to Aruba, Martinique, Grenada, and Trinidad in the southern Caribbean. Through associate Avior Turisticas it also offers holiday packages to the tropical Margarita Island and sightseeing tours to some of Venezuela's spectacular natural wonders. Avior Airlines was formed in 1994 to provide air transport for petroleum companies and travel agents in the eastern part of Venezuela and started flying that same year with charters to Margarita Island and Canaima.

FLEET:
2 X B737-200A, 10 x Beech 1900D, 2 x Cessna 208B Grand Caravan, 2 X EMB 120ER Brasilia

FEATURES:
This clean bright red and white aircraft sends a clear message, with a bold white A on the red tailfin, and red *Avior Airlines* lettering on the forward fuselage. The horizontal stroke in the letter A has been drawn to represent an aircraft in flight with its condensation trails. The aircraft engines are painted in red to ensure a balanced design.

Axis Airways (AXY)

FRANCE (F)

French airline operating domestic and international passenger and cargo charter flights throughout Europe, the countries bordering the Mediterranean, and across the Atlantic, from bases at Paris Charles de Gaulle and Marseille Provence airports. An operation is also conducted out of Pescara in Italy, from where regular flights serve Paris and Brussels. Axis Airways was created by Axis Partners at Marseille in March 2001 and began charter operations the following month with a single Boeing 737-200QC. The first transatlantic flight was inaugurated on 15 May that year.

FLEET:
2 X BAE 146-200QC,
3 X B737-300QC, 1 X B737-400,
1 X B757-200

FEATURES:
This design is unusual and not unattractive in two respects. The blue and gold tail design incorporating two sketched letter AS arranged to read both as AS and as an X stops abruptly at an angle two-thirds of the way up, and the large blue web address slopes across the fuselage. The blue engines help to balance the overall effect, but the airline name forward is overpowered by the web address and appears as if it has been added only as an afterthought.

Azerbaijan Airlines (J2/AHY)

AZERBAIJAN (4K)

State-owned national carrier of Azerbaijan operating a growing network of international services from Baku's Heydar Aliyev International to destinations in Europe, the Commonwealth of Independent States, North and South America, and the Middle and Far East. Domestic flights and regional charters are also offered. Aviation in Azerbaijan dates back as far as 1923, but the airline was reconstituted out of the former Aeroflot directorate on 7 April 1992 following the collapse of the Soviet Union and the country's subsequent independence.

FLEET:
1 (2) X A319-100, 1 X A320-200,
2 (2) X AN-140-100, 2 X B727-200,
4 X B757-200, 5 X TU-134B-3,
1 X TU-154M, 9 X Yak-40,
1 x Yak-40K

FEATURES:
The highly visible bright blue is applied to the tailfin and backed up by a windowline and lower cheatline, with additional speed lines under the cockpit. The tailfin has a ringed delta-wing arrow in the national colors of sky blue, red, and green, together with AZAL initials. *Azerbaijan* lettering is supplemented by AHY initials aft, standing for its local name, Acerbaycan Hava Yollari.

Azteca Airlines (Lineas Aéreas Azteca) (ZE/LCD)

MEXICO (XA)

Privately owned domestic scheduled airline linking Mexico City and a secondary hub at Tijuana to more than 10 other Mexican cities. A cross-border link is also maintained to Los Angeles in California. Lineas Aéreas Azteca was established on 9 May 2000, taking over some assets and staff of Transportes Aéreos Ejecutivos SA (TAESA) following that airline's collapse. TAESA had been founded on 28 April 1988 and quickly grew into the third-largest airline in Mexico. Azteca started domestic operations on 2 June 2001 with a service between Mexico City and Tijuana using a leased Boeing 737-300.

FLEET:
5 x B737-300, 3 x B737-700

FEATURES:
This unpretensious yet elegant scheme uses the green, white, and red colors of the Mexican tricolor, derived from the flag of the "Three Guarantees" flown during the war of independence from Spain. The airline name, applied in green on the cabin roof, and the twin pyramids of red and green on the tailfin and forward, recall the Aztec civilization that flourished in Mexico until the sixteenth century. The fresh red and green are offset beautifully on the all-white aircraft.

Bahamasair (UP/BHS)

BAHAMAS (C6)

National airline of the Bahamas providing a network of scheduled services linking several cities in Florida, as well as the Turks and Caicos Islands, with the capital Nassau. From there, onward connections are available on its domestic flights to the main Bahamian islands and inhabited Out Islands. Bahamasair was established on 18 June 1973 and began operations the same day as the national airline when the newly independent Commonwealth of the Bahamas acquired the operations of two private airlines, Flamingo Airlines and Out Island Airways.

FLEET:
4 x B737-200A, 7 x Dash 8 300

FEATURES:
This tropical scheme is appropriate for the carefree paradise ambience of the Caribbean. A colorful mixture of leaves, petals, and fruit tumbles down the white tailfin and is contrasted by the blue aircraft belly and engines with the web address. *Bahamasair* titles in aquamarine blue and orange cover the cabin roof. The aquamarine, yellow, and black Bahamian flag follows the aircraft registration at the rear. The black triangle is considered a symbol of the unity of the islands.

BAL Bashkirian Airlines (V9/BTC)

RUSSIAN FEDERATION (RA)

Main airline in the Republic of Bashkortostan providing scheduled passenger and cargo services from Ufa to other main cities within Russia and to the now independent Caucasian republics of Armenia and Azerbaijan, as well as to Tajikistan in Central Asia. Regular charter flights are also carried out to destinations in Europe, Asia, and North Africa. The airline was established in 1991 as a major Aeroflot unit and was formerly part of Samara-based Aerovolga. The airline operation was separated from Ufa Airport on 1 January 2000.

FLEET:

1 X AN-74, 1 X AN-74-200,
1 x Mil MI-8T, 2 X TU-134A-3,
6 X TU-154M

FEATURES:

This notable blue and white livery is dominated by large BAL initials in Cyrillic script across the forward fuselage, emphasized by a broad blue band ahead of the lettering. The blue tailfin displays the airline's symbol of a stylized bee, referring to the republic's reputation as a purveyor of high-quality honey. The sky blue, white, and green Bashkortostan flag, with the gold *kurai* flower signifying the seven original tribes, is carried on the roof.

Bangkok Airways (PG/BKP)

THAILAND (HS)

Major Thai regional carrier operating a domestic network from Bangkok International Airport to several major towns and cities, together with services to Cambodia, China, Laos, Vietnam, and Singapore. Bangkok Airways can trace its history back to 1968 and the establishment of Sahakol Air, which provided air-taxi services in support of oil and gas exploration in the Gulf of Thailand. Scheduled services were added in January 1986, leading to the adoption of the present title in 1989, to more accurately reflect its expanded activities. It has built its own resort airports on Koh Samui.

FLEET:

3 X A320-200, 2 X ATR 72-200,
9 X ATR 72-500, 4 X B717-200

FEATURES:

All the aircraft designs feature the unique beauty of each of the destinations served by Bangkok Airways. The aircraft illustrated carries the name of the Chinese city of Guilin, highlighting the pine-covered mountains, dhows, Pagoda Hill, and the Li River. The airline's attractive corporate blue, gold, and red wing symbol is applied on the tailfin and engines.

Batavia Air (7P/BTV)

INDONESIA (PK)

Private Indonesian airline operating a strong domestic network out of Jakarta, reaching some 15 destinations on all the main islands. Among the principal destinations served are Jakarta, Denpasar, Medan, Surabaya, Balikpapan, and Yogyakarta. International routes are also flown to China. The airline obtained its air operator's certificate in January 2002 and began flying that same month. International flights were introduced in June 2003 with the service to Guangzhou in China.

FLEET:
16 x B737-200A, 1 x B737-300, 4 x B737-400, 1 x F28 MK4000

FEATURES:
A curvaceous blue and orange floral design on the tailfin forms the most eye-catching feature of the livery, contrasted by *Batavia Air* titles linked by an orange flourish on the forward roof. The straight-through orange windowline and dark blue line below are framed by white. Some aircraft are operated without the cheatlines and with large *Batavia Air* lettering on the front fuselage.

Bearskin Airlines (JV/BLS)

CANADA (C)

Northern Ontario's largest regional airline serving nearly 40 points ranging from First Nation communities to the major markets of Toronto, Ottawa, and Winnipeg. The network radiates from bases at Sioux Lookout, Thunder Bay, and Sudbury. The airline was founded on 17 July 1963 by pilot and free trader John Hegland as Bearskin Lake Air Service and named after a remote northern Ontario community, known as Maquan in the local dialect. Charter operations began with two Cessna 180s. The present name was adopted in 1993 when the airline picked up a scheduled network following the collapse of NorOntair.

FLEET:
3 x Beech 99, 1 x Beech 99A, 5 x SA227AC Metro III, 2 x SA227DC Metro 23

FEATURES:
The two-tone burnt sienna colors of the livery, as applied to the aircraft in the shape of three cheatlines that splay out and across the tailfin, are a reminder that the airline's roots can be found deep in the soil of northern Ontario. Both the airline name on the roof and aircraft registration at the rear are drawn in the same colors, complementing the simple corporate design.

Belair Airlines (4T/BBB)

SWITZERLAND (HB)

Zurich-based Swiss charter airline offering a mix of year-round and seasonal flights to destinations in the Mediterranean basin, the Black Sea, and the Canary Islands, as well as across the Atlantic to North America and the Caribbean, and eastwards to Goa and the Maldives. Flights are operated for its parent company Hotelplan, Switzerland's largest tour operator. Belair Airlines was established in 2001 out of the remnants of charter company Balair, a subsidiary of the now defunct Swissair, when the latter found itself in financial difficulties and ceased flying.

FLEET:
2 X B757-200ER, 1 X B767-300ER

FEATURES:
The centerpiece of the Belair livery is the tailfin, which promotes the traditional white Holy Cross on a red shield, effectively the Swiss flag, dating back to the Battle of Laupen in 1339 when the Helvetic armies united under a single banner. The white of the upper fuselage is reminiscent of the snow-covered Swiss mountains, and the blue underside of the aircraft of the clear mountain lakes, which are abundant in this alpine country. The large *Belair* titling is applied in blue.

Belavia Belarusian Airlines (B2/BRU)

BELARUS (EW)

National airline of the Republic of Belarus operating an extensive network of scheduled passenger and cargo services from the capital Minsk to more than 25 destinations in Europe and the Comonwealth of Independent States. Numerous charter flights are also undertaken. Belavia was established in November 1993 but reformed on 5 March 1996 upon a restructuring of air transport in Belarus, which had previously been based on the Aeroflot directorate in this former Soviet republic. In September 1998 another operator, Minskavia, was integrated, adding a large number of ex-Soviet aircraft.

FLEET:
3 X AN-24RV, 2 X B737-500, 7 X TU-134A-3, 4 X TU-154B-2, 4 X TU-154M, 3 X Yak-40

FEATURES:
In the center of the bright blue tailfin is the airline's red feathered-arrow symbol, complemented by a straight-through windowline and blue engines lightened by thin white lines. Red *Belavia* titles sit above the forward windows, as does the Belarus flag further back. The red in the flag stands for the blood of the country's defenders, green for hope and its forests, and the traditional pattern for its rich cultural heritage.

Bellview Airlines (B3/BLV)

NIGERIA (5N)

Private Nigerian airline providing scheduled passenger and cargo services based in Lagos and Amsterdam and serving the major cities within Nigeria and destinations in East and West Africa and the Indian subcontinent. Domestic destinations include Abuja, Kano, Lagos, and Port Harcourt. Charter flights are also offered to points throughout Africa. Bellview Airlines was formed in 1991 and began scheduled flights from Lagos, initially with ex-Soviet equipment, in 1993.

FLEET:
4 X B737-200A, 2 X B767-200ER

FEATURES:
Two white fairy terns soar into the skies, represented by the blue tailfin, whose coloring extends through the rear fuselage. The shadow of the terns in flight is projected ahead of the *Bellview* titles midway along the aircraft. Each aircraft is named after virtues, such as hope, resilience, charity, fortitude, peace, and unity.

Big Sky Airlines (GQ/BSY)

UNITED STATES (N)

u.s. regional airline serving four western states from its base at Billings in Montana. Scheduled passenger and cargo flights reach some 20 destinations in Idaho, Montana, North Dakota, and Washington. Big Sky Airlines was established on 1 June 1978 and began operations in its home state on 11 September that same year linking Billings with Helena and Kalispell. On 15 July 1985, it started connecting flights at Billings under the Northwest Airlink banner, but these have since been discontinued. Essential Air Service routes in the west were taken over from Aspen Mountain Air in October 1998.

FLEET:
8 x Beech 1900D, 3 x SA227AC Metro III, 5 x SA227DC Metro 23

FEATURES:
A sweep of royal blue from the nose to the underside of the aircraft and back up to cover the tailfin, together with the blue engines and winglets, creates a classy image, further enhanced by the silver-gray pencil line above the blue. *Big Sky* titles in black freehand writing stand out strongly on the glacier-white fuselage, as does the blue aircraft registration.

Biman Bangladesh Airlines (BG/BBC)

BANGLADESH (S2)

Government-owned national airline operating scheduled international flag services from the capital Dhaka to 25 destinations in 20 countries in Asia, the Middle East, Europe, and the United States. Also serves a domestic flight network connecting eight major towns and cities. The airline was established on 4 January 1972, soon after the country's independence from Pakistan, and began operations a month later with domestic flights, before adding a London route on 5 March that year with leased Boeing 707s. Biman Bangladesh Airlines is based at Dhaka's Zia International Airport.

FLEET:
4 x A310-300, 3 x F28-4000, 4 x DC-10-30, 1 x DC-10-30ER

FEATURES:
The national colors of red and dark green are used in the form of a cheatline running at window level along the whole length of the all-white fuselage, coming to a point at the front. Dark green *Bangladesh Airlines* titles are carried in English and Bengali on the port and starboard side respectively. A white stork, flying across the rising sun, represented by a crimson disc, is positioned centrally between horizontal fin bands in red and green, and on the engines.

Binter Canarias (NT/IBB)

SPAIN (EC)

Regional airline providing extensive inter-island services in the Canary Islands, a group of volcanic islands belonging to Spain and lying off the coast of Morocco. High-frequency flights connect the seven larger islands of Gran Canaria, Fuerteventura, Lanzarote, Tenerife, La Palma, Gomera, and Hierro to the airline's main bases at Las Palmas de Gran Canaria and Tenerife North. Binter Canarias was set up as a subsidiary of flag-carrier Iberia on 18 February 1988 and started operations on 26 March 1989 with a CASA CN-235 turboprop aircraft. It was privatized in late 1999.

FLEET:
4 x ATR 72-200, 1 x ATR 72-210, 8 x ATR 72-500, 2 x Beech 1900D

FEATURES:
Binter's latest color scheme of two-tone flowing green and white suggests the verdant hills and valleys and beaches of the Canary Islands. The central symbol of two stylistic birds with wings spread wide is prominently displayed on the tailfin and also flies ahead of the *Binter* name on the forward fuselage. The light green underside of the aircraft is accompanied by an undulating darker green band, which stretches from nose to tail.

Blue Dart Aviation (BZ/BDA)

INDIA (VT)

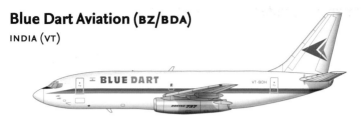

Major Indian cargo logistics company providing domestic scheduled overnight express cargo flights, alongside local and regional charter activities, from hubs at Bangalore, Mumbai, Delhi, Kolkata, Chennai, and Hyderabad. It has its own in-house maintenance facility and also provides aircraft maintenance and engineering support to third parties. Cargo handling and consultancy services complete the service. Blue Dart Aviation was established by Blue Dart Express on 31 May 1994 and began operations on 17 June 1996.

FLEET:
5 X B737-200(F)

FEATURES:
As the name would suggest, the airline has focused on a dart symbol to present an image of speed. This is applied in a two-color arrangement in blue and green on the tailfin, as is the airline name ahead of the wings and the mid-fuselage cheatline, the latter ending in a sharp downward-angled point to reinforce forward movement. The Indian flag precedes the airline name.

Blue Line (BLE)

FRANCE (F)

French charter airline offering VIP flights, ad hoc charters with two hours' notice, and inclusive-tour services for leading package-tour operators from its base at Paris Charles de Gaulle to destinations in the Mediterranean basin, Europe, Africa, and the Middle East. Wet-lease services on an aircraft, crew, maintenance, and insurance basis are also undertaken. Blue Line was formed in January 2002 by a group of aviation professionals led by Xavier Remondeau and began operations in May that same year.

FLEET:
1 X B737-400, 1 X B757-200, 2 X F100, 2 X MD-83, 1 X MD-90-30

FEATURES:
Blue and white imbues a touch of class, with simplicity often the key to a successful corporate identity. The flowing sky blue B on the dark blue tailfin and the dark blue engines are underscored by a thin blue line suggesting an unlimited horizon for the airline. The first letter in the airline name repeats the tail design, although the B in this case is drawn differently.

Blue Panorama Airlines (BV/BPA)
ITALY (I)

Private Italian airline operating domestic and Europe-wide charters, serving especially the resorts around the Mediterranean, together with long-haul flights across the Atlantic to Mexico, Guatemala, and Cuba, and eastwards to Thailand, Indonesia, and the Maldives. Extensive flights also operate to destinations throughout Africa. Blue Panorama Airlines was founded in Rome by tour operator Astra Travel on 26 December 1998 and began operations with a single Boeing 737-400.

FLEET:
5 x B737-400, 1 x B757-200, 3 x B767-300ER, (4) x B7E7-8

FEATURES:
Two birds in flight are hinted at by the white design on the dark blue tailfin, which is duplicated in blue on the engine cowlings and in front of the *Blue Panorama* titles on the forward cabin roof. The solid blue nose and thin blue line mirror the tail arrangement.

Blue Wings (QW/BWG)
GERMANY (D)

German charter airline providing a variety of services for businesses and tourists from its Düsseldorf base on both an ad hoc and contract basis. The Bosphorus metropolis of Istanbul and Turkish resorts on the Aegean Sea and Black Sea are flown to on behalf of Öger Tours, while other flights frequently operate to Iran, Dubai, India, and Sri Lanka. Another major activity is the transport of migrant workers from Germany to their home countries. Blue Wings was founded in February 2002 and started operations with a single Airbus A320 in July 2003.

FLEET:
1 x A320-200, 1 x A321-100

FEATURES:
Two aerofoil shapes in two shades of blue on the tailfin and *Blue Wings* titles forward in a lighter blue color make up the understated corporate identity. The only other color on the mostly white aircraft is the dark blue underside and the black, red, and gold German flag at the top of the fin. The colors are derived from the coat of arms of the Holy Roman Empire of the German nation, which comprised a black eagle with red claws and beak on a gold field.

Blue1 (KF/BLF)
FINLAND (OH)

Regional subsidiary of SAS Scandinavian Airlines feeding traffic into the parent company's hubs at Stockholm, Copenhagen, and Oslo from six Finnish cities, and linking Helsinki to destinations in Germany, Belgium, and the Netherlands. Blue1 was formed at Seinäjoki in Finland in 1988 as Air Botnia and adopted the present title in January 2004. In January 1998, it was purchased by SAS and on 4 October 2004 became the first regional member of the global Star Alliance.

FLEET:
7 X BAE RJ85, 2 X BAE RJ100,
5 x Saab 2000

FEATURES:
The mid-blue tailfin and engine cowlings incorporate the word *Blue* in white, with the figure 1 constructed from seven gray squares following the *Blue* on the fin, thus completing the airline name. The full name also appears above the first row of windows, this time in gray and blue. The SAS logo refers to the airline's association with the tri-national Scandinavian flag-carrier.

Bluebird Cargo (BF/BBD)
ICELAND (TF)

Keflavik-based Icelandic carrier providing capacity to major express parcel companies, freight forwarders, and airlines such as UPS and Cargolux, mainly on an ACMI (aircraft, crew, maintenance, and insurance) wet-lease basis. The airline also offers blocked-space agreements and part-charters. Bluebird Cargo was established in 2000 by a group of local businessmen but has since been acquired by the FL Group, the owner of Icelandair. Operations started in March 2001, with a single Boeing 737-300 freighter routing daily from Iceland via the United States to Cologne in Germany.

FLEET:
5 X B737-300(F), 1 X B757-200(F)

FEATURES:
As its name suggests, the aircraft is painted largely in blue, with the exception of a gray strip separating the belly from the rest of the aircraft, and a thin white edge to the tailfin across which fly three blue, white, and red stylized birds in formation. White *Bluebird Cargo* titles are written in a natural script across the forward fuselage. Blue, white, and red are the colors of the Icelandic flag.

BMED (British Mediterranean Airways) (KJ/LAJ)

UNITED KINGDOM (G)

Independent British Airways franchise partner operating an expanding route structure, which now services some 15 destinations in the Levant, Central Asia, Iran, and northeast Africa from London Heathrow Airport. The schedule allows passengers to connect at Heathrow with British Airways long-haul flights. British Mediterranean Airways, since October 2004 trading as BMED, started operations on 28 October 1994 using a single Airbus A320-200 on a service to Beirut, with extensions to Amman and Damascus following six months later. A franchise agreement with BA took effect from 30 March 1997.

FLEET:
4 x A320-200, 3 (7) x A321-200

FEATURES:
As a franchise operation, BMED aircraft are painted in British Airways colors. The BA corporate palette of red, white, and blue is drawn from the British flag, a fluttering adaptation of which is depicted on the tailfin. The airline name is applied in a soft and rounded typeface, and the speedwing symbol has evolved into a three-dimensional speedmarque. Both are applied in a large format on the front fuselage, which is white above wing level and blue below.

bmibaby (WW/BMI)

UNITED KINGDOM (G)

Low-cost arm of BMI british midland operating scheduled services within the United Kingdom and to more than 25 destinations in Europe and the Channel Islands. Apart from its main base at Nottingham East Midlands, the airline also operates from Cardiff, Manchester, Birmingham, London Gatwick, and Durham Tees Valley airports. bmibaby, promoted as "the airline with tiny fares," was formed on 17 January 2002 and began flying on 20 March that same year with a service between the East Midlands and Malaga in Spain. It obtained its own air operator's certificate on 15 March 2004.

FLEET:
10 x B737-300, 6 x B737-500

FEATURES:
The bmibaby livery complements the master brand and is based on a more economic model of "speed and charm – basic but full of character." It has been highly successful and is said to deliver "price with attitude." Acclaimed American design firm Landor Associates has used "Tiny," a seven-month-old angelic baby with the attitude of a 17-year-old, and infused it with a personality that comes alive in the minds of the customers.

bmi british midland (MD/BMA)

UNITED KINGDOM (G)

bmi, a member of the Star Alliance, is one of Europe's leading scheduled airlines, serving nearly 30 destinations on the continent, including 11 within the UK. It has also added long-haul services across the North Atlantic and to India. Its main operational base is London Heathrow, where it is now the second-biggest operator after British Airways. A long history goes back to 1938 when it began life as Air Schools, becoming Derby Aviation and Derby Airways, before adopting the British Midland Airways (BMA) name in 1964. A rebranding exercise in early 2001 resulted in the present attractive identity.

FLEET:
6 (3) X A319-100, 11 X A320-200, 8 X A321-200, 3 X A330-200

FEATURES:
The bmi brand, which subtly uses the national colors and the stylized representation of the British flag on the tailfin has been designed by Landor Associates to reflect "speed with charm and style." It was intended to highlight the airline's core values. These are stated to be its Britishness, can-do spirit and innovation, and reputation for offering warm and friendly customer service. It was introduced in February 2001.

bmi regional (WW/GNT)

UNITED KINGDOM (G)

Regional airline subsidiary of bmi providing scheduled services from Aberdeen, Edinburgh, Glasgow, Leeds Bradford, and Manchester, primarily within the UK, but also to several destinations in Europe. The airline was formed by Ian Woodley in July 1987 as Business Air with a small fleet of twin-engined Embraer Bandeirantes, flying charters by day and Royal Mail services by night, before adding scheduled passenger services. It was bought by Airlines of Britain Group in April 1996 and became a subsidiary of British Midland Airways in January 1998, initially trading as British Midland Commuter.

FLEET:
3 X ERJ 135ER, 8 X ERJ 145EP, 2 X ERJ 145ER, 1 X ERJ 145MP

FEATURES:
The bmi regional branding is identical to that of the parent company. The subtle use of the national colors and the stylized representation on the tailfin of the British flag are the key elements and have been designed to reflect speed with charm and style.

Bouraq Indonesia Airlines (BO/BOU)

INDONESIA (PK)

Privately owned regional airline flying scheduled services to eastern parts of the Indonesian archipelago, linking major points in Java, Kalimantan, Sulawesi, Maluku, Bali, and the Nusa Tenggara Islands. There is also a connection between Jakarta and neighboring Singapore. Bouraq was established in April 1970 and began operations with three Douglas DC-3s flying from Jakarta to Banjarmasin, Balikpapan, and Surabaya.

FLEET:
9 x B737-200A, 1 x MD-82

FEATURES:
The teal green color scheme, made up of a broad band and thin pencil line starts at the cockpit and curves down low, before sweeping up again to fill the entire tailfin. A black B in a white circular disc is set into the fin, and bold black *Bouraq* titles cover the forward cabin roof. A small red and white Indonesian flag is carried behind the cockpit.

BRA Transportes Aéreos (BR/BRB)

BRAZIL (PP/PT)

Brazilian airline offering low-fare scheduled passenger services from São Paulo to some 30 destinations, the majority in the northeast of the country. Among the main destinations are São Paulo, Brasilia, Rio de Janeiro, Porto Alegre, Natal, Recife, Salvador, and the tourist destinations of the famous Iguaçú Falls in the south of the country. Maceió, Salvador, and Porto Seguro are also connected across the South Atlantic to Lisbon in Portugal. BRA Transported Aéreos was established in 1999.

FLEET:
5 x B737-300, 3 x B737-400, 1 x B767-300ER

FEATURES:
The bold BRA initials in blue and yellow, standing for Brasil Rodeo Aéreo, the full name of the company, feature large on the tailfin, forward fuselage, and engine cowlings, with a fringe on the B added to give the impression of movement. The aircraft is otherwise all white. Additional *Rotatur* titles of the airline's owner are carried by some aircraft.

Brit Air (DB/BZH)

FRANCE (F)

Morlaix, Brittany–based French regional airline providing scheduled services within metropolitan France and to Denmark, Germany, Italy, Spain, and the United Kingdom, both in its own right and for parent company Air France. Its route network covers 20 cities in its home country, plus 15 in Europe, from hubs at Lyon St.-Exupery, Paris Orly, and Paris Charles de Gaulle airports. Brit Air was founded in 1973 and began scheduled services in April 1979. It operated for a time as an Air France Express partner, but became a wholly owned subsidiary of Air France in October 2000.

FLEET:
19 X CRJ100ER, 12 X CRJ700, 10 X F100

FEATURES:
Brit Air's aircraft are painted in the Air France livery but carry the airline's symbol on the engines. The motif comprises two parts: the Triskele, a Celtic symbol representing the three elements of earth, fire, and water, and the Hermine, the emblem of Brittany. Colors were selected from the region's natural environment, including the yellow broom for Triskele, the white of the Breton flag as the main color of the aircraft, and European blue.

Britannia Airways (6B/BLX)

SWEDEN (SE)

Holiday airline operating charter flights from Norway and Sweden to destinations around the Mediterranean and the Canary Islands, and in Thailand and other Indian Ocean resorts. Flights originate primarily from Oslo, Bergen, Malmö, Gothenburg, and Stockholm. The airline was originally formed to handle the charter operations of Transwede Airways and was renamed Blue Scandinavia when acquired by tour operator Fritidsresor, and to the present title in 1998 after they came under the control of Thomson Travel. Britannia Airways is now owned by TUI Airline Management.

FLEET:
4 X B737-800, 1 X B757-200

FEATURES:
Aircraft are painted in the standard "World of TUI" colors, comprising a blue upper fuselage and tailfin, a gray underside, and, of course, the red "smile" now so well-known at European airports and further afield. The fleet carries large red *Fritidsresor* titles and those of other travel agents along the fuselage.

British Airways (BA/BAW)

UNITED KINGDOM (G)

One of the world's leading airlines, operating the largest global network of scheduled passenger and cargo services, linking the UK with more than 180 destinations in 80 countries on all continents. It also provides a comprehensive domestic network including the "Super Shuttle" from London, the Scottish Highlands and Islands routes, and regional flights through BA CitiExpress. The network is further extended through its membership of the oneworld alliance and franchise operations in the UK, Denmark, and South Africa. British Airways was founded as Imperial Airways on 31 March 1924 through the amalgamation of Handley Page Transport, Instone Air Line, Daimler Airways, and British Marine Air Navigation. Daimler Airways was the successor to Aircraft Transport & Travel, which had launched the world's first international scheduled service on 25 August 1919 between London and Paris. On 1 April 1940, Imperial merged with the original British Airways (founded on 30 September 1935) to form British Overseas Airways Corporation (BOAC). The present airline came into being on 1 April 1972 from the merger of BOAC and the other state corporation British European Airways, which had been set up on 1 January 1946. British Airways was privatized in February 1987, and in April 1988 controversially took over British Caledonian.

FLEET:
36 X A319-100, 5 X A320-100, 24 X A320-200, 7 X A321-200, 5 X B737-300, 18 X B737-400, 9 X B737-500, 57 X B747-400, 13 X B757-200, 21 X B767-300ER, 3 X B777-200, 40 X 777-200ER

FEATURES:
The corporate palette of red, white, and blue is drawn closely from the British flag, a fluttering adaption of which takes up the tailfin. The airline name is applied in a soft, round typeface, and the flat red speedwing symbol has evolved into a new three-dimensional speedmarque. Both are applied on the front fuselage, which is white above wing level and blue below. Some aircraft may still be seen in the "World Colours," a design created by London consultancy Newell and Sorrell but now discarded. The tail colors created by artists from across the world were intended to depict British Airways as a global, cosmopolitan company but proud of its "Britishness."

British Airways CitiExpress (TH/BRT)

UNITED KINGDOM (G)

Europe's second-largest regional airline operating a dense cross-country network within the UK, and to points in Scandinavia and Continental Europe. The airline operates from hubs at London Gatwick, Belfast, Birmingham, Bristol, Edinburgh, Glasgow, Manchester, Newcastle, and Southampton. The regional subsidiary of British Airways began operations on 31 March 2002, combining British Regional Airlines, created on 1 September 1996 via a merger, and Brymon Airways, which started in England on 15 June 1972. Manx Airlines and BA Regional were integrated in 2002. The airline changed its name to BA Connect on 3rd February 2006.

FLEET:
1 X BAE 146-100, 2 X BAE 146-200, 1 X BAE 146-300, 8 X Dash 8 300, 8 X ERJ 145EP, 20 X ERJ 145EU, 16 X RJ100

FEATURES:
The livery is identical to that of the parent company, with the three-dimensional speedmarque and *British Airways* titles applied in a large format on the front fuselage, which is white above wing level and blue below. The entire tailfin is taken up by the fluttering adaptation of the British flag.

BritishJet.com

MALTA (9H)

Malta-based low-fare airline operating several flights a week between the Mediterranean islands and London Gatwick in support of tourism between the two nations. The airline was established on 29 September 2004 by Malta Bargains, formerly Malta Sun Holidays, a leading tour company and hotel operator. The inaugural flight was operated on 1 May 2005 with a McDonnell Douglas MD-90-30 leased from Hello of Switzerland.

FLEET:
1 X MD-90-30

FEATURES:
As the British market is the airline's main target, the livery is loosely based on the British flag, with the red and white crosses on the flag cleverly transformed into a flaming sun on the blue tailfin. The sun reflects the holiday environment in Malta. A red ribbon floats over the *BritishJet.com* title under the front windows of the white fuselage, and on the aft roof.

Buddha Air (BHA)

NEPAL (9N)

Nepalese domestic airline operating a network of scheduled passenger services radiating from the capital Kathmandu to 10 destinations, five at each end of the country. The airline also operates charter flights and mountain-experience flights in the Himalayas, taking in some of the highest peaks, with a close-up view of Mount Everest a Buddha Air speciality. Buddha Air was founded in 1997 and began operations in October that year with a single Beech 1900D.

FLEET:
4 x Beech 1900D

FEATURES:
A pair of gold and white doves are highlighted on the deep blue tailfin to form the visual element of the airline's presentation, while the similarly colored engines and low cheatline and aircraft belly add a streamlining effect. *Buddha Air* titling, also in blue, is painted on the mid-cabin roof. The unique shape of the Nepali flag can be seen ahead of the first window. The airline name derives from the founder of Buddhism, which seeks to attain a perfect state of enlightenment.

Buffalo Airways (J4/BFL)

CANADA (C)

Diversified northern Canadian aviation company operating within the Northwest Territories and the Yukon. Among its many activities are a scheduled passenger service between its base at Hay River and Yellowknife, together with passenger and cargo charters, fuel supply, pollution and pest control, fire suppression, aircraft conversions, maintenance, and flying training. Aircraft and parts sale are also offered. Buffalo Airways was established in 1969.

FLEET:
4 x Bombardier CL-215, 2 X C-46A Commando, 10 x DC-3, 4 X DC-4, 4 x PBY-5A Canso

FEATURES:
There are several variations in the livery on different aircraft, but the DC-3 is distinguished by the bluey-green tailfin and a broad windowline edged in black on each side, with the lower pencil line separating the upper white from the gray underside of the aircraft. Bold black *Buffalo* titles are painted along the cabin roof.

Bulgaria Air (FB/LZB)

BULGARIA (LZ)

State-owned national airline of Bulgaria maintaining
passenger and cargo schedules from the capital
Sofia to key cities in 18 European countries. Bulgaria
Air was established in November 2002 as the successor to the collapsed flag-carrier Balkan Bulgarian
Airlines, whose history dated back to fall 1948 and
the foundation of a joint Bulgarian–Soviet undertaking under the name of TABSO, to take over the
operation of Bulgarshe Vazdusne Sobstenie, which
had inaugurated a domestic service on 29 July 1947.
Bulgaria Air began operations began on 4 December
2002 with a service from Sofia to London and Paris.

FLEET:
5 × B737-300, 4 × B737-500

FEATURES:
The largely white aircraft has few
decorations, but what there is
pleases the eye. The fresh red and
green colors, which together with
the white make up the Bulgarian
tricolor, are used in the tailfin
design in the shape of an aircraft.
At the rear of the fuselage, the
airline's Web site address is also
applied in red and green. The
underside and engines are
painted in gray.

Bulgarian Air Charter (BAC)

BULGARIA (LZ)

Private Sofia-based carrier providing passenger
charter flights for tour operators from European
countries, especially from Germany, to the principal
Bulgarian summer resorts of Varna and Bourgas on
the Black Sea and the popular skiing centers in the
mountains. Cargo charter flights are also
undertaken, and the airline's aircraft are available
for wet-lease services. Bulgarian Air Charter was
registered on 26 June 2000 and started flying on
14 December that same year.

FLEET:
6 × MD-82, 2 × MD-83, 6 × TU-154M

FEATURES:
Bulgarian Air Charter also uses
the white, red, and green colors
of the Bulgarian flag to good
effect, especially in the airline
symbol of two aerofoil sections,
which form a circular sun design
on the tailfin. This is reiterated in
front of the airline name in red
and green on the cabin roof. A
rather heavy green windowline
and red pencil line run the length
of the aircraft and terminate in a
point under the cockpit windows.

BWIA West Indies Airways (BW/BWA)

TRINIDAD AND TOBAGO (9Y)

National carrier of Trinidad and Tobago, providing passenger and cargo flights from Piarco Airport, Port of Spain, to many Caribbean islands, South America, North America, and across the Atlantic to the UK. An air bridge between Trinidad and Tobago is also operated. The airline's history goes back to 27 November 1939 and the foundation of British West Indian Airways (BWIA), but the present company dates to 1 January 1980 and the merger of BWIA and Trinidad and Tobago Air Services. The latter had been established in June 1974 to operate the air bridge between the two islands.

FLEET:
2 X A340-300, 7 X B737-800,
2 x Dash 8 Q300

FEATURES:
The bright yellow and turquoise colors reflect the golden sands, clear seas, and cloudless skies of the Caribbean, and also capture West Indian warmth. But the greatest visual impact is provided by the silver representation of the steelpan, the country's well-known national instrument, which wraps itself around the forward underside and the tailfin of the aircraft. The design was created by Wayne Leal, of 2 Communicate, a West Indian resident in London.

CAL Cargo Air Lines (5C/ICL)

ISRAEL (4X)

Israeli all-cargo airline providing a mix of scheduled and charter flights from its main base at Tel Aviv's Ben Gurion International Airport and its logistics center at Liège in Belgium. Scheduled flights are operated to the United States, Hong Kong, and East Africa, exporting fresh produce and industrial materials, and importing heavy machinery, scientific equipment, high-value items, and livestock from around the world. CAL Cargo Air Lines was established by agricultural marketing boards in June 1976 and began operations on 2 November. Scheduled services were started on 1 December 1999.

FLEET:
2 X B747-200F

FEATURES:
A highly stylized bird carrying a small box in its beak flies ahead of the black *Cargo Air Lines* titles at the front of the aircraft. The airline's initials are prominently displayed on the tailfin, and more modestly on the engine cowlings. The main symbol and tail design are presented in three shades of blue, ranging from medium to sky blue.

Calm Air (MO/CAV)

CANADA (C)

Central Canada's regional airline operating scheduled passenger and cargo services to some 18 communities throughout Manitoba and the Kivalliq District of the new Nunavut Territory. Charter flights for both passengers and cargo are also provided. Calm Air was founded in 1962 by Arnold and Gail Morberg with flights to its president's fishing lodge near Stony Rapids in northern Saskatchewan using a single-engined floatplane. In 1976 it took over the passenger services of Transair in the Nunavut area.

FLEET:
5 x BAE 748-2A, 1 x BAE 748-2B, 5 x Saab 340B

FEATURES:
A forest green tailfin with gold CA initials tops the all-white fuselage, which carries only red *Calm Air* titles on the cabin roof. The airline's name is derived from the initials of its founder – Carl Arnold Lawrence Morberg – but also makes a statement about the comfortable, worry-free service the airline strives to provide.

Cameroon Airlines (UY/UYC)

CAMEROON (TJ)

National flag-carrier maintaining scheduled passenger and cargo links with Paris from its Douala hub and several West African capital cities, together with a small domestic network. The airline also operates out of Johannesburg with flight connections to West Africa. Cameroon Airlines was established on 26 July 1971 following Cameroon's withdrawal from the Air Afrique consortium, which had provided air links since 1961. Operations began on 1 November 1971 from Douala, the country's largest city and principal port and commercial center, to Yaounde with Boeing 737s.

FLEET:
1 x B737-200A, 1 x B737-300, 1 x B757-200, 1 x B767-200ER, 1 x B767-300ER

FEATURES:
The main points of interest are the green flamingo becoming airborne beneath the Cameroon Star encircled in red on the tailfin, and the exotic *Cameroon Airlines* titles on the forward upper fuselage. The ribboned triple cheatline borrows its colors from the national flag, being predominantly red but trimmed above and below in green and yellow respectively.

Canadian North (5T/ANX)

CANADA (C)

Yellowknife-based airline operating scheduled passenger services to major communities in the northwestern part of Canada's Northwest Territories and the new territory of Nunavut. Charter flights are also undertaken throughout the region. Canadian North was established in 1989 and operated services for Canadian Airlines until that company was absorbed by Air Canada. It acquired its own air operator's certificate in 2002.

FLEET:
5 X B737-200C, 1 X F28-1000

FEATURES:
The motif displayed prominently on the dark blue tailfin embodies the strength, boldness, beauty, and promise of the north. The northern lights and midnight sun are symbolic of its free spirit and willingness to meet the needs of those who fly. The polar bear, known locally as Nanuk, the ever-wandering one, thrives in a land where opportunities are gained through hard work, smart thinking, and quick action.

CanJet Airlines (C6/CJA)

CANADA (C)

Halifax, Nova Scotia-based Canadian low-fare airline operating scheduled services to more than 10 points in central and eastern Canada and across the border to New York. The airline also serves a number of resorts in Florida during the winter months. A division of the IMP Group, one of Canada's largest aviation and aerospace companies, CanJet Airlines was established in 1999 and began flying on 5 September 2000. After an enforced period of inactivity from the end of 2001, the airline was relaunched in summer 2002, inaugurating a first service on 27 June to Montreal and Ottawa.

FLEET:
9 X B737-500

FEATURES:
The mid-blue tailfin and engines contrast beautifully with the snow-white fuselage, as do the large CanJet titles on the tail and CanJet.com web address on the forward fuselage. In both cases, the c wraps around a red maple leaf, giving emphasis to the word can and the airline's Canadian heritage.

Cape Air (9K/KAP)

UNITED STATES (N)

U.S. commuter airline operating scheduled passenger services in the Cape Cod area, southern New England, South Florida and the Keys, Puerto Rico, and the British and U.S. Virgin Islands in the Caribbean. Services out of Guam in Micronesia are flown under the Continental Connection banner. Sister company Nantucket Airlines links Cape Cod with the islands of Martha's Vineyard and Nantucket. Cape Air started flying in 1989 with a first service between Boston and Provincetown.

FLEET:
3 X ATR 42-300, 47 x Cessna 402B II Businessliner

FEATURES:
This elegant two-tone blue livery is distinguished by a mid-blue tailfin presenting a light blue seagull in full flight, and twin curved cheatlines that take up the central part of the aircraft. *Cape Air* titling is applied low on the forward fuselage. Several aircraft carry special paint schemes designed by airbrush artist Jürek. These include a depiction of Nantucket's spring Daffodil Festival Weekend, the beauty of Key West, and the ambiance of Provincetown, where it all began.

Cargojet Airways (W8/WNT)

CANADA (C)

All-cargo airline serving the Canadian market from its main base at Toronto's Pearson International, where scheduled flights operate to 10 major cities. The airline focuses on time-urgent cargo for major courier companies, freight forwarders, and manufacturers. The airline was founded in July 2001 when Cargojet Canada acquired a major interest in Canada 3000 Cargo, taking over fully in February 2002 when the present name was adopted.

FLEET:
10 X B727-200F

FEATURES:
A faint red maple leaf against a gray globe, both outlined in strong red and provided with white speed lines, on the black tailfin, emphasize the airline's country of origin. Black and red cheatlines run from the rear and dip down at the front of the aircraft. Black *Cargojet* titles with a red maple leaf and red aircraft taking off are prominently displayed over the mid-fuselage, while the red web address is applied further forward.

Cargolux Airlines International (CV/CLX)

LUXEMBOURG (LX)

Europe's leading cargo-only airline and logistics business operating scheduled services between Europe, the Americas, the Near and Middle East, Africa, and the Asia Pacific region, together with worldwide charter flights. The scheduled network out of Luxembourg serves more than 50 destinations. Cargolux also provides complementary trucking facilities and offers maintenance and sub-leasing. The airline was founded on 4 March 1970 by Luxair, Salen Shipping, and Loftleidr Icelandic Airlines and took off the following September with a flight to Hong Kong, operated by the Canadair CL-44 swing-tail freighter.

FLEET:
15 X B747-400F

FEATURES:
The light gray fuselage is highlighted by simple straight cheatlines using the blue, white, and red tricolor of Luxembourg, broken on the forward fuselage by bold black *Cargolux* titling in lowercase lettering. The airline's distinctive three-dimensional "triple box" cargo motif, in white outlined in red, dominates the aircraft's massive tailfin.

Caribbean Star Airlines (8B/GFI)

ANTIGUA (V2)

Antigua-based regional airline providing inter-island services throughout the Caribbean from Tortola in the British Virgin Islands in the north to as far south as Trinidad and Tobago, taking in 13 islands. Holiday packages and charter flights are also offered, together with courier services for small parcels. Sister company Caribbean Sun Airlines operates out of Puerto Rico. Caribbean Star Airlines was founded in January 2000 by Texan business-man R. Allen Stanford, who has extensive business interests in the Caribbean. Operations started in June that year.

FLEET:
4 x Dash 8 100, 8 x Dash 8 Q300

FEATURES:
Several floral stars in golden yellow are placed at random along the fuselage in varying sizes, but these are dwarfed by a white star that takes up almost all of the golden tailfin. *Caribbean Star* titles in a dark green freehand script are written at the front and rear of the fuselage. The whole design conveys the free spirit and sunny and verdant islands of the Caribbean.

Caribbean Sun Airlines (zq)

UNITED STATES (N)

San Juan, Puerto Rico-based airline offering inter-island services in the Caribbean from Luis Muñoz Marin International Airport to Antigua, the Netherlands Antilles, and the British and u.s. Virgin Islands, where connections to other islands are available from sister company Caribbean Star Airlines, operating out of Antigua. Caribbean Sun Airlines is an affiliate of the Stanford Financial Group owned by r. Allen Stanford, who founded the airline in September 2002. Its inaugural flights, from San Juan to Tortola, British Virgin Islands, took place on 21 January 2003.

FLEET:
7 x Dash 8 100

FEATURES:
The Caribbean Sun Airlines design is similar to that of its sister company Caribbean Star, but the stars decorating the white aircraft have been replaced by golden sunbursts. The airline title at the rear has been moved up into the golden tailfin and is written below a white sunburst. The emphasis here is on Florida's golden beaches and seemingly endless sunshine.

Carpatair (v3/krp)

ROMANIA (YR)

Private Romanian-Swiss regional airline based in Timisoara in Romania, from where it operates a scheduled network to destinations in Italy, Germany, Hungary, Croatia, and the Republic of Moldova. All flights connect at Timisoara to five other Romanian cities. Charter flights are also offered. Carpatair was established in September 1998 as Veg Air and started flying on 15 March 1999 between Cluj and Treviso with a Yakovlev Yak-40 leased from Moldavian Airlines. The present title was adopted in December 1999 when Swiss investors bought into the company.

FLEET:
4 x Saab 340B, 8 x Saab 2000

FEATURES:
A dark green swathe of color fronted by light green starts towards the base of the tailfin and changes into thin cheatlines below the windowline, fading away to a point at the front. Depicted in the white part of the fin is a representation of the Carpathian Mountains enclosed in a green square outline. Over the forward cabin windows are green *Carpatair* titles, with the blue, yellow, and red Romanian flag at the rear.

Caspian Airlines (CPN)
IRAN (EP)

Iranian carrier operating a small domestic network and international flights from its main base at Tehran to the Persian Gulf area, and to Syria, Georgia, Armenia, and the Ukraine. Charter flights also form a large part of its business. Caspian Airlines was established in mid-1993 as a joint venture between Iranian and Russian interests and started operations in September that year.

FLEET:
3 x TU-154M

FEATURES:
The mid-blue tailfin and rear fuselage have been transformed into a homogenous arrow design creating a strong impression of free forward movement. At the top of the fin, a blue bird is outlined against a golden sun in a white circle. Understated *Caspian Airlines* titles sit atop the forward cabin windows, with the Arabic name in gold below. The Iranian flag has been added behind the cockpit windows.

Cathay Pacific Airways (CX/CPA)
HONG KONG (B-H)

Principal privately owned Hong Kong airline operating scheduled passenger and cargo services to some 50 destinations in Australia, New Zealand, the Middle and Far East, Europe, Africa, and North America. Another 18 cities are served in China through associate Dragonair, while a strong cargo business is further enhanced through its ownership of all-cargo airline Air Hongkong. Cathay Pacific Airways was founded by two wartime pilots on 24 September 1946 and began operations with a Douglas DC-3 on 1 July 1948. In September 1998, it became a member of the oneworld alliance.

FLEET:
26 (3) x A330-300, 15 x A340-300, 3 x A340-600, 8 x B747-200F, 20 x B747-400, 6 x B747-400F, 5 x B777-200, 12 x B777-300, (16) x B777-300ER

FEATURES:
Centerpiece of the Landor-designed identity is the "brush-wing" suggestion of the wing of a bird taking up most of the tailfin. A red "speed bar" encloses the bottom of the logo. The image is said to symbolize modern energy, confident elegance, and exacting standards of service, while its oriental feel is intended to appeal to both its Asian and Western customers.

Cayman Airways (KX/CAY)

CAYMAN ISLANDS (VP-C)

National airline of the Cayman Islands, a self-governing British Overseas Territory in the western Caribbean Sea, providing a scheduled passenger and cargo service to destinations in Cuba, Jamaica, and the United States. Services also link the three islands of Grand Cayman, Cayman Brac, and Little Cayman. A limited charter service is also offered. Cayman Airways was founded in July 1968 as the successor to the LACSA subsidiary Cayman Brac Airways, dating from 1955. It became wholly government owned in December 1977.

FLEET:
2 x B737-200A, 1 x B737-200C, 2 x B737-300, 2 x DHC-6 Twin Otter 300

FEATURES:
The highlight of the airline's visual image is the remarkable and amusing pirate turtle caricature on the tailfin, complete with peg leg and saber. The remainder of the scheme on the largely white aircraft is more conventional, with a triple straight-through cheatline of varying widths in green, red, and dark blue, and dark blue *Cayman Airways* titles on the cabin roof.

CCM Airlines (XK/CCM)

FRANCE (F)

Corsican regional airline linking this French Mediteranean island to the major cities in metropolitan France, and to Rome. Services connect at Paris and Lyon with intercontinental flights of Air France, a minor shareholder in the airline, and at Rome with those of Alitalia. CCM Airlines was established on 1 January 1989 and began operations in June 1990. Initially known as Compagnie Corse Mediterranée, it changed its name and identity in November 2000.

FLEET:
2 x A319-100, 2 x A320-200, 1 x ATR 42-500, 5 x ATR 72-200, (6) x ATR 72-500, 1 x F100

FEATURES:
The waves on the tailfin suggest the Mediterranean's blue waters washing the shores of the island, while the initials CCM and the flowing line are said to convey an impression of dynamic efficiency. CCM's values are symbolized by the emblem of Corsica on the aircraft engines. The Moor's head represents the airline's wish to be open to the outside world, while remaining attached to the history of Corsica.

Cebu Pacific Air (5J/CPI)

PHILIPPINES (RP)

Second national carrier of the Philippines providing low-fare services from Manila's Ninoy Aqino International Airport and from the island of Cebu to 15 domestic destinations. Main destinations are Bacolod, Cagayan de Oro, Davao, Iloilo, Luzon Island, Tacloban, and Zamboanga. International services are also flown to Hong Kong and South Korea. Cebu Pacific Air was founded on 26 August 1988 but did not start operating until 8 March 1996, when it inaugurated high-frequency flights between Manila and Cebu.

FLEET:
(12) X A319-100, 2 X A320-200, 3 X B757-200, 15 X DC-9-30

FEATURES:
The artistic corporate eagle motif in blue and green dominates the forward fuselage, flying ahead of green *Cebu Pacific* titling. The eagle also straddles the gold and yellow tailfin, whose colors descend to the underside of the aircraft before re-emerging in a peak on the forward fuselage, with an inset Philippine flag. The airline has several additional special liveries with a Filipino theme, including "Centennial Plane" and "Tropical Island Fun."

Centralwings (CO/CLW)

POLAND (SP)

Low-fare subsidiary of Polish flag-carrier LOT operating scheduled services from its main base at Warsaw-Okeçie and from Krakow, Poznan, Katowice, and Wroclaw to more than 20 destinations in Europe. Charter flights are also undertaken to the Mediterranean basin and the Black Sea from the same points of origin, as well as to a number of other Polish cities including Wroclaw and Poznan. Centralwings was established by LOT following the collapse of privately owned Air Polonia and began operations on 1 February 2005, initially linking Warsaw and Krakow with London.

FLEET:
2 X B737-300, 3 X B737-400

FEATURES:
The red and white livery using the national colors features an elegantly stylized bird in flight, taking off from the largely red tailfin. The logo is repeated in a smaller rendition on the forward fuselage flying ahead of the airline title.

Centurion Air Cargo (WE/CWC)

UNITED STATES (N)

U.S. cargo airline offering services to Central and South America, serving more than 15 scheduled destinations from its base at Miami in Florida. The company specializes in the carriage of seafood and other perishable products, such as vegetables and fresh flowers, and livestock, particularly horses. Its history goes back to the formation of Challenge Air Cargo on 23 December 1986, but when financial difficulties forced a cessation of services, UPS bought the assets, excluding the name and air operator's certificate in June 1999. Centurion Air Cargo was then formed the following month, taking over the AOC of Challenge Air Cargo.

FLEET:
4 X DC-10-30F

FEATURES:
The airline name, as shown on the forward fuselage, is associated with the commanding Roman soldier, whose helmet sported a massive plume of feathers. This is alluded to by the yellow initial C, which has been drawn to resemble the plumed helmet. The body of the aircraft is otherwise all white, except for the yellow tailfin, which makes the aircraft highly visible.

Chalk's Ocean Airways (OP/CHK)

UNITED STATES (N)

One of the world's oldest airlines, operating scheduled seaplane services from Miami's Watson Island Seaplane Base and Fort Lauderdale International Airport to Paradise Island and Bimini in the nearby Bahamas. Founded as long ago as 1919 by "Pappy" Chalks as Chalk's Airlines, it has continuously served the Bahamas since that date. Several ownership changes in the last decade led first to a short-lived operation under the Pan Am Air Bridge name, followed by a rebranding to Chalk's Ocean Airways after restructuring and re-capitalization in July 1999.

FLEET:
5 x Grumman G-73 Turbo Mallard

FEATURES:
This latest of many previous schemes is rather undemonstrative, with the emphasis on simple titles in which *Ocean* is prominent, riding waves created by the reflection in the water on the white fuselage. This simple design is applied on the tailfin and lower forward fuselage of the mainly white aircraft. The only contrast is offered by the high-mounted engines, painted like the titling in purple.

Chanchangi Airlines (3U/NCH)

NIGERIA (5N)

Kaduna-based private domestic and regional airline operating high-frequency connections between all the main centers of population within Nigeria. Regional charter flights are also undertaken, but the airline has now also received authority from the Ministry of Transport for scheduled flights between Nigeria and Equatorial Guinea, Cameroon, Senegal, Côte d'Ivoire, and Ghana. Chanchangi Airlines was established by Alhaji Chanchangi on 5 January 1994 and started operations on 2 May 1997 between Kaduna, Lagos, Abuja, and Port Harcourt.

FLEET:
3 X B727-200A, 3 X B737-200A

FEATURES:
The white tailfin carries the airline's simple motif constructed out of the initials CAL and given wings to speed the aircraft along. The red in the symbol is matched by the aircraft belly, which is separated from the white upper fuselage by a gold cheatline. Winged *Chanchangi Airlines* titles provide color on the forward cabin roof.

Channel Express (LS/EXS)

UNITED KINGDOM (G)

All-cargo airline operating scheduled cargo flights between Bournemouth and the Channel Islands, together with contract, wet-lease, and ad hoc charter flights throughout Europe, the Middle East, and Africa on behalf of overnight express parcel companies, postal authorities, scheduled airlines, and tour operators. Founded in January 1978 as Express Air Services, it began operations with a service to the Channel Islands. The name was changed to the present title in 1982. In early 2006 Channel Express was rebranded to Jet2, which provides low-fare flights out of Leeds Bradford.

FLEET:
1 X A300B4-100F, 3 X A300B4-200F, 1 X B737-300C, 3 X B737-300QC

FEATURES:
The white aircraft is driven by a bright green tail, which wraps around the rear fuselage. *Channel Express* titles in two-tone green appear on the forward fuselage and are reversed out in white on the tailfin, with the first letter N carrying the Rose of Sarnia, symbol of the Bailiwick of Guernsey, the second-largest of the Channel Islands, lying off the northern coast of France. The word *express* is graduated to create an expression of speed.

China Airlines (CI/CAL)

TAIWAN (B)

Taiwan's flag-carrier providing international passenger services from Taipei to some 45 cities throughout Asia and to Australia, Europe, and the United States, together with the domestic trunk route between Taipei and Kaohsiung. The airline also has an extensive international cargo network. It was founded on 10 December 1959 by retired air force officers with two PBY-5 Catalina flying boats. It was designated the national airline on 29 May 1968 after the demise of Civil Air Transport.

FLEET:
12 X A300-600R, 7 X A340-300, 14 X A330-300, 14 X B737-800, 19 X B747-400, 19 X B747-400F

FEATURES:
This attractive identity was developed by Singaporean consultancy Addison Design to illustrate the airline's commitment to sincerity, caring, innovation, sense of responsibility, and pursuit of excellence. The essence of the scheme is the pink plum blossom, the national flower of Taiwan, which adorns the tailfin of the aircraft, floating on a purple haze. The otherwise all-white aircraft also features an unusual two-tone blue chinstrap.

China Cargo Airlines (CK/CKK)

CHINA (B)

China's first all-cargo airline, operating dedicated freight services based on China Eastern's route structure out of Shanghai's Honqiao and Pudong international airports. Apart from domestic flights, the network includes several destinations in the United States, and Luxembourg in Europe. The airline was established on 30 July 1998 as a joint venture between China Eastern Airlines and China Ocean Shipping Company and began operations the following October.

FLEET:
1 X A300B4-200F, (2) X B747-400F, 6 X MD-11F

FEATURES:
The scheme is very similar to that of China Eastern, with aircraft painted in white and gray, the two colors separated by red and blue cheatlines enclosing a golden pencil line. China Cargo titles are applied on the mid-fuselage roof in red Chinese characters and blue English wording. The tailfin is dominated by a red sun rising from a blue sea at dawn, through which flies a white stylized bird.

China Eastern Airlines (MU/CES)

CHINA (B)

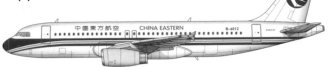

One of the largest air enterprises in China, serving a network of domestic trunk routes to some 60 cities from its main bases at Shanghai's Pudong and Hongqiao airports, and from regional centers at Hefei City, Nanchang, Nanjing, Qingdao, Wuhan, and Xi'an. The airline also operates a fast-expanding regional network, together with long-haul routes to Europe and the United States. China Eastern was established on 25 June 1988 on the basis of the CAAC Huadong Administration and became one of three major airline groups following the consolidation of China's airline industry in October 2002. It has several local subsidiaries.

FLEET:
10 x A300-600R, 10 (5) x A319-100, 54 x A320-200, 4 x A321-200, (5) x A330-200, (15) x A330-300, 5 x A340-300, 5 x A340-600, 25 x B737-300, 16 x B737-700, 5 x B737-800, 3 x B767-300ER, (15) x B787-8, 5 x CRJ200LR, 5 x ERJ 145LI, 3 x MD-82, 9 x MD-90-30

FEATURES:
Aircraft are painted in white and gray, separated by red, gold, and blue cheatlines. *China Eastern* titles are applied on the mid-fuselage, in red Chinese characters and blue English wording. The tailfin is dominated by a red sun rising at dawn from a blue sea, through which flies a white stylized bird.

China Postal Airlines (8Y/CYZ)

CHINA (B)

Joint venture between the China State Post Bureau and China Southern Airlines providing overnight, next-day mail and parcel-delivery flights in the heavily populated eastern part of China. The network of postal flights links the main base of Shanghai with Beijing, Chengdu, Guangzhou, Shenyang, and Shenzhen. The convertible fleet can be used on passenger flights during the day. The airline started flying in 1997 and began its cooperation with China Southern on 18 June 2000, before the latter acquired a 49% stake in the airline from the Post Bureau in June 2002.

FLEET:
2 x B737-300QC, 2 x B737-300F, 5 x SACY8F-100

FEATURES:
An intriguing white geometrical design transformed into a bird on the bright green tailfin takes the attention away from the rest of the scheme, which comprises a broad green band supported by a triple cheatline of blue, red, and yellow. Black *China Postal Airlines* titling on the cabin roof in English is preceded by the same in Chinese characters.

China Southern Airlines (CZ/CSN)

CHINA (B)

Largest airline group in China operating from Guangzhou and 10 regional bases to more than 20 cities in Asia, Australia, and the U.S. West Coast, and to 65 points within China, covering all major cities. Part of its domestic network is served by subsidiary and associated airlines, including Xiamen Airlines, Shantou Airlines, Guangxi Airlines, Guizhou Airlines, Zhongyuan Airlines and China Postal Airlines. China Southern was established on 1 February 1991 from the CAAC Guangzhou Regional Administration. China Northern Airlines and China Xinjiang Airlines were absorbed in January 2003.

FLEET:
17 (3) X A319-100, 15 (16) X A320-200, (10) X A321-200, 4 X A330-200, (5) X A380-800, 26 X B737-300, 2 X B737-300QC, 11 X B737-500, 8 X B737-700, 14 X B737-800, 2 X B747-400F, 25 X B757-200, 4 X B777-200, 6 X B777-200ER, (10) X B787-8, 6 X ERJ 145LI, 9 X MD-90-30

FEATURES:
China Southern uses bold reds and blues as the main color palette of its aircraft paint scheme. The striking symbol on the tailfin is a representation of the beautiful scarlet bloom of the kapok tree, here set into a bright blue, which symbolizes the sky.

China Xinhua Airlines (XW/CXH)

CHINA (B)

Beijing-based airline operating trunk routes to 30 major cities from Beijing and branches at Tianjin and Shenzhen, using an all-Boeing fleet. Charter flights also form part of its activities. The airline was established in August 1992 as a joint venture between the Beijing municipal government and financial institutions but is now a subsidiary of Hainan Airlines. Operations began on 6 June 1993.

FLEET:
6 X B737-300, 3 X B737-400, 3 X B737-800

FEATURES:
As a member of the Hainan Airlines group, China Xinhua's aircraft are painted with the same tailfin design of mid-blue sporting the stylized red and gold mythical bird. The corporate symbol behind the cabin door is followed by the airline name, first in Chinese characters and then in English. The name *Xinhua* means "New (Xin) China (hua)."

China Yunnan Airlines (3Q/CYH)

CHINA (B)

Chinese regional carrier with an extensive domestic route system linking Kunming Wu Jiabao Airport with more than 40 major cities and smaller provincial points. A few international routes serve principally the tourist markets in Laos, Malaysia, Thailand, and Singapore. The airline was founded by the Civil Aviation Administration of China (CAAC) on 28 July 1992 at Kunming, based on the CAAC Yunnan Regional Authority. It became part of the China Eastern Group in October 2002.

FLEET:
13 X B737-300, 10 X B737-700, 3 X B767-300ER, 5 X CRJ200LR

FEATURES:
A golden feather floating down the tailfin forms the central element of this smart green and gold livery. Twin gold and green cheatlines divide the upper white from the lower gray fuselage and support black *China Yunnan Airlines* titles in black, applied both in English and Chinese.

Cielos Airlines (Cielos del Peru) (A2/CIU)

PERU (OB)

Private Peruvian cargo airline operating a mix of scheduled and charter services from its base at Lima's Jorge Chavéz International. The scheduled network serves cities in South America and the United States, while charter flights are operated throughout the Americas and to Europe and Asia. The airline specializes in the carriage of perishables, livestock, and dangerous and high-value goods. Cielos del Peru was formed on 30 November 1997 and started flying after acquiring Export Air on 31 January 1998.

FLEET:
1 X DC-10-10F, 2 X DC-10-30CF, 6 X DC-10-30F

FEATURES:
The company symbol is an ornate golden Inca sun protected by the condor with its wings wrapped around it. The Spanish word *Cielos*, meaning "heaven," is written across the center engine and also along the yellow cheatline that turns down at an angle. The Peruvian flag is applied on the roof. It is said that General Jose de San Martin, upon seeing some flamingoes with white breasts and red wings, declared: "Those shall be the colors of liberty."

Cimber Air (QI/CIM)

DENMARK (OY)

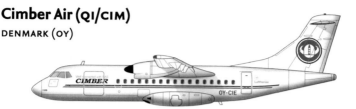

Long-established Danish regional airline operating scheduled domestic flights in cooperation with SAS Scandinavian Airlines, with extensions to mainland Europe. A separate network is flown in Germany on behalf of Lufthansa. Cimber Air was founded by the late Ingolf Nielson on 1 August 1950, after acquiring Sonderjyllands Fyveselskab. Charter flights were initially flown under that name until it was changed to Cimber Air in 1953. Feeder services out of Sonderborg began in 1963. SAS bought a 26% stake on 13 May 1998 but sold it back to the company on 25 February 2003.

FLEET:

1 X ATR 42-300, 1 X ATR 42-500, 5 X ATR 72-200, 1 X ATR 72-210, 1 X ATR 72-500, 2 X CRJ200ER, 5 X CRJ200LR

FEATURES:

A horned viking helmet on a red sun within a blue circle is the company symbol, which reflects the country's heritage, as does the predominantly red and white of the Dannebrog, one of the oldest flags in the world. *Cimber* titling is applied above the blue and red cheatlines. The words *Well connected with* SAS forward and the Lufthansa wording and symbol aft refer to the airline's association with both carriers.

Cirrus Airlines (C9/RUS)

GERMANY (D)

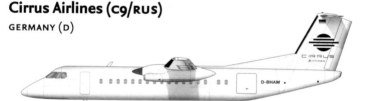

German regional airline operating scheduled passenger services within Germany and to neighboring countries, most routes being flown on behalf of Lufthansa as a Team Lufthansa member. Ad hoc charter flights are also provided from its base at Saarbrücken. Cirrus Airlines was founded as an executive charter company in February 1995, flying business people and VIPs to anywhere in the world. It obtained a licence for scheduled traffic in March 1998, and in 2000 signed a wide-ranging agreement with German flag-carrier Lufthansa.

FLEET:

1 X B737-500, 4 x Dash 8 100, 3 x Dash 8 Q300, 1 X EMB 170LR, 1 X ERJ 145MP, 2 X FD 328JET, 6 x FD 328-110

FEATURES:

The Cirrus Airlines aircraft are sparsely decorated with only the tail design drawing the eye to the white aircraft. This design simply comprises a striated sun symbol under which the airline name resides, applied in a very thin blue typeface that is not easy to read from a distance. Some aircraft carry the description "Team Lufthansa," referring to Cirrus's association with the German flag-carrier.

City Airline (CF/SDR)

SWEDEN (SE)

Regional airline linking Gothenburg, Sweden's major port and second-largest city in the southwest of the country, with destinations in Norway, Finland, Estonia, France, Switzerland, Italy, Hungary, and the United Kingdom. Charter flights and weekend holiday packages are also available. City Airline was founded in 1997 and started flying on 10 September 2001. It is owned by Investment AB Janus, which also owns two major tour operators.

FLEET:
2 X ERJ 135ER, 1 X ERJ 135LR, 1 X ERJ 145ER, 1 X ERJ 145MP, 1 X ERJ 145LR

FEATURES:
The dark blue tailfin displays the Gothenburg city coat of arms showing a golden lion rampant wielding a sword and carrying a blue shield with three golden crowns. Large dark blue *City Airline* titling along the white fuselage complete this smart businesslike livery.

CityJet (WX/BCY)

IRELAND (EI)

Irish-based regional subsidiary of Air France linking Dublin and Paris Charles de Gaulle airports with destinations throughout Europe. It also undertakes wet-lease operations and code-share flights and has a dedicated spare aircraft with crew available for the parent company at Charles de Gaulle Airport. CityJet was established on 28 September 1992 and began flying on 12 January 1994, initially between London City Airport and Dublin under a franchise agreement with Virgin Atlantic. The association with Air France began in 1996 and, after acquiring a stake in May 1999, Air France took full control in February 2000.

FLEET:
15 X BAE 146-200, 2 X BAE 146-300

FEATURES:
The predominantly white aircraft carry the basic Air France markings with additional *CityJet* titling underneath bold blue *Air France* titling in uppercase lettering on the forward fuselage. Based on the French tricolor, the aircraft's major design element is a splash of color in the form of blue and red stripes in varying widths sweeping up the tailfin.

Click Mexicana (MX)

MEXICO (XA/XB)

The establishement of Mexicana's low-fare brand was announced on 11 April 2005 and operations began in July with initial roundtrips between Mexico City and nine other destinations within the country. The network has since been expanded to include all major points in the southern part of the country. Most services radiate from Mexico City, but the airline also operates mini-hubs at Cancun, Guadalajara, and Veracruz. The airline resulted from the rebranding of regional carrier Aerocaribe, which started operations in the Yucatan peninsula on 12 July 1975.

FLEET:
8 X DC-9-30, 7 X F100

FEATURES:
The word *click* is easy to pronounce in any language and communicates speed and technology, and refers to the airline's website sales channel. A yellow keyboard button with a white aircraft taking off, therefore, is the principal emblem, applied on the dark blue tailfin. Large *click* lettering in the same blue, with a gold dot over the *i*, take up the forward fuselage, accompanied by *Grupo Mexicana* titles. The web address appears on the engines.

Coast Air (BX/CST)

NORWAY (N)

Norwegian regional airline, operating a small network of scheduled services linking its base at Haugesund Karmøy to eight scenic destinations in southern Norway, northwards as far as Trondheim, Bergen in the west, and Oslo in the east. Long-term contract and ad hoc charters typically include corporate hospitality, city weekends, and the transportation of sports teams to points in Norway and other northern European countries. Coast Air was established in 1975 and initially concentrated on air-taxi and charter flights, before introducing scheduled services in August 1986.

FLEET:
2 X ATR 42-300, 4 X BAE Jetstream 31, 2 X BAE Jetstream 32EP

FEATURES:
This imaginative arrangement on a dark blue aircraft features a large snowflake on the tailfin and a row of red-roofed Norwegian houses along the fuselage, straddling the gray underside. All of the design elements are created from a series of squares, Lego-style. *Coast Air* titling continues the line of the windows.

Comair (MN/CAW)
SOUTH AFRICA (ZS)

Major South African airline operating domestic and regional services as a British Airways franchise. Apart from the main cities within the country, Comair also serves destinations in Zimbabwe, Zambia, and Namibia. Low-fare services are offered by its Kulula.com brand. The airline was registered in 1943 as Commercial Air Services and operated its first charter flight between Germiston and Durban with Fairchild aircraft on 14 July 1946. Scheduled services were introduced in 1948 and consolidated on 1 November 1967 under the present title. The franchise agreement with British Airways was signed on 27 October 1996.

FLEET:
1 x B727-200A, 8 x B737-200A, 6 x B737-300, 2 x B737-400

FEATURES:
All Comair aircraft carry full British Airways markings with the British flag on the tailfin and the speedmarque and name on the forward fuselage. Additional *Operated by Comair Limited* titles are applied under the cockpit windows.

Condor Flugdienst (DE/CFG)
GERMANY (D)

Germany's leading holiday airline providing extensive inclusive-tour services to resort areas in the Mediterranean basin, together with long-haul flights to the Caribbean, North and Central America, East Africa, points in the Indian Ocean, and the Far East. Flights originate from all major German airports, but mainly from Frankfurt, Berlin, Cologne, Düsseldorf, Munich, Hamburg, and Stuttgart. Now part of Thomas Cook, the airline was founded on 21 December 1955 as Deutsche Flugdienst and began operations on 28 March 1956. The Condor name was adopted on 25 October 1961.

FLEET:
1 x B757-200, 13 x B757-300, 9 x B767-300ER

FEATURES:
Condor aircraft basically carry the Thomas Cook identity developed by global design agency FutureBrand, with the addition of large *Condor* titles in blue on the forward fuselage. The tailfin in the traditional Condor yellow features a globe in the group colors of blue and yellow with the Thomas Cook signature. It symbolizes its "world" as an efficient pan-European and fully integrated leisure group.

Continental Airlines (CO/COA)

UNITED STATES (N)

Major U.S. carrier with an extensive network of scheduled passenger flights serving 125 U.S. cities and 90 international destinations throughout the Americas, Europe, and the Far East from hubs at Houston, Newark, Cleveland, and Guam. The network is further enlarged at home through Continental Express and Continental Connection, and internationally through Continental Micronesia and membership of SkyTeam. Continental Airlines was formed on 15 July 1934 as Varney Speed Lines, which inaugurated a service from El Paso to Denver using a Lockheed Vega. In December that year, the name was changed to Varney Air Transport, and on 1 July 1937 the company became Continental Airlines. Texas Air, parent of Texas International Airlines, formerly Aviation Enterprises and Trans-Texas Airways, acquired a controlling interest, merging the two concerns on 31 October 1982 under the Continental banner. Following the purchase of low-fare carrier People Express (formed 7 April 1980) and the assets of Frontier Airlines in 1986, all services of these two airlines, as well as those of the already owned New York Air, which started operations on 19 December 1980, were fully integrated with effect from January 1987. Frontier Airlines was founded on 1 June 1950 after Monarch Airlines merged with Arizona Airways.

FLEET:

51 x B737-300, 63 x B737-500, 36 (15) x B737-700, 86 (26) x B737-800, 12 (3) x B737-900, 41 x B757-200, 9 x B757-300, 10 x B767-200ER, 16 x B767-400ER, 18 (2) x B777-200ER, (5) x B787-8

FEATURES:

Continental's livery is based on blue, white, and gold, with the blue tailfin the dominant feature, incorporating a stylized three-dimensional globe in white latitudes and gold longitudes. A thin gold pinstripe divides the upper white fuselage from the gray belly. Simple blue *Continental* titles are carried on the forward cabin roof. The corporate identity, unveiled on 12 Feburary 1991, was said to symbolize the progress of the airline after periods in administration and its goals for the future.

Continental Connection (CO)

UNITED STATES (N)

Regional air services network provided by four carriers connecting into Continental Airlines' hubs. Cape Air, founded in 1989, serves Cape Cod, Florida, the Caribbean out of San Juan, and Rota, Saipan, and Guam in Micronesia. Gulfstream International Airlines, founded in October 1988, covers Florida and the Bahamas, while Colgan Air services radiate from Houston's George Bush Intercontinental. Commutair links the Northeast and upper Midwest from hubs at Cleveland and Albany. Colgan Air started operations on 1 December 1991, initially as National Capital Airways. Commutair started flying on 1 August 1989.

FLEET:
3 x ATR 42-300, 2 x Beech 1900C-1, 58 x Beech 1900D, 3 x EMB 120ER Brasilia, 31 x Saab 340B

FEATURES:
The Continental Connection livery is identical to that of Continental Airlines, with additional silver gray *Connection* wording. Based on blue, white, and gold, the blue tailfin is the dominant feature, incorporating a stylized three-dimensional globe in white latitudes and gold longitudes.

Continental Express (CO/BTA)

UNITED STATES (N)

Regional carrier ExpressJet Airlines, operating a large network of services as Continental Express, serving some 140 destinations in the United States, Canada, Mexico, and the Caribbean from Continental Airlines' hubs at Houston, New York/Newark, and Cleveland. Founded in 1956 as Vercoa Air Service, it operated as Britt Airways from late 1968. The airline underwent several ownership changes before starting operations as Continental Express in January 1989 and later becoming a subsidiary of Continental Airlines. It is owned by ExpressJet Holdings.

FLEET:
11 x ERJ 135ER, 19 x ERJ 135LR, 23 x ERJ 145ER, 117 x ERJ 145LR, 91 (13) x ERJ 145XR

FEATURES:
The Continental Express livery is identical to that of the main airline, with additional silver-gray *Express* wording. Based on blue, white, and gold, the blue tailfin is the dominant feature, incorporating a stylized three-dimensional globe in white latitudes and gold longitudes. A thin gold pinstripe divides the upper white fuselage from the gray belly.

Continental Micronesia (cs/cmi) (v6)
MICRONESIA (N)

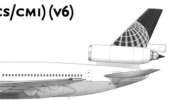

Subsidiary of Continental Airlines operating scheduled passenger services from Guam to other island destinations in the Micronesian basin of the Pacific, and to Australia, Indonesia, the Philippines, Hong Kong, Taipei, and Japan. Guam is an Unincorporated Territory of the United States. The airline was formed in 1966 as Air Micronesia by the United Micronesian Development Association (UMDA), Continental Airlines, and Aloha Airlines to provide interisland services and began operations on 16 May 1968. The present name was adopted when Continental acquired full ownership.

FLEET:
9 x B737-800

FEATURES:
As aircraft are wet-leased from the parent company, the livery is identical, except for additional *Micronesia* wording, although this is not always applied. The livery is based on blue, white, and gold, with the blue tailfin the dominant feature, incorporating a stylized three-dimensional globe in white latitudes and gold longitudes. A thin gold pinstripe divides the upper white fuselage from the gray belly.

Conviasa
VENEZUELA (YV)

Flag-carrier of the Bolivarian Republic of Venezuela, operating scheduled passenger and cargo services from the capital Caracas to 10 domestic destinations and to neighboring Grenada and Trinidad and Tobago in the southern Caribbean and to Bogotá in Colombia. Long-haul routes to Europe are under consideration. Conviasa (Consorcio Venezolano de Industrias Aeronáuticas y Servicios Aéreos) was established on 7 July 2004 by the national goverment and the regional govern-ment of Nueva Esparta and began operations on 11 December that same year.

FLEET:
1 x B737-300, 1 x Dash 7-100

FEATURES:
The aircraft's bright orange tailfin incorporates a golden sun in which resides a specially designed letter v for Venezuela, and a dynamic representation of the country's yellow, blue, and red flag. Large *Conviasa* titles are applied on the forward fuselage, the v in the name again being highlighted, with the web address at the rear.

Copa Airlines (CM/CMP)
PANAMA (HP)

Leading Panamanian airline operating a comprehensive passenger and cargo network from Panama City's Tocumen International Airport, the "Hub of the Americas," to more than 30 destinations in 20 countries within Central America and the Caribbean, and extending to North and South America. Connecting services are available to other parts of the world through its strong alliance with Continental Airlines. The airline was established on 21 June 1944 as Compania Panamena de Aviacion (COPA), with the assistance of Pan American, and began services over local routes on 15 August 1947.

FLEET:
18 (7) x B737-700, 4 x B737-800, (12) EMB 190AR

FEATURES:
The Copa livery of white, blue, and gold mimics that of its alliance partner Continental Airlines with the suggestion of a globe in white latitudes on the blue tailfin. Gold speed lines streak away from the globe giving an impression of movement. Simple blue *Copa Airlines* titles cover the cabin roof. A golden pencil line divides the white from the gray lower fuselage.

Corsair (SS/CRL)
FRANCE (F)

French charter airline operating regular flights from its main base at Paris Orly to more than 60 destinations in Europe, Africa, the Caribbean, North America, and the South Pacific. The airline was founded by the Corsican Rossi family in 1981, flying for small tour operators and other organizations under the name of Corse-Air International, with a fleet of four Sud-Aviation Caravelles from Orly and Ajaccio, starting on 1 July 1981. It was purchased by Nouvelles Frontières in 1990 and rebranded under the present title. In September 2002, Nouvelles Frontières sold Corsair to the TUI Group.

FLEET:
2 x A330-200, 2 x B737-400, 2 x B747-200B, 3 x B747-300, 3 x B747-400

FEATURES:
Following its acquisition by the TUI Group, the colors of the South Sea were replaced by the parent's blue, and smiley red face on the tailfin. Large *corsairfly.com* titles in red and white take up all of the front half of the aircraft. The tailfin design is repeated on the winglets on appropriate aircraft.

Cosmic Air (F5/COZ)

NEPAL (9N)

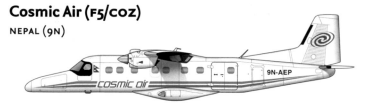

Regional airline operating a comprehensive domestic network from the capital Kathmandu over trunk routes to Biratnagar, Bhairahawa, and Nepalgunj, and to many remote areas in this Himalayan kingdom, including sightseeing flights over Mount Everest. Cross-border services are operated to several destinations in India, and to Dhaka in Bangladesh, with extensions planned to Myanmar, Thailand, and Bhutan. Cosmic Air, a subsidiary of the SOI Group, a leading business house in Nepal, was established in 1997 and started operations on 1 January 1998, initially using two Mil Mi-17 helicopters on tourist flights.

FLEET:
1 x Dornier 228-100, 1 x Dornier 228-200, 4 x F100, 1 x Saab 340A

FEATURES:
The company's symbol of red swirls, suggesting circular movement, is the only decoration on the white tailfin, with red *Cosmic Air* titles on the cabin roof in English on the port side and Nepali script on the starboard side. Turboprop aircraft in the fleet have additional twin cheatlines.

CR Airways (N8/CRK)

HONG KONG (B-H)

Regional jet airline operating an expanding service between Hong Kong, mainland China, the island of Hainan, and several destinations in Southeast Asia, including Cambodia and the Philippines. Business jet charters are also offered by the Rainbowjet associate company. CR Airways was established in 2001 by Robert Yip and China Rich Holdings to provide jet services from the Hong Hong Special Administrative Region of China. Operations started on 5 July 2003.

FLEET:
2 X CRJ200LR, 1 X CRJ700

FEATURES:
This smart scheme focuses on magenta and white, with the magenta tailfin displaying three white flower petals and the white fuselage a beautifully curved splash of magenta. The winglets are also painted in magenta. *CR Airways* titling in black is preceded by the name in Chinese characters in magenta.

Croatia Airlines (OU/CTN)

CROATIA (9A)

Croatian flag-carrier operating international scheduled services from the capital Zagreb to points in Europe. Domestic flights also link Zagreb with all major inland and coastal towns, and there are additional direct summer schedules and charters from northern Europe to the country's holiday resorts on the Adriatic. Croatia Airlines was formed on 7 August 1989 as Zagreb Airlines (Zagal) and adopted the present title on 23 July 1990 following democratic elections in the former Yugoslav republic. Operations started on 5 May 1991 between Zagreb and Split with a leased MD-82.

FLEET:
5 X A319-100, 4 X A320-200, 3 X ATR 42-300

FEATURES:
Croatia Airlines' livery is built around the red, white, and blue colors of the national flag and is notable for the heraldic checkerboard pattern on the tailfin. Developed by in-house designer Ivana Ivankovic, the red and white squares have been separated to create a dynamic expression of a young and modern company. The *Croatia* titling in blue is sped along by a small red and white checkered arrow.

CSA Czech Airlines (OK/CSA)

CZECH REPUBLIC (OK)

Flag-carrier of the Czech Republic providing services to 60 international destinations, its network including intra-European flights and long-haul services to the Middle East, Asia, and North America. Domestic services also link Prague Ruzyne to other major cities. The airline was founded on 29 July 1923 as CSA (Ceskoslovenské Státni Aerolinie) and operated its first flight on 29 October from Prague to Bratislava. The name changed to its present title on 26 March 1995 to take account of the break-up of the Czechoslovak Federation, although it retained the original initials. Member of the SkyTeam Alliance.

FLEET:
4 X A310-300, (6) X A319-100, 2 (6) X A32go-200, 2 X A321-200, 2 X ATR 42-400, 5 X ATR 42-500, 4 X ATR 72-200, 15 X B737-400, 15 X B737-500

FEATURES:
The fresh white overall paint scheme is complemented by the red and blue colors, which make up the national flag. Red and blue cheatlines underscore large red CSA initials (standing for the Czech title of Ceské Aerolinie) and *Czech Airlines* lettering. The same color combination is maintained on the tailfin in the form of three pennants, adding a semblance of speed.

Cubana de Aviación (CU/CUB)
CUBA (CU)

Cuban flag-carrier operating scheduled international services to some 40 destinations in the Caribbean and South America, and across the Atlantic to Europe. A domestic network serves all major points on the island. Cubana was founded by Curtiss Aviation in 1929 as Compania Nacional Cubana de Aviación Curtiss. It began operations on 30 October 1930 with a single Ford Tri-Motor from Havana to the coastal town of Santiago de Cuba. Curtiss was dropped from the name in 1932 when the airline was taken over by Pan Am. It was acquired by the new socialist government of Fidel Castro in 1959.

FLEET:
3 x A320-200, 8 x AN-24RV, 1 x B747-400, 5 x IL-62M, 2 x IL-96-300, 3 x Yak-42D

FEATURES:
The Cubana scheme, which has barely changed since its introduction in 1970, has a surprisingly clean and modern look. Taking up the entire tailfin is a clever representation of the national flag, where the blue and white stripes stand for the original provinces of Cuba and the purity of the revolution, with the red symbolizing liberty and blood shed in defense of freedom.

Cygnus Air (RGN)
SPAIN (EC)

Spanish all-cargo airline offering scheduled flights from its base at Madrid Barajas Airport to various destinations in Europe. Cygnus Air began life as a passenger airline, having been established in 1994 by Regional Airlines of France and Spanish executive operator Gestair as Regional Lineas Aéreas. Passenger flights were operated from Madrid until January 1998, after which the airline lay dormant until reemerging in November that same year as an all-cargo airline under the name of Cygnus Air, operating two McDonnell Douglas DC-8-62F freighters. It is now a full member of Grupo Gestair.

FLEET:
2 x DC-8-62F, 1 x DC-8-73CF

FEATURES:
The attractive two-tone blue and white tailfin and rear fuselage design is highlighted by white swans soaring into the skies. Blue Cygnus Air titles are applied behind the cargo door, with the letter C serving both as the first letter in the airline name and also in the word Corporation above. The aircraft engines are painted in blue and white.

Cyprus Airways (CY/CYP)

CYPRUS (5B)

Flag-carrier operating scheduled international passenger services from Larnaca to more than 30 destinations within Europe, and to the Middle East and Persian Gulf. Some destinations are also served from Paphos. Charter flights are operated through subsidiary Eurocypria Airlines. Cyprus Airways was established on 24 September 1947 as a joint venture between the Cyprus government, British European Airways, and local interests. Operations began on 6 October between Nicosia and Athens. The airline lost its Nicosia base and several aircraft when Turkey invaded Cyprus in July 1974 but restarted operations from Larnaca on 8 February 1975.

FLEET:
2 X A319-100, 7 X A320-200, 2 X A330-200

FEATURES:
The livery provides a striking contrast between the royal blue of the tailfin and engines and the snow white fuselage which is interrupted only by blue *Cyprus Airways* titles, highlighted by the large rendition of the country name. The tailfin and engines display the airline's winged mouflon symbol in ocher. The mouflon is a graceful, hardy, and powerful native mountain goat, once widespread throughout the island, but now found only in the Troodos Mountains.

Daallo Airlines (D3/DAO)

DJIBOUTI (J2)

Private African airline connecting the Horn of Africa with some 15 regional destinations in Somalia, Eritrea, Ethiopia, Kenya, Saudi Arabia, and the United Arab Emirates. The airline also links Djibouti with France and the United Kingdom. Daallo Airlines was established in 1991 and began operations on 20 March that same year, initially using only ex-Soviet equipment.

FLEET:
1 X AN-24, 1 X AN-24RV, 1 X Let L-410 UVP-E

FEATURES:
The white upper fuselage is contrasted by the green tailfin, belly, engines, and wings of the aircraft, together with a blue cheatline that starts thin at the front and broadens out towards the rear. The airline logo is applied on the tailfin. The blue and green come from the Djibouti flag, where the blue is symbolic of the Issa and the green of the Afar people.

Dalavia Far East Airways (H8/KHB)

RUSSIAN FEDERATION (RA)

Largest airline in Russia's far east operating scheduled passenger and cargo services from Khabarovsk to major cities throughout Russia and to China, Japan, South Korea, Uzbekistan, and Azerbaijan. International destinations include Guangzhou, Harbin, Seoul, Niigata, Osaka, Baku, and Tashkent. The state-owned company also provides a variety of other aviation-related services and owns and manages Khabarovsk Novy Airport. It was founded as Khabarovsk Aviation Enterprise in 1953 and changed its name to Dalavia in January 1999.

FLEET:
7 X AN-24RV, 9 X AN-24V,
5 X AN-26, 1 X AN-26B, 7 X IL-62M,
11 X TU-154B-2, 5 X TU-154M,
3 (5) X TU-214

FEATURES:
There are variations among the aircraft fleet, although all feature a blue windowline and lower cheatline, with two flying wings outlined against the blue sky on the tailfin, the symbol being rendered in several different versions. *Dalavia* titles are carried on the cabin roof in English on the starboard with additional small *Dalavia Far East Airways – Khabarovsk* titles in English and in Cyrillic.

Danish Air Transport (DAT) (DX/DTR)

DENMARK (OY)

Danish aviation concern offering a diverse portfolio of activities from scheduled passenger flights to charters and specialized transport such as air ambulance. Scheduled passenger services link points in Norway, France, and the UK. Ad hoc, contract, and short-notice cargo transport is also available, with flights carried out for FedEx, DHL, PostDenmark, and others, carrying mail, livestock, and general freight. DAT was founded by Jesper and Kirsten Rungholm in 1989 and began flying all types of cargo and mail with a Shorts SC-7 Skyvan. Scheduled passenger services were added on 18 November 1996.

FLEET:
4 X ATR 42-300, 1 X ATR 42-320,
2 X ATR 72-200, 1 X Beech
1900C-1, 1 X Beech 1900D

FEATURES:
The airline's logo and highly visible multicolored aircraft painted in blue, yellow, red, and green, illustrate the diversity of its product range. DAT also wants to project the fact that it is an unconventional and flexible airline. A central symbol is an aircraft taking off, featured on the tailfin and under the cockpit windows.

Darwin Airline (DWT)

SWITZERLAND (HB)

Swiss regional airline operating scheduled services from its base at Lugano Agno in the canton of Ticino to other Swiss cities, with extensions to London, mainland Italy, and the island of Sardinia. International points on the network are London, Rome, and Olbia. Darwin Airline was founded on 12 August 2003 and started operations on 28 July 2004 with a service to Geneva.

FLEET:
2 x Saab 2000

FEATURES:
The creator of this corporate identity has taken a different path to most others, reversing the general trend towards a dark underside and white upper fuselage. A gray roof line opens out to fill the dorsal fin and tail, leaving the major part of the fuselage below in white. The airline's symbol of swirls of red and blue, drawn to suggest birds in flight, are displayed on the tailfin and forward in front of the name. The name underlines the airline's willingness to evolve.

DAS Air Cargo (WD/DSR)

UGANDA (5X)

All-cargo airline specializing in providing regular connections between Europe and Africa, where it serves 40 destinations, but its scheduled network also extends to the Middle East and the Indian sub-continent. The airline operates out of hubs at Amsterdam, London Gatwick, Dubai, and Entebbe. DAS Air Cargo was established in 1983 by Captain Joe Roy and began operations in June that year, flying between Europe and West African cities with a single Boeing 707-320C.

FLEET:
1 X AN-12, 7 X DC-10-30F

FEATURES:
The colors used by DAS Air Cargo are essentially those of the Ugandan flag, with the black changed to a chocolate brown, particularly recognizable in the triple straight-through cheatlines. A leaping lion is outlined against a winged sun on the tailfin and underslung engines, while the airline's red DAS initials stand out on the center engine. The winged ANA initials ahead of the full name refer to the airline's owners.

Dauair (D5/DAU)

GERMANY (D)

German regional airline headquartered at Lübeck in northern Germany, with an operational base at Dortmund in the Ruhr area. Scheduled passenger services are targeted primarily at the business traveler, offering fair prices from Berlin and Dortmund to other destinations within the country and to neighboring Poland and Switzerland. Dauair was established in March 2005 by Hans-Jörg Dau, from whom the airline takes its name. Inaugural flights took off on 25 April that same year, providing a link between Berlin and Poznan, and Dortmund and Poznan.

FLEET:
2 x Saab 340B

FEATURES:
A color scheme that means business, as displayed by the smart red and sober gray *Dauair* titles on the clean white fuselage and two gray flying wing symbols assembled to form a *D*. On the lower forward fuselage, the *Dauair* titles have an additional slogan in German, translating as "We give you wings." Aircraft are given names of the destinations served and these can be found under the cockpit window.

dba (Deutsche BA) (DI/BAG)

GERMANY (D)

Second-largest scheduled airline in Germany, concentrating its flying activities on intra-German routes, where it provides low-fare connections between all major cities. Additionally, dba flies to Scandinavia and Russia, and also operates leisure routes to the Mediterranean. The airline's history goes back to the founding of Delta Air in Friedrichshafen in April 1978. In March 1992, British Airways acquired a major stake, increased to full ownership in April 1997, and renamed the airline Deutsche BA. Another change of ownership on 1 June 2003 resulted in the present trading name.

FLEET:
13 x Boeing 737-300,
1 x B737-500, (40) x B737-700/800

FEATURES:
Lime green is a rare choice for airlines, but in dba's case, where large blue initials are spread across the base of the tailfin, it makes for a new and refreshing image. The lime green engines with the blue web address, repeated in a larger typeface on the forward upper fuselage, create a harmonious balance to the design.

Delta Air Lines (DL/DAL)

UNITED STATES (N)

Major U.S. airline operating a vast domestic passenger network from six main hubs at Atlanta, Cincinnati, Dallas Fort Worth, Los Angeles, New York, Orlando, and Salt Lake City, together with international services throughout the Americas and to Europe and the Far East. Its international reach is extended through the SkyTeam Alliance, in which it was a founding member. An extensive domestic feeder network is also flown by regional airlines under the Delta Connection banner, with low-fare services provided by Song. Founded in 1924 as Huff Daland Dusters, using a fleet of 18 "Duster" crop-spraying aircraft, it moved its operations to Peru during the winter months and later also opened a mail service between Peru and Ecuador. It became Delta Air Service in 1927, taking its name from the Mississippi Delta. It operated its first passenger service on 17 June 1929 from Dallas to Jackson. The name was changed to Delta Air Corp in 1930, and again in 1945 to Delta Air Lines. The airline's subsequent growth was marked by three major acquisitions and mergers. The first was Chicago & Southern Air Lines, formed in 1933 as Pacific Seaboard Airlines, which was absorbed on 1 May 1953. This was followed by Northeast Airlines in 1972 and by another pioneer dating back to 13 July 1925, Western Airlines, formerly Western Air Express, on 1 April 1987.

FLEET:
40 X 737-200A, 22 X 737-300, 71 (50) X 737-800, 85 X 757-200, 12 X 767-200, 28 X 767-300, 59 X 767-300ER, 8 (5) X B777-200ER, 120 X MD-88, 16 X MD-90-30

FEATURES:
The Landor-developed "flowing fabric" branding features a colorful, vibrant tail in dark blue and red, contrasted against the white fuselage. The simple *Delta* wording, without the *Air Lines*, is said to reflect an assumptive pride in its heritage and leadership role. The triangular heritage mark, long referred to as the "widget," has been softened, symbolizing a more human approach.

Delta Connection (DL)

UNITED STATES (N)

Extensive feeder network throughout the United States, Canada, and Mexico, provided by five independent regional airlines under contract to Delta Air Lines, plus wholly owned subsidiary Comair. From its Cincinnati and Orlando hubs, Comair serves 95 cities from Canada to the Bahamas, and from the Great Plains to the Atlantic. SkyWest covers 66 cities in 14 western states from Salt Lake City and Dallas Fort Worth, while its subsidiary Atlantic Southeast Airlines (ASA) has a network from Atlanta and Dallas Fort Worth that takes in 100 cities across the USA, Canada, Mexico, and the Bahamas. Shuttle America also flies Delta Connection services out of Salt Lake City. Chautauqua Airlines serves the Florida market, as does Mesa Air Group member Freedom Airlines. Comair was founded in 1976 as Wings Airways and began flying in April 1977. It became a Delta Connection carrier on 1 September 1984. ASA was established in March 1979 and started commuter services on 27 June that same year. It became a wholly owned subsidiary of Delta in 1999 but was sold to SkyWest Airlines in 2005. Chautauqua was established on 3 May 1973 and started scheduled Allegheny Commuter services on 1 August 1974. Shuttle America was founded in 1995 and began flying on 12 November 1998.

FLEET:
12 X ATR 72-210, 79 X CRJ100ER, 42 X CRJ100LR, 121 X CRJ200ER, 62 X CRJ700ER, 30 X FD 328-100

FEATURES:
All Delta Connection carriers have adopted the Delta "flowing fabric" brand to offer a seamless transfer to the mainline operation, both visually and in terms of service standards, with additional *Connection* titling in gray. Some aircraft also carry the individual airline name on the lower forward fuselage or tailfin.

Denim Airways (3D/DNM)

NETHERLANDS (PH)

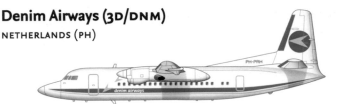

Airline arm of multi-discipline Dutch group that now focuses entirely on regional airline ACMI (aircraft, crew, maintenance, and insurance) wet-lease services for other airlines. Denim Air is also developing its ACMI Plus service, which offers start-up airlines full operational support. The company's history dates back to 1996. Charter operations began on 26 April that year. It was owned for a time by Spanish regional Air Nostrum but was bought out by its management in October 2002. For a time the airline operated scheduled regional services in Germany and Switzerland.

FLEET:
1 X ATR 42-300, 8 X F50

FEATURES:
Blue and gold are a favorite choice, adding a touch of class to the design. The large golden arrow in a blue disc on the tailfin is the dominant element, while the *Denim Airways* titles set in white into the blue cheatline are by contrast exceptionally small. The golden arrows tumbling towards the lower golden cheatline add a modicum of extra interest to the visual display.

DHL Air (DHK)

UNITED KINGDOM (G)

Operating arm of DHL Aviation (UK), based at Nottingham East Midlands Airport, providing air express and logistics uplift for DHL customers across more than 100 countries in its Europe and Africa regions. DHL Air was established in March 2001 and began operations in December that year after receiving its air operator's certificate from the UK authorities.

FLEET:
22 X B757-200(SF)

FEATURES:
The red DHL initials are among the most recognized of company signatures right across the world. Adding them to an almost totally yellow aircraft, with the exception of the red underbelly, ensures that the airline will be noticed wherever one of its aircraft touches down. Set into a red triple speed line, the large initials proclaim its guarantee for a fast delivery service.

Domodedovo Airlines (E3/DMO)

RUSSIAN FEDERATION (RA)

Moscow-based Russian airline operating an extensive network of scheduled services from Moscow's Domodedovo International Airport to destinations throughout Russia and to Uzbekistan and Thailand. Charter flights are also operated to Spain, the Canary Islands, Indonesia, Seychelles, Thailand, India, and Malaysia. The airline's history goes back to 1960 when it was part of the airport. The present carrier was created in January 1998, following the restructuring of the airport and separation of airline activities.

FLEET:
11 X IL-62M, 2 X IL-96-300,
2 X TU-154M, 2 X Yak-42D

FEATURES:
The white, blue, and red winged DMO logo on the tailfin and lower forward fuselage is derived from the airline's ICAO designator. It forms the key element of the livery, which also includes a blue straight-through windowline above a red cheatline, and *Domodedovo Airlines* titles in English on one side of the aircraft and in Cyrillic lettering on the other, accompanied by the Russian flag in both locations.

Donbassaero (7D/UDC)

UKRAINE (UR)

Prominent Ukrainian airline operating scheduled and charter passenger flights from Kiev to destinations in Russia, the Commonwealth of Independent States, the Baltic countries, the United Arab Emirates, Greece, Turkey, Germany, and Austria. Charter-only flights are undertaken to other countries. The airline also serves the main domestic centers. Donbassaero's history goes back to 1933.

FLEET:
1 X A320-200, 2 X AN-24RV,
5 X AN-24V, 6 X Yak-42,
4 x Yak-42D

FEATURES:
The major design element uses the blue, yellow, and white of the national flag to present a splash of color, with lines of varying widths sweeping up from the underside of the rear fuselage to the top of the tailfin. Bold blue *Donbassaero* titles are angled the same way, maintaining the streamlining impression.

Dragonair (Hong Kong Dragon Airlines) (KA/HDA)

HONG KONG (B-H)

Second-largest Hong Kong airline serving more than 30 destinations, with an emphasis on linking Hong Kong with mainland cities in China. Also served are regional destinations in Japan and Taiwan, and in Southeast Asia, taking in cities in Thailand, Cambodia, and Malaysia. A growing cargo business serves markets in Europe, the Middle East, China, and Japan. Dragonair (Hong Kong Dragon Airlines) was founded in May 1985 and began operations the following July with a flight to Kota Kinabalu. The airline was granted a licence to serve China in 1986.

FLEET:

1 X A300B4-200F, 10 X A320-200, 6 X A321-200, 11 (4) X A330-300, 1 X B747-200F, 3 X B747-300SF, 1 X B747-400F

FEATURES:

As its name implies, the central motif is a beautifully drawn Chinese dragon that climbs up the white tailfin and, on a smaller scale, the engines. The name is applied to the forward fuselage in red Chinese characters, and below in black English lettering. All cabin doors and emergency exits are highlighted in red, as are the winglets on the airbuses. Large *Dragonair Cargo* titles replace the normal design on freight aircraft.

Druk Air (Royal Bhutan Airlines) (KB/DRK)

BHUTAN (A5)

National airline of the Himalayan Kingdom of Bhutan, known locally as Druk Yul or "Land of the Thundering Dragon." A small network of scheduled services is operated from the capital Thimphu to points in India, Nepal, Myanmar, and Thailand. Druk Air was established by royal decree on 5 April 1981 and began operations on 11 February 1983 with a flight to Calcutta, using a Dornier 228-200. Until then, the only way to the capital of this isolated kingdom was a 16-hour overnight journey along precipitous mountain roads from Bagdoara in the tea-growing center of north Bengal.

FLEET:

2 X A319-100, 2 X BAE 146-200

FEATURES:

The tailfin of the aircraft represents the national flag, which traces its origin back to Bhutan's former links with China. The fin is divided diagonally, the upper half of saffron yellow denoting the royal authority, with the lower reddish-orange alluding to the Buddhist faith. The dragon, a benevolent figure in the East, is associated with power and generosity. Popular tradition ascribes the thunder of the mountain valleys to the voice of the dragon.

Eastern Airways (T3/EZE)

UNITED KINGDOM (G)

Expanding regional airline operating a growing network of scheduled services, which spread right across the UK from Wick in Scotland's far north to Southampton on the south coast. Strong hub operations are maintained at Humberside, Aberdeen, and Newcastle. In addition to scheduled services, the airline has a thriving charter business, covering ad hoc executive flights, crew movements for major carriers, and occasional freight charters. Eastern Airways started flying in December 1997 with daily services between Humberside and Aberdeen. It purchased Air Kilroe in February 1999.

FLEET:
1 X BAE Jetstream 31, 4 X BAE Jetstream 32, 2 X BAE Jetstream 32EP, 15 BAE Jetstream 41, 2 X ERJ 145EP, 4 X Saab 2000

FEATURES:
The emphasis on this patriotic red, white, and blue design concept is on the Eastern Airways name, which, together with the stylized crowned bird, takes up a large part of the white fuselage. The red and blue arrangement at the rear underlines the shape of the tailfin.

easyJet (U2/EZY)

UNITED KINGDOM (G)

Europe's biggest low-fare, no-frills airline operating more than 130 routes to 40 key European cities from hubs at London Gatwick, Luton, Nottingham East Midlands, Liverpool, Berlin Schönefeld, Amsterdam, and Paris Orly, carrying in excess of 20 million passengers a year. Services are also operated out of Geneva by associate easyJet Switzerland. EasyJet was formed on 18 October 1995 by Greek shipping magnate Stelios Haji-Ioannou and began operations on 10 November that year. On 16 May 2003, it acquired London Stansted-based low-fare carrier Go, which has been fully integrated.

FLEET:
47 (65) X A319-100, 22 B737-300, 32 X B737-700

FEATURES:
The bright orange rendering of the tailfin and engine cowlings with the airline's name reversed out in white are unmistakable, as is the prominent orange lettering that covers virtually the whole length of the otherwise largely white fuselage. This either represents the telephone number or web address through which flight bookings can be made, or a variety of topical slogans. The name infers a relaxed attitude and a desire to make flying a pleasurable experience.

EAT-European Air Transport (QY/BCS)

BELGIUM (OO)

Subsidiary of DHL Worldwide Express operating express parcel services throughout Europe and to destinations in the Middle East and Africa on behalf of its parent company. It also offers ad hoc cargo flights including the transportation of livestock. EAT was established on 9 December 1971 by four pilots to operate a flying school, but activities were soon expanded to include air-taxi work, air-ambulance flights, general passenger and cargo charters, and, for a time from April 1976, scheduled passenger services out of Brussels on behalf of Sabena. It was bought by DHL in 1986 to transport urgent shipments across Europe.

FLEET:
13 X A300B4-200F, 1 X B727-100F, 1 X B757-200PF, 12 X B757-200SF

FEATURES:
All EAT aircraft are painted in the full yellow and red colors of DHL. The red DHL mark is among the most recognized of company signatures right across the world and is prominently displayed within triple red cheatlines on the almost totally yellow aircraft, ensuring that the airline will be noticed wherever one of its aircraft touches down. The very base of the aircraft is painted in red.

Edelweiss Air (8R/EDW)

SWITZERLAND (HB)

Charter arm of the Swiss-owned Kuoni Travel Group, operating holiday flights to the popular resorts in the Mediterranean, Red Sea, Canary Islands, Maldives, Kenya, the Caribbean, and the United States. Most of its flying activities are undertaken for its parent company, although other tour operators are also serviced. The airline was founded on 19 October 1995 by Kuoni Reisen and Niklaus Grob and operated its first flight with an MD-83 from Manchester to Zurich. The first commercial flight followed on 10 February 1996 with a round-trip between Zurich and Paphos and Larnaca in Cyprus.

FLEET:
3 X A320-200, 1 X A330-300

FEATURES:
The airline's livery, dominated by a large representation of the edelweiss, the Swiss national flower, on the red tailfin and forward fuselage, suggest the reliability, punctuality, and friendliness associated with the Swiss psyche. The corporate philosophy of Edelweiss Air is a determination to be as unique and unmistakable as the edelweiss, growing high in the Alpine meadows, as it reaches proudly for the stars.

EgyptAir (MS/MSR)
EGYPT (SU)

Egyptian flag-carrier operating scheduled services from Cairo to more than 50 destinations throughout the Middle East and to the Far East, Africa, the United States, and Europe. Domestic flights serve 11 points, including all the major tourist attractions. Charter and tourist flights are also undertaken by wholly owned subsidiary Air Sinai. EgyptAir was founded on 1 June 1932 as Misrair and operated its first service the following month. During a short-lived union between Egypt and Syria, it operated as United Arab Airlines. The present name was adopted on 10 October 1974.

FLEET:
2 X A300B4-200, 5 X A300-600R, 12 X A320-200, 2 X A321-200, 7 X A330-200, 3 X A340-200, 2 X B707-320C, 4 X B737-500, (6) X B737-800, 5 X B777-200ER

FEATURES:
Key element of the EgyptAir identity is the ancient symbol of Horus, the falcon-headed god of the sun and the moon of Egyptian mythology, depicted on the royal blue tailfin in red and gold, and repeated on the similarly painted engine cowlings. *Egyptair* titles in blue are followed by Arabic script painted in red.

Eirjet (EIR)
IRELAND (EI)

Irish charter airline serving the holiday resorts around the Mediterranean basin from bases at Dublin and Shannon. The airline was formed in 2004 and started operations on 23 December 2004 with an inaugural flight to Agadir in Morocco.

FLEET:
3 X A320-200

FEATURES:
The emerald green and name of the carrier identifies this jet airline as coming from Eire, which is the Gaelic name for Ireland. This uncomplicated arrangement, where the green tailfin and engine contrast beautifully with the pristine white of the rest of the aircraft, vividly brings to mind spring freshness and the green vales of this emerald isle.

EL AL Israel Airlines (LY/ELY)

ISRAEL (4X)

National airline providing scheduled passenger and cargo services from Tel Aviv's Ben Gurion International Airport. The network is dominated by European connections and extends to the United States, Canada, Africa, and the Far East. Subsidiary Sun D'Or International operates regular, ad hoc, and seasonal charter flights with aircraft leased from the parent company as and when required. EL AL was formed on 15 November 1948 as the flag-carrier of the newly established state of Israel. Operations began in August 1949 with a Douglas DC-4 service from Tel Aviv to Rome and Paris.

FLEET:
2 x B737-700, 3 x B737-800,
1 x B747-200B, 2 x B747-200C,
3 x B747-200F, 5 x B747-400,
4 x B757-200, 2 x B767-200,
4 x B767-200ER, 1 x B767-300ER,
4 (2) x B777-200ER

FEATURES:
The predominantly white aircraft is wrapped in a dark blue and gray ribbon ending at the base and top of the tailfin. In between the bands, the six-pointed Star of David provides instant recognition. Bold EL AL titling, meaning "to the skies," is interspersed with the Hebrew equivalent in a lighter shade.

Emerald Airways (JEM)

UNITED KINGDOM (G)

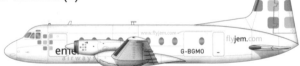

Predominantly a cargo carrier, operating converted freighters on long-term contracts with post and parcel carriers and major consolidators. Ad hoc cargo charter flights, wet and dry leasing, and aircraft maintenance are also offered. Scheduled passenger and freight services connect Liverpool with the Isle of Man across the Irish Sea. Bases are maintained at Liverpool and Blackpool. Emerald Airways was established on 1 December 1987 as Janes Aviation, and adopted the present title in recognition of business generated across the Irish Sea. Streamline Aviation was bought in August 2002.

FLEET:
2 x BAE ATP, 2 x BAE ATP(F),
13 x BAE (HS) 748 SRS 2,
3 x Shorts 360-100, 4 x Shorts
360-200

FEATURES:
The purpose of the attractive arrangement of squares with rounded corners in shades of emerald on the tailfin and behind the cockpit windows is to convey that the major business of the airline is the carriage of cargo across the Irish Sea. The name adds further to this clear statement. The presentation of the web address is almost a must these days, and Emerald opted to display it twice!

Emirates Airline (EK/UAE)

UNITED ARAB EMIRATES (A6)

Dubai flag-carrier operating scheduled passenger and cargo flights to more than 50 destinations throughout the Middle East and to Europe, Asia, Africa, points in the Indian Ocean, Australia, and the Commonwealth of Independent States. Emirates was established by the Dubai government in May 1985 and began operations on 25 October that year to Karachi, using Boeing 727s and Airbus A300s leased from Pakistan International. Since then, it has won a reputation for quality and innovative passenger service. It also has a strong cargo business operated under the Emirates SkyCargo name.

FLEET:
29 x A330-200, 8 x A340-300, 10 x A340-500, (20) x A340-600, (43) x A380-800, (2) x A380-800F, 4 x B747-400F, 3 x B777-200, 6 x B777-200ER, 12 x B777-300, 5 (47) x B777-300ER, (10) x B777-200LR, (8) x B777F

FEATURES:
The colors of the UAE flag are emblazoned on the tailfin in a flowing rendition, with an emphatic sweep to the red, black, and green, designed to create the feel of a modern and dynamic airline. Prominent gold *Emirates* titles dominate the forward fuselage, while the intricate Arabic logo is also seen on the wingtips and engines.

Era Aviation (7H/ERH)

UNITED STATES (N)

Alaskan air carrier operating scheduled passenger services in cooperation with Alaska Airlines out of Anchorage, together with an extensive network of routes serving 17 destinations in western Alaskan villages. Era also provides important air cargo links throughout the state and offers flightseeing tours to a variety of spectacular locations from bases at Denali and Juneau. It is also one of the world's oldest continuously operating helicopter companies. Era Aviation was established in 1948.

FLEET:
2 x Bell 212, 10 x Bell 412, 4 x Dash 8 100, 2 x DC-3C, 1 x DHC-6 Twin Otter 100, 1 x DHC-6 Twin Otter 200, 6 x DHC-6 Twin Otter 300, 2 x AS 332L Super Puma, 4 x Sikorsky S-61N, 7 x S-76A++

FEATURES:
The red tailfin incorporates a white encircled *Era* logo and is finished off neatly at the base with twin red and black lines. This detail is repeated as cheatlines along the fuselage. Black *Era Aviation* script is applied below. The red and black features also add some interest to the aircraft engines.

Eritrean Airlines (B8/ERT)

ERITREA (E3)

National airline of Eritrea operating a small number of passenger routes from the capital Asmara to points in East Africa and Europe. Cargo activity includes transporting relief supplies to the region and exporting fresh fish. The airline started life in 1991 as a ground-handling company at Asmara, Assab, and Mssawa and was converted into the national airline following independence of this East African country along the Red Sea from Ethiopia on 24 May 1993. Eritrean Airlines inaugurated passenger services the month before with a single Boeing 767-300ER.

FLEET:
1 X B767-200ER, 1 X B767-300ER

FEATURES:
The letter E for *Eritrea* on the dark blue tailfin is formed by a golden olive leaf, signifying peace, and three horizontal stripes in the national colors of green, red, and blue. It is also used as the first letter in the blue *Eritrean Airlines* titles on the forward fuselage. The tailfin design is mirrored on the aircraft engines. The green, red, and blue are the official colors of the Eritrean People's Liberation Front.

Estafeta Carga Aérea (E7/ESF)

MEXICO (XA/XB)

San Luis Potosi-based Mexican cargo airline operating scheduled domestic cargo services to 12 destinations, with two cross-border routes into the United States. Domestic and international charter services are also offered, together with capacity for special contract cargo flights. Estafeta Carga is part of the Estafeta Group, which is the leading express-shipping company in Mexico. Operations on the domestic front started in November 2000, with the first international connection to Miami added in January 2002.

FLEET:
3 X B737-200C, 1 X B737-200QC, 1 X B737-200F, 2 X B737-300QC

FEATURES:
Estafeta translates from the Spanish as "post office," but the airline is a commercial undertaking, transporting all types of cargo and mail. Apart from the bold red *Estafeta* titles on the forward fuselage, the only other form of decoration is a simple letter *e* in white over a white contrail on the red tailfin. A small Mexican flag accompanies the name.

Estonian Air (OV/ELL)

ESTONIA (ES)

National carrier of Estonia operating flag-services
from the capital Tallinn on the Baltic Sea to a small
number of cities in northern Europe, Russia, and
the Ukraine. No domestic services are scheduled.
Estonian Air was set up on 1 December 1991 by the
government following the country's newly won
independence and was based on the remains of the
local Aeroflot division. The first service was
operated the same day to Helsinki with an inherited
Tupolev TU-134A. It was partially privatized in
September 1996 with SAS Scandinavian Airlines
having a 49% stake.

FLEET:
5 X B737-500

FEATURES:
Estonian Air uses the national
colors of blue, black, and white to
good effect, although the black
has been replaced by a deep
shade of blue. The two-tone blue
covers the upper half of the
aircraft with white below, an
unusual reversal of traditional
concepts. The light blue and
white tailfin, divided by the
company's stylized bird motif in
dark blue, is an imaginative
portrayal of the national flag.
Estonian Air titles are preceded by
the airline symbol.

Ethiopian Airlines (ET/ETH)

ETHIOPIA (ET)

One of Africa's most prominent airlines, operating
flag services from Addis Ababa to almost 50 points
throughout Africa and to the Middle and Far East,
Europe, and across the Atlantic to the United States.
It also serves a vital domestic network incorporating
more than 25 destinations. Ethiopian Airlines was
founded on 30 December 1945 by proclamation of
Emperor Haile Selassie I to develop international
services and link the capital to communities in
isolated mountain areas. Operations began on 8
April 1946 with local services and a Douglas DC-3
flight between Addis Ababa and Cairo in Egypt.

FLEET:
1 X B737-200A, 5 X B737-700,
4 X B757-200, 1 X B757-200PF,
1 X B767-200ER, 6 X B767-300ER,
(10) X B787-8, 3 X DHC-6 Twin
Otter 300, 5 X F50, 2 X L100-30
Hercules

FEATURES:
The smart livery is dominated by
three attractive tail feathers in the
national colors of green, yellow,
and red. The rampant lion of the
days of the emperor has been
retained in gold on the forward
fuselage. Large red *Ethiopean*
lettering is displayed in English
across the front fuselage and in a
smaller rendition at the rear in
Amharic, the official language.

Etihad Airways (EY)
UNITED ARAB EMIRATES (A6)

Fast-growing Abu Dhabi-based national airline of the United Arab Emirates operating scheduled flag services to a growing number of destinations in the Middle East, the Indian subcontinent, the Far East, and Europe. The airline was set up by the government of Abu Dhabi in 2003 and made a first ceremonial flight to Al Ain on 5 November that year. The inaugural commercial passenger service took place on 12 November with a flight from Abu Dhabi to Beirut. The first commercial cargo flight was operated on 3 February by Etihad's Crystal Cargo division between Abu Dhabi and Frankfurt.

FLEET:
2 X A300-600F, 1 X A310-300F, 6 (14) X A330-200, 1 X A340-300, (4) X A340-500, (4) X A340-600, (4) X A380-800, 1 X B767-300ER, (5) X B777-300ER

FEATURES:
The main element is the coat of arms of the UAE in the shape of a falcon, incorporating the traditional dhow sailing boat used in the Persian Gulf. It is shown on the tailfin under the representative sweep of the flag in the national colors of red, green, white, and black. The word *Etihad*, applied prominently in gold in English and Arabic on the fuselage, refers to the unity of the Emirates.

Eurocypria Airlines (UI/ECA)
CYPRUS (5B)

Charter subsidiary of flag-carrier Cyprus Airways established on 12 June 1991. Operations began on 25 March 1992, initially with Airbus A320s, and these now provide services from over 50 European airports in 14 countries to Larnaca and Paphos. The majority of flights serve regional airports, offering direct connections to Cyprus in support of the growing tourist industry. Eurocypria Airlines also provides flights for specific interest groups and private charters.

FLEET:
4 X B737-800

FEATURES:
The fleet has been named after Mediterranean winds, each being distinguished by a different tail color. All incorporate a yellow sun logo crossed by a blue flash. Zephyrus, a light wind blowing from the west and a god in Greek mythology, is symbolized by the blue fin, while Levantes, denoted in light blue, is a strong east wind. Gray Maestros is a low-intensity northwesterly that brings coolness during the summer. Northeast Grecos is a wind blowing from Greece. It is highlighted in white.

Eurofly (GJ/EEZ)

ITALY (I)

Independent Italian airline providing a network of short-haul scheduled and charter flights from Milan, Rome, Bologna, and Verona to points in Europe, the eastern Mediterranean, and North Africa, together with long-haul leisure services to the Caribbean, Central and South America, East Africa, the Maldives, and Sri Lanka. A business class-only service has also linked Milan with New York since June 2005. Eurofly was established on 26 May 1989, initially with Alitalia and Olivetti having a 45% stake each, primarily to develop the Italian flag-carrier's charter business. Operations began on 26 February 1990.

FLEET:
8 x A320-200, 4 x A330-200, (3) x A350

FEATURES:
The bold and uncluttered livery provides a striking contrast between the red company color and the pristine white aircraft. A lowercase *e* in red is painted right across the slim tailfin, while simple *eurofly* titles are applied above the windows on the forward fuselage. Unusual is the triple curved cheatline in two shades of gray.

euroLOT (K2/ELO)

POLAND (SP)

Regional subsidiary of flag-carrier LOT Polish Airlines serving some 20 domestic and secondary international cities with frequent scheduled flights. Cross-border flights link destinations in Austria, Germany, Ukraine, the Czech Republic, Latvia, and Lithuania. Ad hoc charters and flight training are also offered. euroLOT was established on 19 December 1996 and began operations with turboprop aircraft on 1 July 1997.

FLEET:
5 x ATR 42-500, 8 x ATR 72-200

FEATURES:
A large red lowercase *e*, being the first letter in the name while also suggesting its European origin, is surrounded by two concentric circles, which illustrate the range of the airline's operations. The red *euro* in the title on the forward fuselage is followed by the logo of euroLOT's parent company.

EuroManx (3W/EMX)
ISLE OF MAN (G)

Regional airline operating a growing network of scheduled passenger services from the Isle of Man, a British Crown Dependency in the Irish Sea, to destinations in Ireland and the United Kingdom. The airline also has a thriving charter business. EuroManx was established at Ronaldsway Airport in the capital Ballasalla at the start of August 2002 by Allan Keen, and began operations on 19 August, initially to Dublin and Edinburgh, using a leased Beech 1900D. The airline was acquired by Warren Seymour, CEO of executive jet operator club328, and a group of UK investors in September 2004.

FLEET:
2 x Avro RJ70, 2 x BAE Jetstream 31, 1 x Dash 8 300, 1 x FD 328-100

FEATURES:
The tailfin of the EuroManx aircraft is representative of the red Isle of Man flag, which in its center features the triskelion emblem dating back to the thirteenth century, depicting the unmistakable "Three Legs of Man" conjoined at the thigh and bent at the knee. The gold and red *EuroManx* titles are split above and below the forward windows, to take account of the high-wing configuration of its aircraft.

Europe Airpost (50/FPO)
FRANCE (F)

Wholly owned subsidiary of La Poste, the French Post Office, operating nightly mail and cargo flights over 20 regular lines throughout metropolitan France and the island of Corsica. Scheduled and charter services for both passengers and freight are provided during the day. Aircraft are stationed throughout the country, but the main base is located at Paris Charles de Gaulle Airport. The airline was founded and started operations in 1991. It was formerly known as Intercargo Service.

FLEET:
4 X ATR 72-200F, 12 x B737-300QC, 2 x B737-300SF

FEATURES:
The latest livery is a bright yellow with a wavy mauve and white design resembling a fish, which covers most of the lower fuselage and much of the tailfin. The underside of the aircraft is finished in deep blue and shaped to add further dynamism to the design. The engines are also painted deep blue.

European Air Express (EAE) (EA/NRX)

GERMANY (D)

German regional airline operating scheduled passenger and cargo services from hubs at Mönchengladbach and Cologne Bonn. The route network serves 10 destinations within Germany, and in neighboring Belgium, Poland, Switzerland, and the United Kingdom. European Air Express was founded in early 1999 and entered the scheduled market in February that year.

FLEET:
5 X ATR 42-300, 2 X SA227AC Metro III, 1 X SA227DC Metro 23

FEATURES:
Five blue stars with a comet trail across the red and blue EAE initials signify the airline's European credentials, highlighted both on the white forward fuselage and the white tailfin. An interesting addition is the dark blue cheatline arrangement in which lines of varying thickness commence at the undercarriage bulge and sweep up to the base of the fin. The blue lower rear of the aircraft is balanced by the blue engines on the high wing.

Eurowings (EW/EWG)

GERMANY (D)

German regional airline providing scheduled passenger and cargo services within Germany and to neighboring countries as part of the Lufthansa Regional system from bases at Dortmund, Frankfurt, and Munich. Eurowings also has a busy summer and winter charter program serving the Mediterranean area and the Canary Islands. Eurowings was established on 1 January 1993 from the merger of NFD Luftverkehrs of Nuremberg and RFG Regionalflug of Dortmund, which had been in business since 1975 and 1976 respectively.

FLEET:
2 X ATR 72-200, 3 X ATR 72-210, 1 X ATR 72-500, 4 X BAE 146-200, 6 X BAE 146-300, 12 X CRJ200ER, 4 X CRJ200LR

FEATURES:
Two speedwing arrows in red and blue, the latter with a curved contrail, form the principal element of the standard design, applied on the white tailfin, engines, and forward fuselage, with black Eurowings titling applied on the forward upper fuselage. The majority of the fleet, however, operates in Lufthansa Regional colors, and there are some special schemes.

EVA Air (BR/EVA)

TAIWAN (B)

Major privately owned Taiwanese carrier serving an expanding global network of some 40 destinations in Asia, Australia, New Zealand, the Indian subcontinent, the Middle East, Europe, and North America. A dedicated international cargo network is also operated. Domestic services are flown by associate UNI Airways. The airline was established by Evergreen Corporation in March 1989 and began international passenger and cargo services on 1 July 1991 with leased Boeing 767-200ERs.

FLEET:
9 (2) X A330-200, 5 X B747-400,
3 X B747-400F, 10 X B747-400M,
1 X B767-200, 2 X B767-300ER,
11 X MD-11F, (3) X B777-200LR,
2 (10) X B777-300ER, 3 X MD-90-30

FEATURES:
The tailfin features a globe displayed against dark green, the color of durability, suggesting stability and reliability. It is positioned so that the upper left-hand corner is cut off at an angle, stated to represent new vistas of service innovation. A vertical strip of orange at the fin's outer edge is said to impart a sense of high-tech innovation.

Evergreen International Airlines (EZ/EIA)

UNITED STATES (N)

Diverse U.S. company providing passenger and cargo services on an ad hoc and contract charter basis, or operating subservices for other airlines on wet lease and dry lease. A major part of its operation is flying for the Air Mobility Command, providing rapid global mobility for America's armed forces and humanitarian support missions. It is also a Civilian Reserve Air fleet, supporting Department of Defense emergency airlift requirements. It was set up on 28 November 1975 when Evergreen Helicopters acquired the certificate of Johnson Flying Service, whose history dated to 1924.

FLEET:
3 X B747-100F, 2 X B747SR-100F,
2 X B747-200C, 4 X B747-200F

FEATURES:
A pair of broad straight-through cheatlines in two shades of green divide the fuselage, which is white above and a natural metal finish below. The green circle motif, behind what originally represented the bow of a boat incorporating the *Evergreen* name, has been tilted to follow the angle of the leading edge of the fin and now resembles a check mark. Large *Evergreen International* titles occupy much of the cabin roof.

Excel Airways (JN/XLA)

UNITED KINGDOM (G)

Holiday charter airline providing flights to Mediterranean leisure destinations, serving Egypt, the Greek Islands, Cyprus, Turkey, Italy, France, Spain, Portugal, and the Canary Islands. Excel Airways operates from three main UK bases at London Gatwick, Manchester, and Glasgow, but regular inclusive-tour flights are also operated from another seven provincial airports. The airline's history goes back to the foundation of Sabre Airways on 17 December 1994, but it was relaunched as Excel Airways on 1 May 2001 following the acquisition of a stake by Libra Holidays. It is now owned by the Icelandic Avion Group.

FLEET:
9 (2) x B737-800, 2 x B747-200B, 1 x B747-300, 4 x B757-200, 2 x B767-200ER, 3 x B767-300ER

FEATURES:
Blue for sky and sea is the dominant color applied to the tailfin and engines of the aircraft. Large *Excel* titles, suggesting exceptional service, are written along the leading edge of the tailfin, with the letter *x* drawn in red and sky blue. The same design element has been used in the blue *excelairways.com* wording on the cabin roof.

Express.Net Airlines (XNA)

UNITED STATES (N)

Contract cargo airline serving the express and overnight freight markets in the United States, Canada, Mexico, South America, and the Far East. It also provides flights on an aircraft, crew, maintenance, and insurance basis. The airline's history dates back to June 1972 when it was founded as International Airlines Academy, organized out of the former Universal Airlines Training Center. It received its commercial operator's certificate in 1975 and began cargo flights with eight Curtiss C-46 Commandos under the name of Trans Continental Airlines. It was renamed in March 2000.

FLEET:
8 x A300B4-200F, 3 x B727-100C

FEATURES:
Blue and black lines broaden from a point at the nose to wide bands at the rear, giving the impression of a slim, long, speeding arrow. Riding on the forward part of the arrow is the *express.net* name in black. Prominent on the white fin is the black hand-drawn letter *e*, given a flourish with a long wraparound tail.

Falcon Air (IH/FCN)

SWEDEN (SE)

Airline arm of the Swedish Post Office, operating domestic night mail flights throughout Sweden from its main base at Malmö-Sturup Airport, with daytime flights undertaken for other airlines together with charters in cooperation with several Scandinavian tour operators. Falcon Air's history goes back to the 1960s, when it operated an air-taxi service with small aircraft out of Gothenburg. Services for the Post Office started on 6 October 1986 with a flight along the length of the country from Malmö to Stockholm, Umeå, and Luleå.

FLEET:
2 X B737-300QC

FEATURES:
Given its name, the airline focus is on the falcon, a strong bird of prey that flies fast and has great aerial agility. The head of a falcon forms the core of the red and white striped tailfin, and each aircraft carries the name of a different species of this bird family. A red cheatline separates the white upper fuselage, which also carries blue *Falcon Air* titles, from the gray underside.

Falcon Air Express (F2/FAO)

UNITED STATES (N)

Private u.s. airline operating ad hoc and contract charter and wet-lease services from its main hub of Miami in Florida to destinations throughout the Americas, together with the transportation of military personnel on behalf of the Department of Defense. Falcon Air Express was established by industry veteran Emilio Dirube in 1995 and began flying in March 1996.

FLEET:
4 X B727-200A, 2 X B737-300, 1 X MD-82

FEATURES:
A rather unusual scheme with a gold cummerbund wrapped around the center fuselage after dark blue *Falcon Air* titles. This color combination is also used for the tailfin, with three gold bands sweeping across a dark blue background. The u.s. flag is also carried.

Far Eastern Air Transport (FAT) (EF/FEA)
TAIWAN (B)

Taiwan's largest domestic passenger and cargo carrier with more than one-third of the market, serving all principal points from its main base at Taipei Sungshan Airport. Its network also extends to neighboring regions, flying to Macau and several cities in Malaysia, Thailand, the Philippines, and the Pacific, operated on both a scheduled and charter basis. The airline was organized on 5 June 1957 by former pilots of Civil Air Transport. Charters were carried out for some years until January 1965, when scheduled passenger services were introduced between Taipei and Kaohsiung.

FLEET:
7 X B757-200, 1 X B757-200PF,
6 X MD-82, 5 X MD-83,
2 X MD-90-30

FEATURES:
The gold and red design, which goes from thin lines to broad red, both on the lower fuselage and engine cowlings, is reversed on the tailfin, where the broad red is applied at the top. This arrangement enhances the long, slim shape of the aircraft, making it anything but FAT, as the airline's initials proclaim on the fin. The full *Far Eastern Air Transport* titles are applied on the cabin roof in English and Chinese lettering.

Farnair Europe (FAH/FAT)
HUNGARY (HA)/SWITZERLAND (HB)

European airline consortium comprising Farnair Hungary and Farnair Switzerland, engaged in scheduled express parcel flights, services for humanitarian relief organizations, and ad hoc and contract passenger and cargo charters. Farnair Hungary was formed in 1990 as Nawa Air Transport and was acquired in 1993 by Farner Air Transport, the ancestor of Farnair Switzerland, which had been established in 1984.

FLEET:
1 X ATR 42-300, 1 X ATR 42-300F,
1 X ATR 72-200, 3 X ATR 72-200F,
6 X F27-500, 1 X Let L-410M,
1 X Let L-410 UVP, 4 X Let L-410
UVP-E

FEATURES:
The Swiss-based cargo carrier uses the colors of the European Union to good effect. The blue tailfin incorporates five golden stars of graduating sizes, indicating that it is firmly based and operating within Europe. The only other decoration on the otherwise white aircraft is the airline name on the lower forward fuselage in the same color combination.

FedEx (Federal Express) (FM/FDX)

UNITED STATES (N)

World's largest express transportation company providing scheduled air cargo and express freight delivery to over 300 airports in more than 200 countries across the globe, from a superhub at Memphis; regional hubs at Newark, Oakland, Fort Worth, Chicago, and Los Angeles; and the Anchorage gateway. Major overseas facilities are operated at London Stansted, Frankfurt, Paris, Subic Bay, and Tokyo. The domestic network is supplemented by a number of contract carriers operating small freighters. Federal Express was founded in 1972 by Frederick Smith and began overnight express package delivery flights on 17 April 1973.

FLEET:
46 x A300-600F, 49 x A310-200F, 6 x A310-300F, (10) x A380-800F, 28 x B727-100F, 90 x B727-200F, 42 x MD-11F, 56 x DC-10-10F, 18 x DC-10-30F

FEATURES:
The Landor-designed brand is said to embrace speed, reliability, innovative technology, and customer service. It is characterized by a bold typeface in dynamic shades of purple and orange, applied in large letters on the white fuselage and in smaller letters on the all-purple tailfin and engines.

Finnair (AY/FIN)

FINLAND (OH)

Finnish flag-carrier serving 50 international destinations, mainly in Europe, but also covering points in North America and Asia. With one of the densest domestic networks in the world in relation to population, it serves 16 towns. In addition to scheduled traffic, Finnair also provides leisure flights to more than 60 resorts in the Mediterranean, Canary Islands, Southeast Asia, the Caribbean, and South America. Founded on 1 November 1923 as Aero Oy, Finnair began operations, initially with floatplanes, on 20 March 1924. The present name was adopted on 25 June 1968 but had been used since 1953.

FLEET:
11 x A319-100, 12 x A320-200, 6 x A321-200, 5 x B757-200, 1(9) x EMB 170LR, (6) x EMB 190, 6 x MD-11, 4 x MD-82, 5 x MD-83

FEATURES:
The latest livery, introduced in May 2000, retains the national colors of white and blue, signifying snow and sky, accentuated by a more softly drawn "Flying F" symbol reversed out in white on the dark blue tail and underlined by a bright blue flash. It was designed by Finnish agency SEK & Gray to convey a message of safety, reliability, Finnishness, and freshness, and reflecting the spirit of the time.

Finncomm Airlines (FC/WBA)

FINLAND (OH)

Finnish commuter airline operating services within Finland on behalf of Finnair and Swedish carrier Golden Air but also flying in its own right from Helsinki to domestic points and to Germany and Norway. The domestic network serves 13 towns and cities across the country. Finncomm was established in 1993 and started flying in 1995.

FLEET:
(8) X ATR 42-500, 2 X ERJ 145LU

FEATURES:
The predominant white and blue scheme, signifying snow and sky, is derived from the Finnish flag. The biggest splash of color is on the tailfin, where three large white curved contrails make a track across the blue sky. *Finncomm Airlines* titles in blue and red can be seen on the lower forward fuselage and the rear engines.

First Air (7F/FAB)

CANADA (C)

Division of Bradley Air Services, one of Canada's largest independent aviation companies, providing scheduled passenger and cargo services to 24 communities in Canada's Arctic regions, together with connections to Ottawa, Montreal, Winnipeg, and Edmonton. Charter services worldwide are also offered. Now owned by the 9,000 Inuit of northern Quebec through the Makivik Corporation, the company's history goes back to the formation of Bradley Flying School in 1946, renamed Bradley Air Services in 1954. Northwest Territorial Airways (NWT Air) was merged into First Air in 1998.

FLEET:
6 X ATR 42-300, 2 X B727-100C, 1 X B727-200C, 2 X B727-200F, 3 X B737-200C, 3 X BAE 748-2A, 1 x Dash 7-150, 1 x L100-30 Hercules

FEATURES:
The choice of four rainbow colors, graduating from yellow to orange, magenta, and black, makes for an attractive scheme. The quadruple windowlines, ending in an arrow point at the front, are complemented by the airline symbol showing the figure 1 cut into a sun, drawn in the same four colors. The symbol is repeated ahead of the airline name on the forward cabin roof.

First Choice Airways (DP/AMM)

UNITED KINGDOM (G)

One of the UK's largest charter airlines, serving more than 60 of the most popular holiday destinations around the Mediterranean basin, Madeira, and the Canary Islands, together with long-haul flights to across the Atlantic to Florida, Mexico, and the Caribbean, and eastwards to the Maldives. Flights originate from 18 UK and Irish airports. The airline also operates scheduled leisure routes from UK cities to Cyprus, and operates a VIP-configured Boeing 757 on prestige around-the-world charters. Operations started on 11 April 1987 as Air 2000, with the present name being adopted in spring 2004.

FLEET:
7 x A320-200, 4 x A321-200, 18 x B757-200, 3 x B767-300ER, (6) x B787-8

FEATURES:
There is no mistaking the tropical attributes of the First Choice livery. The magenta star-shaped flower on the turquoise tailfin is instantly recognizable, but another attractive aspect is the wavy cheatline that graduates from turquoise to magenta. Aquamarine *First Choice* titles are preceded by the corporate symbol, which depicts a tableau comprising a golden sun, blue sky, tropical flower, white sandy beach and turquoise sea.

Fischer Air Polska (8F/FFR)

POLAND (SP)

Polish charter airline providing package holiday services to destinations in European and North African countries along the Mediterranean. Flights are operated out of Warsaw and other Polish cities. Charter flights for other travel companies are also available. The airline was set up by Czech operator Fischer Air, which has ceased operations. Fischer Air was established on 26 July 1996 by Václav Fischer and inaugurated its first commercial flight on 30 April 1997 between Prague and Palma de Mallorca using a Boeing 737-300.

FLEET:
2 x B737-300, 1 x B757-200

FEATURES:
The modern new livery comprises an attractive tailfin in bright blue, graduating at the base into sky blue and light blue, and incorporating a fan shape in three shades of blue with a golden dot that can be loosely interpreted as the letter F. Blue *Fischer Air* titles are applied on the cabin roof, with the additional *Polska* title for its Polish operation. A small version of the airline name and tailfin symbol is also carried on the aircraft engines.

Flightline (B5/FLT)

UNITED KINGDOM (G)

UK charter company operating ad hoc and contract passenger charters out of its hub at Southend Airport, together with branded aircraft, crew, maintenance, and insurance wet-lease contracts and subservices for major airlines. Flights are also operated on behalf of Premiership football clubs, car manufacturers, and major recording artists, and the airline is also a prime contractor to the oil industry, providing air services from Aberdeen to support North Sea installations. A VIP product is also part of its expanding portfolio. Flightline was established in April 1989, initially for the purchase and sale of executive aircraft.

FLEET:
4 X BAE 146-200, 1 X BAE 146-300

FEATURES:
As the aircraft are operated mostly for other clients, the only paint scheme that refers to the airline are small *Flightline* titles above or below the forward cabin windows. The name is displayed in black, with a green triangle above the letter *F* and green dots above both letters *i* and after the final *e*.

Florida West International Airways (RF/FWL)

UNITED STATES (N)

All-cargo carrier, operating scheduled services between Miami and several destinations in Latin America, including Bogota, Guatemala City, Medellin, Panama City, Quito, and San Jose. The airline also offers worldwide charter flights, transporting general cargo, perishables, valuables, and livestock. Formerly known as Pan Aero International, Aero Exchange, and Florida West Airlines, the company gained its charter authority from the Civil Aeronautics Board in 1981. Domestic scheduled flights were authorised in 1984, and international scheduled flights some time later.

FLEET:
1 X B767-300F

FEATURES:
The central motif of the airline is a representation of the globe, drawn in blue longitudes and red latitudes on the white tail. The white upper fuselage is separated from the gray underside by curtailed blue and red cheatlines. Large *Florida West* titles, also in blue and red, take up much of the forward fuselage.

Fly Air (Fly Airlines) (F2/FLM)
TURKEY (TC)

Private Turkish airline, providing a mix of holiday charter flights and domestic scheduled services. Charter flights connect Turkey with destinations in Belgium, the Netherlands, France, Germany, Italy, Switzerland, Israel, Lebanon, Iran, Syria, Armenia, Northern Cyprus, the United Arab Emirates, Pakistan, Afghanistan, Egypt, Niger, Nigeria, and Sudan, while scheduled flights link Trabzon and Istanbul with several major cities. Fly Air was founded in 2002 and is part of the Trabzon-based Peksen Group. Scheduled domestic services were inaugurated in October 2003.

FLEET:
2 X A300B2K-3C, 1 X A300B4-200, 2 X A300B4-2C, 1 X B737-300, 1 X MD-83

FEATURES:
This complicated scheme on a white aircraft uses stripes of blue, red, orange, and yellow on the tailfin and along the fuselage. The large red *flyair* titles forward are a highly visible signature, while the two-tone blue "eye in the sky" emblem dominates the tailfin. A small red Turkish flag with its crescent moon and stars is shown on the front fuselage.

FlyGlobespan (GSM)
UNITED KINGDOM (G)

Scottish no-frills airline operating low-fare services from Glasgow, Edinburgh, and London Stansted to some 15 European cities, reaching as far as the Canary Islands. FlyGlobespan was launched on 7 November 2002 by travel group Globespan and inaugurated services from Glasgow Prestwick to Malaga, Nice, Palma de Mallorca, and Rome in April 2003. These services were soon moved to Glasgow International, with a second base at Edinburgh established on 30 October 2003.

FLEET:
4 X B737-300, 1 X B737-400, 4 X B737-600, 3 X B737-800

FEATURES:
The huge *flyglobespan.com* titles, taking up almost all of the aircraft fuselage, make a strong statement of the airline's policy of booking flights on the Internet. The web address is repeated on the red engine cowlings, which complement the wavy red underside of the aircraft and winglets. White letter *gs* are floating on the red tailfin against the background of the same letter in outline reflection.

FlyBaboo (F7/BBO)

SWITZERLAND (HB)

Geneva-based Swiss regional airline operating a small network of services linking Geneva to Lugano and to points in nearby Italy, France, Spain, and the Czech Republic. Special "Escape" packages including hotels and excursions are also offered. FlyBaboo was established by Julian Cook on 21 August 2003 and started flying on 2 November that same year with a service between Geneva and Lugano using a Bombardier Dash 8 300 wet-leased from German carrier Cirrus Airlines.

FLEET:
2 x Dash 8 Q300

FEATURES:
The unusual name reflects the idiosyncratic approach of its founder, who wanted to provide a different flying experience for his passengers. The word *baboo* comes from Hindi and is a respectful and honorary title or form of address given to educated people. Only upon close examination can the unusual tailfin design be recognized as a stylistic representation of the Indian turban.

FlyBE (British European) (BE/BEE)

UNITED KINGDOM (G)

Large independent low-fare airline operating from principal hubs in London, Birmingham, Belfast, Bristol, Exeter, Liverpool, Southampton, the Channel Islands, and Scotland, from where it serves 17 domestic and more than 20 international destinations. A thriving charter business is operated at weekends. The airline came into being as Jersey European Airways on 1 November 1979, taking over the operations of Intra Airways. On 1 June 2000 the name was changed to British European, with the present brand adopted on 18 July 2002 to reflect its relaunch as a low-fare, full-service airline.

FLEET:
7 x BAE 146-200, 8 x BAE 146-300, 18 (27) x Dash 8 Q400, (14) x EMB 175LR

FEATURES:
The emphasis of the livery is to provide reminders of the airline name and web address. Huge *flyBE* titles in sky blue and dark blue are applied on the tailfin and rear fuselage, as well as across the forward cabin, with additional *British European* lettering underlined by a line graduating across part of the color spectrum from red to yellow. The belly of the aircraft and underside of the engines help to reinforce the sky blue theme.

189

FlyJet (FJE)
UNITED KINGDOM (G)

London Gatwick-based airline offering holiday charter flights from London and Manchester, taking in the major resort areas in Cyprus, Finland, Greece, Italy, Portugal, Spain, the Canary Islands, Turkey, and Israel. Long-haul flights are also undertaken to India and Ghana. FlyJet was established in 2002 and acquired its air operator's certificate on 13 June 2003. Services were launched with a 233-seat Boeing 757-200.

FLEET:
2 X B757-200

FEATURES:
The FlyJet design comprises two elements, which appear on the tailfin, engine cowlings, and forward fuselage. It consists of the airline name, either in white or blue depending on the background, preceded by an orange flash. The logo is strongly promoted on the white fuselage and on the blue tailfin. The airline's web address can be seen at the rear.

FlyLAL (Lithuanian Airlines) (TE/LIL)
LITHUANIA (LY)

National carrier of Lithuania operating a modest international network from the capital Vilnius to points in Western Europe and to Russia and the Ukraine. A domestic link is also provided between Vilnius and Palanga. The airline's history dates back to 20 September 1938 and the formation of Lietuvos oro linijos, which operated as a regional branch of Aeroflot during the Soviet occupation. It was re-established on 21 December 1991 as Lietuvos Avia-linijos (Lithuanian Airlines) following the country's independence. The new trademark was adopted in late 2005 following the airline's privatization.

FLEET:
1 X B737-200A, 5 X B737-500, 2 X Saab 2000

FEATURES:
The livery reflects the national colors of red, green, and yellow, which are painted in stripes of varying thickness diagonally across the white fuselage to the base of the fin. The effect of speed is created by three graduated yellow stripes. The company motif of two encircled red letter LS forming a stylized bird is featured on the largely white tailfin. The FlyLAL trademark, designed by Vaidotas Skolevičius, is short and simple, as befits a modern airline.

FlyMe (SH/FLY)
SWEDEN (SE)

Low-fare airline, operating a network of scheduled services aimed at the business traveler and linking its main base of Gothenburg, as well as Malmö and Stockholm, to other Scandinavian cities, with a connection to Helsinki in Finland. Contract and ad hoc charter flights are also provided to increase the utilization of its leased fleet. The airline originated under the title Array but was registered as FlyMe in November 2003. Operations began between Gothenburg, Malmö, and Stockholm on 1 March 2004 with Boeing 737-300s.

FLEET:
3 x B737-300

FEATURES:
This catchy name probably does not need further embellishment and the airline could not have kept its corporate identity much simpler. Large *FlyMe* titles in full on the forward fuselage and curtailed on the tailfin, together with the front half of the engines, are painted in dark red on the all-white aircraft.

FlyNordic (LF/NDC)
SWEDEN (SE)

Swedish-based airline operating low-fare flights within Scandinavia from its main base at Stockholm Arlanda Airport. The network serves destinations in Sweden, Denmark, and Norway. The airline offers ticketless travel by telephone or via its website www.flynordic.com. FlyNordic was established on 1 November 2000 as Nordic Airlink, beginning regional services on 1 December that year. It was transformed into a low-cost, low-fare airline in fall 2003 when purchased by Finnish flag-carrier Finnair.

FLEET:
5 x MD-82, 3 x MD-83

FEATURES:
The two delta-wing arrows design in blue and red has been replaced by a smart red and white scheme centered on a floral motif, in which the petals represent the airline's route network in Scandinavia. It is applied on the tailfin and ahead of the airline name on the cabin roof. The blue and yellow Swedish flag follows the aircraft registration at the rear.

Focus Air (F2)

UNITED STATES (N)

Cargo charter carrier operating on a domestic and worldwide basis out of Fort Lauderdale Hollywood International Airport in Florida. Focus Air also provides subservices for other airlines including Cargolux and China Eastern. The airline was established by Omega Air Holdings in March 2004.

FLEET:
1 X B747-300SF

FEATURES:
The tailfin is divided by a curved gold line, which separates the upper midnight blue from the lower mid-blue paint scheme. The lower blue is transformed into two broad bands that speed along the rear fuselage before quickly fading into white. The mid-blue also highlights the aircraft engines. A thin blue cheatline provides a border to the gray underside. A curved gold horizon is superimposed on the blue *Focus Air* titles on the fuselage.

Four Star Air Cargo (HK/FSC)

U.S. VIRGIN ISLANDS (N)

Scheduled all-cargo airline based at St. Thomas in the U.S. Virgin Islands providing frequent links with the British Virgin Islands, Puerto Rico, and Miami in Florida, carrying general cargo, express freight, perishable goods, and hazardous material. Custom charters are also undertaken throughout the Caribbean. Four Star Air Cargo started operations on 1 January 1982 and is part of Four Star Aviation.

FLEET:
3 x Convair 440, 6 x DC-3C

FEATURES:
The only color used on this white livery is in the airline title on the cabin roof. This comprises the words *Four Star*, surrounding four five-pointed stars in outline, all rendered in the same blue.

Free Bird Airlines (FHY)

TURKEY (TC)

Turkish charter airline serving the popular resorts on the country's Aegean coast from more than 50 European points, and transporting Turkish holidaymakers to other Mediterranean tourist destinations. The airline was formed in June 2001 by the Gözen Group, which provides ground services, fuel supply, and aircraft brokerage. Free Bird started flying on 5 April 2001 with three McDonnell Douglas MD-83 aircraft, flying between Istanbul and Lyon in France.

FLEET:
3 X A320-200, 4 X MD-83

FEATURES:
The emblem of the Gözen Group is made up of the letter g in blue and red, set into a white field on the red tailfin. A large red flash crosses the *Free Bird* titles, rendered in a blue outline along the forward fuselage. The red Turkish flag is applied behind the cabin door.

Freedom Air (FOM)

NEW ZEALAND (ZK)

Auckland, New Zealand-based airline offering value-for-money scheduled services between major cities on New Zealand's North and South islands, across the Tasman Sea to Australia, and to Fiji in the South Pacific. The airline traces its history to 1995 and the establishment of South Pacific Air Charters by the Mount Cook Group. Charters only were operated at first, but the trading name of Freedom Air International was introduced with the inauguration of scheduled services. The *International* has since been dropped from the title.

FLEET:
2 X A320-200, 2 X B737-300

FEATURES:
A yellow and blue spinning sun with red rays covers the central part of the blue tailfin, indicating the fact that the airline serves the leisure industry. This is further enhanced by the orange-yellow body of the aircraft, with the red *freedomair.com* web address covering most of the upper fuselage. The tail design and color combination is repeated on the engines with additional *Freedom Air* titles.

Frontier Airlines (F9/FFT)

UNITED STATES (N)

Major u.s. low-fare airline operating an extensive network of scheduled passenger services from its hub at Denver International, where it is the second-largest jet user. Services extend to almost 50 destinations in more than 20 u.s. states, spanning the nation coast-to-coast, and to five cities in Mexico. Regional services under the name of Frontier JetExpress are flown by Horizon Air with CRJ700 regional jets. Frontier Airlines was established on 8 February 1994 to fill the gap left in the Denver market by the downsizing of Continental Airlines at that airport. Operations began on 5 July that year with two Boeing 737-200s.

FLEET:
8 x A318-100, 42 (11) x A319-100

FEATURES:
Large *Frontier* titles with the inset slogan *A whole different animal* are splashed across the white aircraft and can be seen from afar, but the most recognizable feature is the colorful tail. A growing number of stunning photographs are used to depict various native animals (mountain goat shown) found in the western u.s. Most aircraft have the same photograph on both sides of the tailfin, but different animals, or the same in an altered rendition, are applied on some aircraft.

Frontier Flying Service (2F/FTA)

UNITED STATES (N)

u.s. commuter airline operating an extensive network of scheduled commuter services for passengers and freight to more than 30 communities in central and northern Alaska from its main base at Fairbanks and hubs at Anchorage, Barrow, and Bethel. Statewide charters and flights into neighboring Canada are also provided, as are air-ambulance services. Frontier Flying Service was established in 1950 by John Hajdukovich to offer a charter service from Fairbanks. Scheduled services were added in December 1983, initially serving Bettles, Wiseman, Chandalar, Allakakeet, and Anatuvik Pass.

FLEET:
8 x Beech 1900C-1, 1 x Beech C99

FEATURES:
Displayed to good effect on the black tailfin is the company's motif of an eagle flying against a red sun, with the red and black combination carried through to the underside of the aircraft in the form of a red cheatline over black. Red *Frontier* titles in natural handwriting cover the white mid-cabin roof.

Futura International Airways (FH/FUA)
SPAIN (EC)

Spanish charter airline serving all the popular resorts on the Spanish mainland, the Balearic and Canary islands from more than 50 points in northern and Eastern Europe. It also operates a scheduled interisland route from its main base at Palma de Mallorca to Mahon on the smaller Balearic island of Minorca. Futura International was set up in 1989 as a joint venture between Aer Lingus, Belton Air, and Spanish interests, initially to fly tourists from Ireland to Spain. The first flight was operated on 17 February 1990 between Dublin and Palma de Mallorca with two leased Boeing 737-300s. The airline is now owned by its management.

FLEET:
6 x B737-400, 10 x B737-800

FEATURES:
This is not a typical color scheme for a holiday airline. The blue and white has been used well to create a smart and sober appearance with strong business ethics. The orbiting-planet design on the blue tailfin is repeated on the winglets of specific aircraft types, while the blue *Futura* lettering on the forward upper fuselage is given a flourish with the unifying planet leitmotiv.

Garuda Indonesia (GA/GIA)
INDONESIA (PK)

Indonesian flag-carrier providing international scheduled passenger and cargo services to many regional destinations in Asia, Australia, and New Zealand, together with long-haul flights to the Middle East, Europe, and the United States. The airline also operates an extensive domestic network linking Jakarta and its hubs at Medan, Bali, and Surabaya with 30 points throughout the Indonesian archipelago. Founded as Indonesian Airways on 28 December 1949, one day after Indonesia's independence, it was formally incorporated as Garuda Indonesian Airways on 31 March 1950.

FLEET:
6 (3) x A330-300, 13 x B737-300, 26 x B737-400, 5 x B737-500, (18) x B737-700, 3 x B747-400, (6) x B777-200ER, 2 x DC-10-30

FEATURES:
This is one of the of the most attractive airline liveries designed by Landor Associates. Its center-piece is a modern representation of the garuda, the sacred bird of Hinduism, which is displayed on the deep blue fin in progressive shades of blue to turquoise. The five wing feathers symbolize the five national ideals: Belief in one god, a just and civilized humanity, unity, democracy guided by inner wisdom, and social justice.

GB Airways (GT/GBL)

GIBRALTAR (VP-G)

British flag-carrier to Gibraltar, Madeira, Morocco, and Tunisia, operating from London Heathrow, London Gatwick, and Manchester to some 30 leisure destinations in France, Spain, the Canary Islands, Gibraltar, Portugal, Morocco, Tunisia, Malta, Croatia, Cyprus, and Greece. All services are flown in full British Airways branding following a franchise agreement signed on 1 February 1995. GB Airways was founded in 1931 as an offshoot of Gibraltar shipping company M. H. Bland, and started operations to Tangier, using a single Saro Windhover flying boat. It traded as Gibair until 1 November 1981.

FLEET:
11 (1) X A320-200,
4 (6) X A321-200

FEATURES:
As a franchise operation, the entire GB Airways fleet is painted in the livery of British Airways, with the three-dimensional speedmarque and *British Airways* titles applied in a large format on the front fuselage, which is white above wing level and blue below. The entire tailfin is taken up by the fluttering adaptation of the British flag. Small *Operated by GB Airways* titles around the Bland Group corporate symbol are added under the cockpit windows.

Gemini Air Cargo (GR/GCO)

UNITED STATES (N)

Major Washington-based U.S. all-cargo airline operating worldwide cargo scheduled and charter services on an aircraft, crew, maintenance, and insurance wet-lease basis for many leading airlines, as well as for the United States Postal Service and the Air Mobility Command, providing global mobility for the U.S. armed forces and humanitarian relief missions. Gemini Air Cargo was founded in 1995 and began flight operations on 18 November that year, using the McDonnell Douglas DC-10-30F on behalf of Swissair Cargo.

FLEET:
7 X DC-10-30F

FEATURES:
A large medallion-type symbol on the dark blue tailfin and blue and gold *Gemini Air Cargo* titles on mid-fuselage stand out very well against the white of the aircraft. Set into a white base surrounded by a yellow ring is a large blue G enclosing a representation of the Earth, graduated to generate a spherical effect. An aircraft flies along the equator and *Gemini Air Cargo* titles are written around the edge of the white circle.

Georgian Airlines (A9/TGZ)

GEORGIA (4L)

Private airline operating a small network of scheduled services from Tbilisi, capital of the Black Sea Republic of Georgia, to destinations in Russia, Western Europe, and Israel. Charter flights are also undertaken. The airline was founded as Airzena in September 1997 and started with business and charter flights before adding scheduled services in cooperation with Austrian Airlines and Uzbekistan Airways. On 31 October 1999, Airzena merged with Air Georgia under the new name of Airzena Georgian Airlines. The trading name of Georgian Airlines was adopted on 1 October 2004.

FLEET:
1 x B737-300, 1 x B737-400, 1 x B737-500, 1 x Yak-42D

FEATURES:
The red tailfin carries a white windrose, balanced against the red *Georgian Airlines* titles with a gray shadow above the cabin windows and the red cheatline below. The word *Airzena* set into the cheatline refers to the airline's full name. Red and white are the colors of the Georgian flag.

Germanwings (4U/GWI)

GERMANY (D)

Low-fare subsidiary of regional airline Eurowings operating scheduled services from its home base at Cologne Bonn Konrad Adenauer Airport and from Berlin Schönefeld, Dresden, Leipzig, and Munich to some 35 destinations throughout Europe. Internal German services are also flown. Germanwings was established in 2002 and began flying on 27 October that same year.

FLEET:
18 (3) x a319-100, 3 x a320-20

FEATURES:
The all-silver fuselage and leading edge of the tailfin offsets the dark red and yellow that colors the remainder of the fin and wraps around the rear of the aircraft. Small red *germanwings* lettering is set into the yellow field but scaled up on the cabin roof. Some aircraft are painted in special paint schemes, including "Spirit of T-Com," and "Spirit of Cologne."

Global Supply Systems (XH/GSS)

UNITED KINGDOM (G)

All-cargo carrier whose principal business is providing aircraft on long-term leases to other airlines on an aircraft, crew, maintenance, and insurance wet-lease basis. Its aircraft are fully occupied flying cargo for British Airways to Hong Kong, South Africa, and the United States. Global Supply Systems was set up in April 2001 and commenced operations on 29 June 2002 flying for British Airways between London Stansted, Frankfurt, and Hong Kong, using a single Boeing 747-400F leased from large minority shareholder Atlas Air.

FLEET:
1 X B747-200SF, 3 X B747-400F

FEATURES:
As its name implies, the main feature of this smart and clean livery is a stylized golden globe that is displayed prominently on the dark blue tailfin and in a commensurate smaller size in front of the blue *Global Supply Systems* title on the forward white fuselage. The paint scheme on the winglets is a reduced version of the tail. Matching blue engines help to add equilibrium to the design.

GOL Linhas Aéreas Inteligentes (G3/GLO)

BRAZIL (PP/PT)

Brazil's leading and fast-growing low-fare airline offering scheduled services from its home base at São Paulo Congonhas Airport to some 50 business and leisure destinations in Brazil and Argentina, with other high-value South American destinations planned to be added reguarly. A Mexican operation is also being set up. The airline was founded as GOL Transportes Aéreas in 2000 and started flying on 15 January 2001 to seven points in Brazil with Boeing 737-300s. The airline revolutionized low-cost travel in Brazil and the new title, meaning "the intelligent airline," reflects this rapid success.

FLEET:
8 X B737-300, 21 X B737-700, 8 (60) X B737-800

FEATURES:
The airline's attractive orange and silver gray corporate identity has stimulated its brand recognition. The silver shadow application of the O in GOL's name across the forward fuselage is repeated in large all-silver paint on the orange tailfin. The web address in both colors is printed along the cabin roof.

Golden Air (DC/GAO)

SWEDEN (SE)

Regional airline operating scheduled passenger and cargo flights to several destinations within Sweden and Finland, the latter flown in association with Finncomm Airlines. Its aircraft are also available for ad hoc and contract charters and air-taxi flights. Golden Air, based at Trollhättan in southern Sweden, was registered on 16 September 1976 and began operations with air-taxi and charter flights. It underwent several changes throughout its history until being restructured under the present ownership on 15 August 1993. It is now part of Thunbolaget, whose core businesses are in ship-owning and real estate.

FLEET:
7 x Saab 340A, 4 x Saab 340B, 4 x Saab 2000

FEATURES:
Four thin pencil lines graduating in color from a bright red to chocolate brown start from a point at the nose and widen out into graceful curves up the rear fuselage and tailfin of the aircraft. The four pencil lines are duplicated on the engine cowlings. Simple *Golden Air* titles, in golden yellow, of course, are applied above the forward cabin, with only the word *Golden* cut into the tailfin.

Great Lakes Airlines (ZK/GLA)

UNITED STATES (N)

u.s. regional airline operating domestic scheduled passenger services based on Denver and Chicago, serving more than 45 destinations. Its history goes back to the foundation on 15 April 1977 of Spirit Lake Airways, which undertook charter and flight training. A name change to Great Lakes Aviation on 25 October 1979 reflected its expansion in the Great Lakes region of northwest Iowa. Scheduled flights were started on 12 October 1981 between Spencer and Des Moines. For almost 10 years, the airline operated as a United Express carrier until being rebranded as an independent airline on 1 May 2001.

FLEET:
25 x Beech 1900D, 5 x EMB 120ER Brasilia

FEATURES:
The midnight blue tailfin is equalized by the similarly dark underside of the aircraft, which is separated from the white upper fuselage by a red cheatline. *Great Lakes* titles are painted on the cabin roof in a cursive font.

Gulf Air (GF/GFA)
BAHRAIN (A9C)/OMAN (A4O)

Bi-national flag-carrier of the Kingdom of Bahrain and the Sultanate of Oman, serving an international network centered on Abu Dhabi, Bahrain, Doha, and Muscat to destinations within the Middle East and to Africa, Asia, Australia, Europe, and the United States. Gulf Air was founded on 24 March 1950 by UK aviator Freddy Bosworth as Gulf Aviation Company and began operations with Avro Ansons on a local network on 5 July that year. The present name was adopted on 1 April 1974, when it became the national carrier of four Persian Gulf States. Qatar and Abu Dhabi have since pulled out.

FLEET:
10 X A320-200, 6 X A330-200, 10 X A340-300, 4 X B767-300ER

FEATURES:
The bold brand builds on the airline's strong geographic, historic, and rich cultural traditions, associated with energy, entrepreneurship, and professionalism, while putting Arab hospitality at the heart of its service. The focal point is the golden falcon, uniquely associated with Arabia, which spreads its enormous wings on the tailfin of the aircraft. The primary palette of gold, blue, and white suggests the rich colors of the Arabian Peninsula.

Gulf Traveller (GF)
BAHRAIN (A9C)/OMAN (A4O)

Low-fare, all-economy full-service airline division of Gulf Air connecting Abu Dhabi with destinations in Nepal, Pakistan, Bangladesh, India, and Sri Lanka, and with Kenya and Tanzania in East Africa. A service is also provided to Bahrain and Saudi Arabia. The division was established in May 2003 and began operations the following month. A new operational hub will most likely be established following the recent withdrawal of Abu Dhabi from Gulf Air.

FLEET:
6 X B767-300ER

FEATURES:
The Gulf Traveller aircraft use the same palette of gold, blue, and white as the parent company but in a different configuration, establishing the blue as the predominant color, rather than gold. The golden falcon, uniquely associated with Arabia, remains the focal point. The gold-edged blue continues over the rear upper and lower fuselage, ending in a razor point under the forward windows. *Gulf Traveller* titles in English and Arabic are displayed on the cabin roof.

Hainan Airlines (HU/CHH)

CHINA (B)

Independent airline operating scheduled services from Haikou on the island of Hainan and Ningbo on the Chinese mainland, from where its network takes in more than 40 major provincial cities. An international route to South Korea is also flown. The airline also has a business jet division known as Deer Jet, and has financial interests in Changan Airlines, China Xinhua Airlines, Shanxi Airlines, and Yangtse River Express. Hainan Airlines was founded in October 1989 as Hainan Tour and Aviation Services and began operations on 2 May 1993 under the present name using three Boeing 737s.

FLEET:
(8) x A319-100, 5 x B737-300, 7 x B737-400, 16 (10) x B737-800, 5 x B767-300ER, (8) x B787-8, 27 x FD 328JET

FEATURES:
The airline's well-known red and golden mythical-bird symbol dominates the blue tailfin and is also applied on the engines and forward of the airline name in Chinese characters. Blue *Hainan Airlines* titles cover the mid-fuselage roof. Some of the aircraft are painted with tropical trees and flowers spread across the lower fuselage.

Hamburg International (4R/HHI)

GERMANY (D)

German holiday airline operating passenger flights from Germany and Luxembourg under contract to European tour operators to destinations in Europe, Africa, and Asia, with European and Mediterranean resort areas served most frequently. Ad hoc and executive charters, as well as subservices, are also offered. Hamburg International was established in July 1998 and started operations on 28 April 1999 with a flight from Luxembourg to Heraklion on the island of Crete, using a single Boeing 737-700.

FLEET:
6 x B737-700

FEATURES:
The striated sun symbol in graduating colors from warm yellow to orange lights up the blue tailfin of the aircraft and forms the most noticeable element of the design. The only other color on the white aircraft are *Hamburg International* titles in blue and yellow. Aircraft operated by the airline's Chilean arm are slightly different, with the word *international* replaced by the word *Chile* in red script.

Hapag-Lloyd Express (X3/HLX)

GERMANY (D)

German low-fare airline providing scheduled passenger services from its key hubs of Cologne Bonn, Hanover, Hamburg, Berlin, Munich, and Stuttgart, some of which are also linked to each other. The network includes frequent schedules to close on 30 cities across nine European countries, including Germany, Austria, Croatia, France, Ireland, Italy, Spain, Sweden, Switzerland, and the UK. A subsidiary of the world's largest tour operator TUI, Hapag-Lloyd Express was founded in August 2002 and began operations on 3 December that same year.

FLEET:
5 X B737-500, 8 X B737-700, 2 X F100

FEATURES:
The airline's unusual but highly visible corporate identity, highlighted by yellow bordered by a black checkerboard pattern, was inspired by the famous New York cab, referencing its claim that throughout Europe its prices are cheaper than taking a taxi. The web address on the tail conveys the message that all flights can be booked online.

Hapagfly (Hapag-Lloyd Flug) (HF/HLF)

GERMANY (D)

Major German holiday airline providing scheduled passenger flights to some 40 leisure destinations around the Mediterranean, southern Atlantic coast, Madeira, and the Canary Islands, primarily for its parent company TUI, the world's leading travel group. Destinations are served from its main base at Hannover Langenhagen and another 15 German airports. The airline was established as Hapag-Lloyd Flug on 20 June 1972 as the air-charter arm of the Hapag-Lloyd shipping group and started flying in March 1973 with three Boeing 727-100s. It became part of TUI in 1997 and now trades as Hapagfly.

FLEET:
2 X A310-200, 2 X A310-300, 29 (10) X B737-800

FEATURES:
As part of brand harmonization, the Hapag-Lloyd aircraft are painted in sky blue, with the exception of the underside, and sport TUI's famous "smile" on the tailfin. The airline now trades as Hapagfly and this is reflected in the web address in white, which takes up the center of the upper fuselage.

Harbour Air Seaplanes (H3)

CANADA (C)

Seaplane operation in British Columbia providing a wide variety of scheduled and charter services out of Vancouver and Richmond. Scheduled flights serve Victoria, Nanaimo, and the Gulf Islands, while scenic flights offer trips to the fjords, alpine lakes and glaciers, the Khutzeymateen Valley, and other scenic locations. Fly 'n' drive packages and tailor-made charters are also offered. Harbour Air was founded in 1981 as Windoak Air Service, initially to provide charter services for the forest industry in British Columbia. Commercial charter flights and scheduled services were added later.

FLEET:
9 x DHC-2 Beaver I, 10 x DHC-3 Turbine Otter, 1 x DHC-6 Twin Otter 300

FEATURES:
The color scheme varies slightly between different aircraft but essentially comprises a bright yellow tailfin with blue edging and large blue intertwined HA initials. A blue cheatline with a narrow yellow edge runs the full length of the fuselage.

Harmony Airways (HQ/HMY)

CANADA (C)

Canadian full-service, low-fare scheduled airline providing direct flights from Vancouver, capital of Canada's western British Columbia province, to Toronto and to destinations in the western USA and the Hawaiian Islands. Through its sister tour operator, Companion Holidays, it also offers package tours, accommodation, and other ground arrangements. Harmony Airways was established in February 2000 as HMY Airways and operated its inaugural flight to Mazatlan in Mexico in November that same year. In May 2004, HMY Airways became Harmony Airways.

FLEET:
4 x B757-200

FEATURES:
Three streaks of yellow run across the gray tailfin, with the lower curving down to form an edge to the dark blue underside of the aircraft. Large Harmony titles traverse the forward fuselage, with smaller HMY Airways lettering above the cabin windows. The red and white Canadian flag with its national maple-leaf symbol is shown behind the cockpit.

Hawaiian Airlines (HA/HAL)

UNITED STATES (N)

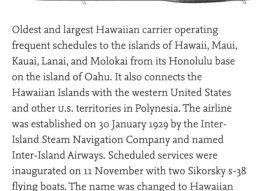

Oldest and largest Hawaiian carrier operating frequent schedules to the islands of Hawaii, Maui, Kauai, Lanai, and Molokai from its Honolulu base on the island of Oahu. It also connects the Hawaiian Islands with the western United States and other U.S. territories in Polynesia. The airline was established on 30 January 1929 by the Inter-Island Steam Navigation Company and named Inter-Island Airways. Scheduled services were inaugurated on 11 November with two Sikorsky S-38 flying boats. The name was changed to Hawaiian Airlines on 1 October 1941.

FLEET:
11 x B717-200, 14 x B767-300ER

FEATURES:
The traditional purple hues of the Pualani logo featured on the tailfin make for a striking scheme that is strongly representative of the colorful Hawaiian Islands. Pualani is an island woman with an orange flower in her hair set against the colors of the hibiscus flower. She has a persona of her own and reflects Hawaii's proud island heritage with a sense of grace, elegance, and caring. At the same time, her expression is seen to capture the strength, determination, spirit, and confidence of its people.

HeavyLift Cargo Airlines (HN/HVY)

AUSTRALIA (VH)

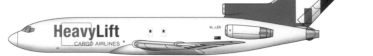

All-cargo operator providing a mix of scheduled and charter services out of a main base at Brisbane International Airport, specializing in the carriage of outsize cargo and dangerous goods. Scheduled services link Australia with Papua New Guinea, Vanuatu, and the Solomon Islands, while on-demand, urgent, and emergency charters are operated worldwide for governments, military agencies and contractors, mining companies, and freight forwarders. The airline was established in 2003 and began flight operations the following year.

FLEET:
2 x B727-100F, 1 x Shorts SC.5 Belfast

FEATURES:
This bold livery depicts a large white H, which divides the red and blue tailfin of the largely white aircraft. Equally prominent *HeavyLift* titles in the same blue and red are displayed on the forward fuselage, with smaller *Cargo Airlines* lettering in black underneath.

Helios Airways (ZU/HCY)

CYPRUS (5B)

Cypriot leisure airline operating scheduled passenger services from Larnaca and Paphos to 10 destinations in the United Kingdom, Ireland, Greece, Bulgaria, and Poland. Charter flights are also operated between Cyprus and the UK, Sweden, Norway, the Netherlands, and Egypt. Helios Airways was founded on 23 September 1998 and began operations with a charter flight to London Gatwick on 15 May 2000. Scheduled services were inaugurated in May 2001. The airline is now owned by the Libra Holidays Group.

FLEET:
1 x B737-300, 1 x B737-800

FEATURES:
The key element of the livery is a gold medallion of Helios, the young Greek god of the sun, after whom the airline was named. He is depicted on the blue tailfin set into concentric circles, with the color blue, alluding to sea and sky, also applied to the aircraft's engines. Each morning at dawn, Helios rises from the ocean in the east and rides in his chariot through the sky, to descend in the west at night. Prominent gold *Helios* titles on the forward fuselage reinforce the sun theme.

Hello (HW/FHE)

SWITZERLAND (HB)

Swiss charter airline serving the holiday destinations around the Mediterranean and the Canary Islands, together with the Red Sea resorts in Egypt. Flights are operated out of the airline's main base at Basel and from Geneva and Zürich. Hello also operates subservices for other airlines. Hello was registered by private interests in February 2004 and started flying on 6 August that same year, with its MD-90-30 initially operating for French charter airline Blue Line out of Paris Charles de Gaulle.

FLEET:
1 x MD-90-30, 1 x MD-90-30ER

FEATURES:
Blue and gold colors are welcoming and so is the airline's name, with which it wants to greet and serve its passengers in a friendly manner. Blue *Hello* titles with a yellow shadow are drawn in an exuberant style across the forward fuselage, with the flourish at the end representing an aircraft taking off. This is repeated in gold on the blue tailfin, which also incorporates the web address.

Helvetic Airways (2L/OAW)
SWITZERLAND (HB)

Swiss low-fare airline operating morning and evening scheduled flights radiating from Zürich to some 20 major European cities, with midday flights operated to leisure destinations, primarily in southern Spain. Helvetic Airways was first founded as Odette Airways in 2001 and began operations on 15 February 2002. A major restructuring in September 2003 resulted in the establishment of Helvetic Airways, which began operations under the new name on 28 November 2003 with a service from Zürich to Alicante on Spain's Costa Blanca.

FLEET:
6 x F100

FEATURES:
Helvetic certainly does not blend into the background and makes a strong statement. Its aircraft are painted in intense magenta, relieved only by *helvetic.com* titling on the forward fuselage and, in a smaller rendition, on the tailfin. The only other areas not in magenta are the wings, whose gray metal finish matches the internal anthracite seat fabric, which alternates with magenta.

Hemus Air (DU/HMS)
BULGARIA (LZ)

Bulgarian state airline providing scheduled passenger and cargo services from the capital Sofia to destinations in Europe, North Africa, and the Middle East, while tourist charters offer connections to the Bulgarian Black Sea and mountain resorts from Scandinavia, central and Eastern Europe, the Middle East, and North Africa. A domestic schedule serves Bourgas and Varna on the Black Sea. Other activities are air-ambulance flights and wet-leasing operations. Hemus Air began flying in 1986 as a division of then flag-carrier Balkan Bulgarian Airlines but became a separate legal entity in 1991.

FLEET:
2 x BAE 146-200, 1 x B737-400, 2 x TU-134A-3, 2 x TU-154M, 4 x Yak-40

FEATURES:
As a state-owned airline, Hemus Air uses the national colors of white, green, and red, respectively representing love of peace, products of the earth, and the people's courage. The green and red on the tail and rear fuselage are shaped to form an arrow, while the same colors create a ribbon, wrapped around the forward body of the aircraft. Green and red *Hemus Air* titles are accompanied by its web address in black.

Hewa Bora Airways (HBA) (EO/ALX)

CONGO, DEMOCRATIC REPUBLIC (9Q)

One of Congo's largest airlines operating scheduled flights to all major domestic points and also linking the capital Kinshasa with Belgium and South Africa. Charter flights are offered to destinations throughout the African continent and further afield. The airline was established in 1994 and began operations that same year under the name of Zaire Express. The name was soon changed to Zaire Airlines, and then to Congo Airlines after the successful rebellion in 1997, when Zaire became the Democratic Republic of Congo.

FLEET:
1 X B707-320C, 1 X B727-100F,
1 X B727-200, 2 X B727-200F,
1 X B737-200A, 1 X DC-9-50,
1 X L1011-500 Tristar

FEATURES:
The blue and gold colors of the national flag provide the basic palette for the airline's identity. Simple blue HBA intials edged in gold on the tailfin are backed by a blue field. A single gold and two blue pencil lines run down the tailfin and along the fuselage to the aircraft nose, supporting the airline name, which derives from the eastern part of the country. The six gold stars in the flag at the rear represent the original provinces of the former Zaire.

Hifly (LK/LXR)

PORTUGAL (CS)

Portuguese airline operating a network of services from Lisbon and Oporto to France, Madeira, Porto Santo, and further along the West African coast to Guinea-Bissau and São Tomé e Principe. Medium- and long-haul destinations are served on a regular charter basis, principal markets being Spain, France, Ireland, Austria, the UK, Thailand, Brazil, Cuba, the Dominican Republic, and United States. The airline was founded as Air Luxor on 14 December 1988 with small private and business aircraft. Airline operations with larger passenger aircraft were launched in 1997. The present name was adopted in October 2005.

FLEET:
3 X A320-200, 2 X A330-300

FEATURES:
Elegant two-tone blue features are set off against the white aircraft, highlighting an arc of sky blue stars on the dark blue tailfin and *Hifly* titles on the forward fuselage. The airline's web address can be found on the rear cabin roof, followed by the Portuguese and EU flags. Blue engines balance this attractive corporate image.

Hola Airlines (HOA)
SPAIN (EC)

Spanish charter airline operating from main bases at Madrid, Palma de Mallorca, and Tenerife South and serving all of Western Europe, as well as North Africa, including popular destinations in Morocco, Tunisia, and Egypt. VIP charters are also offered. Hola Airlines was established in early 2002 by Mario Hidalgo, a Spaniard who had previous experience with Air Europa, and began flying on 15 May that same year.

FLEET:
2 X B737-300, 1 X B757-200

FEATURES:
The Hola Airlines white aircraft are sparsely decorated, with only the airline name on the forward fuselage and five stars on the tailfin and after the name providing color. Both are rendered in dark green. The word *hola* means "hello" in Spanish and is intended to offer a warm welcome to its passengers.

Hongkong Express (UO/HKE)
HONG KONG (B-H)

Regional airline with a focus on business travelers, linking the Special Administrative Region of Hong Kong to a growing number of cities in mainland China. Hongkong Express is the fixed-wing jet operation of HeliExpress, which flies helicopter services between Hong Kong, Macau, and Shenzhen. Formerly known as Helicopters Hong Kong, founded in 1997, the operation of the regional jet airline was officially announced on 3 August 2005 and the inaugural service between Hong Kong and Guangzhou's New Baiyun International Airport was flown on 8 September 2005.

FLEET:
1 (3) X EMB 170LR

FEATURES:
The airline's x symbol is drawn in golden orange and blue with arrows pointing to the four corners, making a statement of the airline's intention to comprehensively serve the region. It is used in the *Express* part of the title on the forward fuselage and is spread across the bright blue tailfin in a lighter sky blue, with one half rendered in orange. Engines and winglets are also painted in blue, as are the Chinese characters of the name at the rear.

Hooters Air (H1)

UNITED STATES (N)

U.S. low-fare jet airline serving Myrtle Beach, a popular beach resort in Florida, from five major U.S. cities, and also flying scheduled services to Nassau on Paradise Island in the Bahamas. Charter flights and special golf packages are also offered. Hooters Air was established in early 2003 by Bob Brooks, founder of Hooters Inc., a franchise chain of over 375 beach-style restaurants in 46 U.S. states and abroad, after purchasing North Carolina-based charter carrier Pace Airlines in December 2002. Flight operations under the distinctive Hooters name started on 6 March 2003. Commercial flights ceased on 17 April 2006.

FLEET:
2 × B737-200A, 4 × B737-300, 1 × B757-200

FEATURES:
The livery uses the Hooters signature orange color, which fills the lower half of the aircraft and sweeps up the rear of the tailfin surmounted by a blue cheatline. Sitting on the fin is Hooters' company symbol of an owl, from where the name originates. Large orange *Hooters Air* titles cover a large part of the white upper fuselage. Both airline and restaurants have become famous for the presence of the attractive "Hooters Girls."

Horizon Air (QX/QXE)

UNITED STATES (N)

Seattle-based large U.S. regional airline and dominant regional carrier in the Pacific Northwest serving 45 destinations in the states of Washington, Oregon, Idaho, Montana, and California, as well as six points in British Columbia and Alberta in neighboring Canada. Horizon Air, part of the Alaska Air Group since 1986, was founded in May 1981 and began operations on 1 September that year with a service from Seattle to Yakima and Pasco in Washington state. It greatly extended its network with the purchase of Air Oregon in July 1982 and Transwestern Airlines of Utah in 1983.

FLEET:
19 (8) × CRJ700, 28 × Dash 8 Q200, 18 (12) × Dash 8 Q400

FEATURES:
An impression of a shimmering sun rises above the horizon on the tailfin, while prominent *Horizon* titles in italic script cut the straight-through cheatlines, the latter being repeated on the engine cowlings. The airline uses bright and dark red on a largely white aircraft.

Iberia (IB/IBE)
SPAIN (EC)

Spanish flag-carrier, providing international services to major European destinations and to Africa, the Middle East, Japan, and points in the Americas, with a strong emphasis on Spanish-speaking Central and South America. A domestic network is backed up by franchise partner Air Nostrum, operating as Iberia Regional. Iberia's history goes back to 28 June 1927 and the start of services on 14 December that year between Madrid and Barcelona with Rohrbach Roland tri-motors. It merged with CETA and UAE on 31 December 1928 as CLASSA, before being re-formed on 7 July 1940 under the present title.

FLEET:
(10) X A318, 7 (7) X A319-100, 60 (14) X A320-200, 13 (5) X A321-200, 18 X A340-300, 9 (4) X A340-600, 2 X B747-300, 2 X B747-400, 18 X B757-200, 21 X MD-87, 12 X MD-88

FEATURES:
A bright sunshine livery combines the red and gold of the national flag with an allusion to the country's holiday attractions. Triple cheatlines of red, orange, and gold sweep down from behind the cockpit and along the fuselage. A quartered IB logo in red and gold on the white tail carries a royal crown.

Iberia Regional (Air Nostrum) (YW/ANS)
SPAIN (EC)

Regional airline operating a dense network of services that cover all of Spain and extend to the Canary Islands, several European countries, and the exclave of Mellila on the North African coast. A total of 55 destinations are served from hubs at Madrid, Barcelona, and a main base at Valencia by Air Nostrum, operating under the Iberia Regional brand. Charter flights are also undertaken. Air Nostrum was established on 23 May 1994 and inaugurated services on 15 December that year with a Fokker 50 flight from Valencia to Bilbao. The franchise agreement with Iberia was signed in May 1997.

FLEET:
7 X ATR 72-500, 32 (19) X CRJ200ER, 19 X Dash 8 Q300

FEATURES:
Spain's major regional airline uses the Iberia sunshine colors, reflecting its franchise operation for the national airline. *Iberia Regional operado por Air Nostrum*, or simpler *Iberia Regional Air Nostrum* titles are painted on the forward fuselage. The red and blue *Air Nostrum* wording is preceded by the airline's symbol of a blue wing embracing a bright red sun.

Iberworld Airlines (TY/IWD)

SPAIN (EC)

Spanish charter airline serving resort areas in mainland Spain, Portugal, Madeira, the Balearic and Canary islands, as well as numerous points in Europe, from its main base at Palma de Mallorca. Long-haul flights from Madrid operate to popular destinations in Cuba, Mexico, and the Dominican Republic. Iberworld Airlines was founded in early April 1998 as a subsidiary of Grupo Iberostar, one of Spain's largest tourist enterprises with a history dating back more than 70 years. Operations started on 12 April with a flight from Palma de Mallorca to Bilbao using an Airbus A320.

FLEET:
6 x A320-200, 1 x A330-200, 1 (1) x A330-300

FEATURES:
The livery uses the Mediterranean blue and yellow sun colors of its parent company Iberostar. Prominent on the blue tailfin and engines is the company motif of a yellow star, modified to symbolize movement within a series of rings. A yellow straight-through windowline separates the upper and lower fuselage, with large blue *Iberworld* titles on the roof.

Ibex Airlines (FW/FRI)

JAPAN (JA)

Japanese regional airline operating a small network of domestic passenger and cargo schedules out of Osaka International Airport (Itami) and Tokyo Narita International. Flights out of Tokyo are operated as an ANA Connection service, operated in conjunction with All Nippon Airways (ANA), with which it has a wide-ranging cooperation agreement. The airline was established on 29 January 1999 and began operations as Fair Inc. on 7 August 2000, initially flying between its home base of Sendai and Osaka's Kansai International Airport. The change of name to Ibex Airlines was effected in October 2004.

FLEET:
2 x CRJ100ER, 2 x CRJ200ER

FEATURES:
The airline's name is set into a cerise band on the dark blue tailfin and repeated on the forward fuselage, with two-tone blue ANA Connection titling below the cabin windows, referring to its association with Japan's second-largest airline. Also of interest is the triple silver, sky blue, and cerise cheatline above the dark blue belly of the aircraft. This color spread is duplicated on the winglets of its regional jets.

Icelandair (FI/ICE)
ICELAND (TF)

Flag-carrier providing international scheduled flights between North America and Europe, taking in 18 cities in 13 countries. The airline uses Keflavik, rather than Reykjavik, as a hub, saving flying time across the Atlantic. The airline came into being on 1 August 1973 through the merger of Flugfélag Islands, whose history went back to the foundation of Flugfélag Akureyrar in Akureyri on the north coast on 3 June 1937, and the world's first truly low-cost transatlantic carrier Loftleidr, which was established on 10 March 1944. The name Icelandair has been in use since 1956. Charter and wet-lease services are operated by Loftleidir Icelandic.

FLEET:
11 X B757-200, 1 X B757-200PF, 2 X B757-200SF, 1 X B757-300, 1 X B767-300ER, (2) X B787-8

FEATURES:
The Discovery brand emphasizes five core values: learning, experience, internationalism, efficiency, and dynamism. The signature colors of bright gold and deep blue are said to be the colors of quality. The gold reflects the renowned warmth of the Icelandic people, while the blue alludes to the airline's international role. A stylized flowing F, standing for its Icelandic name, *Flugleidr*, rides the blue tail.

Iceland Express (AEU)
ICELAND (TF)

Iceland's first low-fare airline, offering daily scheduled services from the United Kingdom and Scandinavia to Iceland's capital Reykjavik. Several new destinations in Sweden, Germany, and Spain were due to be added in May 2006. Iceland Express was established in 2002 and started operations on 27 February 2003 linking Reykjavik to London Stansted and Copenhagen. It was previously known under the marketing name of Pro and is owned by investment company Fons Eignarhaldsfélag HF.

FLEET:
2 X MD-82

FEATURES:
The light green airline symbol of encircled double arrows is displayed in a large size across the tailfin where it is set into a mid-blue field. The gray web address above the cabin windows follows the airline name in blue. The symbol also appears on the blue aircraft engines.

Independence Air (DH/BLR)

UNITED STATES (N)

U.S. low-fare airline operating in the eastern half of the country, serving more than 40 points from its hub at Washington Dulles Airport, with cross-country connections to the West Coast. Frequent services are also available to resort areas in Florida. The airline's history goes back to 15 December 1989 when Atlantic Coast Airlines (ACA) began operating feeder routes as a United Express carrier, later also flying for a time as Delta Connection. The agreement with United was terminated in 2003 and ACA reinvented itself as a low-fare airline under the Independence Air name on 19 November that year. The airline ceased operations on 5 January 2006.

FLEET:
12 (16) x A319-100,
66 x CRJ200ER

FEATURES:
The two-tone blue *i*, being the first letter in the airline name and highlighting the independence angle, is set into a white disc on a light blue tail. Two interesting aspects of the scheme are the circular perforations at the rear, which provide a gradual transition from the blue of the fin to the white fuselage. The design is reinforced by the blue surrounds to the cabin windows. Blue *Independence Air* titling in a classic typeface graces the cabin roof, with the web address painted beneath the cockpit.

Indian Airlines (IC/IAC)

INDIA (VT)

Principal government-owned airline whose internal passenger network is one of the largest in the world, encompassing 45 towns and cities throughout India. The regional network serves 15 cities in Southeast Asia and the Persian Gulf. Some services are flown by low-fare subsidiary Alliance Air. Indian Airlines was set up as a state corporation on 28 May 1953 and on 1 August that year took over the operations of eight private companies including Airways (India), Bharat Airways, Himalayan Aviation, Kalinga Airlines, Indian National Airways, Deccan Airways, Air-India, and Air-Services of India.

FLEET:
3 x A300B4-200, 3 (16) x A319-100,
47 (4) x A320-200, (20) x
A321-200, 2 x Dornier 228-200

FEATURES:
The all-orange tailfin displays the airline's modern IA initials in white. Based on the "Golden Section" of Ancient Greece, the letter *I* and first stroke of the *A* have been italicized to suggest speed, further accentuated by truncating the first stroke, a device that also suggests the horizontal bar. The second stroke of the *A* is vertical to suggest reliability. *Indian Airlines* titling is worn on the starboard in English and on the port in Hindi script.

Inter Airlines (INX)
TURKEY (TC)

Antalya-based charter airline serving the Turkish holiday resorts around the cities of Antalya, Istanbul, Izmir, Bodrum, and Dalaman from some 20 cities in Germany and the Netherlands. Flights are operated for a number of specialist tour operators in all three countries. Inter Airlines was established in December 1999 and began operations on 4 April 2002.

FLEET:
2 X B737-800, 3 X F100

FEATURES:
Three swirls in the national colors of red and white combine to present the wings of a bird. This attractive design commands the blue tailfin, which is balanced by large blue *Inter* above smaller red *Airlines* titling across the forward fuselage. The red Turkish flag behind the aircraft registration at the rear dates from the time of the Ottomans and incorporates a white crescent moon and star, symbolic of Islam.

InterSky (3L/ISK)
AUSTRIA (OE)

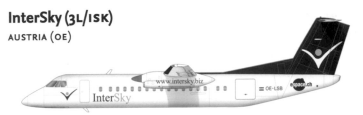

Austrian regional airline operating scheduled services out of Bern in Switzerland and Friedrichshafen in Germany, linking the Lake Constance/Rhein Valley area to various cities in Austria, Germany, northern Italy, and the Czech Republic. Charter flights are undertaken in summer to Corsica, Elba, and Mallorca, while winter ski flights bring tourists from northern Europe to the Austrian and Swiss mountains. InterSky was formed in November 2001 and began operations on 25 March 2002.

FLEET:
2 x Dash 8 Q300

FEATURES:
This smart blue and gold livery centers on the airline's symbol, which represents a check mark and golden sun, applied on the blue tailfin and the white forward fuselage. *InterSky* titling in the same color combination is painted on the lower forward fuselage, while the web address appears on the high-mounted engines.

IranAir (IR/IRA)
IRAN (EP)

Flag-carrier of Iran providing scheduled passenger and cargo services from the capital Tehran to 35 destinations within the Middle East, and to Europe, the Far East, and the Asian republics of the Commonwealth of Independent States. A domestic passenger and cargo network also links 20 towns and cities in Iran. The airline was established on 24 February 1962 as the Iran National Airlines Corporation as the successor to two privately owned carriers, Iranian Airways, which dated to May 1944, and Persian Air Services, which had been founded in 1954. The new national airline commenced operations in April 1962.

FLEET:
4 X A300B2-200, 4 X A300-600R,
6 X A310-200, 2 X A310-300,
4 X B727-200A, 1 X B747-100,
2 X B747-200C, 2 X 747SP, 9 X F100

FEATURES:
A deep blue line sweeps up the leading edge of the tailfin and flows around to fill the upper third, forming a dynamic and distinctive fin design. Below flies the homa, the mythical bird of ancient Persia, which symbolizes good fortune and great strength. *IranAir* titles are carried on the forward cabin roof.

Iran Air Tour (B9/IRB)
IRAN (EP)

Government-owned affiliate of IranAir operating scheduled domestic services from the holy city of Mashad and the capital Tehran to more than 15 towns and cities, together with charter flights to destinations in the Middle East and Europe. IranAir Tour was established in 1973 under the auspices of IranAir with the aim of expanding tourism to the country through charter flights, using aircraft from the parent company. Services stagnated after the 1979 Islamic Revolution and during the lengthy war with Iraq, but were restarted on 19 May 1992 out of Mashad with two leased Tupolev TU-154s.

FLEET:
6 X TU-154M

FEATURES:
The golden homa, the mythical bird of ancient Persia symbolizing great strength and good fortune, commands the striking cobalt blue tailfin. The blue sweeps down to the underside of the rear fuselage and contrasts sharply with the mostly white aircraft. A balancing effect is provided by the blue nose. Small *Iran Air Tour* titles are applied on the forward cabin roof, preceded by the green, white, and red national flag with its four red crescents and sword symbolizing the Islamic faith and strength.

215

Iran Aseman Airlines (EP/IRC)

IRAN (EP)

Government-owned carrier providing a mix of services from Tehran and Shiraz, ranging from domestic schedules and regional flights to air-taxi and charters and air-ambulance flights. The domestic network reaches more than 20 points, while regional schedules connect Tehran to the central Asian republics and the Persian Gulf. Iran Aseman was founded on 26 June 1980 by merging four established air transport companies: Air Taxi Co., whose history dated back to 1958; Air Service, founded in 1962; Pars Air, which had been in existence since 1969; and Hoor Asseman. The name was formerly written as Iran Asseman Airlines.

FLEET:
3 X ATR 72-210, 2 X ATR 72-500, 4 X B727-200A, 11 X F100, 2 X BN-2A Islander

FEATURES:
A stylized bird in flight with feathers splayed wide hovers in the blue sky, which is represented by four bands of blue graduating from light to dark. These cover the lower half of the tailfin and wrap around the rear fuselage. Small black titling and the national flag are applied above the forward cabin windows.

Iraqi Airways (IA/IAW)

IRAQ (YI)

National flag-carrier operating a limited domestic and regional service. Iraqi Airways was founded in December 1945 by the State Railways and inaugurated its first service on 29 January 1946 with a flight between Baghdad and Basra. International services followed on 14 June that year. The airline was largely inactive as a result of UN suspension of cross-border flights and the establishment of no-fly zones in the north and south of Iraq following the first Gulf War in 1991, a situation that persisted until well after the removal of the Baathist regime in 2003. Services recommenced in October 2004.

FLEET:
(5) X A310-300, 2 X B727-200A, 4 X B737-200A, 1 X B767-200ER

FEATURES:
The distinctive "dolphin style" livery, using the traditional green of Islam in two shades, sets the Iraqi aircraft apart. The fuselage roof is colored dark green and tapers at the "waist" before sweeping up to encompass the tailfin. A brighter green window-line runs straight through. Set into a white disc is a bird motif, believed to be of Mesopotamian origin. The airline tiles are applied in English on the starboard side and in Arabic on the port side of the aircraft.

Ishtar Airlines

IRAQ (YI)

Privately owned Iraqi airline that began operations in 2005 with a service between Baghdad and Dubai, with flights from Arbil and Basra inaugurated later. The new airline has applied for services to Frankfurt and London and also intends to add several new destinations in the Middle East. It was founded by a group of former Iraqi Airways pilots.

FLEET:
1 X B727-200A, 1 X B737-200QC

FEATURES:
This smart livery of gray and gold is notable for the unusual arrangement of the gold cheatline that divides the upper white fuselage and lower gray in a sweeping curve, which rises at the front and descends towards the rear of the aircraft. *Ishtar* titles sit on the tailfin above a flash of gold. The name derives from the Mesopotamian goddess Ishtar, the lunar goddess of light, also referred to as "the light of the world."

Island Air (WP/PRI)

UNITED STATES (N)

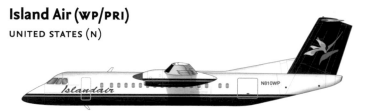

Hawaiian regional airline operating daily flights from its home base of Honolulu on Oahu to destinations on the Big Island of Hawaii, and the islands of Maui, Kauai, Molokai, and Lanai. Island Air was incorporated in 1980 by Colorado-based Consolidated Oil and Gas and began operations as Princeville Airways on 9 September that year with Twin Otters between Honolulu and Princeville. It was purchased by the Aloha AirGroup in May 1987 and renamed Aloha IslandAir but adopted the present name following its purchase from Aloha by Gavernie Holdings on 11 May 2004.

FLEET:
4 x Dash 8 100

FEATURES:
A beautiful bird-of-paradise flower in yellow, red, and blue adorns the dark blue tailfin, forming the central symbol of the color scheme. A magenta pencil line is set into the dark blue base of the aircraft and supports freely written *Islandair* titling in red. The attractive magenta and blue arrangement is reiterated at the base of the high-wing engines.

Island Aviation Services (Q2/DQA)
MALDIVES (8Q)

Government-owned carrier of the Maldives, an archipelago in the Indian Ocean formed by 1,190 low-lying coral islands stretching some 500 miles north to south. The airline operates scheduled domestic flights from the capital Male to four islands, including Gan, and is also responsible for ground handling, general sales, operation of the lounge at Male International Airport, and aerial photography, medical evacuation, and freight flights. Island Aviation Services was formed by presidential decree and commenced flying on 13 April 2000.

FLEET:
2 x Dornier 228-200, 1 x Dash 8 Q200

FEATURES:
The *i* for islands is set into a red sun disc, with the Muslim crescent forming the dot over the *i*, and the word *Island* applied low on the fuselage. The crescent has been borrowed from the Maldives flag, which is applied at the top of the fin. But the most interesting features are the two-tone blue waves of the Indian Ocean along the base of the aircraft, with fish and dolphins leaping from the water. The airline's web address is written forward.

Isles of Scilly Skybus (5Y/IOS)
UNITED KINGDOM (G)

Small regional airline operating year-round scheduled passenger and freight services linking Land's End on the UK mainland to the Scilly Isles, lying off the southwestern tip of the Cornish coast. The islands are also served from other west-coast points during the summer season. Isles of Scilly Skybus is an offshoot of the Isles of Scilly Steamship Company and was founded in July 1984. Operations began the following month.

FLEET:
3 x BN-2A Islander, 2 x DHC-6 Twin Otter 300

FEATURES:
The Twin Otter features the company colors of red and blue in the form of a waistband and on each side of the *Isles of Scilly* name on the lower part of the forward fuselage. The ensign of the Isles of Scilly Steamship Company is painted high on the tailfin, with red *Skybus* titles along the rudder. The Islanders are painted somewhat differently, but use the same colors in a sweep up the tailfin.

Israir Airlines (6H/ISR)

ISRAEL (4X)

Israeli domestic airline providing a scheduled passenger service between Tel Aviv and Eilat on the Red Sea, together with international charter flights from Tel Aviv's Ben Gurion and Dov Hoz airports to major destinations in Europe and the Mediterranean basin. VIP flights, cargo services, and a variety of tourism products, such as holiday packages, are also offered. Israir was first established in 1989 as Emek Wings and adopted the present title in 1996. International flights were started in 1999.

FLEET:
4 X ATR 42-300, 2 X B757-200, 1 X B767-300ER

FEATURES:
The six-pointed Star of David, drawn in a rather interesting "split" fashion, is scattered in varying sizes across the tailfin and rear fuselage, either on a plain white or blue tailfin, leaving no doubt about the airline's origin. Blue *Israir* titles in English are preceded by the orange star and the airline name in the Hebrew alphabet written from right to left.

Jagson Airlines (JA/JGN)

INDIA (VT)

Indian regional airline serving a number of towns and cities in the northern states of Himachal Pradesh and Rajasthan from New Delhi. Also operated is the Shri Amarnath Helicopter Service in Jammu and Kashmir providing a high-frequency round-trip service from Srinagar. Charter flights are available to destinations in India, Nepal, and Bhutan. Jagson Airlines was founded in November 1991 as the first private air-taxi service following domestic deregulation and began flying that same month. Its first scheduled helicopter service was inaugurated with a locally built HAL Chetak on 21 June 2005.

FLEET:
3 x Dornier 228-200, 1 x Hal (Aerospatiale SA 316B) Chetak

FEATURES:
The company colors of blue, red, and yellow start at the nose of the aircraft and run along the fuselage as narrow cheatlines, before widening out to entirely fill the tailfin. Set into the upper blue field are the winged initials VA. Red *Jagson Airlines* titles are cut into the cheatlines midway along the aircraft.

J-Air (JL)

JAPAN (JA)

Regional subsidiary of Japan Airlines operating feeder services for the parent company and scheduled passenger flights from Nagoya's Komaki Airport and Osaka Itami to 10 secondary cities. A longer connection is also flown to Sapporo on the northernmost island of Hokkaido. J-Air was established in early 1991 and began operations in April that year.

FLEET:
6 (2) X CRJ200ER

FEATURES:
The J-Air aircraft are painted in the full Japan Airlines livery with additional gray *J-Air* titles on the cabin roof. The livery is derived from the rising sun, one of the best-known icons of Japan and the focal point of the national flag. The red sun, which shades a large part of the tailfin of the aircraft, is set in a creamy parchment-colored background reminiscent of handmade Japanese paper.

JAL Express (JC/JEX)

JAPAN (JA)

Member of the Japan Airlines Group operating low-fare domestic services out of Osaka to some of Japan's major cities on the main islands and to Okinawa. JAL Express was formed on 1 April 1997 and began flying on 1 July 1998, initially serving Miyazaki and Kagoshima from Osaka with a fleet of two Boeing 737-400s. The network was quickly expanded with mainline routes transferred from the parent company.

FLEET:
8 X B737-400, 4 X MD-81

FEATURES:
As the low-fare arm of Japan Airlines, the JAL Express aircraft also carry the full markings of the parent company with additional gray *JAL Express* titles on the cabin roof.

JALways (JO/JAZ)
JAPAN (JA)

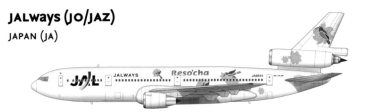

Subsidiary of Japan Airlines Group serving the leisure markets at home and in Southeast Asia and the Pacific. International destinations include Bangkok in Thailand and Honolulu and Kona in the Hawaiian Islands. It also undertakes wet-lease services for the parent company. JALways was established as a charter airline on 5 October 1990 under the name of Japan Air Charter and began operations in July 1991. The transformation into a scheduled leisure airline under the present name was completed on 1 October 1999.

FLEET:
2 X B747-300

FEATURES:
The JALways aircraft are bedecked with birds and tropical flowers, alluding to the airline's leisure business. As a subsidiary of Japan Airlines, the JAL initials appear across the forward fuselage, followed by small JALways titles.

Japan Air Commuter (3X/JAC)
JAPAN (JA)

Commuter airline providing feeder services for Japan Airlines Domestic into Kagoshima on Kyushu, the southernmost main island of Japan. Scheduled passenger and cargo services are operated from a number of islands in the Amami archipelago, together with charter flights. Japan Air Commuter was established on 1 July 1983 by Toa Domestic Airlines, later Japan Air System, and 14 municipalities in Kagoshima Prefecture. Operations started on 10 December 1985 with Dornier 228s to Amami Oshima, Tokunoshima, and Yorn Island.

FLEET:
6 (3) x Dash 8 Q400, 6 x NAMC YS-11A-500, 11 x Saab 340B

FEATURES:
The Japan Air Commuter aircraft carry the identical livery to those of Japan Airlines with additional *Japan Air Commuter* wording in gray on the fuselage.

Japan Airlines Domestic (JL/JLJ)

JAPAN (JA)

Japan's principal domestic carrier, combining the networks of Japan Airlines and Japan Air System (JAS). The extensive domestic route system covers high-frequency trunk routes between the major cities and connections to another 60 points on the main islands and smaller outlying islands. JAS was founded as Toa Domestic Airlines on 15 May 1971 from the merger of Japan Domestic Airlines, itself an amalgamation of feeder carriers Nitto Aviation, Fuji Airlines, and North Japan Airlines, and Toa Airways, founded on 30 November 1953. It was renamed Japan Air System on 1 April 1988.

FLEET:
3 × A300B2K, 1 × A300B4-200,
22 × A300-600R, 7 × B777-200,
2 × B777-300, 14 × MD-81,
8 × MD-87, 16 × MD-90-30

FEATURES:
The Landor-developed airline mark, made up of the initials JAL, is derived from the rising sun, one of the best-known icons of Japan and the focal point of the national flag, and reaches dynamically to the sky. It is reflected in the red sun, which shades a large part of the tailfin of the aircraft and is set in a creamy parchment-colored background reminiscent of handmade Japanese paper.

Japan Airlines International (JL/JAL)

JAPAN (JA)

Japan's biggest international airline providing passenger and cargo services worldwide from Tokyo and Osaka, serving 50 cities on all continents except Africa. Japan Airlines was founded on 1 August 1951 and began operations with a flight from Tokyo to Osaka using a Douglas DC-4. Japan Airlines System, now Japan Airlines Corporation, was created on 2 October 2002 with the merger of Japan Airlines and Japan Air System. Following full integration on 1 April 2004, operations were split into international and domestic businesses.

FLEET:
2 × B737-400, (30) × B737-800,
3 × B747-100, 4 × B747-200B,
10 × B747-200F, 11 × B747-300,
34 × B747-400, 8 × B747-400D,
2 × B747-400F, 3 × B767-200,
19 × B767-300, 18 × B767-300ER,
(3) × B767-300ERF, 8 × B777-200,
11 × B777-200ER, 5 × B777-300,
4 (4) × B777-300ER, (13) × B787-3,
(17) × B787-8, 4 × DC-10-40

FEATURES:
The color markings are identical for both domestic and international operations.

Japan Asia Airways (EG/JAA)

JAPAN (JA)

Subsidiary of the Japan Airlines Group, operating supplemental scheduled services for passengers and cargo to Hong Kong, Taipei, and Kaohsiung, together with charters throughout the Asia Pacific region. Services operate from hubs at Nagoya, Okinawa, Osaka, and Tokyo. Japan Asia Airways was founded on 8 August 1975, initially to take over, for political reasons, the parent company's routes to Taiwan, but has since expanded its activities to other areas in Asia.

FLEET:
4 X B747-200B, 1 X B747-300, 3 X B767-300

FEATURES:
The livery is dominated by the red sun, which shades a large part of the tailfin of the aircraft and is set in a creamy parchment-colored background reminiscent of handmade Japanese paper. It differs from that of Japan Airlines by using JAA initials instead of JAL on the forward fuselage. The full name is painted on the mid-cabin roof.

Japan TransOcean Air (NU/JTA)

JAPAN (JA)

Member of the Japan Airlines Group providing links to major cities on Japan's main islands from its base at Naha on Okinawa Island. Subsidiary Ryukyu Air Commuter provides feeder services from the smaller islands. Japan TransOcean Air was established on 20 June 1967 as Southwest Air Lines and began flying on 1 July that year, serving the Ryukyu archipelago. It adopted its present name in July 1993.

FLEET:
15 X B737-400

FEATURES:
A very similar livery to that of Japan Airlines, with the red sun shading a large part of the tailfin of the aircraft and set in a creamy parchment-colored background. However, the JAL initials on the forward fuselage are replaced by JTA initials, and the full *Japan TransOcean Air* titles are carried on the cabin roof in gray.

Jat Airways (JU/JAT)

SERBIA AND MONTENEGRO (YU)

National airline operating flag services from the capital Belgrade to domestic destinations and to points within Europe and the Middle East and North Africa. Charter flights are provided by subsidiary Air Yugoslavia. Jat also operates a flight academy and agricultural division. The airline was organized by the then Yugoslav government on 1 April 1947 as Jugoslovenski Aerotransport (JAT) to take over interim services that had been flown since November 1945 by the Yugoslav air force. Operations began with Junkers JU52/3MS and Douglas DC-3s over a domestic network and an international route to Warsaw.

FLEET:
(8) X A319-100, 4 X ATR 72-200, 2 X B727-200A, 7 X B737-300, 3 X B737-400, 4 X DC-9-32

FEATURES:
As the national carrier, Jat Airways uses the Pan-Slavic colors of red, blue, and white. The eye is drawn to the three large discs, two blue and one red, on the white tailfin, and to the large *Jat Airways* titles, also in blue and red, across the forward all-white fuselage. *Jat* is derived from the airline's original name of Jugoslovenski Aerotransport.

Jatayu Airlines (VJ/JTY)

INDONESIA (PK)

Regional airline linking the capital Jakarta with major cities on the main islands of Indonesia, and with the island of Penang in Malaysia. Principal domestic destinations are Banjarmasin, Balikpapan, Medan, Padang, and Pekanbaru. Jatayu Airlines (Jatayu Gelang Sejahtera) was established in 2000 and received its air operator's certificate in December that year.

FLEET:
9 X B727-200A, 1 X B737-200, 3 X B737-200A

FEATURES:
The name of the airline derives from Hindu mythology. Jatayu was the king of birds and steed of Vishnu and other gods, speedily traversing the skies. He is depicted with golden wings on the cerise tailfin, which extends down and around the rear of the aircraft. Prominent *Jatayu* titles are painted low across the forward fuselage.

Jazeera Airways (J9)

KUWAIT (9K)

First privately owned Kuwaiti no-frills airline, operating an expanding network of services from Kuwait City to destinations in the Persian Gulf, Syria, Lebanon, Jordan, Egypt, India, and Southeast Asia. It was established in early 2004 by the Boodai Group, an industrial conglomerate, but 70% of the shares are now held by institutional and public investors following a successful flotation in June 2004. The new airline began operations on 30 October 2005 with inaugural flights to Dubai, Damascus, Beirut, Amman, and Bahrain.

FLEET:
4 X A320-200

FEATURES:
This clean and unfussy scheme is based around a computer keyboard key, alluding to the airline's Internet-based ticketing. It is applied in sky blue on the tailfin of the white aircraft, with the airline name set into the key. The title is also painted on the forward fuselage in an artistic typeface in English and in Arabic. A similar design appears on the engines, and other splashes of sky blue feature on the winglets and the tail cone.

Jet Airways (9W/JAI)

INDIA (VT)

Largest privately owned Indian carrier, providing daily scheduled flights to more than 40 towns and cities from its main hub of Mumbai, and secondary bases at Bangalore, Delhi, Chennai, and Kolkata, giving the airline a large share of the domestic market. International flights have also been added to regional points and to London. Jet Airways came into being on 1 April 1992 and began operations on 5 May the following year, initially under air-taxi regulations. Scheduled airline status was granted in late 1994, after the repeal of the Air Corporations Act (1953).

FLEET:
2 X A340-300, 8 X ATR 72-500, 5 X B737-400, 13 X B737-700, 19 (10) X B737-800, 2 X B737-900, (10) X B777-300ER

FEATURES:
The golden sun with speed arrows on the royal blue tailfin is the highlight of the airline's identity, with this color combination maintained through the blue windowline, which separates the bare metal underside from the white upper fuselage and is underscored by a golden cheatline. The orange, white, and green Indian flag precedes blue *Jet Airways* titles.

Jetair (TUI Airlines Belgium) (TB/TUB)

BELGIUM (OO)

Belgian charter airline flying for tour operator TUI to all the holiday resort areas around the Mediterranean basin and the Canary Islands. Long-haul flights are also operated to Cuba, the Dominican Republic, Jamaica, and Mexico, as well as eastwards to Thailand. The airline was established on 13 November 2003 by the TUI Group following the demise of Sobelair, which had previously served the Belgian charter market. The first service was flown on 1 April 2004.

FLEET:
3 x B737-400, 2 x B737-800, 1 x B767-300ER

FEATURES:
In line with other airlines under the TUI Airline Management, the Jetair aircraft are painted in the "World of TUI colors," notable for the largely blue aircraft with its red "smile" on the tailfin. Large *Jetairfly* titles are painted across the forward fuselage.

JetBlue Airways (B6/JBU)

UNITED STATES (N)

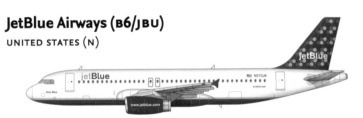

New York-based low-fare airline operating a continuously expanding network out of New York J.F. Kennedy International and Boston Logan International reaching from the West Coast right across America and down to Florida, Puerto Rico, the Bahamas, and the Dominican Republic. JetBlue was founded by David Neeleman, former head of Morris Air and WestJet, in February 1999 and started flying on 11 February 2000 with a service from New York to Fort Lauderdale using an Airbus A320. The airline has built up an enviable reputation for its service standards. It is the only all-ticketless airline in the U.S.

FLEET:
81 (102) x A320-200, 1 (99) x EMB 190AR

FEATURES:
The blue theme encompasses all aspects of the airline's identity. Several designs have been adopted for the tailfin, including champagne bubbles (illustrated), stripes, harlequin, windowpane, plaid, and fabric, all in shades of blue. The name is reversed out in white on the fin, and applied in silver and blue above the forward cabin windows. Aircraft carry names, all containing the word *blue*, examples being Blue Suede Shoes, Blue Sapphire, Mystic Blue, and many more.

Jetstar (JQ/JST)
AUSTRALIA (VH)

Low-fare subsidiary of Qantas Airways, Australia's principal airline, serving the leisure traveler with frequent services from Brisbane, Sydney, and Melbourne to 10 of the most popular resort areas such as the Gold Coast, the Whitsunday Coast, and Hamilton Island. Jetstar was formed in November 2003 out of regional carrier Impulse Airlines, which was operating under the QantasLink brand. Services were launched on 25 May 2004 with a fleet of 14 Boeing 717-200s. Associated Jetstar Asia provides low-fare services out of Singapore.

FLEET:
12 (11) x A320-200,
11 x B717-200, (10) x B787-8

FEATURES:
The solid black *Jet* name takes up almost all of the tailfin and is followed by a bright orange five-pointed star, applied equally prominently. A splash of orange colors part of the underside of the silver aircraft and, where appropriate, the aircraft winglets. The airline's web address, rather than its name, appears on the upper forward fuselage, with the words *All day, every day, low fares* beneath.

Jetx (GX/JXX)
ICELAND (TF)

Icelandic wet-lease operator flying scheduled and charter passenger services for a number of other airlines. Regular services to European destinations are flown out of Trieste, Olbia, and Farli Bologna in Italy. Jetx was founded in 2003 and obtained its air operator's certificate from the Icelandic Civil Aviation Administration on 5 May 2004. Operations began on 2 July 2004.

FLEET:
2 x MD-82

FEATURES:
The gray and gold scheme on the all-white aircraft has been executed in a smart fashion, with large *Jetx* titles across the forward fuselage balanced by the golden rays of a sun on the tailfin.

Jet2 (LS)
UNITED KINGDOM (G)

Low-fare passenger airline, serving more than 20 domestic and European destinations from its main base at Leeds Bradford Airport, and hubs at Manchester and Belfast International. Jet2 was established by Bournemouth-based freight carrier Channel Express (Air Services), which operates aircraft on its behalf. Operations commenced on 12 February 2003 with a service from Leeds Bradford to Amsterdam. Since then the network has expanded considerably.

FLEET:
14 X B737-300, 4 X B737-300QC, 1 X B737-400

FEATURES:
Red and white are the prime colors on the airline's silver aircraft, with the dominant feature being large red Jet titles followed by a white figure 2 over the forward fuselage. The web address is painted down the red tailfin and across the red engines.

Jordan Aviation (JAV)
JORDAN (JY)

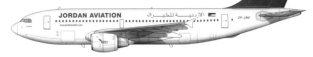

Privately owned airline operating charter flights from Amman's Queen Alia International and Aquaba airports, serving the tourist industry in Jordan, the Middle East, Africa, and Europe. Among its varied activities are inclusive-tour and ad hoc passenger charters, special events and student charters, general cargo and express parcels flights, courier services, executive VIP and air-taxi flights, and air-ambulance services. It also provides ACMI leasing services on behalf of other airlines during peak demand. Jordan Aviation was founded in 1998 and began operations in October 2000 with a Boeing 737-400.

FLEET:
1 X A310-200, 1 X A310-300, 1 X B727-200A, 1 X B737-200A, 1 X B737-300, 1 X L1011-500 Tristar

FEATURES:
Although the overall impression of the blue and white livery is positive, the amateurish blue and red aircraft logo encompassing the initials ATE and the words Jordan Aviation in a white disc on the blue tailfin detracts somewhat. The blue Jordan Aviation titles and web address above and below the forward cabin windows is followed by the name in Arabic and the Jordanian flag.

Kabo Air (QNK)
NIGERIA (5N)

Non-scheduled Nigerian airline providing regular flights between all major cities within the country and charter flights throughout Africa. It is also a participant in the annual Haj pilgrimage flights for Nigeria's Muslims to the holy shrines in Saudi Arabia. Other activities include special charter services for corporate bodies, executives, and government officials. Kabo Air was founded by the late Dan Kabo as the first indigenous private airline in February 1980 and began operations in April 1981 with a fleet of five Sud-Aviation Caravelle twin-jets.

FLEET:
2 X B747-100, 2 X B747-200B

FEATURES:
The two most salient aspects of the airline, the name of the founder Kabo and N for *Nigeria* are strongly promoted on its aircraft. The white N is set into a red disc and surrounded by a white circle on the charcoal tailfin of the otherwise white aircraft, while *Kabo* titling in red and charcoal stands out on the forward fuselage.

Kalitta Air (K4/CKS)
UNITED STATES (N)

Major U.S. charter airline operating scheduled and on-demand flights out of Willow Run Airport for customers in the United States and around the world. The airline's history dates back to 1967, when Connie Kalitta began transporting parts for the automotive industry with a twin-engine Cessna 310. The operation grew into a substantial airline, American International Airways, which was reformed into Kitty Hawk International in 1997. When Kitty Hawk closed down in April 2000, Connie Kalitta purchased the operating rights and set up Kalitta Air, restarting operations the following November.

FLEET:
3 X B727-200F, 5 X B747-100, 9 X B747-200F

FEATURES:
A triple cheatline of burnt sienna enclosing gold starts at a point below the nose of the aircraft and progresses straight along the fuselage before sweeping up and widening to take up most of the tailfin. Black *Kalitta Air* titling enclosed in black wings stretches across the mid-cabin roof.

Karat Air (v2/akt)
RUSSIAN FEDERATION (RA)

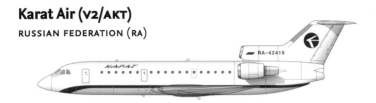

Scheduled airline operating passenger and cargo services from Moscow Vnukovo to several cities within Russia and to Baku in Azerbaijan. Charter flights are also undertaken, particularly from Kazan in the Tatarstan Republic, together with vip flights and other business aviation services. Karat Air was formed in 1993 as Rikor Airlines and in 2004 merged with Kazan-based Tulpar Aviation, with which it had established a strong alliance, to form the present Karat Air. Tulpar (the name means "winged steed" in the Tartarian language), had been founded in 1991 by a team of aviation specialists.

FLEET:
4 x AN-24RV, 6 x TU-134A-3, 3 x TU-154B-2, 4 x Yak-40, 1 x Yak-40K, 10 x Yak-42D

FEATURES:
As with most Russian airlines, color schemes vary widely between different aircraft, but the cleanest arrangement is that illustrated, which shows a white arrow in a red disc on the white aircraft tailfin, with the word *Karat* written largely in blue on the forward fuselage in the Cyrillic alphabet. The name has been given prominence by the transformation of part of the initial letter к into a red arrow, matching the tailfin design.

Karthago Airlines (5R/KAJ)
TUNISIA (TS)

Private Tunisian charter airline operating from the main Tunisian cities of Tunis, Djerba, and Monastir to points in Europe. Karthago Airlines was established in January 2002 by the Karthago Group, which also runs hotels and tourist services, and other tour-operating companies. It began flying in March that same year with a single Boeing 737-300.

FLEET:
4 x B737-300

FEATURES:
The tailfin and rear fuselage are colored by one blue and two orange bands, with a beautifully stylized bird, drawn in the same colors, flying on the white field in between. *Karthago Airlines* titles are applied on the cabin roof in English and Arabic, followed at the rear by the Tunisian flag. The airline takes its name from the Phoenician city whose ruins on the outskirts of Tunis are of major archaeological and touristic interest.

κD-Avia (Kaliningradavia) (κD/κNI)
RUSSIAN FEDERATION (RA)

Russian scheduled and charter carrier based at
Kaliningrad, a Russian exclave sandwiched between
Poland and Lithuania. Scheduled passenger and
cargo services link the city with Moscow, St.
Petersburg, and other points in Russia, and with
Kiev in the Ukraine. The airline was first established
on 8 October 1945 as part of Aeroflot's Belarussian
Civil Aviation Directorate Kaliningrad Detachment
following the ceding of Königsberg, as it was then
known, to Russia, and began operations in 1946. It
later became known as Kaliningradavia and
changed to the present identity in 2005 to
distinguish itself from the airport operator.

FLEET:
4 x B737-300, 4 x TU-134A,
3 x TU-134A-3, 2 x TU-154M

FEATURES:
Superimposed on the white
aircraft is an unusual purple paint
scheme that itself represents the
shape of an aircraft. Set into the
purple are gold κD initials on the
mid-fuselage and a delta-wing
taking off on the tailfin.

Kenn Borek Air (4K/KBA)
CANADA (C)

Highly diversified Canadian operator providing
scheduled passenger and cargo services, domestic
and international charter flights, contracts in
support of exploration companies and for UN peace-
keeping missions, aircraft leasing and maintenance,
and overhaul services from several bases in the
Northwest Territories, British Columbia, and
Alberta. Kenn Borek is also a specialist in Arctic and
Antarctic support for scientific research. Founded as
a subsidiary of Borek Construction, the airline
began operations in 1970, initially providing air
support for oil exploration.

FLEET:
1 x Beech 99, 2 x Beech B99,
1 x DC-3 Super, 12 x DHC-6 Twin
Otter 300, 1 x EMB 110P1
Bandeirante + smaller Beechcraft

FEATURES:
The aircraft are painted mostly in
terracotta red, with a black
lightning flash separating the red
from the lower snow white
underside. The red and black
scheme is carried over to the
engines. Black *Kenn Borek Air Ltd*
titling is applied at the rear, with
the registration (unusually) at
mid-level on the black-edged
tailfin. The Canadian flag is
painted at the top of the fin.

Kenya Airways (KQ/KQA)
KENYA (5Y)

Flag-carrier operating regional services within Africa, together with schedules from Nairobi and Mombasa to Europe, the Middle East, the Indian subcontinent, and Asia. Long-haul connections are available at Amsterdam through its associate KLM, which has a 26% stake in the airline. Domestic routes serve all major towns including the popular tourist areas. Kenya Airways was established by the Kenyan government on 22 January 1977 following the collapse of the tripartite East African Airways Corporation. Operations began on 4 February from London to Nairobi with leased Boeing 707s.

FLEET:
2 x B737-200A, 1 x B737-200QC, 4 x B737-300, 4 x B737-700, 5 x B767-300ER, 3 x B777-200ER, 2 x Saab 340B

FEATURES:
The livery uses the national colors in a dramatic design on the tailfin with red and green flowing down to the belly of the aircraft. Attendant strips of white split the bright colors to form artistic bands. The letter K is also a key feature on the red engines. *Kenya Airways* and *The Pride of Africa* slogan in a lively font are preceded by the flag, which includes a Masai shield and two spears symbolizing the defense of freedom.

Kibris Türk Hava Yollari (Cyprus Turkish Airlines) (YK/KYV)
NORTHERN CYPRUS (TC)

National airline of the largely unrecognized Turkish Republic of Northern Cyprus, operating scheduled and charter passenger services from Nicosia to points in Europe, with an emphasis on Germany and the United Kingdom. All flights operate via the Turkish mainland. The airline was established on 4 December 1974 and operated its first scheduled flight on 3 February 1975. Originally partially owned by Turkish Airlines, its shares were transferred to the Ministry of Privatization on 1 April 2003.

FLEET:
2 x A310-200, 1 x A321-200, 3 x B737-800

FEATURES:
The centerpiece of the livery is an intriguing flowing and interlinked design in bright green and orange set into a white disc on the dark blue tailfin. Large blue KTHY lettering covers most of the forward fuselage, followed by the airline's English equivalent *Cyprus Turkish Airlines* titling. Aircraft are named after towns in Northern Cyprus.

Kingfisher Airlines (IT/KFR)

INDIA (VT)

One of India's newest low-fare airlines, which made its inaugural flight on 7 May 2005, followed by the first commercial flight two days later with an Airbus A320 between Mumbai and Delhi. The network has since been expanded to take in more than 20 destinations across the length and breadth of the country from bases at Mumbai's Chhatrapati Shivaji Airport and at Bangalore. Kingfisher Airlines was established in summer 2004 by United Breweries, a diversified group best known around the world for its branded Kingfisher lager.

FLEET:
(4) x A319-100, 6 (8) x A320-200, (5) x A380-800, (20) x ATR 72-500

FEATURES:
The Kingfisher "Funliners" are unmistakably linked to the parent company's premium lager brand, with its colorful kingfisher motif strikingly displayed on the red tailfin and red engines. The *Kingfisher* name in red covers most of the central part of the aircraft. The underside of the aircraft is red, as are the engines and winglets. The orange, white, and green Indian flag is painted at roof level towards the rear.

Kinshasa Airways (KNS)

DEMOCRATIC REPUBLIC OF CONGO (9Q)

One of the Congo's main charter airlines, operating throughout Africa from its principal base at the capital Kinshasa, from which it takes its name, and in the Middle East from a secondary base at Sharjah International Airport in the United Arab Emirates. Both passenger and cargo charter flights are undertaken. The airline was established in 2002.

FLEET:
1 x B707-320B, 1 x B707-320C, 1 x B727-200A, 1 x B747SP, 2 x DC-8-55JT

FEATURES:
A beautifully stylized flower in two shades of blue that grows out of the dark blue tailfin is the central element in this elegant design. The two-tone blue theme is repeated in the dark blue *Kinshasa* titles in English and Arabic on the cabin roof and the slogan *Spirit of Congo* underneath the flower.

Kish Air (Y9/IRK)
IRAN (EP)

Iranian scheduled and charter carrier linking Kish Island with several major domestic points, and with neighboring Bahrain and Dubai across the Gulf. Seasonal services are also flown to Cyprus and Turkey. The airline was established on 16 December 1989 by the Kish Free Zone Organization and obtained its air operator's certificate in 1990. Operations began with leased aircraft.

FLEET:
2 x Iran-140, 6 x F50, 1 x MD-82, 1 x MD-83, 2 x TU-154M

FEATURES:
The highlight of the livery is the eye-catching design on the dark blue tailfin, where a golden sun rises above earth and sea, expertly modeled into the shape of a bird. Colorful *Kish Air* titling in red, blue, gold, and green brightens up the white fuselage, which also contains the Iranian flag. The blue engines balance the design.

Kitty Hawk Aircargo (KR/KHC)
UNITED STATES (N)

All-cargo operator providing a domestic overnight express freight service from its sortation hub in Fort Wayne, Indiana. Apart from general cargo, the airline also provides transportation of oversize products and equipment, live animals, and dangerous goods. Capacity for a number of customers through ACMI wet leases is another part of its business. The carrier was founded in 1976 by Tom Christopher as Kitty Hawk Airways. Various mergers and acquisitions eventually led the owner to file for bankruptcy protection on 1 May 2000, from which it emerged on 31 August 2002.

FLEET:
19 x B727-200F, 7 x B737-300SF

FEATURES:
A simple blue and white design uses two blue ribbons across the *Kitty Hawk Aircargo* titles along mid-fuselage and a bold blue tailfin with large KHA initials inset in white. The airline's web address is shown on the center engine above the U.S. flag.

KLM Royal Dutch Airlines (KL/KLM)

NETHERLANDS (PH)

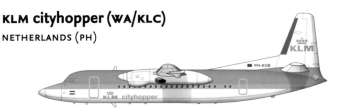

Dutch flag-carrier and one of the oldest operating airlines in the world, serving an extensive European and long-haul network of passenger and cargo flights from Amsterdam to more than 150 cities on all continents. The domestic and European network is further extended through subsidiary KLM cityhopper. The airline was incorporated on 7 October 1919 as Koninklijke Luchtvaart Maatschappij (KLM) and operated its first service from Croydon to Amsterdam with a de Havilland DH.16 on 17 May 1920. It merged with Air France in May 2004 but retains its own brand. Member of the SkyTeam Alliance.

FLEET:
1 (7) X A330-200, 14 X B737-300,
13 X B737-400, 14 X B737-800,
5 X B737-900, 5 X B747-400,
17 X B747-400M, 3 X B747-400ERF,
11 X B767-300ER,
10 (4) X B777-200ER, 10 X MD-11

FEATURES:
A deep blue cheatline divides the gray underside of the aircraft and the light blue cabin roof above. The KLM logotype, topped by a royal crown, is painted in light blue on the white tailfin and also appears in white on the forward cabin roof. Cargo aircraft carry additional *Cargo* titles in a stenciled format.

KLM cityhopper (WA/KLC)

NETHERLANDS (PH)

Regional subsidiary of KLM Royal Dutch Airlines, providing passenger and cargo services from Amsterdam to some 40 destinations across Europe. Charter flights and special package deals are also available. KLM cityhopper was established in April 1991 through the merger of NLM CityHopper and Netherlines. NLM's history went back to August 1966 when it started operating two scheduled domestic routes. Netherlines was founded on 1 February 1984 and started scheduled flights on 8 January 1985. The operations of KLM UK, formerly Air UK, were integrated into KLM cityhopper in November 2002.

FLEET:
14 X F50, 21 X F70, 16 X F100

FEATURES:
Aircraft carry the KLM livery with additional *cityhopper* titles in blue below the gray windowline that divides the white underside of the aircraft and the light blue cabin roof above. The KLM logotype, topped by a royal crown, is painted in light blue on the all-white tailfin.

KMV (Kavminvodyavia) (KV/MVD)

RUSSIAN FEDERATION (RA)

Major Russian carrier operating a large network of scheduled passenger and cargo services to some 50 domestic and CIS destinations from Mineralnye Vody, the largest city in southern Russia and gateway to famous mineral springs with curative properties, and the Caucasus Mountains ski resorts. International flights extend to Bulgaria, Germany, Greece, Syria, Israel, Turkey, and the United Arab Emirates. The airline was established on 2 June 1962 as the North Caucasian CAD/Mineralnye Vody Civil Aviation Production Association. It was re-organized under the present name in August 1995.

FLEET:
5 x TU-134A-3, 10 x TU-154B-2, 3 x TU-154M, 2 (1) x TU-204-100, (2) x TU-234

FEATURES:
The huge red KMV initials taking up almost the full height of the fuselage are unmistakable and can be read from a great distance. The airline's full title, however, is applied in comparatively small lettering in Cyrillic script only. The mid-blue tailfin incorporates a golden eagle motif, with the Russian flag painted alongside the rudder. A blue windowline and narrower cheatline below run along the length of the aircraft.

Kolavia (Kogalymavia) (7K/KGL)

RUSSIAN FEDERATION (RA)

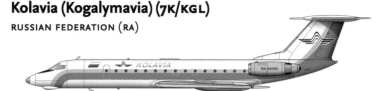

Diverse Russian airline operating domestic passenger schedules serving a number of communities in the oil-rich Tyumen region in western Siberia and providing links to cities in other parts of the country. International charter flights are also undertaken to points in Africa, Europe, and Asia from bases at Kogalym (from which the airline takes its name), Surgut, and Moscow Domodedovo. Among other activities are maintenance services at Surgut, aviation consultancy, fuel monitoring at Russian airports, and ground handling. The airline started operations in May 1993.

FLEET:
6 x MI-8T, 3 x MI-17, 6 x TU-134A-3, 2 x TU-154B-2, 4 x TU-154M

FEATURES:
Broad cheatlines in three shades of blue below a snow white roof are the dominant feature of this attractive scheme. Starting under the chin of the aircraft, the cheatlines run along the mid-fuselage before reaching up to cover two-thirds of the tailfin, which also displays the airline's triple-wing symbol in black and white. Blue *Kolavia* titles with the wing symbol are applied in English on the port side and Cyrillic on the starboard side.

Korean Air (KE/KAL)
SOUTH KOREA (HL)

Privately owned flag-carrier maintaining an extensive schedule of international passenger services to more than 80 destinations regionally, and in Europe, North and South America, the Middle East, Africa, Australia, and New Zealand. The airline also provides international all-cargo services and domestic flights. It was founded in June 1962 when the government took control of Korean National Airlines, which had been organized by Captain Yong Wook Shinn in 1945, but came under the control of the Ministry of Defence in June 1950. The Hanjin Group took over on 1 March 1969. Member of the SkyTeam Alliance.

FLEET:
10 X A300-600R, 3 X A330-200,
16 X A330-300, (5) X A380-800,
14 X B737-800, 15 X B737-900,
2 X B747-200F, 1 X B747-300SF,
23 X B747-400, 10 X B747-400F,
1 X B747-400M, 5 (3) X B747-400ERF, 18 X B777-200ER,
4 X B777-300, (10) X B787-8

FEATURES:
A pale shade of sky blue colors the entire upper fuselage and tail unit, below which runs a silver cheatline, representing the sea. The *Taeguk* symbol combines the red yin and blue yang symbols representing the opposing forces of nature, in this case heaven and earth, with white to show "endless strength of progress."

KrasAir (Krasnoyarsk Airlines) (7B/KJC)
RUSSIAN FEDERATION (RA)

One of Russia's leading airlines operating a network of scheduled services from Krasnoyarsk in Siberia to more than 20 major cities in Russia, with regional flights extending to capital cities of several former Soviet republics. The airline is the official carrier between Russia and Germany, South Korea, and China. A seasonal charter program serves resorts in the Mediterranean basin. KrasAir was established in 1993, although its history dates back to 1982 when the Krasnoyarsk United Aviation Wing, which under various guises dated back to 11 May 1934, was re-structured into the present organization.

FLEET:
(15) X AN-148-100,
2 X B767-200ER, 2 X IL-76T,
2 X IL-76TD, 6 X IL-86,
1 X IL-96-300, 1 X TU-154B-1,
5 X TU-154B-2, 12 X TU-154M,
3 X TU-204-100, 2 X Yak-42D

FEATURES:
This airline has a large variety of color schemes, especially on its older aircraft, but the most modern application is a simple wing symbol in three shades of blue and turquoise on the tailfin of the all-white aircraft and blue *KrasAir* titling on the forward roof. The Russian flag is painted at the rear.

Kuban Airlines (GW/KIL)

RUSSIAN FEDERATION (RA)

Domestic and international passenger and cargo airline, linking its main base of Krasnodar on the western edge of the Caucasus to other major Russian cities and to Germany, Armenia, and Uzbekistan. Regular charter flights are also operated to Europe, in particular to several German cities, and to points in Asia. Other activities include the operation of its home airport of Krasnodar, and nearby Gelendzik on the Black Sea, and aviation engineering. Founded in 1932 as a division of Aeroflot, it later operated as Krasnodaravia, before adopting the present title. It was partially privatized in 1992.

FLEET:
1 x AN-24V, 2 x AN-26,
2 x TU-154B-2, 2 x TU-154M,
6 x Yak-42, 5 x Yak-42D

FEATURES:
A white crane in a blue disc on the tailfin is the main feature on the largely white aircraft, with blue *Kuban Airlines* titling and the Russian flag on the forward roof. The initials ALK, standing for the Russian name of Aviatsionnye linii Kubani, are set into the blue cheatline in the Russian colors of white, blue, and red. The name of the airline is derived from the Kuban River, which flows through its home city and thence into the Black Sea.

Kulula.com (MN/CAW)

SOUTH AFRICA (ZS)

Low-fare carrier set up in July 2001 by long-established Comair as a low-cost alternative. Operations started on 1 August 2001 with three daily flights between Johannesburg and Cape Town. Frequent services now link the five largest cities in South Africa, including the "Golden Triangle" between Johannesburg, Durban, and Cape Town. All flights can be booked on the Internet. A hire-car service is also offered, and on 1 November 2004 the airline introduced experience and adventure packages, such as shark-cage diving.

FLEET:
2 x B737-200A, 1 x B737-400,
6 x MD-82

FEATURES:
A striking bright green fuselage with white and blue highlights at the nose and tail of the aircraft differentiates this airline from others in the country, greatly aiding recognition. Bold *kulula.com* titles in blue are set into the front half of the fuselage ahead of the wings.

Kuwait Airways (KU/KAC)

KUWAIT (9K)

National carrier of the Persian Gulf State of Kuwait operating scheduled passenger and cargo services predominantly throughout the Middle East and to Europe, with some services extending to the Far East and the United States. The airline was founded in March 1954 by private interests as Kuwait National Airways and began operations on 16 March between Kuwait and Iraq with one Douglas DC-3 operated and maintained by BOAC. The government acquired a half share in the struggling carrier and renamed it in June 1958, before taking full control on 1 June 1963.

FLEET:
5 X A300-600R, 3 X A310-300, 3 X A320-200, 4 X A340-300, 2 X B747-200C, 1 X B747-400M, 2 X B777-200ER

FEATURES:
The black bird symbol flies reversed out in white on the largely blue tail band trimmed in black and darker blue. *Kuwait Airways* titles are applied in blue on the cabin roof, in both English and Arabic, and are repeated at the base of the tailfin in English only. The national flag, whose colors of green, white, red, and black attest to Kuwait's membership of the Arab world, appears on top of the fin.

Kuzu Airlines Cargo (GO/KZU)

TURKEY (TC)

Istanbul-based all-cargo airline operating scheduled flights from Atatürk Airport to a number of commercial centers in Europe and the Middle East, which are used as transit points for interline air traffic to other parts of the world, and extensive road-trucking services. The airline also offers full charters for all types of cargo, together with wet-lease services. Kuzu Airlines Cargo was established in January 2004 by the Kuzu Construction Group and started operations in June that year under the name of Baron Hava Cargo. The airline was rebranded under the present title in October 2004.

FLEET:
2 X A300B4-100F, 1 X A300B4-200F

FEATURES:
The white aircraft are adorned with large blue *Kuzu Cargo* titles over a red flash covering a large part of the fuselage, the airline's motif of a blue K set into white and blue boxes stressing its cargo business. The motif is applied on the tailfin and the aircraft engines.

Kyrgyzstan Airlines (R8/KGA)
KYRGYZSTAN (EX)

National carrier operating a small network of services to destinations in Russia, other Asian CIS republics, Europe, the Indian subcontinent, and the Middle East. A domestic route system also links the capital Bishkek with five other towns on a scheduled basis and more with regular charter flights. The airline is also responsible for aerial work, air-ambulance flights, and search-and-rescue operations with fixed-wing aircraft and helicopters. Kyrgyzstan Airlines was established by presidential decree on 29 December 1992, based on the former Aeroflot directorate.

FLEET:
1 X AN-28, 1 X IL-76T, 5 X MI-8T, 2 X TU-134A-3, 4 X TU-154B-1, 4 X TU-154B-2, 1 X TU-154M, 8 x Yak-40

FEATURES:
The blue tailfin and red band narrow into a sharp speed arrow, with the blue bird symbol set into the fin. The airline's local name, *Kyrgyzstan Aba Zoldoru* in Cyrillic script takes up most of the fuselage roof. The red flag incorporates a stylized representation of the roof of a Kyrgyz yurt (tent) surrounded by 40 rays of a golden sun.

LAB–Lloyd Aéreo Boliviano (LB/LLB)
BOLIVIA (CP)

Bolivian flag-carrier operating scheduled services from La Paz and Santa Cruz de la Sierra to some 20 destinations throughout Central and South America, together with extensions to Miami and Washington, D.C., in the United States. A transatlantic route links La Paz with Madrid in Spain. A comprehensive domestic network reaches all the main centers of population. One of the oldest airlines in South America, LAB was founded on 15 September 1925 by a group of German residents and began commercial operations on 23 September with a service between Cochabamba and Santa Cruz with a Junkers F 13.

FLEET:
1 X B727-100, 8 X B727-200A, 1 X B727-200F, 1 X B737-300, 2 X B767-300ER

FEATURES:
The mid-blue color on the tailfin and the huge LAB lettering on the fuselage is said to represent stability and consistency, alluding to the airline's long and unbroken history. A contrasting tone of orange and coral has been added to some aircraft, representing warmth and congeniality. The airline symbol includes the condor, the world's largest bird of prey, which soars high over the Andes of South America.

LADE–Lineas Aéreas del Estado (5U/LDE)

ARGENTINA (LV)

Public-service airline operated by the Argentine air force, providing a vital passenger and cargo service to some 30 communities, mostly in the provinces of Patagonia and Buenos Aires. It was founded in July 1940 as LASO (Lineas Aéreas del Sudoeste) and began operations on 4 September that year between Palomar and Esquel with intermediate stopovers, using a three-engined Junkers JU 52/3M. Another branch, LANE (Lineas Aéreas del Noreste), started on 6 January 1944 serving the Iguaçú Falls from Buenos Aires. The two branches were amalgamated under the LADE name on 23 October 1944.

FLEET:
1 X B707-320C, 10 X DHC-6 Twin Otter 200, 1 X F27-500, 2 X F28-1000C, 1 X L100-30 Hercules

FEATURES:
LADE's aircraft carry basic Argentine air force (Fuerza Aérea Argentina) markings, together with the brigade operating the public-service flights. At the rear is the air-force roundel, and on the tailfin the blue and white Argentine flag with the golden "Sun of May." A black cheatline separates the gray underside from the white upper fuselage, which also carries titles in black.

LAI–Linea Aérea IAACA (KG/BNX)

VENEZUELA (YV)

Regional airline providing scheduled connections between its base in Venezuela's southwestern state of Barinas and nine other major cities. Charter flights are also operated. The airline's history goes back to 1954 and the foundation of Industría Aérea Agricola CA (IAACA), which specialized in agricultural spraying and evolved to become the largest air-taxi operation in Venezuela. Following deregulation of the domestic market, IAACA was transformed into a scheduled airline in 1995.

FLEET:
2 X ATR 72-210

FEATURES:
The airline's initials in black with a white outline are superimposed on an orange sun on the sage green tailfin of its aircraft. The same design is prominently displayed behind the cockpit, partially set into the two-tone green cheatlines above the sage green belly. The full airline title is written in a cursive style on the forward upper roof.

LAM–Linhas Aéreas de Moçambique (TM/LAM)
MOZAMBIQUE (C9)

National airline operating scheduled passenger and cargo services to points in southern Africa, with a northward extension to Portugal. A domestic network is also flown. The airline was established by the colonial government of Mozambique in 1936 as a division of the Department of Railways, Harbors, and Airways under the title of Direcçao de Exploraçao dos Transportes Aéreos (DETA). Operations began on 22 December 1937 with a mail service between Lourenço Marques (now Maputo) and Johannesburg with de Havilland biplanes. The present title was adopted on 19 November 1980.

FLEET:
4 X B737-200A, 1 X EMB-120ER Brasilia

FEATURES:
Dramatic black and red LAM initials, followed by smaller *Linhas Aéreas de Moçambique* titles and underscored by the web address, lead the eye to the beautifully created white bird symbol flying on the red tail. The red and black colors, standing for the struggle for freedom and the African people, are drawn from the national flag, a small rendition of which appears at the rear of the aircraft. Each aircraft carries the name of a Mozambique town.

LAN Airlines (LA/LAN)
CHILE (CC)

Principal Chilean airline and one of the oldest in South America, having been founded on 5 March 1929 as Linea Aeropostal Santiago-Arica under the Command of the Chilean air force. In 1932, the airline adopted the title of Linea Aérea Nacional de Chile, known as LAN Chile. It was privatized in September 1989 and rebranded on 17 June 2004. Its network of scheduled passenger and cargo services now extends throughout the Americas, and to Europe and across the Pacific to Australasia. Airline associates operate in Peru, Ecuador, and Argentina. LAN Cargo operates a dedicated freighter fleet.

FLEET:
3 (9) X A319-100, 8 X A320-200, 4 (2) X A340-300, 5 X B737-200A, 1 X B737-200F, 15 (6) X B767-300ER, 3 (5) X B767-300ERF

FEATURES:
The identity of LAN Airlines, referred to as "The Spirit of the South of the World," captures the colors and textures of the vast and varied Chilean landscape with a personality that offers friendly and cordial service typical of the people of this Andean country. The aircraft is divided into white with large blue LAN initials, and a mid-blue rear fuselage edged in light blue. The fin carries a five-pointed star.

LAN express (LU/LCO)
CHILE (CC)

Subsidiary of LAN Airlines operating an extensive network of domestic services to all main cities stretching along the full length of this Andean country, with a few routes flown to neighboring Argentina. The airline's history dates back to 3 September 1958, when it was founded as Linea Aérea del Cobre, more commonly known as LADECO, and began operations with Douglas DC-3s over two routes. It was acquired by LAN Chile in August 1995 and in October 1998 was merged with cargo carrier Fast Air, established on 14 August 1978. The present title was adopted following the rebranding of the parent company.

FLEET:
2 X A319-100, 3 X A320-200,
1 X B737-200, 8 X B737-200A

FEATURES:
The corporate identity matches that of the parent LAN Airlines, with additional LAN express titles along the fuselage. The aircraft is divided into white with large blue LAN initials, and a mid-blue rear fuselage and tail edged in light blue. The fin carries a five-pointed star underscored in red.

Lao Airlines (QV/LAO)
LAOS (RDPL)

National airline of Laos in Indochina providing scheduled services, linking the capital Vientiane with all major towns and cities in the country. Regional services are also flown to the neighboring countries of Thailand, Cambodia, Vietnam, and China, as are special charters for government personnel. The airline was founded on 19 January 1976 as the Civil Aviation Company taking over from Royal Air Lao and Lao Air Lines, and began operations in September that year. The name was changed to Lao Aviation in 1979. A re-organization under the present title was implemented in early 2003.

FLEET:
1 X A320-200, 2 X ATR 72-200,
2 X Y-7-100, 4 X Y-12-II

FEATURES:
The attractive focal point of the airline's corporate identity is the Dok Champa flower, or frangipani, which is the national flower of Laos and is used in special ceremonies. Attractively drawn on a striking royal blue tailfin and rear fuselage, it is pivotal in representing the timeless beauty of Laotian culture and hospitality. The national flag, in which the white disc is said to represent the moon over the Mekong River, is displayed ahead of the blue Lao Airlines title.

LASER–Linea Aérea de Servicio Ejecutivo Regional (8z/LER)

VENEZUELA (YV)

Privately owned regional airline providing scheduled passenger and cargo services from Caracas to a small number of cities within Venezuela. Charter flights are also offered, as are special tour packages to the holiday island of Marguerita lying off the country's northern coast. The airline was founded in 1993, and began operations the following year.

FLEET:
1 X DC-9-10, 2 X DC-9-30

FEATURES:
A swathe of green edged in gold runs from the tailfin in a graceful curve down to a point under the nose of the aircraft. The engines are also painted green, but the remainder of the aircraft is white. Set into the tail and ahead of the green LASER titling on the fuselage is the airline's flower symbol comprising a gold diamond surrounded by petals.

LatCharter Airlines (6Y/LTC)

LATVIA (YL)

Charter airline operating flights to Europe, Africa, the Middle East, and Asia from its base at Riga. Flights are operated for government, tour operators, and corporate clients, with regular summer tourist services operated to Turkey, Crete, and Spain, and to the Canary Islands, Austria, northern Italy, Egypt, and Dubai in winter. LatCharter was founded in April 1992 by four pilots and one engineer and began operations the following year, flying tourists from Riga to Rimini with a leased Tupolev TU-134B.

FLEET :
1 X A320-200, 2 X Yak-42D

FEATURES:
The main elements of the scheme are a large blue arrow on the aircraft engines, formed by highly stylized letters L and C, and a flowing ribbon design, with three blue bands covering the tailfin and rear part of the aircraft. Blue LatCharter titles are carried under the forward cabin.

Lauda Air (NG/LDA)
AUSTRIA (OE)

Member of the Austrian Airlines Group, providing leisure flights to holiday destinations around the Mediterranean basin, and to popular resort areas in far-flung countries in Asia, including Sri Lanka, the Maldives, Thailand, Malaysia, Myanmar, Singapore, China, and Australia, as well as the United Arab Emirates in the Persian Gulf and Mauritius in the Indian Ocean. Founded by Formula 1 world motor racing champion Niki Lauda in April 1979, Lauda Air began charter flights on 24 May that year. Austrian Airlines acquired full control on 6 June 2002, having gradually increased its holding since 1997.

FLEET:
2 X A320-200, 1 X B737-600, 2 X B737-700, 6 X B737-800, 3 X B767-300ER, 3 X B777-200

FEATURES:
Attention of the livery is focused on the large red "double L" with a discreet outline, which covers the tailfin and serves as the first letter in the *Lauda* roof title. Of note is the angel motif with the words *Service is our Success* applied in shimmering gold. The dark gray underside of the aircraft is angled in line with the leading edge of the tail, adding elegance and efficiency.

Lauda Air Italia (L4/LDI)
ITALY (I)

Italian charter airline operating long-haul flights from Milan and Rome to a number of leisure destinations in Central America and the Caribbean, particularly in Cuba, Mexico, the Dominican Republic, Brazil, Jamaica, and Guatemala, as well as in East Africa and the Far East. Flights are operated for parent company Viaggi del Ventaglio and other tour operators. The airline was founded in September 1990 by Formula 1 world champion Niki Lauda. Having acquired a 40% stake in March 2002, the Ventaglio Group took full control on 13 March 2003. Livingston is a sister company.

FLEET:
3 X A330-200, 1 X B767-300ER

FEATURES:
The livery uses the famous "double L," but in the green and red colors of the Italian flag, which covers the tailfin and leads the *Lauda* name on the forward roof. Set into the tail and after the title is the angel motif with the words *Service is our Success* applied in shimmering gold. The gray underside of the aircraft is edged in gold and is cut dramatically short in line with the leading edge of the tailfin.

LIAT (LI/LIA)
ANTIGUA (V2)

Regional airline serving 20 destinations in the eastern Caribbean from Santo Domingo in the Dominican Republic in the north to Georgetown, Guyana, in the south, linking the chain of islands in between. Code-share flights are also undertaken with partners Air Caraibes and BWIA. LIAT operates from hubs at Antigua and Barbados. The airline was founded on 1956 by Frank Delisle as Leeward Islands Air Transport (LIAT) and started flying with a single Piper Apache between Montserrat and Antigua. In spite of a history punctuated by owner-ship changes, LIAT has provided unbroken service.

FLEET:
4 x Dash 8 100, 6 x Dash 8 300

FEATURES:
The Caribbean colors of dark blue, orange, and yellow fan out from the beginning of the dorsal fillet to encompass the tailfin and rear fuselage in an elegant sweep. The initials LIAT derived from the airline's original name, are highlighted in white on the fin, with a yellow sun forming the dot on the second letter. Small THE Caribbean Airline titling is almost hidden away at the base of the forward fuselage.

Libyan Arab Airlines (LN/LAA)
LIBYA (5A)

Libyan flag-carrier operating scheduled passenger and cargo services from Tripoli and Benghazi to other domestic points and to destinations in Europe, North Africa, and the Middle East. The airline was organized in September 1964 under the name of Libyan Airlines to succeed NAA Libiavia. Scheduled services were inaugurated in October 1965, by which time the airline became known as Kingdom of Libya Airlines. The present title was adopted on 1 September 1969, although it was later known for a time as Libyan Arab Jamahiriya. UN trade sanctions prevented international flight between 1992 and 1999.

FLEET:
2 x A300-600R, 2 x A310-200,
1 x A320-200, 6 x AN-26,
1 x B707-320B, 1 x B707-320C,
1 x B727-200, 5 x B727-200A,
1 x C212-200 Aviocar, 12 x DHC-6
Twin Otter 300, 1 x F27-600,
3 x F28 MK4000, 9 x IL-76

FEATURES:
The white aircraft is an exemplary blend of gold and Islamic green, with a golden tailfin into which is set the airline's long-standing emblem of a gazelle in full flight. The fin is edged in green at the base, while the green engines have two bands of gold and white. The all-green Libyan flag is followed by the airline name.

Lineas Aéreas Suramericanas (LAU)

COLOMBIA (HK)

All-cargo airline providing regular and domestic charter flights, together with international extensions to Miami and Luxembourg using leased long-haul aircraft as required. The airline was founded in 1972 as Aerovias del Norte (Aeronorte) to provide local services and adopted the present title in 1986 to more accurately reflect its increased sphere of operations. International operations were started in 1987 with a first service between Bogota and Panama City using a Sud-Aviation Caravelle VIR twin-jet.

FLEET:
2 X B727-100C, 2 X B727-100F,
4 X B727-200F, 1 X DC-9-15RC

FEATURES:
Wide bands of black, mid-blue, and golden orange are wrapped around the lower forward fuselage before being transformed into thin pencil lines that curve up to the base of the dark blue tailfin. The fin is accentuated by the yellow letter s and blue L from the airline's name, which appears in full along the roof, followed by the word *Columbia* to emphasize its home base. The lettering on the engines confirms that they have been hushkitted to meet Stage 3 noise requirements.

Lion Air (PT Lion Mentari Airlines) (JT/LNI)

INDONESIA (PK)

Privately owned low-fare airline linking Jakarta's Soekarno Hatta Airport with nearly 20 major domestic cities and across the border to neighboring Malaysia. The airline's license permits it to fly to 50 domestic destinations and additional flights will be added as it grows its business. Lion Air was established by travel agency Lion Tours in October 1999 and began scheduled passenger services on 30 June 2000 between Jakarta and Pontianak using a leased Boeing 737-200.

FLEET:
4 X B737-400, (30) X B737-900ER,
13 X MD-82, 1 X MD-83,
5 X MD-90-30

FEATURES:
A fierce red lion with an artistically drawn mane, signifying power, strength, and fearlessness, forms the central element of the livery on the tailfin of the all-white aircraft. The only other splash of color is the enormous *Lion* titling across the front fuselage.

Livingston (LM/LVG)

ITALY (I)

Leisure airline operating charter services on short-
to medium-haul routes around the Mediterranean
basin to destinations in Egypt, Cyprus, Jordan,
Tunisia, Greece, Turkey, Croatia, and the Balearic
Islands. Longer flights are offered to the Cape Verde
Islands and Madagascar. Flights originate
principally from Milan, Rome, Bologna, Verona, and
Bergamo and are undertaken for parent Viaggi del
Ventaglio and other tour operators. Livingston was
established on 13 January 2003 and started flying
with two Airbus A321s the following May. Lauda Air
Italia is an associate company.

FLEET:
3 X A321-200, 1 X B757-200

FEATURES:
The interesting motif comprises a
humorous matchstick figure in
silver with an orange with green
leaves as the head. It dances on
the white tailfin behind an ocher
cheatline that extends along the
leading edge and down to and
along the gray underbelly of the
aircraft. Large *Livingston* titles in
ocher cover half of the aircraft.
Beneath is written the slogan
Energy Flight.

Loganair (LC/LOG)

UNITED KINGDOM (G)

Scotland's regional airline, operating an extensive
network of passenger services out of Glasgow and
Edinburgh. It also provides vital interisland links in
the Orkney and Shetland isles, night mail services,
and charters, and flies for the Scottish Air Ambulance Service. All scheduled flights are operated in
British Airways colors under a franchise agreement
first signed on 11 July 1994. Loganair was established
on 1 February 1962 and became part of Airlines of
Britain in December 1983. On 27 October 1996 it was
incorporated into British Regional Airlines but
became independent again on 1 March 1997.

FLEET:
6 X BN-2B Islander, 2 X DHC-6
Twin Otter 310, 2 x Saab 340A,
11 x Saab 340B

FEATURES:
Although most of the fleet carries
British Airways colors, some
aircraft retain the original
Loganair livery. This focuses on
red and black, with the design on
the tailfin representing the L and
A from the airline name and the
broad red band and black cheatline extending from the base of
the fin to the aircraft nose. Red
Loganair titling is applied at the
rear, with the additional
Scotland's Airline catchphrase at
the front in black.

LOT Polish Airlines (LO/LOT)

POLAND (SP)

Polish flag-carrier operating a widespread European network, with services extending to the Middle East, North Africa, Asia, and North America. Access to other markets is provided through its membership of the Star Alliance. Domestic and thinner European routes are flown by subsidiary EuroLOT. The airline was founded on 1 January 1929 by the Polish government as Polskie Linie Lotnicze-LOT to take over the operations of private companies Aerolot and Aero, the former dating back to 1922. Services were suspended at the outbreak of war on 1 September 1938 but re-activated on 1 April 1945.

FLEET:

3 x B737-400, 6 x B737-500, 2 x B737-800, 2 x B767-200ER, 4 x B767-300ER, (7) x B787-8, (2) x B787-9, 10 x EMB 170LR, (4) x EMB 175LR, 2 x ERJ 145EP, 11 x ERJ 145MP

FEATURES:

The aircraft livery on an all-white fuselage is centered on a large dark blue LOT fuselage logo (lot means "flight" in Polish), which is followed by a solid windowline, lining up with the top of the lettering. The blue fin contains the Polish flag behind the historic flying crane insignia in a white circle, introduced with the founding of the airline. The airline name is applied in both English and Polish.

Lotus Air (TAS)

EGYPT (SU)

Private Egyptian charter airline bringing European tourists to the Red Sea resorts of Hurghada and Sharm el Sheikh, and to the ancient cities and monuments at Cairo, Luxor, Abu Simbel, and Aswan. VIP flights and wet-lease services for other airlines are also undertaken. Lotus Air was established in 1997 and began operations the following year.

FLEET:

1 x A320-200

FEATURES:

A stylized lotus flower set into a blue sun fading into yellow and orange is the eye-catching symbol of the airline, painted on the tailfin and aircraft engines. The exquisite lotus flower played an important part in ancient Egypt, both in religion and mythology and represents the "Spirit of Egypt" as denoted on the forward cabin roof. Blue *Lotus* titling in an attractive double font is executed below the cabin.

LTA–Línea Turística Aerotuy (TUY)
VENEZUELA (YV)

Private airline providing air travel mainly to remote destinations in Venezuela that can only be reached by air. Most flights are operated to national parks, such as Canaima (Angel Falls) and Los Roques, but also serve Margarita Island, La Blanqilla, the Orinoco Delta, and Grenada and Tobago in the southeastern Caribbean. It is also a full-service safari company with its own lodges, camps, guides, and sailing vessels. Línea Turística Aerotuy was established in 1982 by Peter Bottome and Juan Carlos Márquez, who still own the organization.

FLEET:
3 x Cessna 208B Grand Caravan,
3 x Dash 7-100

FEATURES:
This scheme provides a clear indication of the airline's leisure activities, featuring a large sun and refracted rays in white on a golden field that spreads across the tailfin and rear fuselage. A bright blue for sea and sky colors the aircraft engines and is also used in the airline name along the fuselage.

LTU International Airways (LT/LTU)
GERMANY (D)

One of Europe's largest holiday airlines, providing scheduled European and long-haul leisure flights, supplemented by charters, operated from its main bases at Düsseldorf and Munich and other main German airports. European flights serve all the principal resort areas in the Mediterranean basin, with long-haul services flown to destinations in the Middle and Far East, Africa, and North and Central America. LTU was founded on 20 October 1955 as Lufttransport-Union, initially operating Vickers Vikings on ad hoc charters from spring 1956, by which time the initials LTU had been adopted.

FLEET:
9 x A320-200, 4 x A321-200,
7 (2) x A330-200, 4 x A330-300

FEATURES:
LTU's aircraft are dominated by the corporate color red. A bright red roof extends the whole length of the aircraft fuselage and sweeps up the tailfin, which incorporates a white LTU logo, derived from the airline's original name. This is repeated in red on white behind the cockpit windows. A broad red cheatline below frames the window band.

Lufthansa (LH/DLH)

GERMANY (D)

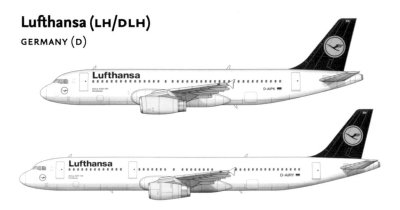

German flag-carrier providing an extensive worldwide system of scheduled services, linking its Frankfurt and Munich hubs with destinations in more than 90 countries on all five continents. Some domestic European routes are flown by a number of airlines operating as Lufthansa Regional. Lufthansa is a founder member of the Star Alliance. The airline was founded as Deutsche Luft Hansa on 6 January 1926 through the consolidation of German air transport, taking over all airlines and affiliates of Deutscher Aero Lloyd and Junkers Luftverkehr. The earliest enterprise, Deutsche Luft-Reederei, dated back to 13 December 1917, but was absorbed, along with Lloyd Luftdienst, to form Deutscher Aero Lloyd on 6 February 1923. Junkers Luftverkehr was established on 13 August 1924 by the Junkers aircraft works and included several airlines within Germany and in neighboring countries. Lufthansa proceeded to pioneer routes to the Far East and across the North and South Atlantic, before the outbreak of World War II curtailed its operations. It made its last flight on 5 May 1945 and was officially liquidated on 1 January 1951 before being reestablished as Luftag on 6 January 1953. On 6 August, Luftag changed its name to Deutsche Lufthansa. The first scheduled services began on 1 April 1955. In 2005, Lufthansa took control over Swiss International Air Lines.

FLEET:
11 x A300-600, 2 x A300-600R,
12 x A319-100, 2 x A319CJ,
36 x A320-200, 20 x A321-100,
6 x A321-200, 2 x A330-200,
10 x A330-300, 30 x A340-300,
10 (7) x A340-600,
(15) x A380-800, 33 x B737-300,
26 x B737-500, 23 x B747-400,
7 x B747-400M

FEATURES:
The centerpoint of the livery is the "flying crane" symbol, which goes back to the earliest days of German aviation when it was carried by Deutscher Aero Lloyd. It is most prominently displayed in a yellow disc within a thin blue circle on the dark blue tailfin, and also appears under the cockpit in blue outline. The famous stylized crane was created in 1918 by Otto Firle to symbolize flying and technical skills.

Lufthansa Cargo (LH/GEC)

GERMANY (D)

Autonomous division of the Lufthansa passenger airline, maintaining an international air freight and logistics buiness, which operates on a worldwide basis from hubs at Frankfurt and Cologne Bonn, serving 450 destinations on all five continents. The airline utilizes its own dedicated freighter fleet but also uses the belly cargo-hold capacity in the passenger aircraft of its parent company. Lufthansa Cargo was established as a separate identity on 30 November 1994 and started operations in 1995. It is a member of the wow cargo alliance.

FLEET:
2 X B747-200F, 19 X MD-11F

FEATURES:
The livery of Lufthansa Cargo is identical to that of the parent company with the exception of the blue title on the roof and the addition of *Member of* wow at the rear.

Lufthansa Regional (LH)

GERMANY (D)/ITALY (I)

Five regional airlines providing a passenger feed into Frankfurt and Munich, and connecting other German cities with each other and with points in Europe. The principal partner is Lufthansa CityLine, now Europe's largest regional airline. Based at Cologne, it was formed in 1958 and was previously known as OLT and DLT. Eurowings, formed on 1 January 1994, is based at Dortmund, while Augsburg Airways, founded in 1980, operates out of southern Germany. Stuttgart-based Contact Air started in 1974. Italy's Air Dolomiti retains its own brand. Lufthansa Regional came into being on 1 January 2004.

FLEET:
8 X ATR 42-500, 2 X ATR 72-200, 2 X ATR 72-210, 6 X ATR 72-500, 4 X BAE 146-200, 6 X BAE 146-300, 12 X CRJ200ER, 33 X CRJ100LR, 10 X CRJ200LR, 20 X CRJ700, 18 RJ85, 6 x Dash 8 Q300, 5 × Dash 8 Q400

FEATURES:
The communal livery uses the blue and yellow colors of Lufthansa, with the blue tail highlighted by yellow dots. Blue *Lufthansa Regional* wording along the upper white fuselage is complemented by additional *operated by* titles to identify the individual airline.

Luxair (LG/LGL)
LUXEMBOURG (LX)

National airline of the Grand Duchy of Luxembourg providing scheduled passenger services within Europe only, focusing especially on leisure flights. It also operates extensive charter flights to the Mediterranean. The airline's history dates to early 1948 and the founding of Luxembourg Airlines, which started flying on 2 February that year with Douglas DC-3s. Services were suspended in 1950, but the company was reconstituted as Luxair-Société Luxembourgeoise de Navigation Aérienne, starting operations on the Luxembourg–Paris route with Fokker F27s on 2 April 1962.

FLEET:
2 X B737-500, 3 X B737-700,
2 X ERJ 135LR, 1 X ERJ 145EP,
7 X ERJ 145LU

FEATURES:
Pale blue and white are the dominant colors of the Luxair livery, with a broad blue window-line separating the upper white and lower gray fuselage, and the blue tail promoting the company's L-shaped arrow emblem. *Luxair* titling is followed by the national and European Union flags. Names of princes and chateaux, together with their coat of arms, are carried on the nose of the aircraft.

Macair Airlines (CC/MCK)
AUSTRALIA (VH)

Regional airline providing a vital network of passenger and cargo services from Townsville, Cairns, and Mount Isa to more than 30 destinations throughout regional Queensland. Some services are flown under a code-share agreement with Qantas. A main part of its business is fly-in, fly-out charters to mines in western Queensland for large mining operators and contractors. The airline commenced operations in 1992 as McKinlay Air Charters, trading as Macair, and introduced regional schedules in northern Queensland in 1998. Transtate Airlines was merged into Macair on 1 June 2000.

FLEET:
2 x Cessna 208B Grand Caravan,
1 x SA227AC Metro III,
7 x SA227DC Metro 23,
3 x Saab 340B

FEATURES:
The royal blue tail and rear fuselage cut diagonally and edged in red is an appealing feature of the Macair livery, which also makes strong use of the initial M. This is set into the tailfin against a white disc fringed in gold. Red *Macair* titles contrast well with the white forward fuselage.

Mahan Air (W5/IRM)

IRAN (EP)

Private Iranian carrier providing international services from several Iranian cities to points in Europe, the Middle East, and Southeast Asia, together with seasonal flights to Thailand, South Korea, India, and Turkey. Passenger charters are also flown to popular destinations in Russia and the Middle East, together with pilgrim services from Kerman. Mahan Air was founded in 1991 by the Mol-Al-Movahedin Organization, which is active in hotel management, and started flying the following year. All-cargo flights were started in 1994.

FLEET:
2 X A300B4-100, 1 X A300B4-200, 1 X A310-300, 2 X A320-200, 2 X TU-154M

FEATURES:
The peacock on the tailfin has deep roots in Iran's history, where it became the dynastic emblem of an early people in the region. In true Islamic tradition, it is drawn in a highly stylized rather than figurative form. The peacock is displayed in a white field surrounded by green, the color of Islam. Black *Mahan Air* titles in English and Arabic are preceded by the national flag, whose red central symbol of four crescents and a sword represents the five principles of Islam.

Malaysia Airlines (MH/MAS)

MALAYSIA (9M)

National carrier operating an extensive domestic and regional network, with services extending to the South Pacific, North Asia, Africa, the Middle East, Europe, and the Americas, reaching more than 70 destinations abroad and 35 at home. The airline was founded as Malayan Airways in 1937, in part by Imperial Airways, but did not start operations until 9 June 1947. It was renamed Malaysian Airways in November 1963 and operated for a time as Malaysia-Singapore Airlines, before being reconstituted as the national airline on 3 April 1971 as Malaysian Airlines System (MAS). MASKargo is the cargo division.

FLEET:
5 X A330-200, 11 X A330-300, (6) X A380-800, 39 X B737-400, 6 X B747-200F, 17 X B747-400, 2 X B747-400F, 17 X B777-200ER, 6 X DHC-6 Twin Otter 300, 9 X F50

FEATURES:
The tailfin displays an aerodynamically drawn Kelantan wau bulan, or moon dragon kite, while the trailing sweep at the rear of the red and mid-blue cheatlines accentuates design symmetry and balance. The letters *m*, *a* and *s* in the title bear red clippings to denote the initials of the airline's full name.

Maldivian Air Taxi

MALDIVES (8Q)

Domestic airline in the Republic of Maldives providing transfer flights on float-equipped de Havilland Canada Twin Otters for arriving passengers at Male's Hulule International Airport to many of the 80-plus tourist resorts scattered along this 1,190-island chain in the Indian Ocean. Charters and government VIP flights are also performed, as are photo flights, excursions, island hopping, and shopping tours. Maldivian Air Taxi was established in 1993 by a group of Danish investors and began operations on 4 November that year with one single-engine Cessna Caravan and two Twin Otters.

FLEET:
3 x DHC-6 Twin Otter 100,
2 x DHC-6 Twin Otter 200,
11 x DHC-6 Twin Otter 300

FEATURES:
Maldivian Air Taxi is leasing all its aircraft from Kenn Borek Air of Canada and has not adopted its own identity, with the exception of its name displayed on the rear fuselage. It is using the rather uninspiring Kenn Borek Twin Otter livery, comprising a terracotta red upper fuselage separated from the lower white by a black flash cheatline.

Malév Hungarian Airlines (MA/MAH)

HUNGARY (HA)

National airline operating a predominantly intra-European and Near East network from Budapest Ferihegy Airport, serving most capital cities and other major industrial and business centers. Long-haul flights reach into Asia and North America. Feeder services are operated under the Malév Express name. Malév was founded on 26 April 1946 as a joint Hungarian/Soviet airline under the name of Maszovlét and began flying on 15 October with Lisunov Li-2s and Polikarpov Po-2s. The present name was assumed on 25 November 1954 when the Soviet interest reverted to the Hungarian state.

FLEET:
6 x B737-600, 7 x B737-700,
5 x B737-800, 2 x B767-200ER,
4 x CRJ200ER, 5 x F70

FEATURES:
The livery features a sweep of blue at the rear of the clean white fuselage and the tail, which carries fin flashes in the national colors of red, white and green, going back to the earliest days of Hungary's history. Blue *Malév* titles are applied on the forward cabin roof, alongside the flag and additional smaller *Hungarian Airlines* lettering. The nose cone is also painted blue.

Malmö Aviation (TF/SCW)
SWEDEN (SE)

Independent regional airline offering scheduled passenger services, mainly from Stockholm's city center Bromma Airport, as well as from the southern city of Gothenburg, to several destinations within Sweden and to points in mainland Europe. Malmö Aviation was founded in 1981, initially providing air-taxi services, freight flights, and flight training. Scheduled passenger services to Hamburg and London were added in 1991 with four-engined BAE 146-200s. The airline has undergone several ownership and name changes in its relatively short history and is now owned by Per G Braathen.

FLEET:
9 x Avro RJ100

FEATURES:
The central emblem of the airline is also that of the city of Malmö, namely a crowned griffin, or in heraldic terms, "argent, a griffin head erased gules, crowned or." It is sketched into the gold tailfin, whose lower perforations provide a neat transition to the white fuselage. A similar design is applied to the aircraft engines. Red *Malmö Aviation* titling on the forward cabin roof is balanced by the web address printed in gray below the rear windows.

Mandala Airlines (RI/MDL)
INDONESIA (PK)

One of the largest privately owned airlines in Indonesia, serving more than 12 major cities within this extensive island chain, stretching from the furthest point west in Sumatra to the easternmost destination in West Papua. Flights originate from its main base at Jakarta's Soekarno Hatta International and hubs at Surabaya and Ujung Pandang. Long-term plans will be to concentrate on entering the international arena, with likely services to Hong Kong and other Asian cities, and to Western Australia. Mandala Airlines was established in April 1969.

FLEET:
1 X B727-200A, 13 X B737-200A, 2 X B737-400

FEATURES:
A modern shade of blue colors the tailfin of the otherwise white aircraft, which incorporates an intricately drawn compass motif in gold. Black *Mandala* titling is displayed above the first row of windows behind the red and white Indonesian flag, which dates back to the late 13th century.

Mandarin Airlines (AE/MDA)

TAIWAN (B)

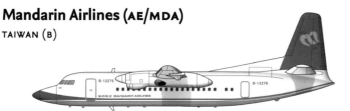

Domestic and regional subsidiary of China Airlines operating flights to Thailand, Myanmar, and the Philippines in Southeast Asia, Hong Kong, South Korea, and several destinations in Japan. The domestic network serves all major points from Taipei's Sungshan Airport. Mandarin Airlines was established on 1 June 1991, initially providing long-haul flights, with the first operated in October that year. Since the merger with Formosa Airlines on 8 August 1999, the airline has focused on domestic and regional flights. Formosa Airlines had been founded in 1966 and was formerly known as Yung Shing Airlines.

FLEET:
1 x B737-800, 2 x DO228-200, 2 x F50, 3 x F50HP, 6 x F100

FEATURES:
Perched on the royal blue tailfin of the aircraft is a representation of the great and agile golden eagle Hai Tung Ching of Chinese legend, conveying a spirit of endeavor and a majestic presence in a small body, which Mandarin Airlines wants to emulate. According to the Annals of Rehol, Hai Tung Ching, who inhabited the lower reaches of the Hai Long River, once flew a thousand miles, overcoming all obstacles in his way.

Martinair (MP/MPH)

NETHERLANDS (PH)

KLM associate operating worldwide cargo charter flights, principally over the Europe-Far East corridor via the Middle East, and to Australia, Africa, and the Americas. The airline also provides passenger services from Amsterdam, serving a number of resorts in Europe, Mexico, Canada, and Thailand, together with scheduled services across the North Atlantic. Contract flights for the government are also undertaken. It was founded on 24 May 1958 by Martin Schröder as Martin's Luchtvervoermaat-schappij (Martin's Air Charter) with a de Havilland Dove and took the present name in April 1968.

FLEET:
3 x A320-200, 1 x B737-800, 2 x 747-200C, 2 x B747-200F, 6 x B767-300ER, 4 x MD-11CF, 3 x MD-11F

FEATURES:
The eye-catching design that covers the entire tailfin of the aircraft is a liberal interpretation of the signature of the airline's founding father, Martin Schröder. Introduced in November 2004, it is said to create a feeling of forward movement of the aircraft. The house colors of red and navy blue have been retained, as has the stylized M ahead of the airline name.

Mas Air (MY/MAA)

MEXICO (XA)

All-cargo airline offering direct flights from Mexico City to the main centers in Central and South America, serving Costa Rica, Guatemala, Colombia, Brazil, and Venezuela. Intercontinental long-haul connections are available at the Los Angeles and Miami gateways, which are also served on a scheduled basis. Apart from the carriage of general and express cargo, the airline also has a specialized department dedicated to the transportation of livestock. Mas Air was founded in early 1992 and started flying in April 1972.

FLEET:
1 X B767-300ER

FEATURES:
A stylized eagle in green flies on the rear of the fuselage, its wings stretching right back across the tailfin. Green and silver gray *Mas Air* titles are applied on the fin and forward above the red cheatline that divides the upper white aircraft from the gray underside. An unusual arrangement has the underside curving up at the rear and wrapping itself around the tail cone of the aircraft.

MAT–Macedonian Airlines (IN/MAK)

MACEDONIA (Z3)

National airline of the Republic of Macedonia linking the capital Skopje and second city Ohrid with several destinations in Western Europe. Apart from scheduled passenger and cargo services, the airline also provides regular charter flights and a number of non-flying activities including airport handling and tourist and transfer services. MAT was established on 16 January 1994 as Makavio and operated its first flight between Skopje and Zürich with a Boeing 737-200 on 23 June that year. It adopted the present, more international name, prior to being designated the national carrier in 2000.

FLEET:
1 X B737-300

FEATURES:
The tailfin is a moving represen-tation of the Macedonian flag, which incorporates a yellow-golden sun with eight thickening rays on a red field. The sun of liberty symbol, although much modified, traces its origin to the sun of Kutle (Vergina), then 16-pointed, symbol of an ancient Macedonian dynasty. Large blue MAT initials, followed by red *Macedonian Airlines* titles, take up most of the aircraft fuselage. A small Macedonian flag is pictured behind the aircraft registration.

MaxJet (MY)
UNITED STATES (N)

International low-cost carrier operating both scheduled and charter flights across the North Atlantic and to points in South America and the Caribbean. The airline is headquartered at Washington Dulles Airport and has operational facilities at New York's John F. Kennedy International and London Stansted airports. MaxJet was established in 2005 and carried out its inaugural flights between New York and London on 1 November 2005.

FLEET:
2 x B767-300ER

FEATURES:
This color scheme emphasizes the word *Max*, which is written large on the sky blue tailfin in white, and scaled down in darker blue with a gold *jet* addition on the front fuselage. The separation of the sky blue fin and rear fuselage from the white body is achieved by a graceful curve that sweeps up from the base to the roof. The web address has been added on the blue engines.

Maya Island Air (MW/MYD)
BELIZE (V3)

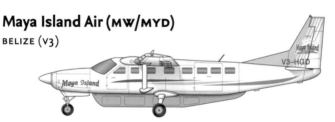

Regional airline providing scheduled passenger and cargo services from Belize City's municipal and international airport to all main points within Belize, as well as offering tourist flights to the local Mayan ruins and those at Tikal in neighboring Guatemala. The airline was created on 1 December 1997 from the merger of Maya Airways and Island Air. Maya Airways had been founded in 1962 to re-establish air services following the demise of BWIA subsidiary British Honduras Airways earlier that year. Island Air's history went back to 1989.

FLEET:
2 x Britten-Norman BN-2A Islander, 7 x Cessna 208B Grand Caravan, 1 x Gippsland G.A8 Airvan

FEATURES:
Purple for sea and sky, yellow for golden sands, and green for the verdant landscape are the prime colors of this "tropic" scheme. All three colors are depicted in broad brushstrokes along the side of the fuselage, while the yellow fills the front half of the tailfin, gradually fading out into the white. A small island with a sandy beach and palm tree is drawn on the fin, together with the airline's name.

MenaJet (IM/MNJ)
UNITED ARAB EMIRATES (A6)

Low-fare airline based at Sharjah in the United Arab Emirates and Beirut in the Lebanon, providing services to points in the Middle East, the eastern Mediterranean, and North Africa. Services also extend to resort areas in France, Italy, and Spain. The airline was formed in May 2003 and began operations with the Airbus A320 on 13 August 2004, making its inaugural flight from Beirut to Dalaman on Turkey's Mediterranean coast.

FLEET:
1 X A320-200

FEATURES:
The MenaJet livery sports vivid blue and yellow, colors of sand, sea, and sky, representing growth and resilience, while reflecting the airline's commitment to deliver a fresh experience to air travelers in the Middle East region. The emblem on the tailfin is the word *mena* in Arabic, meaning "port." It has been drawn using a three-stroke brush, resulting in an innovative, rather than traditional, Arabic calligraphic expression. The corporate identity was developed by Beirut-based design studio Mind the Gap.

Meridiana (IG/ISS)
ITALY (I)

Major Italian airline providing scheduled domestic passenger flights and cross-border services to four European countries from hubs at Verona, Catania, and Florence. Additional seasonal routes are flown from Costa Smeralda Airport in Sardinia. Meridiana was founded on 24 March 1963 by the Aga Khan as an air-taxi and general aviation company under the name of Alisarda, to assist in the development of the tourist industry on the northeast coast of the island of Sardinia. Scheduled services were inaugurated on 1 June 1966 with Nord 262s. The present name was adopted on 3 May 1991.

FLEET:
4 X A319-100, 9 X MD-82, 8 X MD-83

FEATURES:
The color scheme is notable for the white circle on a predominantly warm red tailfin, incorporating the company insignia composed of meridians — imaginary lines joining the North and South poles at right angles to the equator. The base of the fin is supported by a thin yellow and broader blue line. A similar yellow cheatline is sandwiched between the red and purple lines extending the full length of the fuselage below the windows.

Merpati (MZ/MNA)
INDONESIA (PK)

Government-owned airline operating a dense domestic network covering all major provincial capitals and a number of smaller towns, with further destinations served with charter flights. Regional services are also scheduled to Malaysia, Singapore, and East Timor. Merpati (Merpati Nusantara Airlines) was established on 6 September 1962 to take over the internal services developed by the Indonesian air force from 1958 and began operations on 11 September that year from the capital Jakarta. In January 1964 it acquired the routes of former Dutch-controlled De Kroonduif, which had been flown by Garuda since 1962.

FLEET:
9 X B737-200A, 2 X B737-300, 7 X C212-200 Aviocar, 3 X CN-235-10, 5 X DHC-6 Twin Otter 300, 4 X F27-500, 5 X F28-4000, 1 X F100

FEATURES:
Three orange banners fluttering on the blue tailfin give the airline an easily recognizable identity, which has now been in use since 1986. Blue *Merpati* titling in a classic typeface above the forward cabin windows complements the blue of the tailfin. A small red and white Indonesian flag is painted behind the cockpit. *Merpati* means "dove."

Mexicana (Cia Mexicana de Aviación) (MX/MXA)
MEXICO (XA)

One of Mexico's two principal airlines operating an extensive network of scheduled passenger and cargo services to more than 25 cities within Mexico, together with international connections to destinations in the United States, Canada, and Central and South America. The airline was registered on 24 August 1924 and the following month bought Compañia Mexicana de Transportación Aérea, which had begun operation on 12 July 1921 with two Lincoln Standard biplanes, carrying payrolls to the oilfields around Tampico. Scheduled passenger services were started on 15 April 1928.

FLEET:
10 X A318-100, 15 X A319-100, 28 (4) X A320-200, 5 X B757-200, 1 X B767-300ER, 3 X Fokker 100

FEATURES:
Mexicana introduced this more modern livery in spring 2005, replacing the different colors with a unified dark blue tailfin in which is outlined in white the airline's long-standing eagle emblem derived from Mexico's Aztec past. Classic and understated *Mexicana* titling is applied below the forward cabin windows and above the gray underside of the aircraft. A small Mexican flag flies at the rear.

MIAT Mongolian Airlines (OM/MGL)

MONGOLIA (JU)

National flag-carrier of Mongolia operating a comprehensive domestic network that covers all major towns and cities, together with international flights from the capital Ulan Bator to destinations in Russia, Germany, China, South Korea, and Japan. MIAT was established in 1956 with the assistance of Aeroflot, and began operations on 7 July that same year from Ulan Bator to Irkutsk using an Antonov AN-24. The airline, which is part of the Department of Civil Aviation, has been known under various names such as Air Mongol, Mongolflot, and Mongolian Airlines.

FLEET:
1 X A310-300, 1 X AN-24RV, 1 X AN-26B, 1 X B737-800

FEATURES:
The airline's winged-horse symbol on the dark blue tailfin is a visual expression of a country often known as the "land of the horse," although its famous horses are no longer found in the wild. In an unusual arrangement, the low cheatline starts with the airline symbol. Blue MIAT *Mongolian Airlines* titles on the cabin roof are preceded by the red and blue Mongolian flag, which includes a yellow soyonbo ideogram, one of the oldest symbols and rich in mystical connotations.

Middle East Airlines (MEA) (ME/MEA)

LEBANON (OD)

National airline operating scheduled services from Beirut to destinations throughout the Middle East, North and West Africa, and Europe. Connections to North America are provided at Paris in association with strategic partner Air France. MEA was founded on 31 May 1945 and operated its first flight to Nicosia on 30 November that same year. On 7 June 1963 it merged with Air Liban under the title of Middle East Airlines Air Liban, although the latter addition was dropped in 1965. An Israeli commando attack on Beirut Airport on the night of 28/29 December 1968 destroyed most of its aircraft.

FLEET:
6 X A321-200, 3 X A330-200

FEATURES:
These all-white aircraft carry MEA initials in red, green, and turquoise on the lower forward fuselage. The tailfin is dominated by a drawing of a green cedar of Lebanon, mentioned in the Bible, which symbolizes strength, holiness, and eternity, while the red and white, taken from the national flag, stands for self-sacrifice and peace. It is repeated on the engine cowlings.

Midwest Airlines (YX/MEP)

UNITED STATES (N)

Prominent U.S. domestic carrier operating a network of low-fare services from bases at Milwaukee, Omaha, and Kansas City to more than 25 destinations across the country. Connecting flights are operated by subsidiary Skyway Airlines, trading as Midwest Connect. The airline's antecedents go back to 1969 and the formation of K-C Aviation as a division of Kimberley-Clark Corporation. Following deregulation, K-C became Midwest Express Airlines in November 1983, and started flying out of Milwaukee on 29 April 1984. The name was simplified to the present title in March 2003.

FLEET:
20 (5) x B717-200, 8 x MD-81, 3 x MD-82, 2 x MD-88

FEATURES:
The corporate symbol is made up of two wings. One is a solid gold shape evoking the airline's strength as a company, with the other, created from curved blue and white lines, symbolizes flight into the future. It is prominently displayed on the tailfin of the mostly blue aircraft, with a triple gold, white, and red cheatline delineating the upper and lower fuselage.

Midwest Connect (AL/SYX)

UNITED STATES (N)

Regional network of scheduled passenger services operated out of Milwaukee by Skyway Airlines, a wholly owned subsidiary of Midwest Airlines. The regional carrier provides feeder services to its parent's hub airports, as well as point-to-point services between other select markets. The network encompasses some 30 destinations in 11 U.S. states and one point in Canada. Skyway began flying on 17 April 1989 between Milwaukee and Boston. It became part of Astral Aviation, a subsidiary of Midwest Express, in 1994, and adopted the Midwest Connect operating name in March 2003.

FLEET:
12 x Beech 1900D, 20 x ERJ 140, 10 x Fairchild Dornier 328JET

FEATURES:
Midwest Connect aircraft mirror those of the parent company, with the scheme focused on the corporate symbol of two wings on the tailfin and the triple cheatlines separating the upper and lower fuselage. The solid gold wing refers to Midwest's strength, while the curved lines of the other are said to allude to its flight into the future.

мк Airlines (7G/MKA)

GHANA (9G)

All-cargo airline operating scheduled and non-scheduled airfreight services linking Ghana, its licensed base of operations, with other points in Africa and throughout the rest of the world. Other operational bases are maintained at Ostend, Belgium, and Kent International in the UK. MK Airlines was formed by Michael Kruger in November 1990 and began flying in 1991.

FLEET:
6 X B747-200F, 3 X DC-8-F-55, 3 X DC-8-62F, 2 X DC-8-63CF

FEATURES:
The red and blue MK company signature outlined in white has been artistically constructed into an arrow to create a feeling of forward movement. It is displayed on the gray tailfin, where it takes up almost all available space, and on the white fuselage ahead of the wing, followed by small *Airlines* wording. The MK initials are derived from the airline's founder, Michael Kruger.

MNG Airlines/MNG Cargo (MB/MNB)

TURKEY (TC)

Major logistics company providing scheduled cargo services between Istanbul and Germany and the UK, an extensive door-to-door delivery service within Turkey, as well as holiday passenger charters to the popular resorts for leading tour operators. Aircraft maintenance, repair, overhaul, and modifications are also undertaken. MNG Airlines was established in February 1996 by Mehmet Nazif Günal and began scheduled cargo services on 30 November the following year with an Airbus A300B4. Passenger flights were added in May 2001. MNG Cargo was established as a distinct entity in January 2003.

FLEET:
1 X A300B4-200, 6 X A300B4-200F, 1 X A300C4-200, 2 X A300F4-200, 5 X AN-26B, 5 X B737-400, 6 X F27 MK500, 1 X F27-600, 4 X MD-82

FEATURES:
The corporate motif is a stork in full flight, which is depicted in white on the mid-blue tailfin, and asserts the logistics part of the group's business. MNG *cargo* in white and orange is applied on the fin and in blue and orange on a much larger scale on the fuselage. The only difference on passenger aircraft is the word *pax* replacing *cargo*.

Moldavian Airlines (2M/MDV)

MOLDOVA (ER)

Private regional carrier providing a scheduled passenger service from the capital Chisinau to destinations in Hungary and Romania. Regular charter flights are also undertaken to Turkey, Kazakhstan, Turkmenistan, Romania, Hungary, and Portugal. Moldavian Airlines is associated with Romanian carrier Carpatair. It was founded on 26 July 1994 as the first private carrier in Moldova and initiated daily services on 19 August that year between Chisinau and Moscow, using a Yak-42 leased from the Ukraine. Moldavian Airlines became a joint Swiss-Moldovan company in November 1999.

FLEET:
1 x Saab 340B, 2 x Saab 2000

FEATURES:
The attractive two-tone green design features the airline's ICAO three-letter code in white on the tailfin, with the M given speed lines for added interest. *Moldavian Airlines* titling in the darker green is spread along the mid-cabin roof, with the blue, yellow, and red Moldovan flag at the rear. The flag includes an eagle in the center holding a cross and a shield, the latter displaying a bison's head, an old Moldovan symbol of power, independence, and pride.

Monarch Airlines (OM/MON)

UNITED KINGDOM (G)

Major UK holiday airline providing extensive charter flights and inclusive tour packages for leading tour operators, including sister company Cosmos, from Luton, London Gatwick, London Stansted, Manchester, Birmingham, Leeds Bradford, and Glasgow to Europe and the Mediterranean area. Long-haul flights are also undertaken, as are scheduled "leisure" routes from Luton to destinations in Spain and the Canary Islands. Monarch Airlines was founded on 1 June 1967 and began operations with two Bristol Britannias on 5 April 1968.

FLEET:
4 x A300-600R, 6 x A320-200, 7 x A321-200, 2 x A330-200, 7 x B757-200ER, 1 x B767-300ER

FEATURES:
The heart and soul of the livery are the indigo and bright yellow, which have strong echoes of its traditional image but with a contemporary and stylish new look. The soft curves flow gently around the fuselage, while the stylized crown reinforces the airline's name. It is said to project Monarch's standing and ambitions to provide a product to meet today's customer demand.

Montenegro Airlines (YM/MGX)

SERBIA AND MONTENEGRO (YU)

Main airline in the former Yugoslav republic providing connections from the capital Podgorica to a number of European cities. Cargo is carried on passenger services and the airline also undertakes charter flights. Its short history has been eventful. Founded on 24 October 1994 during a period of strife and economic sanctions in the Balkans, the airline was unable to start flying until 7 May 1997, when a Fokker F28 Mk4000 left Podgorica for Bari in Italy. NATO bombings and further sanctions again forced a suspension of all flight activities for most of 1999, with operations restarted on 23 October that year.

FLEET:
4 x Fokker 100

FEATURES:
Blue and white are the dominant colors in this scheme, with the dark blue tailfin sporting the head of a falcon, a reference to the days of the Austro-Hungarian Empire when the "Falcons of the Black Mountains" strove to soar to the heights of the Austrian eagle. Simple *Montenegro Airlines* titles are applied on the upper fuselage, together with a small rendition of the Serbia and Montenegro flag in the pan-Slavic colors of blue, white, and red.

Myair (My Way Airlines) (8I)

ITALY (I)

Italian low-fare airline providing a network of services out of Milan, Bergamo, Venice, and Bologna to some 10 destinations in southern Italy, France, Spain, and Romania. International points served include Barcelona, Madrid, Bucharest, and Paris Orly. Myair was established in 2004.

FLEET:
3 x A320-200, 1 x MD-82

FEATURES:
Bold and highly visible, this patriotic scheme flaunts the green, white, and red of the Italian tricolor. Both the fuselage and the tailfin use all three colors to striking effect, with the red on the fin turned into a forward-piercing arrow. The overpowering red of the fuselage is softened by white and green *myair.com* titles, while the green engines, which also incorporate the name and arrow symbol, add to an overall harmony of design.

Myanma Airways (8M/UBA)

MYANMAR (XY)

Government-owned airline of Myanmar (formerly
Burma), providing an extensive domestic network
linking the capital Yangon with more than 20 points
throughout the country. The history of the airline
goes back to 1948 and the foundation of Union of
Burma Airways (UBA), changed in December 1972 to
Burma Airways Corporation. The name Myanma
Airways was adopted on 1 April 1989 following the
renaming of the country. A new international
carrier was set up in a joint venture with Singapore
and Brunei interests in August 1993 to take over
international services.

FLEET:
1 X ATR 42-300, 2 X ATR 72-210,
1 X F27-100, 1 X F27-400,
4 X F27-600, 1 X F28-1000,
2 X F28-4000

FEATURES:
The golden sun symbol on the
blue tailfin is the main hallmark
of this scheme. The tailfin also
includes *Myanma Airways* titling
in gold, but, unusually, the airline
name does not feature on the
aircraft fuselage. A blue cheatline
bisects the largely white aircraft
body. The country's red and blue
flag flies behind the cabin door.
Its blue canton includes a
cogwheel and rice-paddy ear,
surrounded by 14 stars, one each
for the 14 Myanmar states.

Myanmar Airways International (8M/UBA)

MYANMAR (XY)

International airline of Myanmar (formerly Burma)
providing connections between the capital Yangon
and several destinations in Southeast Asia.
Myanmar Airways International was created in
August 1993 as a joint venture between Myanmar
Airways and Singapore interests, with the support of
Royal Brunei Airlines, and began regional flights on
15 August. It was reformed in January 2001 in a new
joint venture with Region Air Myanmar (HK) and
local Zan Company.

FLEET:
2 X MD-82

FEATURES:
The intriguing symbol, which is
highlighted against an orange
sun on the white tailfin and white
engines, and rendered in sky blue
on the dark rear fuselage, is a
mythical creature called Pyinsa
Rupa, meaning "five beauties." It
is made up of parts from five
animals – the trunk and tusk of
an elephant, a lion's head, the
antlers and legs of a deer, the
wings of a bird, and the body and
tail of a fish. The curtailment of
the orange and blue paint scheme
leaves white space at the front for
the airline's initials and full title.

MyTravel Airways (DK/VKG)

DENMARK (OY)

Scandinavian charter airline providing inclusive-tour services to holiday resorts in Europe and the Mediterranean basin, primarily from Copenhagen and Stockholm. It was established as Premiair on 1 January 1994 from the merger of Conair of Denmark and Scanair of Sweden. Conair's history went back to October 1964, while Scanair had been established by SAS on 30 June 1965. In February 1966, Airtours acquired Scandinavian leisure group Spies, giving it full control of Premiair, which, along with Airtours International in the UK, was rebranded on 1 May 2002.

FLEET:
3 X A320-200, 5 X A321-200, 2 X A330-300

FEATURES:
The MyTravel Group's corporate logo is prominently displayed across the forward fuselage. It is made up of an orange-red ellipse with an inset smaller blue ellipse left, and *MyTravel* titles in white, with a red dot above the Y representing a stylized person with arms stretched out in a welcoming gesture. The logo has been greatly scaled up to partially fill the rear upper fuselage and tailfin to create an interesting design.

MyTravel Airways (VZ/AIH)

UNITED KINGDOM (G)

Major charter airline providing inclusive tour services that cover most of the Mediterranean resorts, as well as long-haul destinations in the Caribbean, Canada, and the United States. Also served are The Gambia in West Africa, India, Sri Lanka, the Maldives, and Australia. Flights originate mainly from London Gatwick and Manchester, and from Dublin in the Irish Republic. The airline began operations as Airtours International on 18 March 1991. Following the renaming of the parent Airtours Group in February 2002, Airtours International was rebranded as MyTravel Airways from 1 May 2002.

FLEET:
12 X A320-200, 3 X A321-200, 4 X A330-200, 1 X A330-300, 2 X B757-200

FEATURES:
The MyTravel Group's corporate logo is prominently displayed across the forward fuselage. It is made up of an orange-red ellipse with an inset smaller blue ellipse left, and *MyTravel* titles in white, with a red dot above the Y representing a stylized person with arms stretched out in a welcoming gesture. The logo has been greatly scaled up to partially fill the rear upper fuse-lage and tailfin to create an interesting design.

MyTravelLite (VZ/LIZ)

UNITED KINGDOM (G)

Low-fare arm of holiday charter carrier MyTravel
Airways operating scheduled passenger services
from its base at Birmingham International Airport
in the West Midlands to some 12 leisure
destinations in Portugal, mainland Spain, and the
Balearic and Canary islands. The foundation of
MyTravelLite was announced by the MyTravel
Group on 7 August 2002 and operations began on
1 October that same year with inaugural services to
Alicante, Belfast International, Geneva, Paris
(Beauvais), and Malaga.

FLEET:
2 x A320-200

FEATURES:
The livery is essentially that of the
parent company, with the partial
scaled-up logo filling most of the
tailfin and rear cabin roof,
although the full logo at the
front has been reduced in size
to make way for the large blue
lite addition.

National Jet Systems (NC/NJS)

AUSTRALIA (VH)

Diversified aviation group providing scheduled
airline operations, charter and resource air services
for major corporate and government organizations,
air cargo flights, aerial survey work, and wet-leasing
of aircraft. Its own scheduled passenger services
link several points in the Northern Territory and
Western Australia, and also connect Perth to the
Cocos (Keeling) Islands and Christmas Island in the
Indian Ocean. National Jet Systems also operates as
a QantasLink carrier. The airline was established at
Adelaide in 1989 and started flying on 1 July 1990.

FLEET:
1 x Avro RJ70, 3 x BAE 146-100,
2 x BAE 146-200, 1 x Dash 8 100,
1 x Dash 8 200, 1 x Dash 8 300

FEATURES:
This Aboriginal design was
adopted in 1995 to tie in with the
airline's push into the regional
market in the Northern Territory
and Western Australia. The dark
blue tailfin carries a red and blue
oval surrounded by multiple dots,
signifying Australia's Red Center
and cloudless sky, and incorporating a woomera, an ancient
aboriginal throwing stick. The
darkness of the fin is lightened by
a silver-gray edge.

Nationwide Airlines (ce/ntw)

SOUTH AFRICA (ZS)

Major airline operating scheduled passenger and cargo services connecting all principal cities within South Africa, including the "Golden Triangle" route between Johannesburg, Cape Town, and Durban. A regional connection is also available to neighboring Zambia, together with a long-haul flight from Johannesburg to London. Other group members undertake aircraft charter, maintenance, and support. Nationwide was founded in 1991 as a charter company providing services within Africa for the United Nations and World Food Program, as well as ad hoc passenger and cargo flights. Scheduled airline services were introduced in 1997.

FLEET:
3 X B727-200A, 10 X B737-200A, 1 X B737-500, 1 X B767-300ER

FEATURES:
A golden stylized letter n given a hint of movement through central speed lines establishes the airline's identity on the mid-blue tailfin. Blue *Nationwide* titling is written across a golden horizon on the cabin roof at the front of the aircraft, with the web address in smaller letters painted below the windows.

NatureAir

COSTA RICA (TI)

Costa Rican domestic airline operating frequent passenger and cargo schedules from Tobías Bolaños International Airport serving the capital San José to 15 destinations reaching all main towns and remote communities in this Central American country. The airline also undertakes charter flights and scenic tour packages to the many national parks, which abound with natural wonders. NatureAir was established in 1991.

FLEET:
3 X BN-2A Islander, 5 X DHC-6 Twin Otter 300, 2 x Let L-410 UVP

FEATURES:
The NatureAir aircraft present a wonderful canvas on which expansive brushstrokes have created a design that incorporates all the warm colors of Central America, from golden sandy beaches, blue sea and sky, to the flaming reds and purples of the hibiscus. NatureAir's Islander aircraft are painted differently if no less colorfully, although the scheme is dominated by deep reds and shades of blue.

Neos (NO/NOS)
ITALY (I)

Italian leisure airline operating scheduled passenger services to tour destinations in the Mediterranean, especially in Greece and Spain, and the mid-Atlantic, where it serves the Canary Islands and the Cape Verde Republic. Flights originate mainly from Milan, Bologna, and Verona. Neos was created on 21 June 2001 following an agreement between IFIL, a leading Italian financial and industrial group and parent company of Alpitour, and German tour operator TUI. The inaugural flight took place on 8 March 2002, linking Milan Malpensa and Cap Skirring, via Dakar. IFIL took full control in January 2004.

FLEET:
4 x B737-800

FEATURES:
Neos aircraft are painted in the TUI sky blue over all the aircraft except the very underside. A red bird outlined in white flies on the tailfin, while similarly colored *neos* titles appear over the first row of cabin windows. The word *neos* originates from the Greek, meaning "new." The airline's web address is shown in small white lettering at the forward blue base. An equally diminutive Italian tricolor accompanies the aircraft registration at the rear.

Nightexpress (EXT)
GERMANY (D)

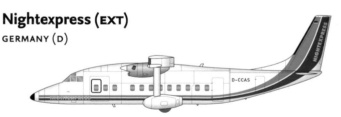

German cargo carrier providing a nightly scheduled service between Frankfurt and Coventry in the West Midlands, with other UK destinations available as required, both on an airport-to-airport and door-to-door basis. Ad hoc and contract charter flights are offered throughout Europe for urgent shipments, general cargo, and hazardous materials. Nightexpress Luftverkehrsgesellschaft was established in June 1984 and began operations that same month.

FLEET:
1 x Beech 99, 2 x Shorts 360-300

FEATURES:
Low cheatlines in light and dark blue on the white aircraft flow along the fuselage and curve up gently to fill the tailfin. Gold *Nightexpress* titles are set into the cheatlines at the front, and into the dark blue band on the fin. A small German flag at the top of the tail identifies the company's origin.

Niki (HG/NLY)
AUSTRIA (OE)

Leisure airline connecting cities in northern Europe to numerous resort areas around the Mediterranean, flown mostly on behalf of tour operator Neckermann Reisen. The airline is partially owned by German low-fare airline Air Berlin, with which Niki has close cooperation. Niki was established on 28 November 2003 by Niki Lauda, twice Formula 1 motor racing world champion for Ferrari and founder of Lauda Air. The first flight on 16 February 2004 in an Airbus a320 from Vienna to Düsseldorf was piloted by Niki Lauda himself.

FLEET:
5 (10) x A320-200, 1 x A321-200

FEATURES:
The airline's title and logo trades on the name and fame of its owner, who is recognized throughout the world. The name is set into a gray field on the silver tailfin surrounded by a red oval. A huge stylized fly takes over the front of the aircraft, refering to the web address *flyniki.com* applied on the gray engines.

Nippon Cargo Airlines (NCA) (KZ/NCA)
JAPAN (JA)

All-cargo carrier providing scheduled flights from Tokyo Narita International and Japan's other major cities to some 20 destinations in the United States, Europe, and Asia. Charter flights are also operated. The airline was founded on 21 September 1978 by All Nippon Airways and several shipping companies as Japan's first all-cargo airline and was initially known as Nippon Air Cargo. It took several years for the airline to battle against state-imposed restrictions and it was not until 8 May 1985 that scheduled services were begun between Tokyo, San Francisco, and New York.

FLEET:
1 x B747-100(F), 10 x B747-200F, 2 (2) x B747-400F

FEATURES:
The airline uses the corporate two-tone blue and white colors of its parent company, All Nippon Airways, promoting the NCA initials in white on a broad mid-blue band on the tailfin. The blue band, supported by a light blue cheatline, follows the line of the leading edge but changes direction at the base of the fin to match the line of a similar but curtailed arrangement at the front. *Nippon Cargo Airlines* titling is applied behind the rising sun of the Japanese flag.

Nok Air (DD)
THAILAND (HS)

Low-fare airline established in December 2003 with a major shareholding by flag-carrier Thai Airways International. The airline operates frequent services linking Bangkok with all major cities, towns, and resort areas in Thailand. Operations began on 23 July 2004 from the capital Bangkok to Chiang Mai, Hat Yai, and Udon Thani with Boeing 737-400s wet-leased from its parent company.

FLEET:
3 X B737-400

FEATURES:
Nok is the Thai word for "bird." It is short, simple, easily remembered, and has a clear association with flying. The airline's friendly culture is expressed by the smiling cartoon-like illustration on the tailfin, which is repeated on the nose of the aircraft, turning it into a funny face. Its Thai heritage is expressed through an exuberant use of purple and magenta, which cover most of the aircraft and are reminiscent of the vibrancy of orchids and the shimmering silks of Thailand.

Nordeste Linhas Aéreas Regionais (JH/NES)
BRAZIL (PP/PT)

Regional subsidiary of VARIG Participações em Transportes Aéreos, operating scheduled services to some 40 destinations in Brazil's north-eastern states under the VARIG brand. Nordeste was established by the Bahia state government and the now long defunct Transbrasil airline as part of the Sistema Integrado de Transportes Aéreos Regional, which was designed to link outlying regions into the main trunk routes. The inaugural flights left Salvador for Lapa, Barreiros, Petrolina, Paulo Afonso, and Recife on 8 June 1976, flown by Embraer Bandeirantes turboprop aircraft.

FLEET:
2 X B737-300, 2 X B737-500

FEATURES:
The livery mirrors that of the parent company VARIG, with the traditional compass-rose symbol in two hues of yellow adding warmth and the luster of gold to the navy blue tailfin. However, the large blue shadowed *Nordeste* lettering across the fuselage, executed in a freely artistic style, is a major distinguishing feature. The aircraft additionally carry small VARIG titles.

Nordic Leisure/Nordic Regional (6N/NRD)

SWEDEN (SE)

Privately owned airline operating a mix of scheduled regional services in central and northern Sweden and leisure flights from Stockholm to Mediterranean resort destinations most popular with Scandinavian holidaymakers. Wet-lease services also form part of the airline's business. Nordic Regional was established in December 2003.

FLEET:
1 x MD-81, 1 x MD-83, 1 x MD-87, 2 x MD-90-30, 1 x Saab 340A

FEATURES:
Aircraft used for holiday charter flights sport a bright yellow, red, and blue design suggesting a palm tree on golden sands below a blue sky. It fills the white tailfin and, in a slightly altered presentation, under blue *Nordic Leisure* titles and the web address in black along the fuselage. Aircraft used on scheduled flights under the Nordic Regional brand include the company symbol of a yellow, red, and blue arrow made up of a folded paper aircraft design.

North American Airlines (NAA) (NA/NAO)

UNITED STATES (N)

U.S. airline providing a mix of scheduled and charter services from its main base at New York's John F. Kennedy International. Scheduled services are operated to Puerto Rico, Hawaii, Mexico, and the Dominican Republic, while domestic and international charters and incentive packages are offered to tour operators, sports teams, and others. The airline is also a certified U.S. Department of Defense air carrier. NAA was established in 1989 and began operations on 20 January 1990 between New York and Los Angeles, using a Boeing 757-200 for Club Med. It is now part of World Air Holdings.

FLEET:
5 x B757-200, 3 x B767-300ER

FEATURES:
This patriotic design features a large Stars and Stripes fluttering on the dark blue tailfin and a small stylized standard ahead of blue italic *North American* titles on the mid-fuselage roof. The engines and belly of the aircraft are painted in the same blue as the fin, with the inset gold cheatline adding a touch of class.

North Cariboo Air (NCB)

CANADA (C)

One of the oldest air carriers in western Canada providing a host of aerial services from Fort St. John in British Columbia and from bases at Calgary and Edmonton, Alberta, and Fort Liard in the Northwest Territories. Flying activities comprise executive transportation, scenic air tours, exploration and survey flights, cargo, medevac, crew changes, and aircraft leasing. Previously known as North Cariboo Flying Service, the company was founded in 1957 and began operations with general charters and oil support flights on 15 May that year.

FLEET:

1 x Beech 1900C, 1 x Beech 1900C-1, 2 x Beech 1900D, 6 x Beech King Air 100, 2 x Beech Catpass 200, 2 x DHC-6 Twin Otter 300 + smaller aircraft

FEATURES:

The diverse fleet is matched by a medley of liveries, none of which could be said to be standard. On the Beech aircraft the tailfin is colored dark blue with a curved red and yellow line, while a triple cheatline of red, yellow, and blue runs along the lower part of the fuselage. The top of each engine is also painted blue, underscored by the three lines.

Northern Air Cargo (NAC) (NC/NAC)

UNITED STATES (N)

U.S. scheduled all-cargo airline operating "flagstop" services from Anchorage to over 40 communities within Alaska and to points in Canada and the Pacific Northwest. The airline is also active in providing transport for the oil and offshore industries in northern Alaska, as well as to remote Eskimo areas. NAC also holds an experimental certificate for charter flights to Russia's far east. Subsidiary Northern Air Fuel provides fuel supply services. NAC was begun in 1956 by Bobby Sholton and Maurice Carlson as Sholton & Carlson and started a freight service with two Fairchild C-82 Flying Boxcars.

FLEET:

1 x ATR 42-300F, 2 x B727-100F, 7 x DC-6A, 1 x DC-6A/C, 1 x DC-6B

FEATURES:

Two simple applications of red are the only color elements on an all-white aircraft and include a fin flash and large NAC initials across the forward fuselage, with the a drawn to include an upward arrow stroke to create a semblance of dynamism.

Northwest Airlines (NW/NWA)

UNITED STATES (N)

World's fourth-largest airline operating an extensive network of scheduled passenger services from its hub at Minneapolis/St. Paul throughout the Americas, across the Atlantic to Europe and Africa, and across the Pacific to Asia and Australia. The network is further enlarged through affiliated airlines Mesaba Airlines, Pinnacle Airlines, and Pacific Island Aviation under the Northwest Airlink banner, bringing to more than 220 the total number of cities served. It is a member of the SkyTeam Alliance. The airline was founded on 1 August 1926 as Northwest Airways, when it was awarded a mail contract covering the Chicago–Minneapolis/St. Paul route. Scheduled services were inaugurated over that sector on 1 October that year, followed by the first passenger service on 1 July 1927 with Stinson Detroiters. On 16 April 1934, the company was re-organized under the present title. Transcontinental routes were inaugurated on 15 July 1947 to Tokyo, the airline then trading as Nortwest Orient Airlines. The acquisition of Republic Airlines on 12 August 1986 gave the airline a vast network of services in the central and southern U.S., as well as routes to Canada, Mexico, and the Cayman Islands. Republic Airlines, based at Minneapolis, was created on 1 July 1979 by the merger of North Central Airlines and Southern Airways.

FLEET:
74 (7) X A319-100, 80 X A320-200,
7 (5) X A330-200,
11 (17) X A330-300, 4 X B747-200B,
13 X B747-200F, 16 X B747-400,
51 X B757-200, 16 X B757-300,
94 X DC-9-30, 11 X DC-9-40,
31 X DC-9-50, 15 X DC-10-30,
4 X DC-10-30ER

FEATURES:
Northwest's trademark red tail, a highly recognizable part of the airline's visual heritage for decades, was retained in the updated livery introduced in April 2003. The black initials NWA running through the signature red "pointer" in the northwest corner of an outline globe have taken on more prominence than the full name featured in the previous scheme. The new design identifies the airline's global reach, innovative use of technology, pioneering track record, and 80 years of heritage.

Northwest Airlink (NW)

UNITED STATES (N)

Feeder network operated by major regional carriers Mesaba Airlines and Pinnacle Airlines, linking some 200 cities in the U.S. and Canada into the Northwest Airlines hubs at Detroit, Minneapolis, and Memphis. Northwest Airlink services are also provided by Pacific Island Aviation in Micronesia. Mesaba Airlines was founded in 1944 as Mesaba Aviation and began scheduled commuter services on 4 February 1973. Pinnacle Airlines began operations as Express Airlines 1 in June 1986 and was renamed on 8 May 2002. Pacific Island Aviation started operating out of Saipan on 21 March 1992.

FLEET:
35 X Avro RJ85, 65 (13) X CRJ200LR, 76 X CRJ440, 7 X Saab 340A, 60 x Saab 340B, 3 x Shorts 360-200

FEATURES:
The paint scheme is virtually identical to that of Northwest Airlines, including its trademark red tail with the signature "pointer" in the northwest corner of an outline globe. The only difference is that the word *Airlink* replaces the Northwest Airlines name under the black NWA initials.

Norwegian (DY/NAX)

NORWAY (LN)

Low-fare point-to-point airline operating a network of services within Norway and to destinations in Sweden, Spain, Portugal, and the United Kingdom. Norwegian's interesting history goes back to 1 January 1966 and the foundation of Busy Bee Air Service, which began flying on 3 May that year. It was known as Air-Executive Norway between 1972 and 1980 and was re-formed as Norwegian Air Shuttle in 1993. In September 2002 the airline adopted the simpler Norwegian brand to concentrate on domestic low-fare operations in competition with Braathens and SAS.

FLEET:
13 X B737-300

FEATURES:
The Norwegian fleet has an unusual scheme, with the forward fuselage painted in bright red and separated from the remaining white aircraft by a narrow blue band. The red and blue is also applied at the top of the tailfin. The most notable aspect to the scheme is that each aircraft features a portrait of a famous Norwegian on the fin. These include, or have included, Fridtjof Nansen, Sonja Henie, Roald Amundsen, Thor Heyerdahl, Henrik Ibsen, Gidsken Jakobsen.

Nouvelair (BJ/LBT)

TUNISIA (TS)

Privately owned Tunisian holiday airline flying tourists from 120 airports in 25 countries in Europe, the Maghreb, the Middle East, and Africa to Tunisia's resorts, regularly serving Tunis, Monastir, and Djerba. The airline was originally established in October 1989 as an affiliate of French operator Air Liberté and named Air Liberté Tunisie. Operations started on 21 March 1990 from Monastir with McDonnell Douglas MD-80s. The company was bought by Tunisian private interests following financial difficulties at Air Liberté and renamed in March 1996.

FLEET:
7 X A320-200, 2 X A321-200

FEATURES:
The airline's symbol represents the sun rising over the blue waters of the Mediterranean, along which coast the country of Tunisia lies. It is applied on the white engine cowlings and on the largely midnight blue tailfin, with the blue sweeping in a narrowing band below the windowline before broadening out again into a chinstrap. Blue *Nouvelair* titles on the forward cabin roof are followed by its name in Arabic script. The red Tunisian flag with its Islamic star and crescent appears at the rear.

Novair (Nova Airlines) (NVR)

SWEDEN (SE)

Swedish charter airline operating from Scandinavia to holiday resorts along the Mediterranean and in the Canary Islands, together with long-haul flights to India, the Dominican Republic, and Thailand. Major departure points are Gothenburg, Copenhagen, Oslo, and Stockholm, but flights also originate from many regional airports in Sweden, Denmark, and Norway. Novair was founded in 1997 by the Swiss-based Kuoni Travel Group. It began operations in November that year from its main base of Stockholm to the Canary Islands and Phuket in Thailand with for sister company Apollo Resor.

FLEET:
3 X A321-200, 2 X A330-200

FEATURES:
Novair has resisted the usual mix of bright holiday colors, focusing instead on the use of gold and mid-blue. The gold tail incorporates the simple white outline of a full sun, the whole picture being repeated on the winglets of some of its aircraft. Bold *Novair* titles cover the forward fuselage followed by a dynamic speed line. Engine cowlings are painted in the same mid-blue.

Ocean Airlines (vc/vcx)

ITALY (I)

All-cargo airline operating scheduled services from Brescia Montichiari Airport in the industrial heartland of northern Italy to destinations in the Far East and Africa. Ad hoc and contract charter flights are also undertaken within Europe and to East and West Africa and the Middle and Far East. Ocean Airlines was established by Austrian and Italian interests in September 2003. It obtained its air operator's certificate on 25 November 2004 and operated its first scheduled flight to Hong Kong on 8 January 2005, using an ex-Lufthansa Cargo Boeing 747-200F.

FLEET:
2 X B747-200F

FEATURES:
The name of the airline provides the inspiration for its visual identity, with two-tone blue for sea and sky dominating the white aircraft. The waves of the warm Mediterranean waters are suggested by the design of the first letter o on the tailfin and ahead of the *Ocean Airlines* titles on the forward fuselage, as well as by the pattern on the blue engines. Two light blue cheatlines accompany the dark blue belly of the aircraft, balancing the dark blue rear of the tailfin and two lines near the base.

OceanAir (ONE)

BRAZIL (PP/PT)

Brazilian regional airline providing scheduled passenger, cargo, and mail flights from Rio's Santos Dumont Airport to several points in the states of Rio de Janeiro and São Paulo. OceanAir was founded in 1998 to operate air-taxi flights, primarily for petroleum companies in the Campos basin. Authorization for regular passenger flights was obtained in 2002.

FLEET:
4 X EMB 120ER Brasilia,
3 X EMB 120RT Brasilia,
3 X Fokker 50

FEATURES:
Red *Ocean Air* titles on the forward fuselage are balanced by red and black forward-pointing paint splashes set into the white tailfin. Several aircraft are painted overall in bright red, sky blue, orange, pink, and gold, with the airline name reversed out in white and the tail design set into a white field.

O'Connor Airlines (UQ/OCM)

AUSTRALIA (VH)

South Australian regional airline operating a small network of scheduled passenger and cargo services from Mount Gambier to points within South Australia and to the neighboring state of Victoria. The network takes in the respective capital cities of Adelaide and Melbourne, as well as smaller towns in between. O'Connor Airlines began operations in 1973 as a single-pilot, single-aircraft flight training school founded by Leigh T. O'Connor.

FLEET:
3 x BAE Jetstream 32EP,
1 x Cessna 441 Conquest II

FEATURES:
The airline symbol comprises a large blue delta wing and long thin arrow superimposed on a red sun, which is applied on the tailfin. A thin blue line with an arrow point supports *O'Connor* titles forward and the full name in a smaller type at the rear.

Odessa Airlines (5K/ODS)

UKRAINE (UR)

Small Ukrainian airline operating scheduled and charter services for both passengers and freight out of Kiev Zhulyany and from its home city of Odessa, a major port on the Black Sea. Scheduled flights are operated to Moscow and St. Petersburg in Russia, and the Bulgarian Black Sea resort of Varna, with charter flights covering Russia, Syria, Turkey, and Germany. Agricultural flying is also undertaken. The airline was segregated from Aeroflot into an independent organization under the name of State Aircompany Odessa Airlines on 29 July 1996. It became a joint-stock company on 20 August 2003.

FLEET:
2 x AN-140, 3 x PZL AN-2,
4 x Yak-40

FEATURES:
The dominant colors are gold and black, applied in bands of varying widths on the tailfin and the lower rear fuselage, creating an impression of speed. The airline's location on the Black Sea is alluded to by two sails in gold and green set into a black ring on the fin. Black *Odessa Airlines* titles are preceded by the blue and yellow Ukrainian flag.

OLT Ostfriesische Luftransport (OL/OLT)

GERMANY (D)

Regional airline operating an internal scheduled service to several cities based in Bremen in northern Germany, together with connections to neighboring countries. Charter flights are also undertaken. Sister companies FLN Frisia Luftverkehr and OFR Ostsee-Flug-Rügen serve the German islands in the North Sea and Baltic respectively. OLT came into being on 1 November 1958 as OLT Ostfriesische Lufttaxi, specializing in air-taxi services to the Frisian Islands lying off Germany's north coast. The present title was adopted on 13 September 1974 when these flights were upgraded to scheduled status.

FLEET:
3 x BN-2B Islander, 1 x Cessna 208B Grand Caravan, 1 x Cessna 404 Titan II, 3 x SA227AC Metro III, 1 x Saab 340A, 1 x Saab 340B, 3 x Saab 2000

FEATURES:
This stylish design is notable for its simplicity, while at the same time describing OLT's operation centered around the Frisian Islands, represented by the white seagull in flight on the red tailfin. The red OLT lettering across the forward fuselage creates the necessary design equilibrium on the all-white fuselage.

Olympic Airlines (OA/OAL)

GREECE (SX)

Greek national airline operating scheduled services from Athens and Thessaloniki to most European and neighboring Middle Eastern cities, as well as to destinations in Africa, the Far East, Australia, and North America. It also serves an extensive domestic route system on the mainland and the Greek islands. Olympic was founded by shipping magnate Aristotle Onassis on 6 April 1957 as Olympic Airways out of former national airline TAE, but was nationalized on 1 January 1975. Olympic Airways, Olympic Aviation, and Macedonian Airlines were integrated under the present name on 12 December 2003.

FLEET:
1 x A300-600R, 4 x A340-300, 6 x ATR 42-500, 6 x ATR 72-200, 3 x B717-200, 1 x B737-300, 14 x B737-400, 4 x Dash 8 100

FEATURES:
The famous six Olympic rings are painted in their traditional colors on the mid-blue tailfin, which is an extension of the narrow pencil line carried above the windows. Expanded *Olympic* lettering, also in mid-blue, is carried on the forward half of the upper white fuselage behind a national blue and white pendant and the EU flag.

Oman Air (WY/OMA)
OMAN (A4O)

Muscat-based carrier operating an international network, linking the Omani capital with some 20 destinations across the Middle East, the Indian subcontinent, and East Africa. A domestic schedule is also operated to Khasab and Salalah, together with local charter flights. Oman Air's history goes back to 24 May 1981 and the foundation of Oman Aviation Services Co. through the merger of the Gulf Air Light Aircraft Division and Oman International Services, both of which had undertaken a multitude of charter flights with light aircraft. It was reorganized under the present name in May 1993.

FLEET:
2 X ATR 42-500, 3 X B737-700, 3 X B737-800

FEATURES:
The national colors of red, green, and white have been used imaginatively to create a fresh and elegant scheme. The red of the tailfin extends down and around the rear fuselage behind a narrow green band. Set into the fin is a sheathed kanjar, the traditional local dagger, which is also shown on the country's flag depicted alongside the aircraft registration. Red *Oman Air* titles are painted below the cabin windows, with the Arabic equivalent above in green.

Omni Air International (OY/OAE)
UNITED STATES (N)

U.S. supplemental carrier operating flights for major tour operators, passenger charters for the U.S. Department of Defense, and special air charters for cruise lines, corporations, and other organizations. A year-round service is flown between Las Vegas and Hawaii and seasonal summer and winter schedules operate to Mexico, the Caribbean, Florida, and other international destinations. Wet-lease services to other airlines are also offered. Founded as Continental Air Transport in 1983, it became Omni Air Transport 10 years later. It has also operated freight services as Omni Air Express.

FLEET:
3 X B757-200, 7 X DC-10-30, 1 X DC-10-30ER

FEATURES:
An undemonstrative design that avoids overt advertising, which is probably useful in its operations for the Department of Defense. Brown OAI initials on the center engine of its aircraft are surrounded by a silver aircraft with its contrail and, together with brown *Omni Air International* titles on the cabin roof, are the only applications of color on the white aircraft.

Omskavia (N3/OMS)

RUSSIAN FEDERATION (RA)

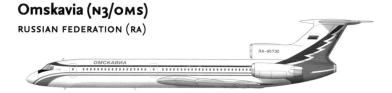

Russian scheduled and charter air carrier operating out of the city of Omsk in western Siberia, from where it offers scheduled passenger, cargo, and mail flights to Moscow and other Russian cities on a year-round and seasonal basis, as well as to destinations in Germany. Charters are also provided to Europe, the Middle East, and Thailand in the Far East. Omskavia was established on 1 February 1994 through the separation of Omsk State Air Enterprise into airline and airport divisions. Operations started with two Tupolev TU-154Bs and a number of ageing Antonov AN-2 biplanes. It has joined with other airlines in the Air Union alliance.

FLEET:
1 X AN-24RV, 1 X TU-154B-2,
5 X TU-154M

FEATURES:
A sweep of red and green on the tailfin is divided by a jagged white line that transitions to the white aircraft fuselage. In a departure from the usual convention, the red extends as a cheatline along the roof of the aircraft before widening and sloping up over the cockpit, while the green continues as twin cheatlines below the windows and turns down under the chin, with one line broadening to provide a counterbalance to the design. Small green *Omskavia* titles are applied above the red roof line.

One-Two-Go (OX/OEA)

THAILAND (HS)

Low-cost domestic arm of Orient Thai Airlines operating scheduled passenger and cargo services from Bangkok to several towns and cities, from Chiang Mai in the far north to Hat Yai in the deep south near the border with Malaysia. One-Two-Go was established in the second half of 2003 and began its first service between Bangkok and Chiang Mai in December that year. Charter flights throughout the region are also offered.

FLEET:
1 X B747-100, 1 X B747-300M,
3 X B757-200, 4 X MD-82

FEATURES:
Red and blue brushstrokes fill the tailfin and part of the rear fuselage and forward roof. *One-Two-Go by Orient Thai* titling in natural writing in blue, red, and black fills the space in between. The blue underside of the aircraft and red front half of the engines harmonize this relaxed design.

Onur Air (8Q/OHY)

TURKEY (TC)

Major Turkish airline operating a mix of holiday charters and inclusive-tour flights from many Western European countries to the most popular resort areas in Turkey, together with scheduled low-fare services from its base at Istanbul to all major domestic cities. Onur Air was founded on 14 April 1992 and began operations on 14 May that same year with two leased Airbus A320s. Scheduled domestic services were added in 2003.

FLEET:
5 X A300-600R, 1 X A300B2K,
2 X A300B4-100, 2 X A300B4-200,
2 X A320-200, 4 X A321-100,
6 X A321-200, 5 X MD-88

FEATURES:
The red arrow piercing a red and blue circle on the white tailfin is a very traditional and even old-fashioned symbol, as is the twin red and blue straight-through cheatline below the cabin windows. The red Turkish flag with its white crescent moon and star is followed by blue *Onur Air* titling. Some aircraft carry the names of Onur Air employees low under the cockpit windows.

Orient Thai Airlines (OX/OEA)

THAILAND (HS)

Major Thai carrier operating scheduled and charter services for passengers and freight from Bangkok to destinations throughout Southeast Asia. Scheduled services link the Thai capital with Hong Kong, South Korea, and mainland China. Domestic low-fare services are provided under the One-Two-Go brand. The airline's ancestry goes back to 1990 and the founding of short-lived Cambodia International Airlines, before the owner moved back to Thailand and founded Orient Express Air, which began flying from Chiang Mai in September 1993 with two Boeing 727s. The name was changed in 1996.

FLEET:
1 X B747-100, 5 X B747-200B,
1 X L1011-1 Tristar,
1 X L1011-50 Tristar

FEATURES:
In a variation from its low-fare One-Two-Go operation, the Orient Thai scheme simply comprises a freehand brushstroke of blue between two splashes of red on the tailfin, and red and blue *Orient Thai* titling in a cursive style on the mid-fuselage. The remainder of the aircraft is white.

Origin Pacific Airways (QO/OGN)

NEW ZEALAND (ZK)

Nelson-based regional airline, operating a scheduled passenger and cargo network to nine destinations throughout New Zealand's North and South islands. The airline offers weekend packages including hotels and car hire to Auckland, Nelson, Wellington, and Christchurch. Same-day and overnight freight flights are also offered throughout its scheduled network, with options for airport-to-door delivery. Origin Pacific Airways was created in 1996 as an air charter service and began operations in April 1997.

FLEET:
3 x Jetstream 31, 3 x Jetstream 32EP, 3 x Jetstream 41

FEATURES:
This elegant scheme is notable for its use of gold and dark blue, which permeates through all elements of the aircraft livery. The dark blue tail incorporates the airline's symbol in white and gold, which represents the initial letters of its name. *Origin Pacific* titles are carried above the dark underside of the aircraft, smartened up with a line of gold. Even the aircraft registration is painted in gold.

Pacific Airlines (BL/PIC)

VIETNAM (VN)

Vietnam's second airline, providing a domestic passenger and cargo service from Ho Chi Minh City in the south of the country, together with regional flights to Taiwan and Hong Kong. Charter flights are also available to destinations throughout the Far East and Southeast Asia. Pacific Airlines was incorporated on 12 December 1990 as the first airline in the country with foreign shareholdings. It started flying in April 1991 with a cargo charter to Europe, and added scheduled services in September that same year. The first service linked Ho Chi Minh City with Taipei.

FLEET:
1 X A320-200, 1 X A321-200, 2 X B737-400

FEATURES:
Pacific Airlines has adopted an economic livery that displays only its star-shaped arrow symbol against the outline of the sun on the tailfin and aircraft engines, and *Pacific Airlines* titles on the cabin roof. Both are applied in dark blue on an overall white aircraft.

Pacific Blue Airlines (DJ/PBI)

NEW ZEALAND (ZK)

International division of Australia's Virgin Blue serving the trans-Tasman market between New Zealand and Australia and also providing low-fare domestic flights, together with a service to Fiji, Vanuatu, and the Cook Islands. The airline was launched on 17 September 2003 and operated its inaugural flights on 29 January 2004 with a service between Christchurch and Brisbane.

FLEET:
3 x B737-800

FEATURES:
The striking Virgin red fuselage is highlighted by large blue and white *flypacificblue.com* titling, which takes up virtually all the fuselage. The red paint scheme is cut off and edged with blue to frame the white tailfin, which has *pacificblue* written up the rudder. Below the cockpit flies a scantily-clad lady carrying a blue flag embroidered with *flypacificblue* lettering. In line with other Virgin airlines, its aircraft carry names such as Pacific Pearl, Territory Tinkerbelle, Bonnie Blue, and others.

Pacific Coastal Airlines (8P/PCO)

CANADA (C)

Major regional airline in western Canada operating scheduled and charter passenger services in British Columbia serving some 16 destinations, primarily coastal logging communities and fishing lodges, from its main base at Vancouver and a hub at Port Hardy. The family-run airline was founded by Daryl Smith in 1979 and was the result of a merger between Powell Air, founded in 1975, and the Port Hardy division of Airbc. Bella Coola-based Wilderness Airlines, also established in 1975, was acquired on 1 April 1998.

FLEET:
3 x Beech 1900C, 3 x DHC-2 Beaver, 3 x EMB-110P1 Bandeirante, 4 x Grumman G-21A Goose, 5 x Shorts 360-200

FEATURES:
The tailfins of the aircraft carry a number of different designs, all relevant to the airline's sphere of operations in the Canadian Pacific. All are sketched in white on a dark blue base and include a grizzly bear, fisherman, yacht, eagle, and a lorry laden with lumber driving through the Canadian pine forests. The blue is repeated on the underside and engines, and is also used in the *Pacific Coastal* titling.

Pakistan International Airlines (PIA) (PK/PIA)

PAKISTAN (AP)

National carrier operating a scheduled network from Karachi to more than 50 destinations in Africa, Europe, the Middle and Far East, and North America. An extensive domestic network is also flown centered on the main cities of Karachi, Lahore, Islamabad, and Peshawar. The airline was founded as a government department in 1954 and began operations between West and East Pakistan (now Bangladesh) on 10 May that year with Lock-heed Super Constellations. It was reorganized on 10 March 1955 by merging PIA and Orient Airways, the latter having been founded on 23 October 1946.

FLEET:
1 X A300B4-200, 12 X A310-300, (7) X ATR 42-500, 7 X B737-300, 4 X B747-200B, 2 X B747-200C, 6 X B747-300, 3 X B777-200ER, (2) X B777-200LR, (3) X B777-300ER, 2 X DHC-6 Twin Otter 300, 4 X F27-200, 1 X F27-500RF

FEATURES:
The green national flag with the Muslim crescent and star in white flutters on the tailfin, while a sash wrapped around the fuselage and large *PIA* titles, preceded by the Arabic equivalent, are the only other elements of green on the pure white and light gold aircraft. White stands for peace and green for prosperity.

Palestinian Airlines (PF/PNW)

PALESTINIAN AUTHORITY

De facto Palestinian flag-carrier trying to maintain a small network of services. Services are currently scheduled from El Arish in Egypt to Amman in Jordan, and there are regular flights to other Middle Eastern countries as well as pilgrim charters to Saudi Arabia. Flights will move back to Gaza when airport facilities destroyed by Israeli forces have been repaired. The airline was established on 1 January 1995 and started charter services initially from Port Said, pending the opening of the new airport at Gaza in late 1998. Scheduled services had been inaugurated on 23 July 1997.

FLEET:
2 X F50

FEATURES:
Flashes of black, red, and green on the white tailfin are the colors of the Palestine flag, where the red stands for Arab unity, black for the prophet Mohammed, and green for Islam. The three flashes are repeated on the lower fuselage between black *Palestinian Airlines* titles in Arabic and English.

Pantanal Linhas Aéreas (P8/PTN)

BRAZIL (PP/PT)

Brazilian regional airline operating a 10-point network of passenger and cargo schedules from São Paulo to a number of cities within São Paulo state, with a few extensions to the neighboring state of Minas Gerais and Bahia in the northeast. It also transports employees of national oil company Petrobas throughout its installations in the Amazon region. Pantanal was established on 12 April 1993 and was one of the first companies to take advantage of partial deregulation of the Brazilian market, which had come into effect in 1992.

FLEET:
3 X ATR 42-300, 3 X ATR 42-320

FEATURES:
A most attractive and bright scheme, notable for the broad red and blue sashes wrapped diagonally around the mid-fuselage, boosted by the blue engines. The same colors are used in the strong chevron on the white tailfin, while *Pantanal* titles on the forward roof, the door surrounds, and the aircraft registration are rendered in blue only.

PBair (9Q/PBA)

THAILAND (HS)

Privately owned airline operating scheduled domestic and international passenger and cargo services. The network includes a growing number of cities in China, as well as in Vietnam, together with 10 destinations within Thailand. PBair was founded on 21 November 1990 by Dr. Piya Bhirom-bhakdi, president of Boonwrad Brewery Company, Thailand's largest brewery. A charter license was obtained on 8 November 1995, enabling a start of operations on 16 March 1998 with a flight between Bangkok and Chumbon. A full scheduled services license was granted on 26 January 1999.

FLEET:
1 X B767-300ER, 2 X ERJ 145LR

FEATURES:
A mythical winged lion, beautifully drawn in blue and white on the golden yellow tailfin, is the noteworthy symbol of this Thai airline. The yellow of the fin is supported by blue and turquoise flashes across the rear fuselage and by the yellow engines. Blue *PBair* titles fill the lower part of the aircraft at the front, with the Thai flag on the cabin roof. Red and white stand for sacrifice and purity, and blue is the royal color.

Pegasus Airlines (PGT)

TURKEY (TC)

Turkey's largest holiday charter airline, operating frequent flights from some 70 European destinations to the Turkish resort areas in and around Antalya, Bodrum, Dalaman, Izmir, and Istanbul. Wet-lease and subcharter work for other airlines is also a major part of the airline's business. Pegasus Airlines was established on 1 December 1989 by Irish flag-carrier Aer Lingus, which also provided technical assistance, to help build up the Turkish tourist industry. The first flight was operated on 15 April 1990 with a single Boeing 737-400. The Aer Lingus shares were acquired by Turkish interests in 1994.

FLEET:
2 × B737-400, 11 (6) × B737-800

FEATURES:
The name and symbol flying proudly on its sunny tailfin leaves no doubt that the airline has chosen the magnificent winged horse of Greek mythology to represent its high-flying ambitions. Pegasus, who was ridden by Bellerophon by the grace of the gods, represents humanity's determination to strive for the impossible.

PenAir (Peninsula Airways) (KS/PEN)

UNITED STATES (N)

Commuter airline operating extensive scheduled passenger and cargo services to some 85 communities in southwestern Alaska, together with charter flights and medevac services. Scheduled flights are operated from hubs at Anchorage, Cold Bay, Dutch Harbor, Dillingham, and King Salmon in a code-share partnership with Alaska Airlines. The airline was founded as a charter operation in 1955 and named Peninsula Airways the following year. Scheduled services were added in 1973 between King Salmon and the Pribilof Islands. The marketing name of PenAir was adopted in November 1991.

FLEET:
2 × Cessna 208B Grand Caravan,
4 × Fairchild SA227AC Metro III,
1 × SA227DC Metro 23,
6 × Saab 340B

FEATURES:
Two red and an enclosed gold band on the upper tailfin converge to simulate speed, and the same arrangement forms narrow cheatlines that speed along the length of the fuselage towards a sharp point. *PenAir* titles are painted midway up the tailfin, with the a extending to form a red and gold ensign.

Perimeter Airlines (UW/PAG)

CANADA (C)

Multifaceted aviation company providing scheduled services in Manitoba, charter and contract flying, aeromedical services, aircraft leasing, full-service maintenance, flight training, and fuel supply through its own fuel depot in Northern Manitoba. Perimeter connects 12 Manitoba communities from its base at Winnipeg, with another four points served by associate Dene Cree Airlines. Perimeter Airlines was established in 1960 and began operations that same year.

FLEET:
1 x Beech 99, 16 x SA226TC Metro II, 2 x SA227AC Metro III

FEATURES:
The light sea green tailfin incorporates the airline motif near the top, together with the aircraft registration. The motif comprises green and orange wing designs interlinked to suggest a bird in flight, set into a white disc and surrounded by a green and orange ring "perimeter." The airline name is applied on the forward fuselage below triple cheatlines comprising an inner orange line trimmed by spring green.

Perm Airlines (9D/PGP)

RUSSIAN FEDERATION (RA)

Russian regional carrier providing scheduled passenger and cargo services from Perm's Bolshoye Savino Airport, which the airline also operates, to destinations within Russia and the Commonwealth of Independent States. Charter flights also are a major part of its business. Perm Airlines is the successor to the Aeroflot Urals Civil Aviation Directorate, itself preceded by Perm Squadron No. 2, whose history dates back to June 1937, when a daily mail flight connected Perm to Sverdlovsk, Kudymar, and Gainy.

FLEET:
1 x AN-24RV, 2 x AN-24V, 2 x AN-26, 3 x TU-134A, 4 x TU-154B-2, 2 x Yak-40

FEATURES:
The airline emblem on the midnight blue tailfin shows a brown bear, a strong and ferocious mammal still found in large numbers west of the Ural Mountains. It is set into a white ellipse within an outline that follows the shape of the fin and also includes white PAL initials.

PGA–Portugália Airlines (N1/PGA)

PORTUGAL (CS)

Portuguese regional airline providing scheduled passenger services from Lisbon and Porto to some 20 European cities. Charter flights are also operated from northern Europe to the Portuguese holiday resorts, particularly in the Algarve. Subsidiary PGA Express connects Lisbon to points in Spain. PGA–Portugália was established by Grupo Espiritu Santo on 25 July 1988, but did not start flying until 7 July 1990 because of delays in the liberalization of the market. The initial routes linked Lisbon, Porto, and Faro with two Fokker 100s, and regular charter flights were also operated to Funchal on Madeira.

FLEET:
1 x Beech 1900D, 8 x ERJ145EP, 6 x Fokker 100, 2 x Saab 2000

FEATURES:
This imaginative use of the colors of the national flag on the tailfin features two brushstrokes in green and red, bisected by a rising sun and underscored by PGA lettering in black. PGA is the airline's three-letter ICAO code and was chosen to be represented on the aircraft as it was considered more memorable than the full name. The red and green colors wrapped around the underside of the fuselage add interest to the black PGA Portugália Airlines title ahead.

Philippine Airlines (PR/PAL)

PHILIPPINES (RP)

National carrier linking Manila with destinations throughout Asia, and with Australia, the Middle East, and the west coast of North America. A few major provincial capitals are also linked into the Asian network and serve as hubs for an extensive domestic route system connecting 18 towns and cities in this archipelago of more than 7,000 islands. The airline's history goes back to 25 February 1941 when it was founded as Philippine Air Lines, after purchasing the franchise of Philippine Aerial Taxi Company. Operations started on 15 March with twin-engined Beech 18s flying between Manila and Baguio.

FLEET:
(2) x A319-100, 6 (11) x A320-200, 8 x A330-300, 4 x A340-300, 4 x B737-300, 3 x B737-400, 4 (4) x B747-400, 1 x B747-400M

FEATURES:
The present livery combines an all-white fuselage with a blue, white, and red "interlocking triangle" tail design inspired by the national flag and features a sun bursting spectacularly from the red. The sun's rays signify the first eight provinces to revolt against Spain during the independence movement.

Phuket Air (9R/VAP)
THAILAND (HS)

Thai carrier providing a mix of domestic and international scheduled passenger and cargo services, together with holiday charter flights to the resort areas in the southern provinces of Thailand. Domestic schedules link Bangkok to a number of destinations along the length of the country, and an international extension is flown to Myanmar. Phuket Air was established in January 2001 to take advantage of the government's open-sky policy and began operations on 19 December that year. The initial service connected Bangkok to Ranong and Phuket in the south, flown with a Boeing 737-200.

FLEET:
1 X B737-200A, 1 X B747-200B,
1 X B747-300M,
2 X Namc YS-11-500

FEATURES:
Stylized fronds of a multi-colored palm tree sway gently in the breeze on the white tailfin. These graduate from yellow to orange, red, brown, blue, turquoise, and green, illustrating the range of colors to be found in this best-known Thai holiday paradise after which the airline was named. The clean white fuselage is punctuated only by blue *Phuket Air* titles along the cabin roof.

PLUNA Líneas Uruguayas de Navegación Aérea (PU/PUA)
URUGUAY (CX)

National airline of Uruguay providing scheduled services from the capital Montevideo to destinations within Latin America, and across the South Atlantic to Europe. A domestic route is also flown between Montevideo and Punta del Este, an important coastal resort. Primeras Líneas Uruguayas de Navegación Aérea (PLUNA) was founded in September 1935 by brothers Jorge and Alberta Marquez Vaeza and operated its first service on 20 November 1936 with a de Havilland Dragonfly between Montevideo, Salto, and Paysandu. It was taken over by the Uruguayan government on 12 November 1951.

FLEET:
1 X ATR 42-320, 3 X B737-200A,
1 X B737-300, 1 X B757-200,
1 X B767-300ER

FEATURES:
The navy blue tailfin and rear fuselage are complemented by the blue engines, affording a lively contrast to the otherwise white aircraft. An artistic interpretation of a bird in flight in gold on the fin adds to the modernity of the color scheme. Blue PLUNA titles are followed by the word *Uruguay* in gold, written in a cursive style.

Polar Air Cargo (PO/PAC)

UNITED STATES (N)

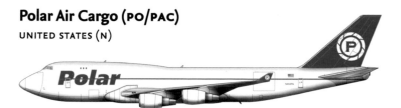

U.S. cargo airline specializing in time-definite scheduled freight flights connecting the major cargo markets in the Americas, Europe, the Far East, and Australasia. Polar also offers charter services, including shipments of livestock. Extensive work is also undertaken for the U.S. Air Force's Air Mobility Command. Polar Air Cargo was formed in January 1993 and began with charter flights the following April, adding scheduled services, initially to Anchorage, Honolulu, and New York, soon after. In November 2001, it was acquired by Atlas Air Worldwide Holdings, parent of Atlas Air.

FLEET:
1 X B747-100F, 4 X B747-200F, 1 X B747-300SF, 6 X B747-400F

FEATURES:
The airline's recognizable "circle P" logo dominates the mid-blue tailfin and can also be seen on the winglets of some of its aircraft. Assertive blue *Polar* titles take up most of the forward part of the aircraft, dissected by a red pencil line that turns into the company blue along the rest of the fuselage. A small U.S. flag is painted at the rear.

Polet Airlines (YQ/POT)

RUSSIAN FEDERATION (RA)

Major Russian airline specializing in the transportation of outsize and heavy cargo on an ad hoc and contract basis to destinations across the world. Passenger services are also scheduled, linking Moscow with several cities within Russia, as is survey work. Polet was established in 1988 and began operations with a single Antonov AN-30, carrying freight and personnel to northern gas exploration sites. Its outsize cargo business was started in 1994 with the acquisition of its first Antonov AN-124-100 Ruslan. Scheduled passenger services were added in August 2003.

FLEET:
8 X AN-124-100, 3 X AN-24RV, 3 X AN-30, 1 X B767-200ER, 3 X TU-134A, 5 X Yak-40, 1 X Yak-40K, 2 X Yak-42D

FEATURES:
Triple white bands are cut into the medium-blue tailfin to imply upward and forward movement, with a similar arrangement on the lower forward fuselage. The blue underside, which is trimmed by a black line, is shaped at the front in line with the upward-opening cargo loading door, and at the rear with the loading ramp. *Polet* titles and its English equivalent, *Flight*, appear at the front and rear.

Polynesian Airlines (PH/PAO)

WESTERN SAMOA (5W)

National airline linking Apia, the capital of Western Samoa, with other islands in the South Pacific, including Fiji, Tonga, Tahiti, and American Samoa, and reaching as far as Australia, New Zealand, and the Hawaiian Islands. Originally founded as a private company on 7 May 1959, the airline came under majority government control in 1971. Operations began with charter flights between Western Samoa and American Samoa in August 1959, using a Percival Prince. Permission to operate scheduled flights was granted on 7 March 1960.

FLEET:
1 x B737-800, 1 x BN-2A Islander, 1 x DHC-6 Twin Otter 300

FEATURES:
A white palm tree superimposed on a sun, which is colored in segments of red, orange, yellow, green, blue, and indigo, is the long-standing symbol of an airline with its home in the South Pacific. It is displayed on the white tailfin above rainbow stripes that rise from the base of the fin and dip down before wrapping themselves around the forward fuselage. Blue *Polynesian* titling in elegant penmanship follows the red Samoan flag.

Precision Air Services (PW/PRF)

TANZANIA (5H)

Private Tanzanian regional airline providing scheduled, charter, and scenic passenger flights out of Dar es Salaam, Arusha, Mwanza, and Zanzibar, serving 18 destinations in Tanzania, Kenya, and South Africa. Arusha is the gateway to many of Tanzania's landmarks and national parks, including the Rift Valley, Ngorongoro Crater, the Serengeti, and Mount Meru and Mount Kilimanjaro. Services are flown in cooperation with Kenya Airways, a major shareholder. Precision Air Services began in 1991 as an air-taxi service and began flying in 1994. Scheduled services were added in November 1999.

FLEET:
4 x ATR 42-300, 2 x ATR 72-200

FEATURES:
The tailfin and rear fuselage are divided vertically into sage green and yellow ocher. The airline's symbol of a leaping impala is emblazoned on the tailfin in white, straddling both colors, which reflect the Tanzanian landscape of forests and dry savannahs. The graceful impala is a small antelope that is renowned for its speed, cunning, and ability to always keep one step ahead. *Precision Air* titles in green and ocher are applied on the lower fuselage and on the aircraft engines.

Provincial Airlines (PB/SPR)

CANADA (C)

Diversified aviation company providing scheduled and charter passenger and cargo services, maritime surveillance, remote sensing, and environmental monitoring. Scheduled services link 14 communities within Newfoundland with its main base at the capital St. John's. Provincial Airlines was founded in August 1972 as a charter and training organization and entered the scheduled-services market in 1980.

FLEET:
2 x Dash 8 100, 2 x DHC-6 Twin Otter 300, 1 x SA227AC Metro III, 2 x Saab 340A

FEATURES:
The airline's symbol, applied to the tailfin of the predominantly white aircraft, features a white bird in flight, speeding along against a striped background of brown and ocher. In a complete change of coloration, the broad red band under the windows is underpinned by a blue pencil line that transforms itself into the head of a wild horse at the nose. The mid-fuselage roof carries blue *Provincial Airlines* titles.

Pulkovo Aviation Enterprise (FV/PLK)

RUSSIAN FEDERATION (RA)

Russia's second-largest airline enterprise, operating a domestic and international network from its base at St. Petersburg Pulkovo Airport. Its extensive network of scheduled and charter passenger and cargo flights takes in 84 cities across the world and nearly 50 within Russia. The airline's history goes back to 24 June 1932 when a first flight arrived carrying passengers from Moscow. Then operating as the Leningrad Civil Aviation Directorate of Aeroflot, it became the Pulkovo Aviation Enterprise in 1993. A merger with state airline Rossiya has been ordered but has not yet taken place.

FLEET:
2 x B737-500, 7 x IL-86, 10 x TU-134A-3, 9 x TU-154B-2, 19 x TU-154M

FEATURES:
The mid-blue color around the aft fuselage sweeps up the rear of the tailfin, providing the backdrop to a large rendition of the red, blue, and white Russian flag. Large blue *Pulkovo* titles are applied in Cyrillic letters on both sides of the forward fuselage.

Qantas Airways (QF/QFA)

AUSTRALIA (VH)

Australia's principal international airline, providing scheduled passenger and cargo services from Sydney and other state capitals to 30 countries in the Asia Pacific region, Europe, North America, and southern Africa. A strong domestic network is boosted by feeder services provided by subsidiary and associated carriers under the QantasLink banner. The airline was founded on 16 November 1920 as Queensland and Northern Territory Aerial Services, from which the Qantas acronym was derived. Australian Airlines, formerly Trans-Australia Airlines, was taken over in September 1992. Member of the oneworld alliance.

FLEET:
4 X A330-200, 7 (3) X A330-300, (12) X A380-800, 1 X B737-300, 21 X B737-400, 28 (5) X B737-800, 24 X B747-400, 6 X B747-400ER, 24 X B767-300ER, (55) X B787-8/9

FEATURES:
The Qantas image, designed by Sydney design consultant Tony Lunn and Associates, features a strong tailfin arrangement in which the warm red is extended down around the fuselage and includes the traditional "flying kangaroo." The red fin is trimmed in gold at the leading edge for added elegance.

QantasLink (QF)

AUSTRALIA (VH)

Regional airline grouping of Qantas-owned subsidiaries Airlink, Eastern Australia Airlines, and Sunstate Airlines, operating a system to 50 destinations throughout Australia from hubs at Tamworth, Newcastle, Cairns, Brisbane, Sydney, Mildura, and Melbourne. Airlink was founded in 1991, while Eastern Australia Airlines' history goes back to 1949 and the formation of East Coast Airlines from the merger of Air Eastland and New England Airways. Sunstate Airlines evolved from Whitaker, and commenced operations on 7 December 1981. Noosa Air was integrated on 1 July 1983.

FLEET:
4 X BAE 146-100, 3 X BAE 146-200, 2 X BAE 146-300, 3 X B717-200, 11 x Dash 8 100, 2 x Dash 8 200, 3 x Dash 8 Q200, 2 x Dash 8 300, 14 x Dash 8 Q300, (7) x Dash 8 Q400

FEATURES:
The QantasLink aircraft retain the warm red and gold tailfin arrangement of Qantas, together with the traditional "flying kangaroo" in white, to provide a common identity. The only change is the application of *QuantasLink* titles in red and black under the mid-cabin windows on the pristine white fuselage.

Qatar Airways (QR/QTR)

QATAR (A7)

Designated national carrier of the Persian Gulf State of Qatar, operating a growing network of scheduled passenger and cargo services from Doha International Airport to 60 destinations throughout the Middle East, and extending to the Indian subcontinent, the Far East, Africa, and Europe. The airline was founded on 20 October 1993 and began flying on 20 January 1994. Originally owned by members of the royal family, it was relaunched with partial private finance in April 1997.

FLEET:
1 X A300-600F, 9 X A300-600R,
2 X A319CJ, 11 X A320-200,
2 X A321-200, 11 (9) X A330-200,
7 X A330-300, 2 X A340-600,
(2) X A380-800

FEATURES:
The attractive livery of Qatar Airways is noticeable for its unusual silver-gray upper fuselage and tailfin above a white lower half. The only other color is the maroon of the national flag, expressed on the titles in English and Arabic, and on the tailfin, where a desert gazelle is superimposed on a graduated gray globe.

Regional Air Lines (FN/RGL)

MOROCCO (CN)

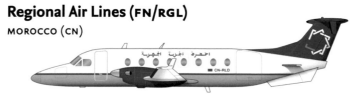

Casablanca-based private regional airline operating a scheduled domestic passenger and freight network, together with international connections to Portugal, mainland Spain, and the Canary Islands. Some services are operated in a code-share agreement with national carrier Royal Air Maroc. Charter flights for tour operators and corporate customers are also undertaken. Regional Air Lines was established in 1996 as the first privately owned airline in Morocco and started flying in July 1997.

FLEET:
2 X ATR 42-300, 4 x Beech 1900D,
1 x Beech King Air 350

FEATURES:
The striking design on the blue tailfin of a white continuous chain in the form of a sun suggests the links the airline provides between communities in Morocco. An interesting touch is the two chain links rendered in Morocco's national colors of red and green. A blue line separating the gray belly of the aircraft adds to the luminosity of the clean white upper fuselage. The airline name appears in English on the starboard side and in Arabic on the port.

Regional Air Services (REG)

TANZANIA (5H)

Tanzanian sister company of neighboring Airkenya Aviation, operating scheduled services from its base at Arusha to several points in the Serengeti for safari tourists. Flights at Arusha link up with Airkenya services from Nairobi, and with flights from Zanzibar, Dar es Salaam, and the Selous. Charters are also offered to anywhere in East, Central and Southern Africa. Regional Air was established in 1997.

FLEET:
2 x Cessna 208B Grand Caravan,
1 x DHC-6 Twin Otter 200,
2 x DHC-6 Twin Otter 300

FEATURES:
A broad cheatline in dark green, recalling the forests of the Tanzanian national parks, trimmed by thin black lines above and below, starts at a point behind the nose cone and flares out at the rear to reach into the base of the tailfin. The airline's initials, an R in black outline joined to the green A, are painted higher up the fin. Additional *Regional Air* titles in black can be found low on the forward fuselage.

Régional Compagnie Aérienne Européenne (YS/RAE)

FRANCE (F)

One of Europe's largest regional airlines based at Nantes and operating scheduled services within France and from provincial hubs such as Bordeaux and Clermont-Ferrand to neighboring European countries, and for parent Air France from its hubs at Paris and Lyon. Régional was created in March 2001 from the amalgamation of Flandre Air, Protéus Airlines, and Regional Airlines, the last having itself been the result of a merger on 1 January 1992 of Air Vendée and Airlec. Flandre Air was founded in 1977 as a charter company, while Protéus Airlines started life in 1986 as Protéus Air System.

FLEET:
10 x EMB 120ER Brasilia,
(6) x EMB 190LR, 8 x ERJ 135ER,
1 x ERJ 135LR, 13 x ERJ 145EU,
15 x ERJ 145MP, 5 x F70, 6 x F100,
6 x Saab 2000

FEATURES:
As a daughter company of Air France, Régional aircraft carry the parent company's tailfin design, a series of blue and red stripes on white based on the French tricolor, with the EU stars set into the broad blue band. Additional *Régional* titles are carried below the Air France name, and also on the engines.

Regional Express (REX) (ZL)

AUSTRALIA (VH)

Australia's largest independent regional airline connecting 30 metropolitan and regional centers from Wagga Wagga across New South Wales, Victoria, Tasmania, and South Australia, and to Australia's capital Canberra. Regional Express was formed in 2002 from the amalagamation of long-established regional airlines Hazelton Airlines and Kendell Airlines, both subsidiaries of the now defunct Ansett, and started operations on 6 August 2002. Hazelton Airlines, founded by Max Hazelton, commenced services in 1953, while Kendell Airlines was founded in 1966 and started scheduled services on 18 October 1971.

FLEET:
5 x SA227DC Metro 23, 6 x Saab 340A, 17 x Saab 340B

FEATURES:
A blue upper tailfin with an orange flash direct the eye to the blue and red *rex* trading name freely and expansively drawn across the rear of the aircraft. The airline's web address on the cabin roof incorporates *rex* in the same style. *Regional Express* titles, also in blue and orange, are applied in a more sober font.

RegionalLink (TL/ANO)

AUSTRALIA (VH)

Regional airline group comprising Darwin-based Airnorth and Adelaide-based Airlines of South Australia and Emu Airways. The three airlines operate under a single brand but retain their individual names. Airnorth, founded in 1978, serves a number of points in the Northern Territory, Queensland, and Western Australia, and also supports ongoing humanitarian aid in East Timor. ASA, founded in 1987, operates a small network in South Australia, while Emu Airways links Adelaide with nearby Kangaroo Island. All three airlines are owned by the aviation-services company Capiteq.

FLEET:
1 x EMB 110P1 Bandeirante,
5 x EMB 120ER Brasilia,
3 x Fairchild SA227DC Metro 23

FEATURES:
The blue, silver, and gold scheme is highlighted by the Southern Cross, which features on the Australian flag, in white on the blue tailfin, with a large central star representing regional Australia and the vertical gold swirl uniting north, south, east, and west.

Rico Linhas Aéreas (RLE)

BRAZIL (PP/PT)

Brazilian regional airline operating an extensive network of scheduled passenger and cargo services from its main base at Manaus's Eduardo Gomes International to 25 points in the Amazon region. Other bases are maintained at Altamira, Belém, Boa Vista, Borba, and Coari. Rico was founded in 1971 as Táxi Aéreo Rondônia, initially transporting workers and equipment for the construction of the Transamazonica highway. It later changed its name to Rico Táxi Aéreo, before adopting the present name following its authorization for scheduled services in northern Brazil on 1 November 1996.

FLEET:
3 X B737-200A, 1 X EMB 110C Bandeirante, 1 X EMB 110E Bandeirante , 2 X EMB 110P1 Bandeirante, 2 X EMB 120ER Brasilia

FEATURES:
This visually striking color scheme is memorable for the large white loop representing the broad waters of the Amazon River on a tailfin painted in the bright red company color. The curved red cheatline that separates the gray belly from the upper white fuselage changes into a similar loop in front of bold red *Rico* titling.

Rio-Sul Serviços Aéreos Regionais (SL/RSL)

BRAZIL (PP/PT)

Regional subsidiary of VARIG Participações em Transportes Aéreos, operating scheduled passenger and cargo services to destinations in Brazil's southern states under the VARIG brand. Operations are centered on São Paulo, Porto Alegre, and Rio de Janeiro. Rio-Sul came into being on 24 August 1976 out of Top Taxi Aéreo, following the establishment of the Sistema Integrado de Transportes Aéreos Regional, designed to develop air links from more remote areas into the main trunk routes. Services began the following September with a service between Rio and São José dos Campos.

FLEET:
4 X B737-300, 5 X B737-500, 2 X B737-700

FEATURES:
The livery is similar to that of the parent company VARIG, with the traditional compass-rose symbol in two hues of yellow adding warmth and the luster of gold to the navy blue tailfin. However, the large golden and shadowed *Rio-Sul* lettering across the fuselage, executed in a wonderfully artistic style, is a major distinguishing feature. The aircraft also carry small VARIG titles.

Rockhopper (XAX)

CHANNEL ISLANDS (G)

Regional airline operating scheduled flights from the Channel Islands, lying in the English Channel off the French coast. Services link the three main islands of Jersey, Guernsey, and Alderney with destinations in southern England and with Brittany in France. Charter flights and short-break holiday packages to the islands are also offered. The airline was formed in 2001 as Le Cocq Airlink to carry perishable goods from Bournemouth in southern England to Alderney. Scheduled passenger services commenced on 1 February 2002, and the present name was adopted on 29 August 2003. The airline was rebranded as Blue Islands in February 2006.

FLEET:
1 x Britten-Norman BN-2A Islander, 1 x BN-2B Islander, 2 x BN-2A MKIII-2 Trislander

FEATURES:
The white and yellow of the airline's prominent web address on the forward fuselage and yellow telephone number and aircraft registration at the rear highlight the deep blue paint scheme, which covers the entire aircraft. The yellow propeller hubs of the three engines on the Trislander also provide some light relief. The Islanders are operated in a similar identity, but the deep blue fuselage is replaced by a bright blue.

Romavia (WQ/RMV)

ROMANIA (YR)

Second Romanian state airline operating government VIP flights, together with scheduled passenger and cargo services to Morocco and Malta. Europe-wide charter flights are offered from major Romanian airports. Aircraft leasing and aircraft and component maintenance also form part of its business enterprise. Romavia was set up on 3 April 1991 and started flying later that year.

FLEET:
2 x BAC One-Eleven 500, 1 x BAE 146-200, 1 x B707-320C

FEATURES:
A most uninspiring design that harks back to the days of Soviet influence, when an airline's home country was highlighted by the national flag on the tailfin of a largely bare aircraft. At least Romavia has added a blue fin flash, cheatline, and partially painted engine cowlings. The title of *Romania*, rather than the airline's name, proclaims it as a government organ.

Royal Air Maroc (AT/RAM)

MOROCCO (CN)

Morocco's national airline providing scheduled passenger and cargo services from Casablanca's Mohammed V International Airport to destinations in North and West Africa, the Middle East, and to most major European destinations, as well as across the Atlantic to North America. Also operates domestic services linking all major cities, and Haj flights to the holy sites in Saudi Arabia. The airline was established on 8 June 1953 as Compagnie Cherifienne de Transports Aériens (CGTA) through the merger of Air Atlas and Air Maroc, both formed by private investors in 1947. It was renamed on 28 June 1957 following independence.

FLEET:
2 (2) x A321-200, 2 x ATR 42-300,
2 x B737-200C, 1 x B737-400,
6 x B737-500, 6 x B737-700,
9 (14) x B737-800, 1 x B747-400,
2 x B757-200, 2 x B767-300ER

FEATURES:
A green, white, and red band separates the upper white, fuselage from the gray underside. It tapers at both ends and promotes strong *Royal Air Maroc* titles in English and Arabic. The centerpiece of the national flag is the green pentangle (or seal of Solomon), which adorns the tail in the form of a shooting star, whose red trail emanates from below bold red RAM initials at the base.

Royal Brunei Airlines (BI/RBA)

BRUNEI DARUSSALAM (V8)

National airline of Brunei Darussalam, providing flag services from the capital Bandar Seri Begawan to regional destinations in Asia and to Australia, the Middle East, and Europe. Additional destinations are accessed through a number of international alliances. The airline also provides flights for the royal family and government officials. Royal Brunei Airlines was established on 18 November 1974 and began operations on 14 May 1975 with a first service to neighboring Singapore using two Boeing 737-200s.

FLEET:
2 x A319-100, 2 x A320-200,
6 x B767-200ER

FEATURES:
Royal Brunei's livery is based strongly on the colors of the national flag, in which yellow represents the sultan and black and white his two chief ministers. The design features a yellow lower fuselage, separated from the white roof by pinstripes in yellow and black, with both colors sweeping upwards over the tailfin. The national arms depicting a vertical winged support on the Muslim crescent form the main feature of the fin.

Royal Jordanian Airlines (RJ/RJA)

JORDAN (JY)

Jordan's flag-carrier operating an international scheduled network from Queen Alia International, serving the capital Amman to destinations throughout the Middle East, and to the Far East, North Africa, Europe, and the USA. Subsidiary Royal Wings operates charter flights, while Royal Jordanian Xpress serves regional destinations. The airline was established on 8 December 1963 as Alia, so named after the king's daughter, meaning "high and exalted one." Operations started on 15 December with one Douglas DC-3 and two Handley Page Heralds, initially to Beirut, Cairo, and Kuwait. The present title was adopted in December 1986.

FLEET:
4 X A310-300, 2 X A310-300F,
5 X A320-200, 2 X A321-200,
4 X A340-200

FEATURES:
The present livery was designed to convey the spirit of Jordan's heritage, using majestic gold and red cheatlines along a charcoal-gray upper fuselage. The gold crown of the Hashemite Kingdom dominates the tailfin, which also features subtly tapered speed bands in dark gray and a red tip. The Jordanian flag, which incorporates a seven-pointed star in a red field signifying the first seven verses of the Koran, is painted on the rear fuselage.

Royal Nepal Airlines (RA/RNA)

NEPAL (9N)

Nepalese flag-carrier operating international scheduled flights from the capital Kathmandu to regional destinations in Asia and the Indian subcontinent. Vital domestic services are provided to points on the southern slopes of the Himalayas and to isolated inland valleys. Royal Nepal Airlines was established on 1 July 1958 as a government corporation to take over local routes which had been operated by Indian Airlines since the early 1950s. Services were started with a leased Douglas DC-3 and international flights were taken over from Indian Airlines on 16 January 1960.

FLEET:
2 X B757-200, 7 X DHC-6
Twin Otter 300

FEATURES:
A pure white fuselage represents the snow-capped peaks of the Himalayas, crossed by twin diagonal fin bands in the national colors of red and blue. Blue *Royal Nepal Airlines* titles, displayed in English on port and Nepali on starboard, are preceded by the "double triangle" flag, which displays the crescent moon and sun, signifying the hope that the country may live as long as these astral bodies. The traditional "winged Buddha" symbol is beneath the cockpit.

Royal Wings Airlines (RWZ)
JORDAN (JY)

Subsidiary of government-owned Royal Jordanian Airlines operating business jet services and charter flights from Amman's Queen Alia International to Aqaba on the Red Sea, gateway to the red rose city of Petra and the Wadi Rum desert landscape. Charter flights also serve the Red Sea resorts in Egypt, the Nile cities of Luxor and Aswan, and Larnaca in Cyprus. Royal Wings was established on 1 January 1996 and began flying on 10 February that year with twice-daily flights to Aqaba. In June 1996, business jet operator Arab Wings was merged into Royal Wings. Scheduled services have been transferred to Royal Jordanian Xpress.

FLEET:
1 x A320-200, 2 x Dash 8 Q300

FEATURES:
The royal crown of the Hashemite Kingdom of Jordan is displayed on the tailfin, where it is emphasized by a series of red lines, and on the forward fuselage ahead of blue *Royal Wings Airlines* titles. The Jordanian flag at the rear is made up of the pan-Arab colors of black, white, green, and red, with a seven-pointed white star in a red field, representing the first seven verses of the Koran.

Russian Sky Airlines (P7/ESL)
RUSSIAN FEDERATION (RA)

Major Russian carrier operating scheduled and charter flights for passengers and cargo out of Moscow's Domodedovo Airport. A number of destinations are serviced within Russia, the CIS, Europe, Africa, and the Middle and Far East. VIP flights are also undertaken, and freight forwarding is another part of the airline's business. The airline was established on 27 November 1995 by the East Line Group, which operates Domodedovo Airport, and was simply known as East Line, then as East Line Airlines from 1997, before being renamed on 21 October 2004 following a change of ownership.

FLEET:
2 x IL-62M, 2 x IL-76MF,
9 x IL-76TD, 4 x IL-86,
1 x TU-134A, 1 x TU-154M

FEATURES:
The tailfin represents a Varangian coat of arms, with dark blue and azure, red, and gold bands, a wing, and arrow. The blue symbolizes greatness and beauty, and the gold power and magnanimity, while the wing suggests speed and freedom, and the arrow energy, momentum, and purpose. Only sky blue *Russian Sky* titles in English on the starboard and Cyrillic on the port side interrupt the clean white fuselage.

Rutaca Airlines (Rutas Aéreas CA) (RUC)

VENEZUELA (YV)

Venezuelan regional airline operating a mix of scheduled and charter services from the capital Caracas serving several major cities within the country, as well as close Caribbean neighbors Trinidad and Tobago and Grenada. Passenger and cargo charters also serve other areas of the Caribbean and South America. Rutaca Airlines was established in 1974.

FLEET:
3 x B737-200A, 4 x Cessna 208B Grand Caravan, 5 x EMB 110P1 Bandeirante

FEATURES:
The large blue *Rutaca* name underscored by a red cheatline dominates the aircraft fuselage, which is mostly white with a dark blue underside. A blue letter R with dynamic red lines is centrally displayed on the tailfin. The yellow, blue, and red Venezuelan flag is painted beside the rear cabin door.

Rwandair Express (WB/RWD)

RWANDA (9XR)

National carrier of the Central African republic of Rwanda, connecting the capital Kigali with Johannesburg in South Africa and cities in the neighboring countries of Kenya, Burundi, Tanzania, and Uganda. Destinations include Nairobi, Entebbe, Kilimanjaro, and Bujumbura. Rwandair Express was established by the government and private interests in early 2003 and started operations on 27 April that year.

FLEET:
1 x B737-500, 1 x MD-81

FEATURES:
The airline has borrowed from the national flag in creating its attractive livery. The yellow sun of enlightenment is partially surrounded by flashes of blue and green, all set into the blue tailfin. The green in the flag, which is displayed behind the forward cabin door, stands for prosperity, the blue for peace and happiness, and the yellow for economic development.

Ryanair (FR/RYR)

IRELAND (EI)

Europe's pioneering low-fare airline providing a still-growing network of no-frills flights linking the Irish Republic, United Kingdom, and Continental Europe from hubs at Dublin, Glasgow Prestwick, London Stansted, Brussels South Charleroi, and Frankfurt Hahn. Other bases are maintained at Luton, Bergamo, Girona, and Stockholm. Ryanair was founded in May 1985 and began low-fare operations with a service between Waterford and London Gatwick. It moved into the European market in 1997 and in early 2003 expanded its activities with the acquisition from KLM of Stansted-based low-fare airline buzz.

FLEET:
10 X B737-200A,
83 (156) X B737-800

FEATURES:
A "flying" variation of the Irish harp, which has been a national symbol since at least the fifteenth century, is displayed in yellow on a mid-blue tailfin. Both colors are repeated along the belly of the aircraft. Blue *Ryanair* titles are carried above the windowline forward of the wing, preceded by a blue harp. A few aircraft are also operated in special advertising markings.

Ryan International Airlines (RD/RYN)

UNITED STATES (N)

Large U.S. airline operating scheduled and non-scheduled passenger and cargo charters on a worldwide basis, deriving a majority of its income from flights for the U.S. Postal Service and overnight freight companies.The airline also makes its aircraft available to tour operators, and has an operation in the Pacific flying fresh fish from Saipan to Japan, and general cargo within Micronesia. The airline was formed in 1972 and began operations on 3 March 1973 as DeBoer Aviation. It later became known as Ryan Aviation and adopted the present title in 1988.

FLEET:
1 X B727-100F, 2 X B727-200F,
2 X B737-400, 6 X B737-800S,
5 X B757-200, 1 X MD-83

FEATURES:
A white stylized letter R, which appears in white on the midnight blue tailfin and in a large silver-gray format on the forward fuselage, is the signature of the airline's identity. Additional *Ryan* titles with an orange symbol appear on the forward cabin roof. The blue of the fin extends down and around the rear fuselage and also colors the engines.

Safair (FA/SFR)
SOUTH AFRICA (ZS)

Africa's largest diverse aviation company, specializing in value-added aircraft leasing and chartering, as well as sale and leaseback transactions, aircraft financing, and contract operations for the United Nations and other organizations. Flight-crew leasing and training, aircraft maintenance and modifications, aviation safety and medical training, and flight planning are among other business activities. The Johannesburg-based airline was formed by Safmarine as Safair Freighters in March 1969 and began cargo charters on 18 March 1970. It was acquired by Imperial Holdings in December 1998.

FLEET:
1 X B727-200A, 3 X B727-200F, 6 X B737-200A, 9 X L100-30 Hercules

FEATURES:
This modest blue and white scheme features the airline's symbol of two birds facing in opposite directions forming the letter s in the center. It is applied on the tailfin and ahead of blue *Safair* titles on the forward cabin roof. The lettering has a white "cut" to imbue speed. The web address resides below the windows.

Samara Airlines (E5/BRZ)
RUSSIAN FEDERATION (RA)

Russian airline connecting the industrial Samara region in the southeastern part of European Russia to many cities in other parts of of the country with scheduled passenger and cargo flights. Regular charters are also flown to Tajikistan, Turkey, Uzbekistan, Ukraine, and the United Arab Emirates. The airline's history dates back to 1961 and the foundation of the Kuybyshev Aviation Enterprise, later transformed into the Kuybyshev Joint Aviation Squadron (KUAO). The privatization of KUAO in 1993 resulted in the establishment of Samara Airlines as a joint-stock company.

FLEET:
2 X IL-76T, 1 X TU-134A, 6 X TU-134A-3, 3 X TU-154B-2, 8 X TU-154M, 1 X Yak-40, 1 X Yak-42, 2 X Yak-42D

FEATURES:
The airline's motif is the letter s superimposed on a blue globe wthin a white disc, the whole being set into the red tailfin of its aircraft. The red is stopped short on the engines to leave space for a blue collar, which is a nice finishing touch. Large red *Samara Airlines* titles take up most of the forward fuselage. A small Russian flag can be found behind the cockpit.

Santa Barbara Airlines (s3/bbr)

VENEZUELA (YV)

Private airline operating a comprehensive domestic network linking the capital Caracas and Maracaibo to most other major cities in Venezuela. Services also extend across the country's borders to Aruba and Curaçao in the Caribbean, to neighboring Colombia, and Florida in the United States. Flights across the Atlantic service Madrid in Spain and Tenerife in the Canary Islands. Santa Barbara Airlines was founded on 1 November 1995 by a group of cattle dealers in the southern region of Maracaibo Lake and inaugurated flights on 1 March 1996 with a service between Santa Barbara del Zulia and Maracaibo.

FLEET:
4 X ATR 42-300, 2 X B727-200A, 1 X B757-200, 3 X Cessna 208B Grand Caravan, 2 X DC-10-30

FEATURES:
A tropical flower symbol on a golden sun disc colors the blue tailfin, which also sports *Venezuela* titles in white across the center engine. The airline's name is written in blue and red above and below the cabin windows over a curtailed blue cheatline. An *SB* logo design is painted on the wing-mounted engines. The yellow, blue, and red Venezuelan flag is at the rear.

Saravia (Saratov Airlines) (6w/sov)

RUSSIAN FEDERATION (RA)

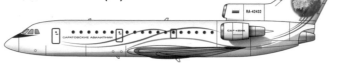

Russian airline linking the Saratov region in the Volga area to the capital Moscow, and other Russian and Commonwealth of Independent States destinations. Charter flights are also offered to anywhere in Russia, the CIS, Europe, and the Middle East. Saravia's history goes back to 1931 when only mail flights were undertaken until the operation became part of the Aeroflot Saratov Directorate.

FLEET:
1 X AN-24RV, 2 X Yak-40K, 3 X Yak-42, 6 X Yak-42D

FEATURES:
Blue wavy lines emanate from the front of the fuselage, culminating in a giant crashing wave against a starry night sky on the tail. The unusual livery is completed by a sky blue underside.

SAS Braathens (BU/BRA)

NORWAY (LN)

Biggest Norwegian airline combining, since 2004, the operations of Braathens and SAS Scandinavian Airlines. An extensive network of services links some 40 communities within Norway and to Spitsbergen, and also provides connections, mainly from Oslo Gardermoen, to 50 European cities reaching south as far as the Balearic Islands in Spain. Founded by Ludvig G Braathen on 26 March 1946 as Braathens South American and Far East Air Transport, soon abbreviated to Braathens SAFE, the airline began operations on 15 May that year. In late 2001, the airline was acquired by SAS.

FLEET:
4 X B737-400, 13 X B737-500, 10 X B737-700

FEATURES:
Although a member of the SAS Group, the airline has retained its strong individual brand. The aircraft is divided cleanly into a white upper part and royal blue underside trimmed in red, with prominent blue *Braathens* titling on the cabin roof. The red, blue, and white Norwegian flag flutters on the tailfin. Each aircraft is named after famous people from the Viking era and the name can be found under the cockpit window.

SAS Scandinavian Airlines (SK/SAS)

NORWAY (LN)/DENMARK (OY)/SWEDEN (ES)

Tri-national airline of Denmark, Norway, and Sweden operating an extensive domestic and intra-Scandinavian route system, together with scheduled services between Scandinavia and Europe, the Middle East and Far East, and the U.S., reaching more than 100 cities. This is further extended through its membership of the Star Alliance. Main bases are maintained at Stockholm Arlanda, Oslo Gardermoen, and Copenhagen. The airline was established as Scandinavian Airlines System (SAS) on 31 July 1946, although predecessor companies in each country date back to the early 1920s.

FLEET:
(4) X A319-100, 8 X A321-200, 4 X A330-300, 7 X A340-300, 27 X B737-600, 6 X B737-700, 13 X B737-800, 24 X Dash 8 Q400, 6 X F50, 13 X MD-81, 20 X MD-82, 15 X MD-87, 6 X MD-90-30

FEATURES:
Developed by Stockholm Design Lab, the livery is said to radiate safety and technical competence. The SAS logo is highlighted in white on a blue tail, setting off the winter white and fall colors of the fuselage on which the word *Airlines* is sketched near the front. Most of the engine cowlings are painted in the colors of an orange-red sunset.

SATA Air Açores (SP/SAT)
AZORES (CS)

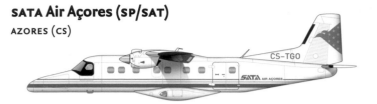

Local airline in the Azores, a volcanic archipelago in the middle of the Atlantic Ocean administered by Portugal. Scheduled services connect the capital Ponta Delgado on the main island of São Miguel with the other eight islands, and there are also direct connections between many of the islands. The airline's history goes back to 21 August 1941 and the foundation of Sociedade Açoreana de Estudos Aéreos to study the possibilities of establishing air services. Operations finally began on 15 June 1947 with a single Beech 18 under the name of Sociedade Açoreana de Transportes Aéreos, or SATA for short.

FLEET:
4 x BAE ATP, 1 x Dornier 228-200

FEATURES:
The blue bird on the tailfin is a depiction of a goshawk, which appears on the Azores flag, together with the nine golden stars standing for the nine islands making up the archipelago, namely São Jorge, Santa Maria, Terceira, Graciosa, Faial, São Miguel, Corvo, Pico, and Flores. The blue and gold is repeated in the cheatline arrangement, with SATA Air Açores titles set into the upper blue line. The airline's ATP aircraft are painted in the more modern symbol of SATA International.

SATA Internacional (S4/RZO)
AZORES (CS)

Subsidiary of SATA Air Açores providing scheduled connections between the capital Ponta Delgada and Madeira and the principal cities on mainland Portugal, and also linking Lisbon with Toronto in Canada. International charter flights are also undertaken. The airline was first incorporated as OceanAir in December 1990 and operated charter flights until it suspended services in 1994. SATA Air Açores acquired the shares and began operations to the U.S. and Canada as Azores Express and SATA Express respectively. On 19 March 1998, it then set up SATA Internacional, which started flying on 8 April.

FLEET:
3 x A310-300, 3 x A320-200,
1 x B737-300, 1 x B737-400

FEATURES:
The goshawk with wings spread wide on the Azores flag is drawn in a modern stylized form in white with light blue feathers, flying on the dark blue tailfin. SATA Internacional titling in blue is displayed on the forward upper roof, with additional Fly Azores lettering at the rear. The airline's goshawk symbol has also been added to the white engine, where it is rendered in two-tone blue, together with the name.

Satena (9N/NSE)
COLOMBIA (HK)

State-owned airline operating an extensive
passenger, cargo, and mail network linking the
main cities to more than 40 smaller destinations
throughout Colombia but specifically in the Amazon
region. Satena (Servicio Aéreo a Territorios Nacionales) was created on 12 April 1962 as a division of
the Colombian air force to develop communications
in the vast Amazon and Orinoco river basins. Operations began in September that year with Douglas
C-47s, C-54s, and de Havilland Beavers, initially
linking Bogotá with Leticia, Tarapacá, El Encanto,
and Puerto Leguízamo. It was transformed into a
commercial airline in 1966.

FLEET:
6 X FD 328-110, 3 X EMB 120ER
Brasilia, 3 X ERJ 145LR,
1 X F28-3000

FEATURES:
The Satena identity features three
major elements and colors, all
designed for high visibility and
recognition. The blue highlights
the waters of the country's Pacific
and Caribbean coasts, while the
amarillo sun rising over the
horizon suggests continuity and
daily renewal. Flying across the
sun is the magnificent *Corocora*,
an indigenous scarlet ibis that
has its home in the Llanos
Orientales, which is the airline's
main sphere of operation.

Saudi Arabian Airlines (SV/SVA)
SAUDI ARABIA (HZ)

National airline of the Kingdom of Saudi Arabia
operating scheduled passenger and cargo services
from its main base at King Abdul Aziz Airport at
Jeddah, and from Riyadh and Dhahran to more
than 70 destinations in the Middle East and Far
East, the Indian subcontinent, Africa, Europe, and
the United States. A 26-point domestic network is
operated. Flights are additionally provided for the
royal family and government institutions with
dedicated aircraft. The airline was founded in 1945
and began operations on 4 March 1947. It used the
Saudia name between 1972 and 1996.

FLEET:
11 X A300-600, 2 X B737-200A,
7 X B747-100, 1 X B747-200F,
9 X B747-300, 5 X B747-400,
23 X B777-200ER,
(15) X EMB 170LR, 4 X MD-11F,
29 X MD-90-30

FEATURES:
The fuselage features shades of
dune-beige and white, separated
by gold, while the royal blue tail is
dominated by a striking representation of the date palm and
crossed swords in gold above a
turquoise sea enclosed by a
golden crescent representing the
Muslim faith. The royal blue and
turquoise colors were inspired by
deep waters of the Red Sea.

Scenic Airlines (YR/YRR)

UNITED STATES (N)

One of the largest and most experienced aerial tour operators in the world, specializing in tours from Las Vegas to the Grand Canyon, taking in Lake Mead, the Hoover Dam, and the Colorado River, as well as Monument Valley, Yosemite National Park, and Bryce Canyon. Essential Air Services are flown to six towns in Nevada and California. High-winged aircraft with oversized windows offer a panoramic view over the great sights of the Southwest. Scenic Airlines was established in 1967. In 1988 it merged with another Las Vegas-based operator, Eagle Canyon Airlines.

FLEET:
1 x Beech 1900C, 14 x DHC-6 Twin Otter 300 (Vistaliner)

FEATURES:
The aircraft and leading part of the vertically divided tailfin are largely painted white, with the rear covered in the colors of the rainbow. The word *Scenic* runs down vertically from the top. A black and red cheatline is underscored by the words *Gateway to the National Parks* referencing the airline's operations.

Scot Airways (CB/SAY)

UNITED KINGDOM (UK)

British regional airline operating a small network of scheduled flights with an emphasis on Scottish services out of London City Airport. It also provides a connection between the south coast and Amsterdam. Scot Airways was established by Roy and Merlyn Suckling as Suckling Airways at Ipswich, East Anglia, in November 1984 and operated its first service to Manchester in April 1986. A permanent move to Cambridge was initiated when the grass strip at Ipswich proved no longer suitable. The present name was adopted on 31 October 1999 following a cash injection from Scottish investors.

FLEET:
2 x BAE 146-200QC, 7 x FD 328-100

FEATURES:
A patriotic rendition of a Scottish tartan forms the central element of the design, taking up most of the tailfin of the otherwise white aircraft and broken by the airline's initials in red. The o in the red *Scot Airways* titles has been cleverly adapted to represent the St. Andrew's cross, a white saltire on blue, which became the Scottish banner early in the thirteenth century, although its history is said to date back to the eighth.

Shaheen Air International (NL/SAI)

PAKISTAN (AP)

Karachi-based second designated national carrier of
Pakistan, operating a small domestic network
between Pakistan's four major cities, together with
regional flights across the Persian Gulf to Kuwait,
Qatar, Oman, and the United Arab Emirates.
Shaheen Air was established as a joint venture
between the Shaheen Foundation and the Pakistan
air force in December 1993 and began commercial
operations that same month. The first international
schedule was added in February 1995, linking
Peshawar and Dubai. The airline is now managed
by Canadian company TAWA International.

FLEET:
3 X B737-200A

FEATURES:
This stunning and memorable
scheme features a golden falcon
with large wings spread across
the blue tailfin and flying fast, as
indicated by the many golden
speed lines behind the wing. The
blue of the tailfin gradually fades
into bands of gold, curving from
the rear base up and over the
mid-fuselage. The predominance
of gold is continued through to
the engines. The design is
balanced by huge blue *Shaheen*
titles, which take up most of the
front half of the aircraft.

Shandong Airlines (SC/CDG)

CHINA (B)

Provincial airline operating a domestic network
across the country serving some 40 destinations,
taking in provincial capitals, major commercial
centers and some smaller communities. The airline
operates out of Jinan Yaoqiang International
Airport, and also has hubs at Jining, Qingdao,
Sanlian, and Yantai. Shandong Airlines was
established on 12 March 1994 and began operations
on 26 December that year from Jinan to Qingdao,
Yantai, and Jining. In September 1997, it jointly
founded the Xinxing (New Star) Aviation Alliance
with five other provincial airlines.

FLEET:
(10) X ARJ-21, 13 X B737-300,
3 X B737-700, 4 X B737-800,
5 X CRJ200ER, 4 X CRJ200LR,
2 X CRJ700, 4 X 340B

FEATURES:
A stylized winged bird is the
symbol of this provincial airline.
It takes up much of the blue
tailfin and also appears on the
blue winglets of appropriate
aircraft. Bold SDA initials cross a
flowing red ribbon on the
forward fuselage, while the full
name in both English and
Chinese characters stretches
along the upper fuselage. The
smart dark blue complements the
mainly snow white paint scheme.

Shanghai Airlines (FM/CSH)

CHINA (B)

Large municipal airline with private shareholding operating an extensive network of domestic routes serving more than 40 destinations, including all provincial capitals, from its bases at Shanghai's Hongqiao and Pudong International airports. Regional routes are also flown to Russia's far east, Cambodia, Macau, and Vietnam. Shanghai Airlines was established in 1985 by the Shanghai municipal government and other interests to become the first independently run airline in China. It was initially limited to domestic flights but finally won approval in September 1997 for international services.

FLEET:
(5) x ARJ-21, 6 x B737-700, 9 (5) x B737-800, 13 x B757-200, 4 x B767-300, 1 (2) x B767-300ER, (9) x B787-8, 3 x CRJ200ER, 2 x CRJ200LR

FEATURES:
A stylized white crane in graceful flight adorns the red tailfin, which sweeps down to form a broad red cheatline under the window level. This cheatline is underscored by thinner straight-through lines in black and red. Prominent black *Shanghai Airlines* titles appear in both English and Chinese lettering on the white cabin roof.

Shenzhen Airlines (ZH/CSZ)

CHINA (B)

Provincial airline operating a domestic network from its base at Shenzhen Huangtian Airport to more than 30 destinations serving most provincial capitals, including Beijing and Shanghai. The airline was established in January 1993 by the Shenzhen government as a local air-transport enterprise with the approval of the Civil Aviation Administration of China and financial participation by Air China and several local banks and corporations. Flights to eight domestic points were inaugurated on 14 October that same year.

FLEET:
(4) x A319-100, 1 (3) x A320-200, 9 x B737-300, 10 x B737-700, 8 x B737-800, 5 x B737-900

FEATURES:
A white boomerang-shaped arrow in a white ring, symbolizing the sun and moon, on a dark green tailfin is the dominant feature. Thin sky blue and dark green cheatlines divide the upper white and lower gray parts of the aircraft, widening at the nose, with the green line creating the effect of a chinstrap. The red stenciled design of the name in English above the windows, preceded by its equivalent in Chinese characters, is unusual.

Siberia Airlines (s7/sbi)

RUSSIAN FEDERATION (RA)

Major Russian airline operating scheduled passenger and cargo flights from its bases at Novosibirsk, Irkutsk, and Moscow to some 60 destinations throughout the Russian Federation and Commonwealth of Independent States, as well as to destinations further away in Europe and Southeast Asia. Siberia Airlines also offers charter flights to Western Europe. Based on the former Aeroflot Novosibirsk division, the airline evolved from the Tolmachevo State Aviation Enterprise, established in May 1992, and formerly traded as Sibir Airlines. Vnukovo Airlines was acquired in May 2001.

FLEET:
2 x A310-200, 3 x A310-300,
3 x B737-500, 10 x IL-86,
4 x TU-154B-2, 29 x TU-154M,
2 (2) x TU-204-100

FEATURES:
The striking two-tone green paint scheme applied over the entire fuselage is highlighted by the airline's s7 IATA-assigned two-letter flight code in white, prominently displayed on the tailfin and forward fuselage, set into a red circle. Along the side of the fuselage, in the darker shade of green, are depicted silhouettes of the "People of s7." The rebranding was designed by Landor Associates.

Sichuan Airlines (3u/csc)

CHINA (B)

Chengdu-based airline operating scheduled services to several destinations within the Sichuan province, and to another 15 cities in other provinces. Flights are centered on its main base of Chengdu and a secondary hub in Chongqing. Sichuan Airlines was established by the provincial government on 19 September 1986 and began operations on 14 July 1988, initially with locally built turboprop aircraft from Chengdu to Wanxian. In September 1997, it joined with five other carriers to form the Xinxing (New Star) Alliance. A shuttle service between its two hubs was added in September 2002.

FLEET:
4 (2) x A319-100,
11 (6) x A320-200, 2 x A321-100,
2 x A321-200, 5 x ERJ 145LR

FEATURES:
The central motif on the red tailfin is an elegant gull, a symbol of ambition, beauty, pragmatism, and strength, depicted flying over the four major rivers in the Sichuan province, namely Ai Jiang, Min Jiang, Jialing Jiang, and Yalong Jiang. The red color on the tail continues along the mid-fuselage, narrowing to a point below the cockpit. Blue *Sichuan Airlines* titles are applied in both English and Chinese characters.

Siem Reap Airways International (FT/SRH)

CAMBODIA (XU)

Cambodian regional airline operating scheduled flights between the capital Phnom Penh and Siem Reap, gateway to the famous Angkor Wat and many other historic temples on this widely spread UNESCO World Heritage site. The airline also flies to neighboring Thailand, Laos, and Vietnam. Siem Reap Airways International is wholly owned by Bangkok Airways and was established in 2000. It operated its first flight on 3 November that same year between Phnom Penh and Siem Reap.

FLEET:
1 X ATR 72-500, 1 X B717-200

FEATURES:
The aircraft of this subsidiary of Bangkok Airways carry the parent company's simple blue, gold, and red wing symbol on the tailfin, but the rest of the aircraft is painted in a stunning representation in gold of temples and sculptures of Angkor Wat. The aircraft is appropriately named *Angkor*, as seen below the cockpit window.

SilkAir (MI/SLK)

SINGAPORE (9V)

Subsidiary of Singapore Airlines serving the business and leisure market in Southeast Asia. Its scheduled network of passenger services now link 25 destinations in Bangladesh, Cambodia, China, India, Indonesia, Malaysia, Myanmar, the Philippines, and Thailand. The airline was founded in 1975 to undertake charter flights for its parent company, but also undertaking flights in support of the oil industry. Initially known as Tradewinds Charters, it became a regional airline, making its first scheduled flight to Pattaya on 21 February 1989, before adopting the present title on 1 April 1992.

FLEET:
6 X A319-100, 9 X A320-200

FEATURES:
A white seagull flies against the mid-blue and turquoise background of the tailfin, with the rear of the wings also edged in turquoise and the turquoise paint enveloping the rear of the aircraft. The only other notable element on the clean white aircraft is the understated *SilkAir* name, applied in blue.

Singapore Airlines (SQ/SIA/SQC)

SINGAPORE (9V)

National flag-carrier operating daily flights from Singapore's Changi International to some 80 cities in Europe, Africa, the Middle East, Asia, southwest Pacific, and North America. Freighter-only services are also operated under the Singapore Airlines Cargo brand, while subsidiary SilkAir provides passenger flights to regional destinations. Singapore Airlines was incorporated on 28 January 1972 as the national airline following the re-structuring of the joint Malaysia-Singapore Airlines. Operations started on 1 October that same year with a fleet of 10 aircraft including five Boeing 707s and five 737-100s.

FLEET:
5 x A340-500, (10) x A380-800, 27 x B747-400, 14 (2) x B747-400F, 46 x B777-200ER, 12 x B777-300, (19) x B777-300ER

FEATURES:
The all-white fuselage displays dramatic foreshortened cheatlines in midnight blue and gold below blue *Singapore Airlines* titles. The lower golden laser line widens to the rear and is repeated on the vertical stabilizer in order to communicate precision. A large stylized gold bird hovers on the blue tailfin and in miniature on each engine. Cargo aircraft carry *Mega Ark* titles forward and *Member of* wow at the rear.

Skippers Aviation (SY)

AUSTRALIA (VH)

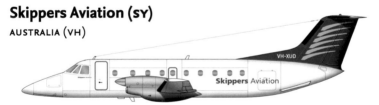

Western Australian airline providing a variety of aerial services out of its main bases at Perth and Broome, including regular passenger transport (RPT) services to several Western Australian communities, charter flights, special incentive packages, search and rescue, and medevac missions. The company is also the largest provider of fly-in, fly-out services to Western Australia's mining industry, operating over 100 flights a week for 14 mining companies in a closed charter arrangement not available to the public. Skippers Aviation was established in 1990 and began operations with a single Cessna 402.

FLEET:
6 x Cessna 441 Conquest II, 3 x Dash 8 100, 5 x EMB 120ER Brasilia, 6 x SA227DC Metro 23

FEATURES:
The polished corporate identity is centered on the tailfin of the aircraft, which features six golden aerofoil shapes set into a midnight blue field. The clean look is enhanced by the classic typeface of the airline name applied in two different fonts at the rear.

Sky Airlines (SHY)

TURKEY (TC)

Turkish holiday charter airline operating services for its parent company the Kayi Group and other tour operators, connecting Antalya and the other major Turkish resorts to over 50 destinations in Europe. Sky Airlines was established in late 2000 and started flying on 12 April 2001 when a Boeing 737-400 left Antalya for the German city of Düsseldorf. Although operations originally concentrated on the German market, the airline has since expanded to other European countries.

FLEET:
4 X B737-400, 1 X B737-800

FEATURES:
Given the name of the airline and its slogan *Smile in the Sky*, the emphasis is clearly on the sky. A red comet with a luminous trail streaks through the firmament amid numerous glowing stars and the Milky Way, as alluded to by the white lines rising from the base of the aircraft. The tailfin design is depicted either against a dark night sky (as shown) or against a sky lit up in orange by the setting sun. Unusually bold *Sky* titles take up a large part of the forward fuselage. Aircraft are named after celestial bodies.

SkyEurope Airlines (NE/ESK)

SLOVAK REPUBLIC (OM)

Central Europe's first and fastest-growing low-fare airline operating a route network covering more 25 European destinations from bases at Bratislava and Kosice in Slovakia, Budapest in Hungary, and Krakow and Warsaw in Poland. The acquisition from 2006 of a large number of new aircraft will facilitate further expansion in the region. SkyEurope was established in November 2001 by Alain Showronek and Christian Mandl, with finance provided by an international consortium including EBRD, ABN Amro Bank, and the European Union. Operations began on 13 February 2002.

FLEET:
7 X B737-500, (14) X B737-700, 4 X EMB 120ER Brasilia

FEATURES:
The unconventional design, where the mid-blue fuselage edged by an angled red band stops about two-thirds along the aircraft, makes this Central European carrier instantly recognizable. *SkyEurope* titles appear prominently on the white tailfin in blue and reversed out in white on the blue fuselage. A red bar atop the vertical stroke of the *k* adds elegance to the rather bold typeface.

SkyKing Airlines (RU/SKI)

TURKS AND CAICOS ISLANDS (VQ-T)

Private regional airline based in the Turks and
Caicos Islands, a British Overseas Territory
southeast of the Bahamas, operating high-
frequency services from its base at Providenciales to
South Caicos and Grand Turk, as well as to points in
neighboring Bahamas, Cuba, Haiti, and the
Dominican Republic. Charter flights are available to
anywhere in the Turks and Caicos and the
Caribbean. SkyKing Airlines was established and
started operations in 1995.

FLEET:
2 x Beech 1900C-1, 2 x Beech
1900D

FEATURES:
An ornate red crown on a deep
blue tailfin conveys a classy,
reliable operation, targeted
equally at business and leisure
traffic. The only other splash of
color on the white fuselage are
modest *SkyKing* titles behind a
smaller rendition of the crown,
and the Turks and Caicos flag
under the cockpit window. The
flag is basically the British Blue
Ensign charged with the colony's
shield, showing typical examples
of the local flora and fauna,
including a conch shell, lobster,
and cactus.

Skymark Airlines (BC/SKY)

JAPAN (JA)

Domestic low-fare airline operating a growing
network from its main base at Tokyo Haneda
International Airport, linking several of Japan's
major cities, reaching as far south as Naha on the
island of Okinawa. Charter flights are also
undertaken within Japan and to neighboring South
Korea. The airline was established by one of Japan's
largest travel agencies, HIS Travel, in 1996 following
deregulation of the domestic market. Operations
began on 19 September 1998 with a flight from
Tokyo to Fukuoka.

FLEET:
(4) x B737-800, 6 x B767-300ER

FEATURES:
A large orange and yellow star in
the night sky is the central theme
of this elegant livery, as depicted
on the tailfin of the aircraft, and
in a slight variation after blue *Sky*
titles on the forward fuselage. The
color rendition provides a sharp
contrast to the otherwise white
aircraft. The airline's full title in
black sits above the rear windows.

Skyservice Airlines (5G/SSV)

CANADA (C)

Major Canadian enterprise operating seasonal
flights primarily from Toronto and Montreal to
destinations in Canada, the United States, the
Caribbean, and Mexico, with long-haul flights
operated across the North Atlantic to Europe.
Specialized charters are operated for corporations,
professional sport teams, governments, relief
agencies, and travel-incentive companies.
Skyservice also provides a worldwide air-ambulance
service under the name of Skyservice Lifeguard.
The airline was founded in 1986 and originally
operated air-taxi and business flights. Larger-scale
charter activities were initiated in 1995.

FLEET:
3 X A319-100, 1 X A320-200,
2 X BAE Jetstream 31,
3 X B757-200, 1 X B767-300ER

FEATURES:
A partially drawn red maple leaf
with a gold edging on a royal
blue tail is the most visible
element of the airline's corporate
identity, reinforced by the red
Skyservice titles low on the
forward fuselage. The maple leaf
is believed to have been adopted
as Canada's national symbol as
early as 1700.

Skyways Express (JZ/SKX)

SWEDEN (SE)

Swedish regional airline operating a large domestic
network serving more than 25 towns and cities
from its main base at Stockholm, with extensions to
Denmark and the United Kingdom. Services are
flown in connection with SAS Scandinavian Airlines,
which is a major shareholder. A thriving charter
business also forms part of its activities. The
Skyways history goes back to the formation in 1939
of Avia on the Baltic island of Gotland, with the
present title adopted in 1993. A steady expansion
followed the acquisitions of Salair in 1991, Highland
Airways in 1997, and Flying Enterprise in 2000.

FLEET:
18 x F50, 6 x Saab 340A

FEATURES:
This simple red and white
color scheme comprises two
basic key features, the white,
freely drawn s fronting a red sun
on the tailfin, and the large
freehand Skyways lettering in red
along the mid-fuselage. The
slogan Well connected with SAS
refers to the airline's equity and
operational partnership with the
tri-national airline.

Skywest Airlines (XR/SLL)

AUSTRALIA (VH)

Largest regional airline in Western Australia, operating scheduled passenger and cargo services to some 15 destinations including an extension to Darwin in the Northern Territory and to Bali, together with charter services to remote locations catering for the needs of government, corporations, and mining companies. The airline provides an essential link for regional communities, tourists, and businesses. Skywest is the result of several mergers since its establishment on 9 April 1963 as Nor-West Air Taxis, later known as Transwest Air Charter. A major regional airline, East-West Airlines, was acquired on 19 December 1983.

FLEET:
5 X F50, 3 X F100

FEATURES:
The sun and sky are visual icons of Western Australia. The Skywest brand, as illustrated on the tailfin, represents a lens flare from the sun in the blue Western Australian sky. Such an image is often sighted from the window of an aircraft. Blue *Skywest* titles are painted across the white fuselage. The corporate image was created by Cato Purnell Partners.

Slok Air International (SO/OKS)

THE GAMBIA (C5)

Banjul-based regional carrier operating regular flights throughout West Africa, serving the capital cities of Mali, Mauritania, Senegal, Guinea, Guinea Bissau, Sierra Leone, Liberia, Côte d'Ivoire, Ghana, Togo, Benin, and the Congo. Corporate and group travel and general charter flights are also operated. The airline was established by the Slok Group as Slok Nigeria and operated out of Lagos, until its Nigerian air operator's certificate was suspended in March 2004. Slok Air then moved to The Gambia in November 2004 and was registered as Slok Air International (Gambia).

FLEET:
5 X B737-200A

FEATURES:
The bright green underside and tailfin top give the aircraft a fresh appearance, the separation from the white being achieved with orange-red and gold cheatlines. A "flying wing" decorates the center of the tail. Black *Slok Air* titles and the Gambian flag are painted on the forward cabin roof. The blue of the flag represents the Gambia River after which the country is named. The red and green symbolize the sun and agriculture. The two white stripes stand for peace and purity.

Slovak Airlines (6Q/SLL)
SLOVAK REPUBLIC (OM)

Slovak flag-carrier operating a small fleet of jet aircraft on passenger and cargo services out of Bratislava's M R Stefanik Airport to domestic and European destinations. Most flights operate on a regular charter basis to points around the Mediterreanean and to Russia, and wet-lease operations are also undertaken. Slovak Airlines was registered on 24 July 1995 by Viliam Veteska and a group of private investors and began operations with a Bratislava–Moscow schedule on 1 May 1998, using a Tupolev TU-154m leased from the government. Star Alliance carrier Austrian Airlines acquired a controlling stake in January 2005.

FLEET:
2 x B737-300, 1 x Fokker 100

FEATURES:
A white dove flies across the blue tailfin, which extends down and sweeps forward to end at a point under the nose of the aircraft. The dove symbol is also painted in blue under the cockpit. *Slovak Airlines* titling in blue above the forward cabin windows is accompanied by the web address in red underneath.

Smart Wings (QS)
CZECH REPUBLIC (OK)

Low-fare scheduled airline brand of charter carrier Travel Service Airlines, linking Prague with a growing number of major European cities in France, the Netherlands, Switzerland, Italy, Spain, Greece, and Cyprus. Smart Wings was set up in 2004 and began operations on 1 May that year.

FLEET:
2 x B737-500

FEATURES:
The large white "squiggle" on the tailfin lightens up the blue and orange scheme and provides symmetry with the white forward fuselage. Orange colors the engines and most of the rear of the aircraft and curves down in a graceful sweep to the underside of the aircraft nose. Blue *SmartWings.net* titling, with the emphasis on *Wings*, takes up the cabin roof.

SN Brussels Airlines (SN/DAT)

BELGIUM (OO)

Belgian flag-carrier operating a predominantly European network from its hub at Brussels National together with long-haul flights to East and West Africa and across the Atlantic to Canada, the United States, and the Netherlands Antilles, serving nearly 100 destinations. Founded out of Delta Air Transport after the collapse of Sabena in 2002, it took its new name on 15 February that year. DAT had been established in 1967 and first concentrated on air-taxi and charter flights before adding scheduled regional services. It was later acquired by then flag-carrier Sabena.

FLEET:
3 X A319-100, 3 X A330-300, 6 X BAE 146-200, 14 X RJ85, 12 X RJ100

FEATURES:
The letter s set into a circle with curved dynamic lines on the mid-blue tailfin was adopted from Sabena whose SN flight code in the airline name also acknowledges its heritage. The word *Brussels* in the title expresses its point-to-point offer and location in the heart of Europe. A mid-fuselage orange pencil line adds warmth to the largely white aircraft.

Snowflake (SK)

DENMARK (OY)/NORWAY (LN)/SWEDEN (SE)

Low-fare brand of SAS Scandinavian Airlines operating extensive services from Copenhagen and Stockholm to more than 50 destinations across the length and breadth of Europe. The new brand was established in October 2002 and operations began on 30 March 2003.

FLEET:
B737, MD-80 as required from SAS

FEATURES:
In line with the trend for simple and catchy names, Snowflake recalls the airline's origin in the winter landscapes of Scandinavia, but rather than using ice blue, the lemon-colored tail invokes the warmer climates of the Mediterranean, to which the airline transports its many passengers. The design expression created by the Stockholm Design Lab is said to convey elegance and boldness and is well connected to the SAS brand.

Solomon Airlines (IE/SOL)
SOLOMON ISLANDS (H4)

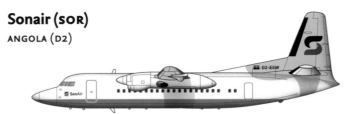

National carrier of the Solomon Islands, a scattered archipelago of nearly 1,000 islands in the Melanesian basin of the southwest Pacific, operating scheduled services from the capital Honiara. Flights serve Australia, Papua New Guinea, Fiji, and Vanuatu, together with a comprehensive domestic network to some 25 destinations. The airline was founded on 1 May 1968 as Solomon Islands Airways (Solair), when Macair of Papua New Guinea took over Megapode Airways, which had been formed in December 1963. The present name was adopted after the government took control in November 1987.

FLEET:
1 x B737-200, 2 x BN-2A Islander, 2 x DHC-6 Twin Otter 300

FEATURES:
The patriotic paint scheme is essentially a representation of the national flag, which fills the tailfin and tapers away towards the front of the aircraft. Bold black *Solomons* titles reinforce the airline's name and origin. The blue, yellow, and green stand for the ocean, sun, and land respectively, while the five white stars refer to the five districts of which the country is composed. The flag was adopted following independence from British rule on 7 July 1978.

Sonair (SOR)
ANGOLA (D2)

Subsidiary of Angola's National Petroleum Company Sonangol, which was registered as a commercial undertaking on 16 February 1998. Sonair provides scheduled commuter flights within Angola for passengers and freight, together with special contract work serving petroleum companies in Africa and Europe. Regular flights are also made between Houston and Luanda in support of the petroleum industry and for the U.S. Africa Energy Association. These flights, known as the Houston Express, were inaugurated on 6 November 2000. Sonair also transports fuel within Angola.

FLEET:
1 x B727-100C, 2 x B727-100QC, 1 x B727-100F, 5 x Beech 1900D, 8 x DHC-6 Twin Otter 300, 2 x F50

FEATURES:
Sonair uses the national colors of red, black, and yellow, with the letter s created in black and red residing in a yellow field that covers most of the tailfin. Small *Sonair* titles with the logo are applied forward above the red underside of the aircraft.

Song (DL)

UNITED STATES (N)

Low-fare arm of Delta Air Lines operating a network of scheduled services from major destinations on the eastern seaboard of the United States to several resort areas in Florida, the Bahamas, and Puerto Rico, together with trans-continental services across the country from the East, to Nevada and California. Song was set up in 2002 and began flying on 15 April 2003. The Song operation was folded into Delta's domestic business in May 2006.

FLEET:
36 x B757-200

FEATURES:
The unusual choice of title alludes to the fact that everyone has a song they love or a song that puts a smile on their face; it is lighthearted and does not take itself too seriously. It is also easy to spell and easy to remember. According to design consultants Landor, the bright green tail color is hard to overlook and broad-casts the brand's outgoing personality and combines style, choice, and fun.

Sosoliso Airlines (SO/SSA)

NIGERIA (5N)

Domestic carrier providing scheduled passenger and cargo services between the five largest cities in Nigeria, from its main base at Lagos. Charter flights are also offered and the airline plans to add cross-border services to other countries in West Africa. Sosoliso Airlines was established by Sosoliso Ltd, at Enugu in eastern Nigeria and inaugurated services on 26 July 2000 with a single Boeing 727-200 operated in a technical partnership with JAT Airways of Serbia and Montenegro.

FLEET:
1 x B737-300, 3 x DC-9-30, 1 x MD-81

FEATURES:
This unpretentious color scheme makes use of the first two letters of the name to form a simple motif, where the red s on the tailfin has been drawn to resemble a flamingo, outlined against the blue letter o alluding to the sun. Sosoliso airlines titles in blue with a red letter o sit atop the forward windows.

South African Airlink (4Z/REJ)

SOUTH AFRICA (ZS)

Regional airline operating feeder services to more than 20 destinations in Southern Africa in conjunction with minority shareholder South African Airways (SAA). The airline was established as Airlink Airline on 10 June 1992 after taking over the defunct Link Airways, itself a fusion of City Air, Border Air, and Magnum Airlines. The last was the principal constituent, which had been formed on 1 March 1978 through the merger of Air Lowveld and Avna Airlines. The present name was adopted in 1995 following cooperation with SAA. Metavia was acquired in December that same year.

FLEET:
12 X BAE Jetstream 41,
5 (15) X ERJ 135LR

FEATURES:
The livery is virtually identical to that of South African Airways, with additional *Airlink* titles under the *South African* on the forward fuselage. The national colors of gold, black, green, red, and white are prominently interpreted on the tailfin. The triangular arrow form suggests speed but also represents the convergence of the diverse South African society into unity. The red band encloses a golden sun disc, symbolizing a new beginning.

South African Airways (SA/SAA)

SOUTH AFRICA (ZS)

National airline operating long-haul flights to Europe, Asia, Australia, and North and South America, together with regional flights within Africa. Domestic trunk routes link all major cities within South Africa and include the "Golden Triangle" between Johannesburg, Cape Town, and Durban. Smaller regional towns and feeder services to its main hubs are provided by affiliates South African Express and South African Airlink. The airline was founded on 1 February 1934 following the acquisition of the assets of private airline Union Airways and began operations that same day.

FLEET:
11 X A319-100, (15) X A320-200,
6 X A340-200, 3 X A340-300,
9 X A340-600, 2 X B737-200A,
2 X B737-200F, 19 X B737-800,
8 X B747-400

FEATURES:
The livery is an interpretation of the flag, using the national colors of gold, black, green, red, and white displayed prominently in the center of the tailfin. The triangular arrow form suggests speed but also represents the convergence of the diverse South African society into unity. The red band encloses a golden sun disc, symbolizing a new beginning.

South African Express Airways (YB/EXY)

SOUTH AFRICA (ZS)

Regional associate of South African Airways (SAA) operating secondary scheduled routes within South Africa and to neighboring Botswana, Namibia, and the Democratic Republic of Congo. Charter flights are also undertaken. It was established on 1 December 1993 under the name of SA Express as a joint venture between South African–based Thebe Investments and a Canadian consortium, to take over unprofitable jet routes from SAA, but has since come under full government control. Services were launched on 24 April 1994, three days before the first democratic elections in South Africa.

FLEET:
6 x CRJ200ER, 7 x Dash 8 Q300

FEATURES:
Almost identical to that of South African Airways, the aircraft carry additional *Express* titles under the *South African* wording on the forward fuselage. The national colors of gold, black, green, red, and white are prominently interpreted in the center of the tailfin. The triangular arrow form suggests speed but also represents the convergence of the diverse South African society into unity. The red band encloses a golden sun disc, symbolizing a new beginning.

Southwest Airlines (WN/SWA)

UNITED STATES (N)

Leading U.S. low-fare airline operating high-frequency point-to-point passenger services linking some 60 major and secondary cities right across the country. Southwest Airlines is regarded as the pioneer of low-fare services and its modus operandi has been admired and copied elsewhere in the world. It was established by Rollin King and Herb Kelleher on 15 March 1967 as Air Southwest but had to overcome several legal hurdles before being able to start services under the present name on 18 June 1971 from Dallas Love Field to Houston and San Antonio. Muse Air was acquired on 25 June 1985.

FLEET:
194 x B737-300, 25 x B737-500, 219 (72) x B737-700

FEATURES:
The majority of the fleet is painted in this standard highly visible scheme of canyon blue, desert gold, orange, and red, with large *Southwest* titles on the tailfin. Special schemes include three flying Shamu killer whales; Lone Star One, Arizona One, California One, Nevada One, and New Mexico One, also known as ZIA, symbolic of the five states; Silver One, the 25th anniversary aircraft; and Triple Crown One, a high-flying tribute to its proud employees.

Spanair (JK/JKK)

SPAIN (EC)

Spanish subsidiary of the SAS Group and member of the Star Alliance operating scheduled passenger services from hubs at Palma de Mallorca, Madrid, and Barcelona to 25 destinations in Europe, and charter flights to over 100 cities, primarily in Scandinavia, the UK, Ireland, and Italy. Aerolineas de Baleares operates for Spanair Link, which flies to and from the Balearic Islands. Spanair was founded in December 1986 by SAS and Spanish tour operator Viajes Marsans and began operations in March 1988, flying Scandinavian holidaymakers to Spain with a fleet of leased McDonnell Douglas MD-83s.

FLEET:
15 X A320-200, 5 (1) X A321-200, 2 X MD-81, 12 X MD-82, 19 X MD-83, 3 X MD-87

FEATURES:
The airline's interesting symbol, displayed on the tailfin and engines of the white aircraft, is made up of two red and blue "petals" conjoined to form a diamond-shaped design that can be interpreted as a stylized flower or a fluttering ensign. Large blue *Spanair* titles are painted across the forward fuselage. One aircraft is painted in the Star Alliance colors.

SpiceJet (OS/SEJ)

INDIA (VT)

Indian low-fare airline, which began operations on 23 May 2005, initially with a fleet of two Boeing 737-800s. The first service linked Delhi, Ahmedabad, and Mumbai, but the network has expanded and now serves more than 15 destinations throughout India. The airline was founded as Royal Airways, itself a reincarnation of Modiluft, which had been established with technical assistance from Lufthansa on 18 March 1993 but ceased operations in 1996. The SpiceJet name was officially adopted on 4 May 2005.

FLEET:
2 (12) X B737-800

FEATURES:
The airline name and image has been chosen to reflect the aspirations of today's fast-paced and technology-savvy traveler, vibrant and energetic, absorbing Indian ethos and flavor. The cinnamon red color starts at the mid-underside of the aircraft and swings up to fill the tailfin, which also incorporates three rows of yellow and orange circles in expanding sizes, suggesting grains of different spices. Large italic *SpiceJet* titles in cinnamon cover the area ahead of the wing.

Spirit Airlines (NK/NKS)

UNITED STATES (N)

U.S. low-fare airline serving 20 destinations within the United States, Mexico, and the Caribbean. The airline's history dates back to 1980, when it was founded as Charter One, which operated travel packages from Detroit to the gambling and entertainment center of Atlantic City, and later also to Las Vegas. This connection was put on a scheduled footing following the acquisition of a license on 8 September 1990. The name was changed to Spirit Airlines on 29 May 1992.

FLEET:
6 (23) X A319-100,
5 (8) X A321-200, 3 X MD-81,
9 X MD-82, 9 X MD-83

FEATURES:
A memorable design that takes a different approach, using a stepped group of squares graduating in color from dark blue towards light gray and white on the tailfin and forward fuselage. One leading square in each location has been changed to red, enclosing the first letter in the airline's name in white, with the remainder of the *Spirit* title following in white.

Spring Airlines (9S/CQH)

CHINA (B)

Shanghai-based private Chinese budget carrier operating scheduled flights from Shanghai's Honqiao Airport to secondary cities. Among destinations are Nanchang, Wenzhou, Guilin, Tianjan, Xiamen, Haikou, Sanya, Kunming, Qingdao, Zhuhai, and Yantai. It was set up in 2005 by leading travel agency Spring International and began operations on 18 July with a flight between Shanghai and the eastern coastal city of Yantai in Shandong province.

FLEET:
1 X A320-200

FEATURES:
Green is the color of spring and of this new Chinese airline. The corporate signature of a triple s is displayed in gold on the fresh green tailfin, with *Spring Airlines* titles along the roof also painted in green, both in English and Chinese characters.

SriLankan Airlines (UL/ALK)
SRI LANKA (4R)

Sri Lankan flag-carrier operating international scheduled passenger and cargo services from Colombo's Bandaranaike International Airport to more than 30 destinations in Asia, the Middle East, and Europe. The airline was established on 10 January 1979 as AirLanka, taking over from the defunct flag-carrier Air Ceylon, which had been founded in 1947. The new airline began operations on 1 September 1979 with two Boeing 707s leased from Singapore Airlines. Emirates Airline acquired a major stake and management control on 1 April 1998, when the present name and corporate identity was adopted.

FLEET:
5 X A320-200, 4 X A330-200, 5 X A340-300

FEATURES:
A graceful peacock with beautiful plumage adorns the tailfin and engine cowlings of the aircraft. For Hindus, the native peacock is special, for Skanda, the god of Katharagama, sits astride a peacock, and Vishnu, another major Hindu deity, is also often shown with a peacock. The Sri Lankan flag, with a golden lion and sword, four Buddhist pipul leaves, and green and orange stripes to represent Hindu and Muslim minorities, is applied ahead of the airline name.

Star Airlines (SE/SEU)
FRANCE (F)

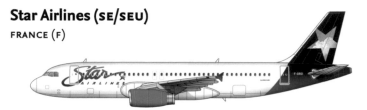

French leisure airline operating a mix of scheduled and charter passenger services from Paris and, in summer only, from Lille. Long-haul scheduled flights are offered to Central America and the Caribbean, Brazil, Sri Lanka, and the islands of Mauritius, Seychelles, and Maldives, while short-haul charters serve the resorts in the Mediterranean and the Canary Islands. The airline was founded by Cédric Pastour on 5 August 1995 as Société de Transport Aérien Régional, trading as Star Europe, and started operations on 22 December that year. The present name was adopted in October 1997.

FLEET:
4 X A320-200, 2 X A330-200

FEATURES:
A sky blue five-pointed star pictured against fair-weather cumulus clouds takes up the center part of the dark blue tailfin. The dark blue extends down and around the rear fuselage, gradually changing to a lighter color. The aircraft engines are sky blue, as is the upper half of the *Star Airlines* titling at the front. A gold star completes the signature. The graduating blue design on the fin is repeated on the winglets.

Sterling (NB/SNB)

DENMARK (OY)

Low-fare airline operating services within Scandinavia and between Scandinavia and leisure destinations in southern Europe. Holiday charters to the Mediterranean area are also flown. The airline was set up in May 1962 by Ejlif Krogager, founder of Tjaerborg Reiser, under the name of Sterling Airways, and began charter operations on 7 July that year with a Douglas DC-6B. After entering bankruptcy, it restarted operations as Sterling European Airlines on 1 May 1994, but reinvented itself as a low-fare airline in 2000. Maersk Air, founded in 1969, was merged into Sterling after both airlines came under the same ownership.

FLEET:
10 X B737-800

FEATURES:
The all-red aircraft is unusually divided below the windowline by a silver stripe, refreshing the airline's name, the inspiration for which the founder was said to have received from his mother. Ejlif Krogager's mother always gave sterling silver as presents, because to her it was a symbol of lasting quality. The interlinked hearts on the tailfin and engines refer to that same perception of the traveling public, as for more than 40 years, Sterling has been "dear to the Scandinavians' hearts."

Styrian Spirit (Z2/STY)

AUSTRIA (OE)

Private Austrian regional airline operating scheduled services from its home base of Graz in Styria to a growing number of business destinations in Europe. The airline has expanded its activities to develop services also out of Salzburg as Salzburg Spirit, and from Ljubljana as Slovenian Spirit, taking advantage of the enlarged Europe. Styrian Spirit was established on 25 December 2002 and started flying on 24 March 2003.

FLEET:
4 X CRJ200LR, 1 X CRJ701LR,
(1) X CRJ900

FEATURES:
The green in the livery stands for Styria (Steiermark), and silver for the spirit of the airline, which is nourished by the flames created by the double s. This also resembles the swept tail of the fabled fire-breathing panther of the Styrian coat of arms set in a field of green, alluding to the fact that more than half of the area of this Austrian province is covered in forests.

Sudan Airways (SD/SUD)

SUDAN (ST)

Sudanese flag-carrier operating international scheduled and charter passenger services from Khartoum to destinations throughout the Middle East and to North and West Africa and Europe. Domestic routes also provide vital links between the capital and many provincial towns. Local charter, air-ambulance flights, VIP services, and agricultural spraying are provided by Sudanair Express. Sudan Airways was established by the government in 1946, with technical assistance from British company Airwork. Proving flights started in April 1947, with commercial operations beginning three months later.

FLEET:
1 X A300B4-100, 1 X A300-600,
1 X A310-300, 1 X AN-24RV,
3 X B707-320C, 1 X B727-200A,
1 x Beech Super King Air B200,
4 X F50, 1 x Yak-42D

FEATURES:
The Sudan Airways scheme has changed little since first introduced in July 1974 but is still memorable for its imaginatively styled elongated *s* (for *Sudan*), which sweeps along in triple bands of nile blue and sand yellow. The design then opens out at the tailfin, where the predominant color is yellow, broken only by *Sudan* titles in Arabic near the leading edge.

Sun Air (PI/SUF)

FIJI (DQ)

Private regional airline serving 10 destinations in Fiji, a chain of 300 islands scattered in the South Pacific to the east of Australia. Scheduled services are operated from hubs at Nadi and Suva on the largest island of Viti Levu. Interisland transfer, daytrips, and package tours are also undertaken. The airline was established in 1980 by Don Collingwood as Sunflower Airlines and began operations in July 1982 with tourist flights to Malololailai and Taveuni.

FLEET:
1 x Beech Queenaire 8800,
5 X BN-2A Islander, 1 x DHC-6
Twin Otter 100, 1 x DHC-6
Twin Otter 200

FEATURES:
Although the airline serves a large number of tourists, the warm orange and yellow "sun" colors are rather understated, with a straight-through triple cheatline and orange and yellow flash on the tailfin of an otherwise white aircraft. A contrast is provided by the blue airline titles, engine cowlings, and belly of the aircraft.

Sun Country Airlines (SY/SCX)

UNITED STATES (N)

U.S. low-fare airline operating a mix of scheduled and charter services from its main base at Minneapolis/St. Paul and a hub at Las Vegas. Services operate right across the United States, with extensive links to several Mexican destinations and points in the Caribbean, including the U.S. Virgin Islands, Puerto Rico, and the Netherlands Antilles. Sun Country Airlines was founded by former Braniff employees on 1 July 1982 and operated its first charter for MLT Tours on 20 January 1983 between Sioux Falls and Las Vegas with a leased Boeing 727-200. Scheduled services were added in June 1999.

FLEET:
7 × B737-800

FEATURES:
Apart from a narrow gray underside trimmed in red, the aircraft is painted in mid-blue all over. The airline's symbol of a letter s forming the center of a flaming orange sun, takes up all of the tailfin and is repeated in light blue on the forward fuselage, which also incorporates white *Sun Country* titles. A small U.S. flag is painted alongside the aircraft registration at the rear.

Sun D'Or International Airlines (7L/ERO)

ISRAEL (4X)

Charter subsidiary of flag-carrier EL AL operating regular, ad hoc, and seasonal charter flights for tour operators to numerous destinations in Europe, Africa, and the Mediterranean basin, using aircraft leased from the parent company. Sun D'Or International was established on 2 October 1977 by EL AL and Teshet under the name OF EL AL Charter Services to enter the Israeli charter market hitherto served by foreign airlines. Operations had already started in April 1977 with a leased BAC One-Eleven between Tel-Aviv and Rome. The Sun D'Or name was adopted on 27 September 1981.

FLEET:
1 × B737-800, 2 × B757-200

FEATURES:
Triple stylized wings in gold, red, and blue on the tailfin and between the airline's name in English and Hebrew on the cabin roof are the only concessions to its sphere of operation, which has its emphasis on flights to holiday destinations. A clue to its origins is offered in the titling and on the engines and underside of the aircraft, all painted in the familiar blue of the Israeli flag.

SunExpress (xq/sxs)
TURKEY (TC)

Leisure airline providing scheduled flights from Antalya on the Turkish Riviera to major cities in Germany and 14 other European capitals with direct Lufthansa connections, reflecting the predominance of German tourists, who account for 70% of the airline's traffic. SunExpress was established on 11 September 1989 by Turkish Airlines, Lufthansa, and private interests and started operations on 4 April 1990 using a leased Boeing 737-300 on a charter flight from Frankfurt to Antalya. Lufthansa's share was passed to Condor, now part of Thomas Cook, in 1995. Scheduled flights started in 2002.

FLEET:
9 x B737-800

FEATURES:
As expected from its name, the airline's symbol on the tailfin and aircraft nose in blue represents a sun with rays bursting forth at the top. The all-white aircraft is otherwise punctuated only by bold blue *Sun Express* titles forward and the red Turkish flag with the white crescent moon and star at the rear.

Sun-Air of Scandinavia (ez/sus)
DENMARK (OY)

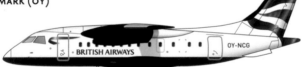

Billund-based regional airline providing scheduled passenger and cargo services, charter and air-taxi flights, specialist aerial work, and aircraft brokerage. All scheduled services are flown under a franchise agreement with British Airways and link Denmark with destinations in Norway, Sweden, Belgium, Germany, the Czech Republic, and the UK. Sun-Air was founded by Neils Sundberg in 1978, initially concentrating on aircraft trading. Scheduled services were initiated in 1987, and these have been operated on behalf of British Airways since the signing of a franchise agreement on 1 August 1996.

FLEET:
3 x BAE ATP, 2 x BAE Jetstream 31, 3 x Jetstream 32, 6 x FD 328-100, 2 x FD 328JET

FEATURES:
Aircraft carry full British Airways markings denoted by the fluttering representation of the British flag on the tailfin and the blue and red speedmarque ahead of blue *British Airways* titles.

Surinam Airways (PY/SLM)

SURINAME (PZ)

National carrier of Suriname operating regional and domestic services from the capital Paramaribo, together with a connection to Amsterdam flown jointly with KLM. The airline was established in 1954 to develop air services in the most populated fertile coastal plain and began services in January 1955 with a Douglas DC-3 between Paramaribo and the small town of Moengo. The date for the official establishment of Surinaamse Luchtvaart Maat-schappij was 30 August 1962. It was designated the national carrier following the country's indepen-dence from the Netherlands on 25 November 1975.

FLEET:
1 X B747-300M, 1 X MD-82

FEATURES:
The elegant red "free" bird symbol, which adorns the tailfin of the white aircraft, was chosen upon independence to indicate that country and airline could now progress unhindered. The eye-catching design shows the wing downbeat producing waves that graduate from sunshine yellow to a deep orange, an arrangement, in a straight rendition, which is also manifested along the fuselage.The national flag precedes the airline title, also in orange.

Swedline Express (SM/SRL)

SWEDEN (SE)

Swedish regional airline operating a small network of scheduled domestic passenger and cargo services from its main base at Hultsfred in southeastern Sweden and from the capital Stockholm. Charter flights are also offered within Scandinavia and to the Baltic countries. The airline was established in 1960 as Värmlandsflyg, which was originally engaged in air-taxi, charter, and prospecting services throughout Sweden. It changed to the present name on 1 December 2002.

FLEET:
3 x Saab 340A, 2 x Saab 2000

FEATURES:
Silver-gray and orange are the signature colors of Swedline, recognizable by the tailfin design and airline name under the cockpit. The web address on the cabin roof uses the same two colors. The orange oval represents Sweden, with the silver dots signifying the islands of Götland and Öland.

Swiss International Air Lines (LX/SWR)
SWITZERLAND (HB)

Principal Swiss airline operating a comprehensive network of scheduled services from Zurich, Geneva, Basel, and Berne to more than 65 destinations in Europe, Africa, North and South America, and the Far East. Charter flights to the Mediterranean basin and Iceland are also provided. Swiss was created when regional airline Crossair replaced the defunct national airline Swissair and began flying under the new guise in 1 April 2002. The airline was founded on 14 February 1975 as Business-Flyers Basel and adopted the Crossair name on 14 November 1978, prior to starting scheduled services on 2 April 1979.

FLEET:
7 X A319-100, 14 X A320-200,
4 X A321-200, 9 X A330-200,
9 X A340-300, 4 X AVRO RJ85,
15 X RJ100, (15) X EMB 170LR,
(15) X EMB 195, 10 X ERJ 145LU

FEATURES:
The white cross emblazoned on a bright red tailfin is instantly recognizable as the Swiss national flag. The history of the cross dates back to the Battle of Laupen in 1339. *Swiss* titles at the front are followed by the country's name in the four spoken languages – German, French, Italian, and Romansch. Two red squares on the engines carry full titles and the white cross.

Syrianair (Syrian Arab Airlines) (RB/SYR)
SYRIA (YK)

National flag-carrier providing international scheduled passenger and cargo services to destinations within Syria and to points in Europe, North Africa, the Middle East, and the Indian subcontinent. The airline was born as a government corporation in October 1961 under the name of Syrian Arab Airlines to succeed Syrian Airways, which had been founded in 1946 as a department within the Ministry of Defense. The short-lived union of Syria and Egypt led to a merger between Syrian Airways and Misrair in January 1961, but this also lasted for less than a year.

FLEET:
6 X A320-200, 6 X B727-200A,
2 X B747SP, 2 X IL-76M,
1 X TU-134B-3

FEATURES:
A bright Mediterranean blue tailfin incorporates the flag-carrier's symbol, a stylized mythical bird flying across the sun, repeated on the engine cowlings. The only other adornment on a fresh white fuselage are *Syrian* titles in the same blue on the forward fuselage followed by Arabic titles in red.

TAAG Linhas Aéreas de Angola (DT/DTA)

ANGOLA (D2)

National carrier providing scheduled services to some 20 points within Angola and international flights to Southern Africa, West Africa, Europe, and South America. The airline was founded at Nova Lisboa (now Huambo) in September 1938 as a division of the Administration of Railways, Harbors, and Air Transport as DTA – Divisão de Exploração dos Transportes Aéreos de Angola – and began operations on 17 July 1940 with de Havilland Dragon Rapides. It was renamed TAAG – Transportes Aéreos de Angola – on 1 October 1973 and changed again to the present title on 13 Febraury 1980.

FLEET:
4 X B737-200, 1 X B737-200C,
(4) X B737-700, 2 X B747-300C,
(2) X B777-200ER

FEATURES:
Twin cheatlines of red and orange commence under the chin and sweep along the fuselage, with the upper red finally encompassing the tail, which also depicts the airline's long-standing antelope symbol. The black head of the antelope is enclosed in an orange disc formed by its long curved horns. The airline name is applied in Portuguese on the port side and in English on starboard, preceded by the red, black, and yellow Angolan flag.

TACA International Airlines (TA/TAI)

EL SALVADOR (YS)

El Salvador and Honduras flag-carrier operating an extensive network of scheduled services to more than 35 destinations, covering all of Central America and extending to cities in North and South America. Operations are centered on three hubs at San Salvador, San José, and Lima. The airline's fascinating history dates back to December 1931 and the establishment by New Zealander Yowell Yerex of Transportes Aéreos Centro-Americanos (TACA), which grew into a powerful air-transport system. It became TACA El Salvador in 1939 and was re-organized under the present title on 29 March 1960.

FLEET:
5 (4) X A319-100,
21 (15) X A320-200, 5 X A321-200

FEATURES:
The image of five golden macaws crossing the sky in formation represents the five airlines that make up the TACA Group, all serving to unite the Americas and now fully integrated. The scarlet macaw is a Central American parrot with a long tail and brilliant red, yellow, and blue plumage. The livery, which also presents the airline's traditional deep blue and red colors on the tailfin and cockpit roof, was designed by Public Image of Miami.

TACA Regional Airlines (TA)
COSTA RICA (TI)/GUATEMALA (TG)/HONDURAS (HR)/ NICARAGUA (YN)/PANAMA (HP)

Regional air transport system in Central America operating scheduled services in association with TACA International Airlines serving 60 destinations in Costa Rica, Guatemala, Honduras, Nicaragua, and Panama, linking smaller cities into the countries' capitals. Participating airlines are Aeroperlas, Panama, established in December 1970; Inter of Guatemala, founded in 1997; La Costeña, Nicaragua, set up in 1991; and Isleña, Honduras, founded at La Ceiba on 16 March 1982 by Arturo Alvarado Wood.

FLEET:
4 X ATR 42-300, 1 x Beech A100 King Air, 23 x Cessna 208B Grand Caravan, 5 x DHC-6 Twin Otter 300, 1 X EMB 110P1 Bandeirante, 1 X EMB 110P2 Bandeirante, 10 x Shorts 360-200

FEATURES:
The tailfins of the aircraft are identical to the main TACA scheme, featuring the five golden macaws flying in formation, with the red crest on the cockpit roof. TACA *Regional* titles, as well as the airlines' individual titles, are applied to the fuselage.

TACV Cabo Verde Airlines (VR/TCV)
CAPE VERDE REPUBLIC (D4)

National airline of the Cape Verde Republic, a group of islands in the central Atlantic facing the coast of Senegal, operating scheduled and charter services from the capital Praia on the largest island of Tiago and from Santa Maria on Sal Island to destinations on the West African mainland and in Europe. A comprehensive interisland service is also flown. The airline was established on 27 December 1958 as Transportes Aéreos de Cabo Verde (TACV) and began interisland links with a Britten-Norman Islander. It was designated the national carrier in July 1975 following independence from Portugal.

FLEET:
3 X ATR 42-300, 2 X B757-200

FEATURES:
A blue motif that is barely recognizable as a stylized bird in flight is the only adornment on the white tailfin, while large red TACV initials take up most of the forward fuselage, followed by the airline's name in English along the mid-cabin roof. Blue, red, and white are the colors of the Cape Verde flag, with the blue symbolizing the infinite expanse of sea and sky, white standing for peace, and red for the effort of its people.

TAF Linhas Aéreas (TSD)

BRAZIL (PP/PT)

Regional airline operating scheduled passenger and cargo services from its base at Fortaleza, capital of Ceará state, to a dozen major points in the northeast of Brazil. A connection is also scheduled from Natal to the nearby island of Fernando de Noronha in the Atlantic Ocean. Charter flights are also offered. The airline was founded in 1957 by Captain Ariston Pessoa de Araujo as Taxi Aéreo Fortaleza (TAF), providing air-taxi and charter flights, but adopted the present title when authorized for scheduled services.

FLEET:
1 x B727-200F, 1 x B737-200A, 2 x B737-200C, 3 x Cessna 208A Caravan I, 1 x Cessna 208B Grand Caravan, 1 x EMB 110 Bandeirante, 1 x EMB 110E Bandeirante

FEATURES:
A bright red colors the tailfin and the large TAF initials on the forward fuselage. The initials also appear on the largely blue tail, where they are reversed out in white.

Tajikistan Airlines (7J/TJK)

TAJIKISTAN (EY)

National flag-carrier of this Central Asian republic linking the capital Dushanbe with regular and charter flights to points in Asia, Europe, and the Middle East. A domestic network is also flown. Services are operated with an ex-Soviet fleet, but the airline intends to acquire Western aircraft for its main services. Tajikistan Airlines, initially known as Tajik Air, was founded on 1 March 1992 and concentrated on domestic flights, until venturing into the international arena with a short-lived service to London on 25 December 1993. International flights have since been resumed.

FLEET:
1 x AN-24, 2 x AN-24RV, 2 x AN-24V, 1 x AN-26, 1 x AN-26B, 4 x AN-28, 2 x MI-8T, 4 x MI-17, 6 x TU-134A-3, 4 x TU-154B-2, 4 x TU-154M, 1 x Yak-40, 5 x Yak-40K

FEATURES:
The airline symbol on the tailfin is made up of the colors of the Tajikistan flag and shows a white dove outlined against a red and green "sun," touching the blue sweep at the rear of the fin and fuselage. Blue *Tajikistan* titles cover the forward cabin roof.

TAM Linhas Aéreas (JJ/TAM)
BRAZIL (PP/PT)

Major Brazilian airline operating an extensive network of domestic services centered on São Paulo to some 40 destinations across the country, together with international flights to neighboring countries, and to Miami in the U.S. and Paris in Europe. TAM Express handles cargo and TAM Jatos Executivos offers air-taxi flights. The airline was formed by Captain Rolim Adolfo Amaro in 1961 as Taxi Aéreo Marilia (TAM) and became TAM Transportes Aéreos Regionais on 12 May 1976. The present title was adopted in 2000 when it merged with TAM Transportes Aéreos Merdionais, formerly Brasil Central and Votec.

FLEET:
13 (5) X A319-100,
35 (20) X A320-200,
(4) X A321-200, 6 (1) X A330-200,
23 X F100

FEATURES:
The TAM initials are well known throughout the South American continent and play a major part in the livery, being applied in red across the forward windows and in white on the red tailfin. A white flash livens up the red engines. Red is also used in the web address along the rear cabin roof and in the surrounds to doors and emergency exits.

TAM Mercosur (PZ/LAP)
PARAGUAY (ZP)

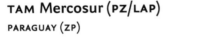

National airline of this land-locked South American state, operating scheduled passenger and cargo services from the capital Asunçion and Ciudad del Este to destinations in Brazil, Bolivia, Argentina, Chile, and Uruguay. Connections to North America and Europe are available via Brazil. The airline was originally established in 1962 by the government as Lineas Aéreas Paraguayas and changed its name to TAM Transportes Aéreos del Mercosur (TAM Mercosur) on 1 September 1996 when TAM Linhas Aéreas of Brazil acquired a 80% stake in the airline from the Paraguayan government.

FLEET:
2 x Cessna 208B Caravan,
2 x Fokker 100

FEATURES:
The livery is identical to that of the parent company, although the red, white, and blue Paraguayan flag with the Sun of May symbol of freedom has been applied in some instances. The TAM initials are applied in red across the forward windows and in white on the red tailfin. A white flash livens up the red engines. Red is also used in the web address along the rear cabin roof and in the surrounds to doors and emergency exits.

TAME Linea Aérea del Ecuador (EQ/TAE)
ECUADOR (HC)

Commercial arm of the Ecuadorean air force providing scheduled passenger and cargo services from Quito and Guayaquil to some 15 domestic destinations, including the Galapagos Islands, which lie in the Pacific Ocean to the west of Ecuador. A cross-border route is also flown to Cali in Colombia. The airline was established as Transportes Aéreos Militares Ecuadorianos (TAME) on 17 December 1962 to fly to more remote communities not served by commercial airlines. The name was changed to Transportes Aéreos Mercantiles Ecuadorianos when it was converted into a separate branch in 1990.

FLEET:

2 X A320-200, 1 X B727-100, 3 X B727-200A, 1 X BAE 748-2A, (2) X EMB 170LR, (1) X EMB 190LR, 2 X F28-4000

FEATURES:

An attractive scheme with pale blue and deep blue bands coloring the forward part of the aircraft together with a gold supporting line that flows upwards to meet the blue at the base of the tailfin, which is also painted in deep blue, as is the tail cone and rear underside of the aircraft. The fin displays the airline's long-standing white encircled bird-of-prey motif. The yellow, blue, and red Ecuadorean flag is applied at the rear.

TAMPA Cargo (QT/TPA)
COLOMBIA (HK)

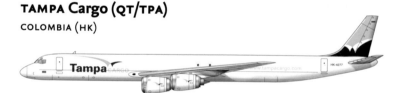

Leading South American cargo and logistics airline providing frequent scheduled and charter flights throughout the Americas from facilities in Bogotá, Barranquilla, Medellin, and Cali in Colombia, and Miami in Florida. TAMPA also provides free cargo transportation for charitable trusts and has signed up to the business anti-smuggling coalition (BASC). The airline was founded in Medellin on 11 March 1973 as Transportes Aéreos Mercantiles Panamericanos (TAMPA) and began carrying fresh flowers between Colombia and Miami. Dutch carrier Martinair is a major shareholder.

FLEET:

4 X B767-200ERF, 3 X DC-8-71F

FEATURES:

A most modern livery highlighted by an old gold and midnight blue tailfin, with the colors divided by a white bird motif that also flies above the blue and gray *Tampa Cargo* titles on the forward fuselage and on the aircraft engines. The web address towards the rear supplements the airline signature.

TANS Perú (T1/ELV)

PERU (OB)

Peruvian domestic airline operating passenger and cargo services from Lima's Jorge Chavez International Airport to nine other major towns and cities in this Andean country on the Pacific coast of South America. TANS Perú was founded by the Peruvian air force in 1963 as Transportes Aéreos Nacionales de Selva (TANS), to provide services exclusively to outlying communities in the Amazon River basin. It received civil authorization on 20 January 1998, and on 19 June that year was designated as a national carrier for the provision of scheduled passenger and cargo services.

FLEET:
3 X B737-200, 3 X B737-200A

FEATURES:
Brick red edged in silver is the dominant theme applied in graceful curves on the forward fuselage, at the rear, and on the tailfin, enclosing the parts of the aircraft left in white. A golden bird is set into the white section of its red tail. TANS *Perú* titles in black and red are carried on the cabin roof, with the web address in small white lettering on the rear red field.

TAP Portugal (TP/TAP)

PORTUGAL (CS)

National carrier operating a European network and flights to Africa, the Far East, and the Americas. A domestic route system includes all major destinations on the mainland and extends into the mid-Atlantic to Madeira and the Azores. The airline was established by the government on 14 March 1945 under the title of Transportes Aéreos Portugueses (TAP). Commercial flights began on the Lisbon–Madrid route with war-surplus Douglas DC-3s on 19 September 1946. It adopted the marketing title of TAP Air Portugal in 1979 and rebranded in February 2005 simply as TAP Portugal.

FLEET:
6 x A310-300, 16 X A319-100, 11 X A320-200, 3 X A321-200, 4 X A340-300

FEATURES:
Interlinking TAP initials in fresh green and red take up virtually the full height of the forward fuselage and are scaled up to such an extent that only part of the initials fill the tailfin. White *TAP Portugal* lettering runs along the upward stroke of the P. Green and red are the national colors, adopted in 1910 as a result of the downfall of the monarchy. The Portuguese flag is depicted aft.

TAROM Romanian Air Transport (RO/ROT)
ROMANIA (YR)

National airline operating scheduled services from
Bucharest Otopeni International to points in Europe,
North Africa, and the Middle East. It also flies a
comprehensive domestic network serving 12 cities
from the capital's other airport of Baneasa. The
airline was founded on 8 August 1945 as Transporturi
Aeriene Romana Sovietica (TARS) under joint ownership of Romania and the Soviet Union. Services
began with domestic flights on 1 February 1946 and
international flights in 1947. The Soviet shares were
bought by Romania in 1954 leading to a renaming
to Transporturile Aeriene Romane (TAROM).

FLEET:
2 x A310-300, (4) x A318-100,
7 x ATR 42-500, 2 x ATR 72-500,
5 x B737-300, 4 x B737-700

FEATURES:
The simple livery displays large
TAROM titles in dark blue below
the windowline and forward of
the all-white fuselage,
underscored by a speed line
extending to the rear. The blue
tail incorporates the airline's
long-standing bird symbol inside
double rings, both in white.

Ted (UA)
UNITED STATES (N)

Low-fare division of United Airlines, operating
scheduled passenger services from the United hubs
at Chicago, Denver, Washington Dulles, San
Francisco, and Los Angeles to popular leisure
destinations such as Las Vegas, Reno, Phoenix,
Orlando, and Tampa, among others, with extensions
to Cabo San Lucas and Puerto Vallarta in Mexico.
Ted was set up in 2003 and started flying in
February 2004, initially out of Denver.

FLEET:
47 x A320-200

FEATURES:
Meet Ted! The unusual name,
taken from the last three letters
of United, was chosen to
emphasise that it is an essential
and integrated part of the parent
company. The vibrant blue of the
name and orange with the
double u on the tailfin, of similar
design to that on mainline
aircraft, is intended to convey a
warm, friendly, and casual
manner, and is said to give the
impression of being United's
spunky kid brother with a distinct
modern personality.

Thai Airways International (TG/THA)

THAILAND (HS)

National airline operating an extensive regional network, together with long-haul flights from Bangkok to Europe, North America, Australia, and New Zealand. A comprehensive domestic network serves all major towns and cities in the country. Thai Airways is part of the Star Alliance. It was founded on 24 August 1959, initially as a joint venture between domestic carrier Thai Airways and Scandinavian airline SAS, and began operations on 1 May 1960. Thai Airways, founded on 1 March 1947 through the amalgamation of Siamese Airways and Pacific Overseas Airlines, was integrated on 1 April 1988.

FLEET:
6 x A300-600, 15 x A300-600R, 12 x A330-300, 2 (2) x A340-500, 2 (4) x A340-600, (6) x A380-800, 2 x ATR 72-200, 7 x B737-400, 2 x B747-300, 18 x B747-400, 8 x B777-200, (6) x B777-200ER, 6 x B777-300, 4 x MD-11

FEATURES:
The Landor-designed livery uses rich and vibrant colors that vividly reflect culture and country. Opulent gold, magenta, and purple tones recall the gold of the temples, the brilliant hues of orchids, and the intensity of Thailand's famous shimmering silks. All are incorporated in a stylized orchid, which dominates the tailfin of the aircraft.

Thomas Cook Airlines (FO/TCW)

BELGIUM (OO)

Brussels-based holiday charter airline serving the main Mediterranean resort areas in Spain, Portugal, Italy, Greece, Turkey, Malta, Egypt, Tunisia, and Morocco. Flights originate from Brussels, Liège, Ostend, Maastricht, Luxembourg, and Lille. The airline was set up by the Thomas Cook Group on 12 December 2001 to access the Belgian charter market and began operations on 13 March 2002 between Brussels and Gran Canaria, Canary Islands.

FLEET:
5 x A320-200

FEATURES:
The corporate signature in an airbrushed representation of the earth is set into the bright blue center of the tailfin, which graduates to darker blue at the top of the tailfin and over the rear fuselage with its scalloped edge. A neat touch is the sky blue underside of the aircraft painted with a gentle curve that contrasts with the dark blue of the engine. The blue *Thomas Cook* titles take up a large part of the aircraft. Each aircraft carries a name at the front, such as *explore*, *discover*, *inspire*, *enjoy*, and more.

Thomas Cook Airlines (MT/TCX)

UNITED KINGDOM (G)

Major UK charter airline serving more than 60 holiday destinations in the Mediterranean, and further afield in the Caribbean, Central America, and the U.S. Winter-only flights serve the Alps, Lapland, Egypt, and The Gambia. Flights originate from main bases at Manchester and London Gatwick, and at London Stansted, Birmingham, Nottingham East Midlands, Glasgow, and Newcastle. The airline was created on 1 September 1999 as JMC Airlines through the merger of Flying Colors Airlines and Caledonian Airways and began operations on 27 March 2000. It was renamed on 30 March 2003.

FLEET:
5 X A320-200, 2 X A330-200,
14 X B757-200, 2 X B757-300

FEATURES:
The corporate signature in an airbrushed representation of the earth is set into the bright blue center of the tailfin, which graduates to darker blue at the top of the tailfin and over the rear fuselage with its scalloped edge. A neat touch is the sky blue underside of the aircraft painted with a gentle curve that contrasts with the dark blue of the engine. The blue *Thomas Cook* titles take up a large part of the aircraft.

Thomsonfly (BY/BAL)

UNITED KINGDOM (G)

Major European airline, formerly trading as Britannia Airways, providing inclusive-tour flights from Luton, London Gatwick, Manchester, Birmingham, and other provincial airports to more than 100 regular destinations throughout Europe and the Mediterranean, and further afield to the U.S., Mexico, the Caribbean, and South America. A low-fare division operates out of Coventry, Bournemouth, and Doncaster. The airline was founded on 1 December 1961 and began operations on 5 May 1962 under the name of Euravia (London). It became Britannia Airways on 16 August 1964.

FLEET:
5 X B737-300, 4 X B737-500,
19 X B757-200, 4 X B 767-200ER,
9 X B767-300ER

FEATURES:
The World of TUI corporate identity is now associated everywhere with the red "smile" on the tailfin of the blue upper part of the aircraft. Standing out from the blue are red and white *Thomsonfly.com* titles.

Tiger Airways (TR/TGW)

SINGAPORE (9V)

Singapore's first low-cost carrier, in which Singapore Airlines has a major shareholding, was incorporated on 9 December 2003 and began operations on 15 September 2004, initially serving the Thai capital of Bangkok and resort areas of Phuket and Hat Yai. Since then, Tiger Airways has added a further 15 destinations in Asia, all within four hours' flying time from Singapore. Countries served include Thailand, Vietnam, Indonesia, Macau, and the Philippines.

FLEET:
4 (8) x A320-200

FEATURES:
This appropriate livery, highlighted by the orange and black tiger stripes covering the tailfin and a leaping tiger ahead of the name and web address, puts the airline firmly in the Singaporean and Asian landscape. Tigers are found only in Asia and represent power, strength, speed, and agility. They are also aggressive and focused when hunting or when challenged, all attributes Tiger Airways wants the traveling public to recognize.

Tikal Jets Airlines (WU/TKC)

GUATEMALA (TG)

National airline operating scheduled passenger services connecting the capital Guatemala City with Flores, gateway to the ancient Mayan ruins of Tikal, one of Central America's premier tourist destinations. Services extend to Mexico, Cuba, Belize, Nicaragua, and El Salvador. The airline also provides sightseeing packages and other ad hoc charters. Tikal Jets was founded in 1992.

FLEET:
1 x DC-9-30, 2 x DC-9-50

FEATURES:
The white aircraft displays a Mayan pyramid outlined against a red canvas painted by the setting sun. Blue and gold cheatlines support the *Tikal Jets* titles on the cabin roof.

Titan Airways (AWC)

UNITED KINGDOM (G)

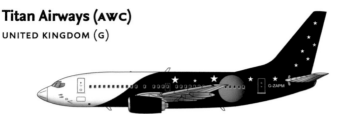

London Stansted-based airline providing contract and ad hoc passenger and cargo charter flights throughout Europe, North Africa, and the Middle East, together with wet-lease services for scheduled airlines. Corporate passenger flights and rapid-response cargo charters are also undertaken, as are regular flights for the Royal Mail. Apart from the Boeings, all other aircraft can be re-configured in 30 minutes to fly as either passenger or cargo aircraft. Titan Airways was established in January 1988 and started operations with a single Cessna Titan on 1 February that year.

FLEET:
1 X BAE 146-200QC,
1 X BAE 146-200QT, 1 X B737-300,
1 X B737-300QC, 1 X B737-300SF,
1 X B757-200, 1 x Beech 200C
Super King Air

FEATURES:
Titan, one of Saturn's moons, has replaced the previous spinning globe and blue fade scheme. It resides in a dark firmament among a galaxy of stars and was created by UK design house Propellor Studios.

TNT Airways (3V/TAY)

BELGIUM (OO)/SPAIN (EC)

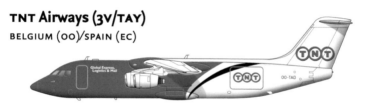

Major express overnight cargo airline based at Liège-Bierset in Belgium, connecting all TNT Express locations across the world and more specifically in Europe in association with sister airline Pan Air of Spain. TNT also provides its fleet and services to third parties for scheduled and non-scheduled cargo flights, wet-lease contracts, and specialized charters focusing on the transportation of thoroughbred racehorses, as well as on newspapers, racing cars, and the automotive industry. TNT's history in Europe goes back to 5 May 1985, but it was incorporated under new ownership in June 1999.

FLEET:
4 X A300B4-200F, 5 X B737-300F,
3 X BAE 146-200QT,
8 X BAE 146-300QT

FEATURES:
TNT replaced the red TNT initials in a compartmentall black box on the tailfin with a new corporate image in 1998. The forward fuselage is now completely surrounded in bright orange, with the rear section in white with a bold black cheek line. The company's new motif of three linked circles containing the letters TNT, both in orange with black shadows, aft of the wings and on the tailfin.

Tobago Express (TBX)

TRINIDAD AND TOBAGO (9Y)

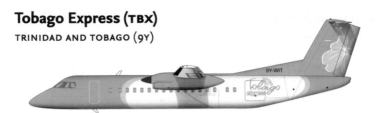

Caribbean airline offering a high-frequency shuttle service between the capital Port of Spain on Trinidad with Crown Point on the tiny island of Tobago. The 20-minute flights, operated 12 times each day, serve the business community traveling between the two islands, and a large number of tourists holidaying at the popular resorts on Tobago. Tobago Express was established by private interests and international carrier BWIA West Indies Airways in 2001.

FLEET:
2 x Dash 8 Q300

FEATURES:
A gold and white hibiscus blossom flowers on the green tailfin, whose coloring extends to the engines and along most of the fuselage. A white, gold-edged window has been cut out of the green in the middle part of the aircraft, including *Tobago Express* lettering, with *Tobago* written in a carefree style, accompanied by the golden hibiscus.

Total Linhas Aéreas (TTL)

BRAZIL (PP/PT)

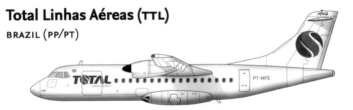

Regional airline operating scheduled passenger and cargo services to some 20 destinations, focusing on linking major cities in the southeastern state of Minas Gerais and the capital Brasilia with destinations in the northern states of Pará and Amazonas. The network is further extended through code-share flights with TAM. The airline also offers passenger and cargo charters, as well as night mail flights on behalf of the Brazilian Post Office. Total was founded in 1988.

FLEET:
7 X ATR 42-300, 2 X ATR 42-500, 2 X ATR 72-210, 3 X B727-200F

FEATURES:
An interesting spherical design in blue and red adds color to the white aircraft, being prominently displayed on the tailfin and as the letter o in the *Total* titles behind the cockpit. Small red *Linhas Aéreas* lettering completes the airline name.

Tradewinds Airlines (wı/tdx)

UNITED STATES (N)

All-cargo airline operating a mix of scheduled and charter services throughout the Americas. Scheduled services provide internal links and extensions to Aguadilla and San Juan in Puerto Rico. The company was set up as Wrangler Aviation in 1969 and began operations in 1973, transporting its trademark jeans and raw materials between manufacturing plants in North Carolina, Florida, and Puerto Rico, using Lockheed L1049H Super Constellations. It was transformed into a commercial air charter operation in 1978 and became an all-cargo airline in 1981. The present name was adopted in November 1991.

FLEET:
5 X A300B4-200F, 3 X B747-200F

FEATURES:
A dark blue cheatline flows along the length of the fuselage at mid-height before flaring out to completely fill the tailfin. Three white waves alluding to the airline's name relieve the starkness of the dark blue. Simple *Tradewinds* titles sit above the cheatline at mid-fuselage.

Trans Maldivian Airways (hum)

MALDIVES (8Q)

Domestic airline providing a variety of aerial services in the Maldives, a chain of 1,190 little coral islands scattered across the Indian Ocean. Apart from scheduled transfers from Male International Airport to some 20 resorts in the Ari, Baa, Alifu, Dhaalu, Male, and Meemu atolls, Trans Maldivian also provides charter flights to island and beach destinations, picnic flights, medical evacuation, and sightseeing services over the spectacular atolls, islands, and lagoons. It began life in 1989 as Hummingbird Island Helicopters but completed the transition to a seaplane fleet in January 1999.

FLEET:
1 X DHC-6 Twin Otter 100,
12 X DHC-6 Twin Otter 300

FEATURES:
This colorful livery depicts the golden sands of the islands surrounded by the still waters of the warm Indian Ocean. A dhoti, the traditional sailing boat of local fishermen, bobs gently on the sea. Dolphins jump playfully on the aircraft's floats.

Transaero Airlines (un/tso)

RUSSIAN FEDERATION (RA)

Moscow-based airline providing services from Moscow Domodedovo Airport to points within Russia and to destinations in the Commonwealth of Independent States, Europe, and the Far East. The domestic network serves more than 10 major cities. The airline was incorporated as a joint-stock company on 28 December 1990 and was the first non-Aeroflot operator to receive approval for scheduled passenger services in Russia. Operations began on 5 November 1991 with a charter flight from Moscow to Tel Aviv. The first scheduled service followed in January 1993 to Norilsk.

FLEET:
2 X B737-300, 4 X B737-400,
2 X B747-200B, 3 X B767-200ER,
4 X B767-300ER, (10) X TU-204-200

FEATURES:
The simple livery of Transaero comprises a graduated arrow in the national colors of red and blue, flying up the white tailfin. Blue *Transaero* titles are painted on the forward cabin roof. The upper fuselage of the aircraft is arctic white, underscored by a blue belly and engines.

Transafrik International (rfk)

SÃO TOMÉ E PRINCIPE (S9)

Cargo charter airline providing flights and logistics services throughout the African continent. Activities focus on servicing the multinational mining and oil-exploration corporations, transport of fuel, medical evacuation, and logistical support and expertise for major relief organizations such as the United Nations and Red Cross. Transafrik was established in November 1984 and began flying the following month. Its main center of operation has been moved from São Tomé e Principe to Luanda in neighboring Angola.

FLEET:
1 X B727-100C, 4 X B727-100F,
1 X B727-200A, 2 X L100-20
Hercules, 6 x L100-30 Hercules

FEATURES:
Transafrik is one of the few airlines still leaving a large part of the aircraft unpainted. Blue and ocher cheatlines along the all-metal fuselage, *Transafrik* titles in a small white block on the forward roof, and a gold map of Africa in an encircled white disc on the tailfin, highlighting the T in the airline's name, are the only concessions to paint.

TransAsia Airways (GE/TNA)

TAIWAN (B)

Domestic and regional carrier of Taiwan providing scheduled passenger services from the capital Taipei to eight other domestic points, and to Macau, Thailand, and Malaysia. Regional charter flights are also undertaken. The airline's history goes back to 1951 when it was established, under the name of Foshing Airlines, as the first private Taiwanese carrier, concentrating for a long time on charter flights before adding scheduled services in the late 1980s. The name was changed to TransAsia Airways to reflect the airline's international ambitions.

FLEET:
3 X A320-200, 5 X A321-100, 3 X ATR 72-200, 7 X ATR 72-500

FEATURES:
The key element of TransAsia's corporate identity is a blue Chinese dragon curled around a golden sun. It fits well into the bright red tailfin, which itself provides a pleasing contrast to the otherwise white aircraft. Simple *TransAsia* airways titling in English and Chinese symbols on the cabin roof is followed by triple bands of red, gold, and blue across the roof. The aircraft registration features not once, but twice on the fuselage. Winglets on appropriate aircraft are highlighted in red.

Transavia Airlines (HV/TRA)

NETHERLANDS (PH)

Subsidiary of KLM Royal Dutch Airlines providing low-fare leisure flights from Amsterdam and Rotterdam to the Mediterranean basin resort areas and to Madeira and the Canary Islands. Charter flights are also operated to over 60 points in Europe, accounting for a large part of the Dutch charter market. The airline was founded in 1965 as Transavia (Limburg) and began operations on 17 November 1966. The name was changed to Transavia Holland in 1967, with the present title coming into force in 1986.

FLEET:
10 X B737-700, 18 X B737-800

FEATURES:
Developed in cooperation with employees, the Transavia scheme emphasizes such concepts as strength, dynamism, enthusiasm, and personal attention. A bold green flash strikes from nose to tail on a brilliant white fuselage, broadening out towards the rear. An elegant and flowing t in blue and green is featured on the tailfin. Blue *Transavia* titles are placed above the forward cabin windows and repeated on the white engine cowlings.

Transmile Air Services (TH/TSE)

MALAYSIA (9M)

Designated national cargo airline of Malaysia providing a network of scheduled and charter freight services linking Kuala Lumpur with destinations in China, India, Indonesia, the Philippines, Singapore, and Thailand. Domestic flights are also operated. Alongside cargo services, the airline also undertakes no-frills passenger flights, introduced in 2000. Aircraft leasing is part of its business too. Transmile began courier services between Peninsular Malaysia and East Malaysia on 27 November 1993 and was designated as the national carrier in 1996. The first international route was opened in May 1998 to Shenzhen in China.

FLEET:
5 X B727-200F, 1 X B737-200C, 1 X B737-200F, 2 X Cessna 208B Grand Caravan, 4 X MD-11F

FEATURES:
This uncluttered and appealing color scheme provides a clean delineation between the white fuselage and the bright red tail and red engines, emphasized by the golden bird symbol. The airline's web address in red stands out particularly well on its windowless cargo aircraft. The Malaysian flag behind the cockpit comprises red and white stripes standing for the states within the federation, and the Islamic golden yellow crescent moon and stars on a blue canton.

Travel Service Airlines (QS/TVS)

CZECH REPUBLIC (OK)

Prominent Czech charter airline operating on behalf of tour operators mainly to the Mediterranean basin and further afield. Regular flights to exotic destinations are also undertaken, together with ad hoc charters. Services originate in Prague, but also in Budapest and the Canary Islands through associate companies Travel Service Hungary and Visig Operaciones Aéreas. Low-fare schedules are flown by subsidiary Smart Wings. Travel Service had its origins in the Czech government Flying Service, SLU Statni letecky utvar, which was commercialized in 1997 through the injection of private capital.

FLEET:
5 X B737-800

FEATURES:
Blue, white, and red are the colors of the Czech flag, which can be seen at the rear. The blue tailfin incorporates the airline emblem of a "speedy" white letter T and red s encircled in white. A red and blue wing symbol flies ahead of Travel Service titles on the forward fuselage. The word Travel is made up of thin lines to create the effect of forward movement. On appropriate aircraft the tail design is repeated on the large winglets.

TRIP Linhas Aéreas (8R)
BRAZIL (PP/PT)

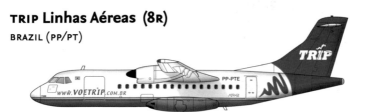

São Paulo-based regional airline operating an extensive network of passenger and cargo services to some 25 destinations within Brazil. Operations are divided into two distinct networks. The larger covers the north and central west regions, making up around half of the country's territory, while the second network covers the northeastern state of Rio Grande do Norte. TRIP Linhas Aéreas was established in 1998 by Grupo Caprioli, a major bus travel and tourism company. TRIP is an abbreviation of Transporte Aéreo Regional do Interior Paulista.

FLEET:
3 X ATR 42-300, 1 X ATR 42-320, 1 X EMB 120ER Brasilia

FEATURES:
A pleasing use of royal blue, red, and white is emphazised by the design of the tailfin and rear fuselage, on which the blue is edged in bright red and from which trails a blue and red ribbon creating a more dynamic effect than if curtailed in a straight line. The web address in blue and red can be found on the forward white fuselage above a red cheatline that separates the lower blue from the upper white fuselage.

Tropic Air (PM/TOS)
BELIZE (V3)

Largest airline in Belize, providing scheduled passenger and cargo services from Belize City's International and Municipal airports to all main towns and tourist destinations within the country. Package tours are operated to the spectacular Mayan ruins of Tikal and Xunantunich, plus adventure trips for cave tubing, diving at the Barrier Reef, and more. Express freight services guaranteed on the next available flight are also offered. Tropic Air was established in 1979 and started flying in November that year.

FLEET:
6 X Cessna 208B Grand Caravan, 1 X DHC-6 Twin Otter 300

FEATURES:
The brick red paint scheme runs from the top of the nose along the fuselage and partially up the rear of the tailfin, being scored by white laser lines to suggest speed. On the tailfin, a road winds into the distance framed by a red sun. *Tropic Air* titles sit behind the windows at the rear. There are some variations.

Tuninter (UG/TUI)

TUNISIA (TS)

Regional airline operating scheduled domestic passenger and cargo services, linking the capital Tunis with other major commercial and tourist centers. All flights are operated in association with parent company Tunisair. Regional charter flights are also undertaken when aircraft are not required to fulfill its scheduled-services obligations. Tuninter was established in August 1991 and started operations in March 1992.

FLEET:
1 x A320-200, 1 x ATR 42-300, 1 x ATR 72-200, 1 x B737-200

FEATURES:
A bright scheme in which the blue tailfin is edged in yellow and displays a yellow design that has been arranged to form the flight of a bird. Large blue *Tuninter* titles are applied along the white fuselage. The red and white Tunisian flag crowns the rear cabin windows.

Tunisair (TU/TAR)

TUNISIA (TS)

Tunisian flag-carrier providing international scheduled services linking Carthage International Airport, gateway to the capital Tunis, to many destinations in Europe, the Middle East, and North and West Africa. Domestic services are also flown, some in association with partially owned Tuninter. Tunisair was established in 1948 as Société Tunisienne de l'Air by the government, Air France, and private interests and began operations over local routes in 1949 with three Douglas DC-3s and two DC-4s. The state acquired a majority holding following the country's independence in 1955.

FLEET:
3 x A300-600R, 3 x A319-100, 12 x A320-200, 2 x B737-300, 4 x B737-500, 7 x B737-600

FEATURES:
The present livery was adopted with the introduction of the Airbus A320 in October 1990. It is centered on an all-white fuselage highlighted by a red leaping gazelle on the tailfin. The impression of speed has been created with red pinstripes trailing down the fin and around the rear fuselage. Red *Tunisair* titles in English and Arabic are displayed on the cabin roof, with the Tunisian flag to the rear.

Tunisavia (TAJ)
TUNISIA (TS)

Tunisian charter airline operating fixed-wing aircraft and helicopters from bases at Tunis, Sfax, Djerba, and Elborama, primarily serving the oil and gas industries, both offshore and onshore, but also providing VIP flights, air-ambulance services, and search and rescue. Helicopters are also used for agricultural spraying, geophysical surveys, power-line patrol, aerial photography, and sightseeing flights. Tunisavia was founded on 27 April 1974 and began operations on 11 July that year with a leased Britten-Norman BN-2A Islander between Tunis and Sfax. Scheduled flights ceased in May 1992.

FLEET:
1 x Dassault Falcon 50, 2 x DHC-6 Twin Otter 300, 2 x AS 365N Dauphin II, 1 x SA318C Alouette II Astazou

FEATURES:
Tunisavia's color scheme comprises a dark blue cheatline, which is unusually subdivided in white and flows above a paler blue belly, and up the rear of the tailfin. The otherwise white fin also displays the airline's two-tone bird motif. *Tunisavia* titles are applied in English on the port side and on the starboard side in Arabic. The two-tone blue design is repeated on the engines.

Turkish Airlines (TK/THY)
TURKEY (TC)

National airline providing scheduled international and domestic services from Istanbul and Ankara to more than 60 cities, with a strong emphasis on Europe and extending to Central Asia, North Africa, the Middle and Far East, and the United States. The airline was established on 20 May 1933 as Hava Yollari Devlet Isletmesi Idaresi and began operations in August that year. The name was changed to Devlet Hava Yollari in June 1938 and a major reorganization on 20 February 1956 resulted in the creation of Turk Hava Yollari, of which the present title is the English equivalent.

FLEET:
5 x A310-300, 1 x A310-300F, 12 (19) x A320-200, 7 (12) x A321-200, (5) x A330-200, 6 x A340-300, 17 x B737-400, 26 (23) x B737-800, 6 x RJ100

FEATURES:
The national colors of red and white predominate in the scheme, with a red tailfin riding the white fuselage. Set into a white circle on the fin is a bird symbol in red. Blue *Turkish* titles are followed by a small Turkish flag, which includes the crescent moon and star on a red field, associated with the Ottoman Empire. All aircraft carry names of Turkish towns and cities.

Turkmenistan Airlines (T5/AKH)

TURKMENISTAN (EZ)

National carrier maintaining a small scheduled network of passenger and cargo services from the capital Ashgabat to a handful of destinations in Asia, Europe, and the Central Asian republics. The airline was established in 1992 following the country's independence. In 1998, the three operating companies, Akhal, Khazar, and Lebap, were integrated into Turkmenistan Airlines.

FLEET:
4 X AN-24RV, 7 X B717-200,
3 X B737-300, 4 X B757-200,
1 X B767-300ER, 4 X IL-76TD,
7 X Yak-40

FEATURES:
Traditional sky blue and mid-blue straight-through cheatlines on the pristine white fuselage and, unusually, on the engines, emphasize the aerodynamic shape of its aircraft. A white dove in a blue disc is the only color on the white tailfin. The interesting green national flag at the front includes a symbolic representation of the country's carpet industry.

Ukraine International Airlines (PS/AUI)

UKRAINE (UR)

Ukrainian international airline providing scheduled passenger services from Kiev Borispol to several European capital cities. Some frequencies are operated via Lvov in the west of the country. Long-haul connections are available at Vienna and Zürich through associated carriers Austrian Airlines and Swiss, who both have financial interests in the airline. Charter flights serve Europe, the Middle East, and North Africa. Ukraine International was established on 1 October 1992 as a joint venture between the government and private foreign investors. Operations began on 25 November 1992.

FLEET:
4 X B737-300, 1 X B737-400,
3 X B737-500

FEATURES:
The blue of the tailfin is carried down in line with the leading edge and wrapped around the fuselage behind a broad band of yellow. Blue and yellow are the national colors. A highly stylized bird symbol flies on a sun disc set into the blue tail. *Ukraine International* titles, preceded by the national flag, take up most of the fuselage, while the full title appears in the local language below the windows.

UM Air (UF/UKM)
UKRAINE (UR)

Ukraine's third-largest airline, operating from Kiev
Borispol Airport to destinations in Russia, the
Commonwealth of Independent States, and the
Middle East. A small domestic network is also
flown, as are international and domestic charters.
The name UM Air is derived from its full title of
Ukrainian-Mediterranean Airlines, was established
in 1998 and obtained its air operator's certificate on
15 September 1999. Operations began in April 2000.

FLEET:
1 X A320-200, 1 x AN-24RV,
4 X DC-9-50, 2 X TU-134A,
1 x Yak-42

FEATURES:
Immediately noticeable is the
cleverly conceived depiction of
waves along the whole of the
white fuselage, with the yellow
ocher reminiscent of the
Ukrainian countryside, and the
blue alluding to the waters of the
Mediterranean Sea, while also
mirroring the colors of the
Ukrainian flag. The scheme has
been designed around the
airline's full name, a shortened
version of which appears on the
forward fuselage. The fluttering
standard on the tailfin is almost
of secondary importance.

UNI Airways (B7/UIA)
TAIWAN (B)

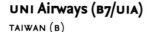

Domestic and regional carrier linking the capital
Taipei with seven major points throughout Taiwan,
and with Malaysia and Thailand. Regional charter
flights are also undertaken. Founded in 1988 as
Makung Airlines, the airline started operations the
following year over a small domestic network. The
present name was adopted in May 1996 when EVA
Air acquired a major shareholding. On 1 July 1998,
Taiwan Airlines and Great China Airlines were
merged into UNI Air. Taiwan Airlines and Great
China had been established in 1966 to initially
provide air-taxi and aerial work services.

FLEET:
1 x Dash 8 200, 8 x Dash 8 300,
3 x Dash 8 Q300, 3 x DO228-200,
7 X MD-90-30, 1 X MD-90-30ER

FEATURES:
The most prominent element of
the design is the corporate
symbol on an orange-red tailfin,
with a green strip along the
rudder. A cheatline emanates
from the *Uni Air* titles on the
forward white fuselage in English
and Chinese characters, all in the
same orange-red.

United Airlines (UA/UAL)

UNITED STATES (N)

World's second-largest airline, providing scheduled passenger and cargo services from hubs at Chicago, Denver, Los Angeles, San Francisco, and Washington Dulles. The network totals 100 U.S. cities and close to 40 international airports, serving 26 countries and two U.S. territories. Its reach is further expanded through its United Express regional partners and through its membership of the Star Alliance. United was founded on 1 July 1931 as the management company for four pioneering airlines, Varney Speed Lines, National Air Transport, Pacific Air Transport, and Boeing Air Transport. Varney Speed Lines had begun mail services between Elko and Pasco with Swallow biplanes on 6 April 1926, followed by National Air Transport between Chicago and Dallas on 12 May that year. Pacific Air Transport followed on 15 September, operating Ryan M-1s on the route between Seattle, San Francisco, and Los Angeles, while Boeing Air Transport began carrying mail and passengers between Chicago and San Francisco, with Boeing 40-AS. On 1 June 1961, Capital Airlines (the successor to Pennsylvania Airlines, formed in 1927 and later known as Pennsylvania-Central Airlines) was merged into United, connecting the primarily east-west route system of United with the north-south routes of Capital.

FLEET:
55 (23) x A319-100,
50 (19) x A320-200,
64 x B737-300, 29 x B737-500,
31 x B747-400, 97 x B757-200,
31 x B767-300ER, 19 x 777-200,
33 x B777-200ER

FEATURES:
United's striking, yet simple, livery was designed to forge an emotional connection with its frequent business travelers and represents the airline's new spirit. The corporate "double U" on the tailfin is drawn in more elegant lines and is offset against the bright white upper part of the aircraft and complemented by the dark blue belly and the bold *United* lettering with the traditional "double U" on the forward fuselage.

United Express (UA)

UNITED STATES (N)

Large regional network provided by four airlines, offering some 2,000 flights a day to 150 cities across the United States and Canada, feeding into the United Airlines hubs at Chicago, Denver, Washington Dulles, San Francisco, and Los Angeles. The four are Chautauqua Airlines, founded on 3 May 1973; Fort Wayne, Indiana-based Shuttle America, which started flying on 12 November 1998; Trans States Airlines, dating from May 1982; and SkyWest Airlines of St. George, Utah, which was incorporated on 2 March 1972 and commenced scheduled services on 19 June that same year.

FLEET:
CRJ200, CJR700, Dash 8, EMB 120ER Brasilia, EMB 170, ERJ 145, Saab 340

FEATURES:
The aircraft operated by United Express carriers are almost identical to that of United Airlines. The emphasis again is on the corporate "double U" on the tailfin that is drawn in elegant lines. The bold *United* lettering on the forward fuselage is followed by the word *Express* in silver-gray.

Universal Airlines (UV/UVG)

GUYANA (8R)

Guyana's international carrier operating scheduled passenger and cargo services from the capital Georgetown to New York and Fort Lauderdale in the United States, as well as to neighboring Trinidad, Suriname, and Northern Brazil. Owned by two ladies, Chandramattie Harpaul and Ramashree Singh, Universal Airlines was founded in 2001 and started operations on 13 December 2001 with a non-stop flight to New York using a leased Boeing 767-300ER. Operations ceased in fall 2005 but are expected to be restarted following restructuring.

FLEET:
1 X A320-200

FEATURES:
The tailfin of the aircraft is dominated by the airline's symbol, which represents the letter U drawn to represent a yellow sun being circum-navigated by a stylized aircraft. This symbol is repeated on the engine cowlings. The unusual Guyanese flag made up of green, yellow, and red triangles, flutters on the top of the fin. *Universal* titles are written across the forward cabin roof.

UPS Airlines (United Parcel Service) (5X/UPS)

UNITED STATES (N)

One of the world's biggest transportation companies, providing cargo and express package delivery services to more than 200 countries and territories, offering next-day and two-day delivery service to anywhere in the world. In addition to its primary hub at Louisville, UPS operates regional hubs across the United States and Canada and international hubs at Cologne Bonn in Germany and Taipei, Taiwan. The company's history dates back to 1907, but its own airline was only launched on 1 February 1988, having previously used contract carriers for its urgent shipments by air.

FLEET:
90 X A300-600F, 15 X B727-100C, 7 X B747-100F, 4 X B747-200F, (8) X B747-400F, 75 X B757-200PF, 32 X B767-300F, 47 X DC-8-70F

FEATURES:
The three-dimensional UPS mark was developed to signal change while retaining the company's proud history. The UPS shield with a simplified but more dynamic golden curve is the cornerstone of the livery and was designed to complement and energize the dark chocolate brown, which has been the company's signature color for nearly 100 years.

Ural Airlines (U6/SVR)

RUSSIAN FEDERATION (RA)

One of Russia's main airlines, operating scheduled passenger and cargo services from Ekaterinburg, formerly Sverdlovsk, to more than 30 cities within Russia, the Commonwealth of Independent States, and Western Europe. Charter flights are regularly carried out to 50 countries in Europe and Asia. Ural Airlines was established as a joint-stock company on 28 December 1993 when the Urals Civil Aviation Directorate/First Sverdlovsk United Air Detachment was separated from Ekaterinburg Koltsovo Airport.

FLEET:
1 X AN-24RV, 2 X AN-24V, 4 X IL-86, 11 X TU-154B-2, 4 X TU-154M

FEATURES:
The emblem of the airline, representing the Cyrillic letters UA, is conspicuously displayed at the nose and on the light blue tailfin, linked by broad blue and red cheatlines. The airline title is carried in English on the cabin roof and in Cyrillic lettering in white within the red band. The white, blue, and red Russian flag fits into the space between Ural Airlines and the large symbol.

US Airways (US/USA)

UNITED STATES (N)

World's largest low-fare, full-service airline, connecting more than 200 destinations coast-to-coast across the United States, and extending to Puerto Rico, the U.S. Virgin Islands, Canada, Central America, the Caribbean, and Europe. The domestic network is further enlarged through regional carriers operating under U.S. Airways Express. The airline came into being on 5 March 1937 as All-American Aviation and began operations on 13 September that year with a unique "pick-up" mail service utilizing Stinson Reliants out of Pittsburgh. It changed its name to Allegheny Airlines in 1953, and mergers with Lake Central Airlines on 1 July 1968 and Mohawk Airlines on 7 April 1972 greatly expanded its operations. Mohawk Airlines had begun operations in 1945 as Robinson Airlines, while Lake Central Airlines started life as Turner Airlines in 1949. It changed its name in 1951. On 28 October 1979 the U.S. Air name was adopted, and changed again to the present title on 27 February 1997. On 27 September 2005 a merger was completed with Phoenix-based America West Airlines, retaining the U.S. Airways name. America West was founded by Edward Beauvais in February 1981 and had begun operations on 1 August 1983. By 1990 it had achieved major airline status and at the time of the merger served nearly 100 destinations.

FLEET:

57 X A319-100, 24 X A320-200, 41 X A321-200, 10 X A330-200, 9 X A330-300, (20) X A350-800, 70 X B737-300, 46 X B737-400, 31 X B757-200, 10 X B767-200ER

FEATURES:

The airline has dispensed with the dark fuselage, which now features a red cheatline separating the dark underside from the upper white, to signify a bright new future. The blue also covers the engines and most of the tailfin, which is topped by white and red, and displays a stylized U.S. flag.

us Airways Express (us/usx)

UNITED STATES (N)

Regional network provided by nine airlines, plus the MidAtlantic division, operating under a code-share agreement with u.s. Airways and serving 130 destinations in the u.s., Canada, and the Bahamas. The nine are Air Midwest Airlines, dating from May 1965; Air Wisconsin, founded in 1963; Chautauqua Airlines, founded on 3 May 1973; Colgan Air, started on 1 December 1991; Mesa Airlines; Piedmont Airlines, founded in 1964 as Henson Airlines; PSA Airlines, dating back to 1969 and Vee Neal Airlines, later Jetstream International; newcomer Republic Airways; and Trans States Airlines.

FLEET:
3 x Beech 1900C, 20 x Beech 1900D, 6 x CRJ100, 52 x CRJ200, 14 x CRJ700, 31 x Dash 8 100, 14 x Dash 8 200, 12 x Dash 8 Q300, 25 EMB 170, 84 x ERJ 145, 5 x Jetstream 41, 19 x Saab 340B

FEATURES:
us Airways Express aircraft have an identical scheme to that of mainline u.s. Airways with the addition of the word *Express* in the title. A red cheatline separates the dark underside from the upper white. The blue tailfin is topped by white and red, and displays a stylized u.s. flag.

us Airways Shuttle (TB/USS)

UNITED STATES (N)

us Airways operation offering high-frequency hourly shuttle services on the eastern seaboard, linking New York La Guardia, Boston, and Washington Reagan National. Its history dates back to October 1988 when it was acquired by New York property tycoon Donald Trump from Eastern Airlines' parent Texas Air. Operations began on 8 June 1989 under The Trump Shuttle banner. On 10 April 1992, another change of ownership was effected when bought by Shuttle and later by u.s. Airways, which adopted the present name on 27 February 1997.

FLEET:
A319-100 and B737-300 from the mainline fleet

FEATURES:
us Airways Shuttle does not have a separate livery as it uses aircraft from the mainline operation. The white upper fuselage is separated from the dark blue underside by a red cheatline, which dips down under the aircraft near the front. The blue tailfin is topped by white and red, and displays a stylized u.s. flag.

USA 3000 Airlines (U5/GWY)

UNITED STATES (N)

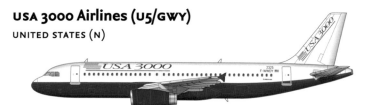

U.S. leisure airline providing scheduled passenger services connecting many northeastern and Midwest cities to resort areas in Florida, Mexico, and the Dominican Republic. In addition, USA 3000 flies charters to the Caribbean and Mexico in conjunction with Apple Vacations, one of the largest tour operators in the United States. It was founded in October 2001 as Brendan Air and began charter operations in December that year under the USA 3000 marketing name. Scheduled services were added in 2002.

FLEET:
12 (1) X A320-200

FEATURES:
This nationalistic livery focuses on blue USA 3000 titling underlined in red and accompanied by an allusion to the U.S. flag, carried both on the forward cabin roof and up the leading edge of the tailfin. A smart red line separates the white upper fuselage from the dark blue belly. The blue engines and red winglets further strengthen the patriotic theme.

USA Jet Airlines (U7/JUS)

UNITED STATES (N)

All-cargo airline arm of logistics and management company Active Aero offering primarily ad hoc charter flights for premium freight. USA Jet Airlines was established in 1994 and began flying in December that same year.

FLEET:
13 X Dassault Falcon 20,
6 X DC-9-10, 4 X DC-9-30

FEATURES:
Red and broader gray and blue cheatlines flow along the white upper part of the fuselage before curving up and over the tailfin. The red line supports blue USA Jet roof titles in the middle, while a U.S. flag flutters on the gray central part of the fin. The engines are painted white to provide some relief from the predominantly gray appearance of the aircraft.

uTair Aviation (P2/TMN)

RUSSIAN FEDERATION (RA)

Major Russian carrier operating a wide variety of
services from its Surgut, Khanty Mansisk, and
Tyumen bases in western Siberia, including
scheduled services to some 30 destinations within
Russia, with a few cross-border routes to countries
of the Commonwealth of Independent States.
Extensive helicopter services in support of the oil
and gas industries in Siberia, and relief operations
for the UN are also undertaken. It was established in
1967 as the Aeroflot Tyumen Directorate but
transformed itself into Tyumenaviatrans Aviation
with private interests in 1991. The present title was
adopted on 1 October 2002.

FLEET:
4 X AN-24RV, 5 X AN-24V,
1 X AN-26, 21 x Mi-8MTV-1,
19 x Mi-26T, 3 x Mi-8P,
110 x Mi-8T, 25 X TU-134A-3,
4 X TU-154B-2, 10 X TU-154M,
10 x Yak-40, 2 x Yak-40K

FEATURES:
An unfussy paint scheme on the
white aircraft memorable only for
the white UT lettering in a blue
disc on the tailfin and large blue
uTair titles across the forward
fuselage. The application of the
Russian flag adds a splash of red.

Uzbekistan Airways (HY/UZB)

UZBEKISTAN (UK)

National airline providing flag services from
Tashkent's Yuzhnyy International Airport and
Uzbekistan's second city of Samarkand to Europe,
the Commonwealth of Independent States, Middle
and Far East, and the United States. A domestic
network is also operated and special aerial work is
provided by associate Spetsialnye Aviatsionnye
Raboty. The airline was established on 28 January
1992 from the Aeroflot Tashkent Directorate
following the country's independence on
1 September 1991.

FLEET:
3 X A310-300, 1 X AN-12B,
3 X AN-24RV, 5 X AN-24V,
6 x B757-200, 4 X B767-300ER,
(4) X IL-114, 2 (9) X IL-114-100,
5 X IL-62M, 10 X IL-76TD, 3 X RJ85,
2 X TU-154B-2, 3 X TU-154M,
8 x Yak-40

FEATURES:
The fuselage paint scheme of
blue, white, and green, separated
by red fimbriations, closely
mirrors the national flag. The sky
blue tail features the airline
symbol of a stylized dove in
green, flying across a golden sun
disc encircled in red. The symbol
is also displayed on the blue
engine cowlings.

Valuair (VF)
SINGAPORE (9V)

Privately owned value-for-money budget airline providing a low-fare, high-quality service from Singapore to regional destinations, serving Thailand, Indonesia, Hong Kong, and Australia. The airline was established on 31 March 2003 and received its air operator's certificate on 14 April 2004. The first flights were inaugurated the following month.

FLEET:
3 X A320-200

FEATURES:
Valuair follows the present trend of extending the color of the tailfin in a gentle sweep down and around the rear fuselage, adding some interest and light relief with the lime green border to the blue. White *Valuair* titles are set into the blue. The otherwise white aircraft carries the airline's web address on the roof in blue behind the red and white Singapore flag with the crescent and five stars, the latter symbolizing the nation's ideals of democracy, peace, progress, justice, and equality.

Vanair (X4/ZHI)
VANUATU (YJ)

Government-owned domestic airline operating frequent scheduled services to many of the 83 islands making up this republic lying in the south-west Pacific between New Caledonia and Fiji. The airline also provides charter flights in support of tourism and to transport much needed supplies to the remote outer islands. International connections are available at Bauerfield Airport, serving the capital Port Vila. Vanair was founded by private interests under the name of Air Melanesiae in 1970 and adopted the present title on 29 November 1989. The Vanuatu government took control in September 2004.

FLEET:
2 X BN-2A Islander, 3 X DHC-6 Twin Otter 300

FEATURES:
A green band with a white swirl against a red sun is the simple design on the white tailfin, with the symbol repeated between *Vanair* titles on the forward fuselage. An interesting stepped green and gold cheatline divides the white aircraft.

VARIG (Viação Aérea Rio-Grandense) (RG/VRG)
BRAZIL (PP/PT)

Principal Brazilian airline, operating regional passenger and cargo services within the Americas, together with long-haul flights to Europe and the Far East. An extensive domestic network from hubs at Rio de Janeiro, São Paulo, Brasilia, Salvador, and Recife, including those of subsidiaries Rio-Sul and Nordeste, encompasses more than 40 towns. VARIG was founded on 7 May 1927 and started flying on 15 July that year with a single Dornier Wal over the Lagoa do Patos (Lake of Ducks) between Porto Alegre, Pelotas, and Rio Grande, taken over from the Kondor-Syndikat. The airline made steady progress but became the largest airline in South America when in 1961 it took over the giant real Consortium, whose network stretched throughout the Americas. REAL had been started as Redes Estaduais Aéreas-REAL by Linnneu Gomes in February 1946 and during the next 15 years acquired 13 other airlines including international carrier Aerovias Brasil. VARIG's strong position in South America was further cemented when it acquired a controlling interest in Cruzeiro do Sul in June 1975. Cruzeiro had started life on 1 December 1927 when founded by Deutsche Luft Hansa under the name of Sindicato Condor and started flying with a Junkers G 24 on 28 January 1928. It was integrated into VARIG in January 1993. Member of the Star Alliance.

FLEET:
24 X B737-300, 4 X B737-400, 2 X B737-800, 4 X B767-300ER, 4 X B777-200, 4 X B777-200ER, 2 X B777-300, 9 X MD-11, 3 X MD-11ER

FEATURES:
The Landor-developed livery represents success, progress, and the Brazilian spirit. The traditional compass-rose symbol on the navy blue tailfin, rendered in two hues of yellow, suggests the warmth of the sun and the luster of gold, with additional compass points added to portray the airline's expanding network. The word *Brasil* is applied in a handwritten, cursive style, lending graceful dynamism.

VARIG Log (LC/VLO)
BRAZIL (PP/PT)

Independent cargo subsidiary of VARIG providing a scheduled freight network that links the main points in Brazil and provides connections to other South American cities and northwards to Mexico and Los Angeles, Miami, and New York in the United States. In addition to scheduled services, VARIG Log offers a door-to-door delivery service, warehousing, stock management, packaging, and transportation and distribution services. VARIG Log was established in October 2000 as an independent subsidiary of the Ruben Berta Foundation out of VARIG Cargo, which had itself been set up as a business unit in 1993.

FLEET:
1 X B727-100C, 1 X B727-100F,
4 X B727-200A(F), 2 X DC-10-30F,
1 X MD-11F, 1 X MD-11ER(F)

FEATURES:
VARIG Log retains the traditional compass-rose symbol on the navy blue tailfin, rendered in two hues of yellow, which suggests the warmth of the sun and the luster of gold, with additional compass points added to portray the airline's expanding network. A two-tone yellow arrow speeds ahead of large blue and gold VARIG Log titles.

Viaggio Air (VM/VOA)
BULGARIA (LZ)

Private Bulgarian airline providing scheduled passenger and cargo flights from Sofia, Varna, Plovdiv, Bourgas, and Gorna Oriahovica airports to several destinations in southern Europe. The airline is the designated carrier to Austria, Greece, Turkey, and the Ukraine. Charter flights are also performed. Viaggio Air was established on 11 September 2002 and operated its first service between Sofia and Vienna on 22 December that same year.

FLEET:
2 X ATR 42-300

FEATURES:
A most interesting design, notable for the unique arrangement in red and blue suggesting the wings of a bird extruded at each end to form thin cheatlines. The sparse blue and red on the tail makes use of the angles of the dorsal fin and leading edge to again allude to the spread wings of a bird in flight. Small Viaggio Air titles have been added at the rear in blue, gold, and red. Viaggio means "journey" in Italian.

Vietnam Airlines (vn/hvn)

VIETNAM (VN)

National carrier operating a growing network of scheduled services from Hanoi and Ho Chi Minh City to destinations throughout Asia and to Australia and Europe. A comprehensive domestic route system is also operated. Until April 1989 the airline was known as Hang Khong Vietnam, having been founded by the Civil Aviation Administration of Vietnam in 1976 after re-unification. At the same time, it took over the assets of Air Vietnam, which had operated in the south since 1 October 1951.

FLEET:
10 X A320-200, 6 (10) X A321-200, 6 X ATR 72-200, 3 X ATR 72-500, 3 X B767-300ER, 8 (1) X B777-200ER, 2 X F70

FEATURES:
The striking blue livery with the golden lotus flower, designed by the U.S.-based Peck/Kubo Partnership, reflects the dramatic improvement made by the airline. The lotus has long been an eloquent symbol of the link between Vietnam's optimism about the future and its reverence for history and tradition. Known as the "flower of the dawn," it stands for steadfastness, purity, and optimism.

Viking Airlines (vic)

SWEDEN (SE)

Private Swedish charter airline operating flights for local tour operators to the Mediterranean resorts in Europe and North Africa. Aircraft are based at Athens on the Greek mainland and at Heraklion on the island of Crete. Viking Airlines was established in early 2003 and started flying on 10 May that year.

FLEET:
2 X MD-83

FEATURES:
As the airline name would suggest, its corporate symbol is a stylized head of a Viking, complete with horned helmet, pictured in yellow with a white outline within a blue gold-ringed disc. Huge *Viking* titles, drawn in blue and yellow, straddle the forward fuselage. Blue and yellow are the colors of the Swedish flag (shown on the rear-mounted engines), which dates back to the sixteenth century.

VIM Airlines (TZ/MOV)
RUSSIAN FEDERATION (RA)

Moscow Domodedovo-based Russian airline operating scheduled and charter passenger and cargo flights, primarily to destinations within Russia and the Commonwealth of Independent States, and to Europe and the Middle East. Holiday flights operate to resorts in Turkey, Egypt, Spain, Cuba, Thailand, and the Seychelles, among others. The airline was established by Viktor Merkulov in 2000 and started flying in December that year, initially specializing in cargo flights.

FLEET:
2 X AN-12B, 12 X B757-200,
9 X IL-62M

FEATURES:
A feathered splash of violet-red on the tailfin and a similar design on the engines could be loosely interpreted as the spread wings of a giant bird, carrying white VIM titles in cursive writing. The full name is written across the forward fuselage, with its Russian equivalent VIM *Avia* in small Cyrillic letters sitting above the second row of windows. The name of the airline derives from the initials of its founder, Viktor Ivanovich Merkulov.

Virgin Atlantic Airways (VS/VIR)
UNITED KINGDOM (G)

The UK's second-largest long-haul carrier, providing scheduled value-for-money passenger services from London Heathrow, London Gatwick, and Manchester. Services are operated to the United States, the Caribbean, West and South Africa, the Indian subcontinent, the Far East, and Australia. A major partnership with Continental Airlines gives Virgin access to Continental's large U.S. network from New York. The airline was established as an offshoot of Richard Branson's Virgin Group and inaugurated operations on 22 June 1984 between London Gatwick and New York Newark.

FLEET:
9 X A340-300, 10 (14) X A340-600,
(6) X A380-800, 13 X B747-400

FEATURES:
Since British Airways' decision to drop the British flag from its aircraft in 1997, Virgin's "Scarlet Lady" has been holding the fluttering Union Jack aloft on the front of the fuselage. The silver aircraft are dominated by the orange-red tailfin, sporting the well-known *Virgin* signature in white. Other distinguishing features, also highly visible from afar, are the orange-red engine cowlings and winglets.

Virgin Blue Airlines (DJ/VOZ)
AUSTRALIA (VH)

Fast-growing low-cost airline providing scheduled services across Australia, connecting all state capitals and other major points. The network now extends to 20 cities. The airline was established by the UK's Virgin Group at Brisbane in 1999 and started flying on 31 August 2000 between Brisbane and Sydney, using a Boeing 737-400.

FLEET:
22 X B737-700, 26 X B737-800

FEATURES:
The Virgin orange-red trademark fuselage is highlighted by large blue and white *virginblue.com.au* titling, which takes up virtually all the fuselage. The paint scheme is cut off and edged with blue to frame the white tailfin, which has the usual *Virgin* signature written across the tail. Below the cockpit flies a scantily clad woman carrying the Australian flag. In line with other Virgin airlines, its aircraft carry names such as *Betty Blue*, *Tropical Temptress*, *Blue Moon*, *Misty Blue*, and others.

Virgin Express (TV/VEX)
BELGIUM (OO)

Low-fare airline operating scheduled passenger services from Brussels and Amsterdam to some 15 destinations in southern Europe, taking in points in Spain, Portugal, France, Switzerland, Italy, and Greece. Ad hoc charter flights are also undertaken throughout Europe and the Mediterranean. Virgin Express was founded in November 1991 by the City Hotels Group as EuroBelgian Airlines and began charter operations on 1 April 1992 with Boeing 737-300s. The present name was adopted following the airline's acquisition in April 1996 by the Virgin Group, who transformed it into a low-fare carrier.

FLEET:
5 X B737-300, 5 X B737-400

FEATURES:
The orange-red fuselage is unmistakable, as is the *Virgin* signature on the white tail that has become a highly recognized trademark across the world. *Virgin Express* titles have been reversed out in white on the forward fuselage, with the *Express* slanted and given speed lines.

Virgin Nigeria (VK/VGN)

NIGERIA (5N)

Latest Nigerian flag-carrier, operating scheduled passenger and cargo services from Lagos to London, and to domestic cities and regional destinations in West Africa. The Nigerian government entered into an agreement with UK carrier Virgin Atlantic in September 2004 to set up a new airline, but delays in obtaining the necessary approvals and authorizations postponed the start of services until 28 June 2005, when the first service left Lagos for London. Domestic routes were added the next day. Virgin Atlantic owns a 49% stake, while the remainder is held by Nigerian institutional investors.

FLEET:
1 X A340-300, 2 X A320-200

FEATURES:
The Virgin Nigeria design is a reverse of the Virgin Blue paint scheme, with the fuselage in white and a red tail, although instead of blue it is edged in the green color of the Nigerian flag. The aircraft engines are also painted in green, as is the airline name on the cabin roof, alongside the green and white flag. The green in the flag stands for agriculture, the country's main source of wealth, while white represents peace.

Vladivostok Air (XF/VLK)

RUSSIAN FEDERATION (RA)

Largest airline in Russia's far eastern Primorski Krai, providing a variety of aviation-related services from its base at Vladivostok's Knevichi Airport, including scheduled passenger services within Russia and to China, Japan, and South Korea, together with VIP flights, mail and cargo flights, helicopter operations, maintenance, and airport management. Vladivostok Air's history dates back as far as 1931, but it was reconstituted on 20 January 1994 as a joint-stock company in compliance with the government schedule of privatization. Abakan-based Khakasia Airlines was absorbed in 2002.

FLEET:
2 X AN-24RV, 1 X KA-32A,
7 X KA-32S, 5 X KA-32T,
3 X Mi-8AMT, 3 X Mi-8MTV-1,
1 X Mi-8PS, 5 X Mi-8T,
5 X TU-154B-2, 9 X TU-154M,
3 (1) X TU-234, 4 X Yak-40,
2 X Yak-40K

FEATURES:
A very typical Russian color scheme with white VA initials in a blue disc on the tailfin, and a blue windowline and thinner red line separating the upper white from the lower gray aircraft. Simple red *Vladivostok Air* titles are painted on the forward roof.

VLM Airlines (VG/VLM)

BELGIUM (OO)

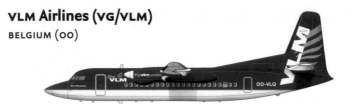

Regional airline operating flights to and within the United Kingdom and to the Netherlands, Luxembourg, France, and Germany, catering primarily for the business passenger. Weekend charter flights are also provided. VLM Airlines was founded on 1 February 1992 with the purpose of connecting smaller regional airports with major economic centers in Western Europe. Scheduled operations began on 15 May 1993. VLM is derived from the initials of the airline's full Flemish name, Vlaamse Luchtvaart Matschappij.

FLEET:
15 x Fokker 50

FEATURES:
Large VLM initials in white with golden wings are proudly displayed on the aircraft tailfin, putting an easily recognizable and highly visible stamp on the navy blue aircraft. The web address is painted in light blue and white on the engines, while *fly VLM* titles incorporating the golden wings are applied behind the cabin door. Aircraft carry names of cities on its network, as well as those of the islands of Jersey and Guernsey.

Volar Airlines (XO/LTE)

SPAIN (EC)

Spanish leisure airline operating passenger services between mainland Spain and the Balearic and Canary islands, and to Europe, primarily to the UK, Ireland, Germany, Switzerland, and Scandinavia. The airline's history dates back to 29 April 1987 and the founding in Palma de Mallorca by German holiday airline LTU and Spanish interests of LTE-Lineas Transportadores Española, later LTE-International Airways. Operations began with two leased Boeing 757s on 1 November that year. The airline was sold on 24 May 2001 to Spanish and Italian businessmen and renamed Volar Airlines in 2003.

FLEET:
5 X A320-200, 1 X A321-200

FEATURES:
The first letter v from the airline's name has been cleverly transformed into a bird. This is the central motif applied in white on the blue tailfin surrounded by gold stars, on the aircraft engines, and in the blue *Volar* titles on the forward fuselage, where it is underlined by a line graduating in color from light to the dark blue used elsewhere. The EU and Spanish flags are carried at the rear. *Volar* means "to fly" in Spanish.

Volareweb.com (Volare Airlines) (VA/VLE)
ITALY (I)

Italian airline operating a predominantly domestic network out of Milan Linate to destinations in southern Italy, with cross-border extensions to other European cities. The airline's history dates back to 1997 and the establishment of Volare Airlines, which started flying on 3 April 1998 with a leased Airbus A320 from Milan and other airports in northern Italy. Volare set up no-frills carrier Volareweb.com on 5 February 2003. Operations began on 30 March that year, but all flying ceased on 19 November 2004 and the airline entered administration. Scheduled services recommenced on 1 June 2005 following reorganization.

FLEET:
2 X A320-200

FEATURES:
The huge *Volareweb.com* titles in white and orange on an overall blue aircraft cannot be missed, as they take up almost the full length of the fuselage, overshadowing the golden winged lion surrounded by 12 stars on the tailfin. The green, white, and red Italian tricolor is represented by a fin flash and a speed line under the cockpit. The airline name, together with an aircraft taking off within an orange outline, covers the blue engines.

Volga-Dnepr Airlines (VI/VDA)
RUSSIAN FEDERATION (RA)

Russian airline operating the world's largest fleet of Antonov AN-124 freighters to transport outsize and heavy cargo on an ad hoc and contract basis to destinations throughout the world. The airline is part of a large group involved in the cargo business through aircraft maintenance, trucking, insurance logistics services and training. Volga-Dnepr Airlines was registered in Ulyanovsk on 22 August 1990 as a joint-stock company, becoming Russia's first private cargo airline. A joint venture was established on 12 September 1991 with UK airline Heavylift, but this was dissolved on 1 February 2001.

FLEET:
9 X AN-124-100, 1 X AN-124-100M, 4 X IL-76TD, (2) X IL-76TD-90, (2) X IL-96-400T, 3 X Yak-40, 2 X Yak-40K

FEATURES:
A broad band of blue, framed by two thin lines, runs down the tailfin and, interestingly, crosses over above the similar horizontal arrangement flowing along the fuselage from nose to tail. Apart from the Russian flag, the fin also supports the airline symbol made up of the entwined Cyrillic letters v and D. It can also be seen in the fuselage band enclosed by the full name in Cyrillic script. English titles are also carried.

Vueling Airlines (VY/VLG)

SPAIN (EC)

Spanish low-fare airline linking the main base of Barcelona and its Valencia hub with several cities in Europe and the western Mediterranean. Vueling was established in 2004 by investment company Apax Partners and Inversiones Hemisferio, part of Grupo Planeta, Spain's largest publishing and media group. Operations began on 1 July 2004.

FLEET:
6 (9) X A320-200

FEATURES:
The tailfin design changes from the solid charcoal at the rear into a progressively lighter perforated order that ends under the rear fuselage in line with the angle of the leading edge. A single yellow dot matches the similarly colored engines and winglets. *Vueling.com* titles in gray and yellow are displayed forward. The overall impression of the design and choice of colors is one of style and harmony. The EU and Spanish flags are carried side by side at the back.

WDL Aviation (WDL)

GERMANY (D)

Cologne-based German carrier engaged in a diverse range of activities including scheduled and charter passenger and cargo services on behalf of other airlines, and VIP and corporate shuttle flights from Frankfurt to all areas in Europe. Another division operates an airship for advertising. WDL Aviation was formed in 1956 as Westdeutsche Luftwerbung (WDL) to provide aerial advertising through banner towing and later air-taxi flights. The name was changed to the present title after the acquisition of larger aircraft for cargo flights. Passenger services were reintroduced in 1998.

FLEET:
1 X BAE 146-100, 2 X BAE 146-200, 1 X F27-400, 8 X F27-600

FEATURES:
The latest livery uses the company's red stylized aircraft symbol to create the outline of a globe on the tailfin of the white aircraft. Prominently displayed at the front are WDL initials crossed by the red aircraft.

Welcome Air (2W/WLC)
AUSTRIA (OE)

Regional airline operating a scheduled domestic service linking its main base of Innsbruck in the Tyrol to Graz, and connecting both cities to destinations in Sweden, Belgium, the Netherlands, Germany, and the Italian holiday island of Sardinia. Charter flights are also undertaken and air-ambulance services are provided under the name of Tyrol Air Ambulance. The group's history dates back to the foundation in 1963 of Aircraft Innsbruck, which operated executive charters. The first ambulance flight took off on 5 July 1976 and scheduled passenger flights were begun in 2000 under the Welcome Air name.

FLEET:
1 x FD 328-100, 1 x FD 328JET

FEATURES:
The name of the airline, written large and underlined on the tailfin and engines, says everything it wants to convey to its customers. Welcome Air has also chosen an unusual color combination that is not easy to forget. A gold upper fuselage and tailfin is separated from the dark magenta lower part by a wavy white band, with the high wing-mounted dark magenta engines reinforcing the design concept.

West Air Sweden (PT/SWN)
SWEDEN (SE)

Gothenburg-based cargo airline operating scheduled and ad hoc freight flights for the main integrators such as FedEx, DHL, TNT, and UPS, and contract night mail flights for the Swedish Post Office. The company also undertakes maintenance and aircraft modification work at Regional Hovby Airport, located outside the lakeside town of Lidköping. West Air Sweden was established by Anders Löfberg in 1962 and was known as Abal Air until the name was changed in 1992.

FLEET:
7 x BAE ATP-F, 6 x BAE 748-2A, 2 x BAE 748-2B

FEATURES:
Dotted across the white aircraft are five blue and gold sketch designs of a Viking winged helmet in varying sizes, making a strong statement about the airline's origins. Black West Air Sweden and Cargo titles are featured above the forward cabin windows and on the tailfin respectively. Some aircraft carry names such as Betty Boop.

West Coast Air (80)

CANADA (C)

Locally owned airline in Canada's western province of British Columbia operating high-frequency floatplane services to Victoria from downtown Vancouver and the Vancouver Airport Floatplane Base, serving both business and leisure traffic. The airline also offers adventure and scenic tours and charter flights from Vancouver and Victoria to south coast destinations including Butchart Gardens, Whistler, Tofino, Campbell River, and more. West Coast Air was founded in 1995 and started flying on 25 January 1996.

FLEET:
2 X DHC-2 Beaver I, 4 X DHC-6 Twin Otter 100, 1 X DHC-6 Twin Otter 200

FEATURES:
A golden eagle soars into the darkening sky, which takes up the entire tailfin of the airline's float-equipped aircraft. Beyond that, the aircraft are pristine white, with the stylish *West Coast Air* titles barely disturbing the clean modern image.

WestJet Airlines (WS/WJA)

CANADA (C)

Canadian low-fare airline providing affordable air travel across western Canada from its main base at Calgary International Airport. The growing network serves more than 20 destinations in Canada, together with transborder flights to the western U.S., Florida, and New York, as well as Hawaii, added in late 2005. WestJet Airlines was set up in June 1995 and began operations on 29 February 1996 with three Boeing 737-200s from Calgary, initially serving Edmonton, Kelowna, Vancouver, and Winnipeg.

FLEET:
9 X B737-200A, 1 (12) X B737-600, 41 (3) X B737-700, 5 X B737-800

FEATURES:
The airline emblem, applied on the fuselage, is projected onto the tailfin, where a white arrow shoots upwards between black and dark cyan, the two signature colors, which are also used in the italic *WestJet* titles along the cabin roof. The red and white Canadian maple-leaf flag is small enough not to disturb the clean lines of this attractive design.

White (YSS)
PORTUGAL (CP)

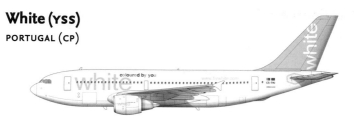

Portuguese charter airline operating services in support of the tourist industry and in partnership with the main tour operators. The airline operates both medium- and long-haul routes to such destinations as the Balearic and Canary islands, Turkey, Tunisia, various European cities, and across the Atlantic to points in Brazil, Mexico, Cuba, and the Dominican Republic. It was formed as Yes Charter Airlines on 19 January 2000 as a joint venture between TAP Air Portugal and tour operator Viagens Abreu and began flying in June that year. The present name was adopted in 2005.

FLEET:
2 X A310-300

FEATURES:
This unconventional livery uses the airline's name as the principal element, being painted in gray on the forward white fuselage, and vertically in white up the gray tailfin. A *coloured by you* slogan is applied in small lettering on the cabin roof. The Portuguese and European Union flags sit above the aircraft registration at the rear.

White Eagle Aviation (WEA)
POLAND (SP)

Private Polish airline offering a variety of aerial services with a mixed fleet of fixed-wing aircraft and helicopters from its base at Warsaw Frederic Chopin Airport. In addition to ad hoc and contract passenger and cargo charters, the company also undertakes air-taxi flights and aerial work. White Eagle Aviation was established in 1992 and started flying in 1993.

FLEET:
1 X ATR 42-300, 1 x Beech 350 King Air, 2 x Let L-410 UVP-E

FEATURES:
Not surprisingly, given the airline name, a beautifully drawn white eagle soars against the blue sky of the tailfin and the engines, urging the white aircraft forward. Large blue WEA initials color the front fuselage, with *White Eagle Aviation* in full aft of the wing.

Widerøe's Flyveselskap (WF/WIF)

NORWAY (LN)

Long-established regional airline and member of the SAS Group, maintaining extensive scheduled passenger services within Norway and to neighboring Denmark, Sweden, and the UK. The majority of services, which link some 40 airfields along Norway's picturesque coastal region from Bergen and Oslo in the south to Kirkenes in the far north, are operated under contract from the government. Widerøe's was formed on 19 February 1934 by aviation pioneer Viggo Widerøe and operated a variety of services until participating in the development of vital rural services from 1970.

FLEET:
16 x Dash 8 100, 9 x Dash 8 Q300, 3 x Dash 8 Q400

FEATURES:
Norway's green hills and valleys on the lower fuselage and engines are outlined in the winter white landscape of the upper fuselage and tailfin, with a stylized bird drawn in a v shape from the first letter in the founder's name, hovering above. Simple dark green *Widerøe* titling is painted on the forward base of the aircraft.

Winair (WM/WIA)

NETHERLANDS ANTILLES (PJ)

Government-owned regional airline in the Netherlands Antilles providing scheduled and charter services throughout the northeastern Caribbean from its main base of Princess Juliana Airport on the island of St. Maarten. Among the destinations are the islands of Saba, St. Eustatius, St. Barths, St. Kitts, Nevis, and Anguilla, as well as Tortola in the British Virgin Islands. Winair (Windward Islands Airways International) was formed on 24 August 1961 and began operations on 5 August 1962.

FLEET:
2 x BN-2A Islander, 3 x DHC-6 Twin Otter 300

FEATURES:
A red cheatline divides the upper white fuselage and lower dark blue belly of the aircraft and then angles up through the middle of the all-blue tailfin. The curved golden line lightens up the dark blue, as do the *Winair* titles on the tail and the lower forward fuselage. The overall impression given is one of serious intent and a businesslike approach to service.

Wind Jet (IV/JET)
ITALY (I)

Italian low-cost airline operating scheduled domestic passenger and cargo services from Catania and Palermo on the southern island of Sicily to major mainland cities and to the nearby island of Lampedusa. International scheduled flights to Monaco and Düsseldorf are also undertaken, together with European charter flights. Wind Jet was established by the Finaria Group in 2003 and inaugurated its first service from Catania on 17 June 2003.

FLEET:
8 x A320-200

FEATURES:
A large blue and orange w outlined in white dominates the orange tailfin of the largely white aircraft. The flowing w design is repeated in front of blue *Wind Jet* titles on the forward roof. The orange engine and nose cone restore the equilibrium of the aircraft livery. The airline's web address can be found on the engines and above the aft cabin windows.

Wizz Air (WZ/WZZ)
HUNGARY (HA)

Hungarian-based Wizz Air is one of the newer low-fare airlines that have taken Europe by storm since the enlargement of the European Union. With bases at Budapest in Hungary and Katowice in southern Poland, the airline has been expanding its routes from both cities since beginning operations from Katowice on 19 May 2004 and from Budapest on 22 June 2004. The network now takes in some 20 European cities. The idea of a low-fare carrier to serve Poland and Hungary, which joined the EU on 1 May, was born in June 2003 and the airline was constituted on 4 September that same year.

FLEET:
7 x A320-200

FEATURES:
Following recent trends, the name of the airline and markings were chosen to make a strong visual impact and to aid instant recognition. The exotic magenta and purple wrapped around the forward fuselage are said to emphazise the dynamic, positive, and differentiated aspects of the Wizz brand.

World Airways (WO/WOA)
UNITED STATES (N)

U.S. supplemental carrier providing worldwide passenger and cargo transport for major international airlines, the U.S. Air Mobility Command, international tour operators and cruise companies, major freight forwarders, and express package delivery companies. Services are flown under wet-lease or full-service contracts. World Airways was established on 29 March 1948 by Benjamin Pepper and taken over in 1950 by Ed Daley, who headed the airline until his death in 1984. Scheduled coast-to-coast and later trans-atlantic passenger services were provided between 11 April 1979 and 15 September 1986.

FLEET:
1 X DC-10-30, 2 X DC-10-30F,
7 X MD-11, 2 X MD-11ER,
1 X MD-11F

FEATURES:
The subdued livery of dark blue is barely noticeable on the white aircraft. It comprises a stylized globe flattened at the poles that rotates at the middle of the tailfin, on the winglets of certain aircraft, and in the *World* titles at the front, where it takes the place of the letter o. A small U.S. flag sits at the top of the fin. A dark blue band around the center of the engines is the only other concession to color.

Xiamen Airlines (MF/CXA)
CHINA (B)

Regional air carrier linking the Xiamen Special Economic Zone in the Fujian province to all provincial capitals and tourist destinations, and to Hong Kong, Macau, Malaysia, Singapore, South Korea, and Thailand. The domestic network encompasses 40 destinations. The airline was founded on 25 July 1984 under China's reform policy in a joint venture between the Fujian province and the city of Xiamen to operate as a commercial enterprise. China Southern Airlines acquired a majority stake on 10 March 1992.

FLEET:
4 X B737-300, 6 X B737-500,
15 X B737-700, 9 X B757-200,
(3) X B787-8

FEATURES:
Although the concept of simple cheatlines is now somewhat dated, the graduating quintuple arrangement of blue and black seems ideally suited to the airline's Boeing 757, giving the already slim and long aircraft an even more aerodynamic shape. The soaring white egret flying against a solid blue disc is also set off beautifully on the white aircraft. *Xiamen Airlines* titles are applied in both English and Chinese characters.

Yakutia Airlines (κ7/SYL)

RUSSIAN FEDERATION (RA)

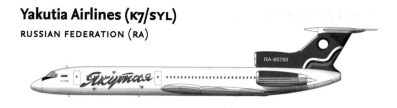

State-controlled Russian airline based at Yakutsk in the Republic of Sakha, an area rich in natural deposits and also known as the cold pole for its extremely cold temperatures. Yakutia Airlines operates scheduled passenger and cargo flights in Russia and the Commonwealth of Independent States, together with charter flights to points in Europe, Asia, and the Middle East. The airline came into being in 1993, based on the former Aeroflot Yakutsk directorate, and was previously known as Yakutaviatrans and Saakhavia. It was reorganized in 2000 and merged with Yakutavia in 2002 when the present name was adopted.

FLEET:
1 X AN-12B, 5 X AN-24RV,
1 X AN-26B, 1 X AN-26-100,
(3) X AN-140-100, 2 X TU-154B-2,
6 x TU-154M, 3 x Yak-40,
1 x Yak-40K

FEATURES:
The appealing livery, derived from the national flag, is full of symbolism. The white sun (*urun'kun*) on a blue field characterizes eternal life in the cold and hard polar climate, while the three lines of white, red, and green attest to hope and snow, strength and courage, and health and joy, respectively. The snaking rendition of the lines also refer to the Lena River.

Yamal Airlines (YL/LLM)

RUSSIAN FEDERATION (RA)

Russian airline based at Salekhard in the Yamal Nenets Autonomous District, providing air services with fixed-wing aircraft and helicopters in the extremely difficult geographical and climatic conditions of Russia's Arctic region. The airline's services reach as far west as Moscow and also serve many of the principal centers of operation in Siberia and other northern districts. Yamal Airlines was formed in spring 1997 as a joint-stock company and began flying on 10 July that year with a Mil Mi-8 helicopter.

FLEET:
2 X AN-24RV, 1 X AN-26B,
1 X AN-74-200D, 1 x Mi-8PS,
19 x Mi-8T, 9 x TU-134A-3,
2 x TU-154B-2, 1 x TU-154M,
5 x Yak-40, 1 x Yak-40K

FEATURES:
The triple cheatline in three different blues starts at the nose and flows along the fuselage towards the tailfin where the lower dark blue line crosses over to form the leading edge of the reversed color arrangement. Set into a white disc is the airline's motif of a red dear leaping ahead of a blue kite over a stylized globe. Winged *Yamal* titles are on the roof in Cyrillic lettering.

Yangon Airways (HK)
MYANMAR (XY)

Domestic airline serving mainly the burgeoning tourist industry through scheduled connections between the capital Yangon and other major cities, giving access to places of historic interest such as Mandalay, Bagan, and many others. Yangon Airways was formed in 1996 by Myanmar Airways and Mayflower Investment and began operations on 15 October that same year.

FLEET:
2 X ATR 72-210

FEATURES:
The aircraft tailfin bears the emblem of the legendary Sin Phyu Taw Pyan, the winged royal white elephant, flying against the sun, which forms part of the Myanmar flag of red, yellow, and green wrapped around the aircraft. The rare white elephant was revered in the days of the ancient Myanmar kingdoms as a symbol of mighty strength and loyal service and was used as the personal mount of the kings for royal occasions. Yangon Airways aims to bring these same attributes to its passenger service.

Yemenia (Yemen Airways) (IY/IYE)
YEMEN (70)

National airline of Yemen operating scheduled international flag-services for passengers and freight from Sana'a and Aden to other points in the Middle East, the Indian subcontinent, Southeast Asia, East Africa, and Europe. A domestic network serves 10 destinations. The airline was founded in 1954 as Yemen Airlines by the then Kingdom of Yemen but was reconstituted as Yemen Airways on 4 August 1961. The present name was adopted on 1 July 1978 and retained following the merger on 15 May 1996 with Aden-based Alyemda as a result of the unification of North and South Yemen in 1990.

FLEET:
4 X A310-300, 2 X A330-200, 2 X AN-26, 1 X B727-200A, 3 X B737-800, 3 X DHC-6 Twin Otter 300, 1 x Dash 7 100, 2 X IL-76, 2 X L382C Hercules

FEATURES:
The aircraft livery alludes to the national flag and employs twin pencil lines in bright red and royal blue, dissecting the all-white fuselage and extending upwards to fill the tailfin, where they are broken by the company motif of a wing section behind the Islamic Red Crescent on an oval white field. *Yemenia* titles are applied in blue, in both English and Arabic.

Yeti Airlines (YA)

NEPAL (9N)

Domestic airline in the mountainous Kingdom of Nepal providing an extensive network of scheduled and charter flights serving the tourist industry and assisting in the economic development of rural areas. Flights radiate from the capital Kathmandu and Nepalganj in the west of the country to some 25 destinations, taking in Lukla, gateway to Mount Everest; Jomsom in the popular Annapurna range; and Simikot, the main gateway to Mansarovar in the Tibet Autonomous Region of China. Yeti Airlines started commercial operations in September 1998.

FLEET:
3 x DHC-6 Twin Otter 300,
3 x Saab 340B

FEATURES:
It would be surprising if the airline symbol did not include the white footprint of the yeti, the legendary and larger-than-life abominable snowman alleged to inhabit the Himalayas. It is pictured against a green disc with the red letter Y. Green *Yeti Airlines* titles sit above the green underside of the aircraft. The unique shape of the blue, red, and white Nepalese flag points to the aircraft registration.

Zambian Airways (Q3/MBN)

ZAMBIA (9J)

Zambia's only scheduled domestic airline operating regular air services between all the main centers of population in the country and from the capital Lusaka to neighboring Malawi, Zimbabwe, and the Democratic Republic of Congo. The airline caters for business traffic but also focuses on flying tourists to some of the most famous areas of Africa, such as the Victoria Falls, Lake Malawi, Lake Tanganyika, and the Lower Zambesi Valley. Zambian Airways was formed in 1988 as Roan Air but changed its name in October 1999 following a major relaunch.

FLEET:
2 x Beech 1900D

FEATURES:
The tailfin of the Zambian Airways aircraft is a clever representation of the national flag. Set into a largely green fin is a depiction of an eagle's head in red, black, and orange. The eagle stands for the nation's hope for the future, while red alludes to the country's struggle for freedom, black to the population, and orange to the mineral resources. Green, which also colors the aircraft engines and the *Zambian* in the airline name on the cabin roof, refers to agriculture.

Zoom Airlines (OOM)
CANADA (C)

Canadian leisure airline operating a combination of scheduled and charter services for its parent company GO Travel Direct and other tour operators to holiday destinations in the Caribbean and southern USA, together with transatlantic flights to France and the United Kingdom. Flights operate from six Canadian cities including the airline's Ottawa base, and from Calgary, Edmonton, Halifax, Toronto, and Vancouver. Ad hoc subcharters for other carriers are also flown. Zoom Airlines was formed in May 2002 and began operations on 14 December that same year.

FLEET:
3 X B767-300ER

FEATURES:
The emphasis of this livery is on the word *zoom*, meaning "to climb and travel rapidly," which is displayed prominently across the forward fuselage and up the tailfin. The letters are drawn and arranged to accentuate the dynamism and stand out beautifully on the overall sky blue aircraft. The web address is shown in white on the mid-fuselage.

1time Airline (1T)
SOUTH AFRICA (ZS)

South African low-fare airline providing high-frequency passenger services from Johannesburg to all other major cities, including flights on the "Golden Triangle" between Johannesburg, Cape Town, and Durban. The airline was established in 2003 and began operations on 25 February 2004 with three daily return flights between Johannesburg and Cape Town, using McDonnell Douglas DC-9s.

FLEET:
1 X B737-200A, 1 X DC-9-10,
4 X DC-9-30, 2 X MD-82

FEATURES:
The overall bright red aircraft incorporates the airline's symbol on the tailfin and on the fuselage alongside the web address. This comprises the figure 1 in red set against an orange and yellow sun. The phrase one time in South Africa is a colloquialism meaning "for real." The airline's slogan *Azokho lo nonsense* (no nonsense) further reflects its determination to offer unconditional low fares.